Impacts of AI on Employment and Skills in Logistics

Thinh Gia Hoang
Ho Chi Minh University of Economics and Finance, Ho Chi Minh City, Vietnam

Umair Tanveer
University of Exeter, UK & Ho Chi Minh City University of Economics and Finance, Ho Chi Minh City, Vietnam

IGI Global
Scientific Publishing
Publishing Tomorrow's Research Today

Vice President of Editorial Melissa Wagner
Director of Acquisitions Mikaela Felty
Director of Book Development Jocelynn Hessler
Production Manager Mike Brehm
Cover Design Jose Rosado

Published in the United States of America by
IGI Global Scientific Publishing
701 East Chocolate Avenue
Hershey, PA, 17033, USA
Tel: 717-533-8845 | Fax: 717-533-7115
Website: https://www.igi-global.com E-mail: cust@igi-global.com

Library of Congress Cataloging-in-Publication Data

LCCN: 2026004231 (CIP Data Pending)
ISBN13: 979-8-3373-7826-8
Isbn13Softcover: 979-8-3373-7827-5
EISBN13: 979-8-3373-7828-2
British Cataloguing in Publication Data
A Cataloguing in Publication record for this book is available from the British Library.

Table of Contents

Detailed Table of Contents

This research explores the evolving strategic tension between the imperatives of environmental sustainability and labour process intensification in the global logistics sector. While the integration of AI in GSCM is often described as a positive development, this paper contends that it is doomed into establishing a green panopticon that will inadvertently erode the well being of workers. Through a qualitative single case study, this study illuminates the process by which algorithmic management to meet carbon reduction targets reduces the temporal porosity, and increases the psychosocial stress. The findings propose a theoretical model of Green Digital Intensification which suggests that without regulatory intervention the cost of carbon neutrality is increasingly met by the human body in the form of accelerated work pacing and diminishes autonomy. This analysis obfuscates the current techno optimist narrative, through revealing the way in which the moral imperative of planetary preservation is being used to legitimate the subjugation of labour to rigid algorithmic control.

This chapter explores the socio-technical transformation of logistics driven by artificial intelligence (AI), focusing on inventory management, automated warehouses, and transport optimization. Beyond technological performance, it examines how AI reshapes employment structures, transforms skills, and redefines job roles within logistics systems. AI reconfigures tasks, redistributes decision-making activities, and increases the importance of cognitive and digital competencies required for algorithmic supervision and human–AI collaboration. It enables predictive inventory planning, intelligent flow management, and optimized routing, while raising managerial and ethical challenges related to workforce adaptation and organizational change. Logistics performance thus depends on the balanced interaction between

Artificial intelligence applications such as intelligent route optimisation, condition based maintenance analytics, and semi autonomous vehicle control are transforming work in road freight transport. This chapter examines how the driver's role shifts from direct mechanical control toward technologically mediated system oversight requiring monitoring capacity, analytical judgement, and structured risk governance. Drawing on four anonymised empirical cases representing advanced AI integration in freight operations, the analysis shows that automation reshapes expertise by redistributing cognitive authority between human operators and algorithmic systems. Tacit experiential knowledge is reconfigured, and occupational identity is renegotiated. The chapter develops a hybrid stewardship model explaining how AI does not merely substitute or augment labour but restructures accountability, decision prerogatives, and skill boundaries in digitally augmented transport systems.

Preface

OVERVIEW OF THE SUBJECT MATTER

Artificial intelligence (AI) has moved from an episodic innovation in logistics to an infrastructural condition of contemporary supply chain coordination. In warehousing, transport operations, inventory management, procurement interfaces, and finance-enabled trade execution, algorithmic systems increasingly participate in decisions that were historically enacted through human discretion, tacit expertise, and negotiated compromise. This volume, *Impacts of AI on Employment and Skills in Logistics*, starts from the premise that AI's significance cannot be adequately apprehended through technical performance metrics alone. The most consequential and durable effects of AI reside in how it reorganises work: how tasks are re-bundled, how decision rights are redistributed, how accountability is intensified through evidence regimes, and how competence is redefined under conditions of heightened visibility, scoring, and auditability.

The chapters collected here therefore address AI as a socio-technical and organisational phenomenon, rather than as a neutral efficiency instrument. Across diverse empirical contexts, a shared pattern emerges: routine work is often partially automated while exception work expands; discretion is relocated from planning into execution under tighter algorithmic constraints; and new forms of "system-facing competence" become consequential for job quality, mobility, and occupational identity. This reframes a central debate in the future of work. Instead of asking only whether AI displaces jobs, the volume asks how AI reconfigures employment structures and skill systems—who is upgraded, who is marginalised, what kinds of competence are legitimised, and which forms of labour become invisible but strategically indispensable. In this regard, the book contributes to scholarship on logistics transformation by treating employment and skills not as downstream "impacts," but as core design stakes of AI-enabled operations.

WHERE THE TOPIC FITS IN THE WORLD TODAY

The salience of this topic is heightened by the convergence of global pressures reshaping logistics as both an economic backbone and a social sustainability frontier. Logistics organisations operate amid decarbonisation mandates and disclosure requirements, persistent volatility and disruption, geopolitical realignment, and intensified customer expectations for speed and reliability. AI is widely positioned as an operational response to these pressures: predictive inventory systems, intelligent routing, telematics and continuous scoring, autonomous mobile robots in fulfilment, and verification infrastructures that embed compliance into everyday execution. However, these solutions also constitute new governance architectures. Optimisation targets become normative performance standards; dashboards, audit trails, and scoring regimes expand; temporal buffers are compressed; and accountability is individualised in ways that can shift risk onto frontline workers.

Consequently, the "AI-in-logistics" agenda is inseparable from pressing questions about job quality, inclusion, and the sustainability of human capital in a sector employing large and heterogeneous workforces. In many organisations, AI does not simply remove work; it reorganises decision-making and redistributes cognitive and moral responsibilities—particularly under sustainability imperatives where ecological legitimacy can be mobilised to normalise intensification. In developing economies, these dynamics are amplified by uneven training infrastructures, variable labour protections, and asymmetries in digital readiness across firms and worker groups. This volume therefore positions AI-enabled logistics as a contemporary site where the future of work is negotiated in practice: through job redesign, reskilling regimes, boundary struggles over expertise, and the institutional conditions under which workforce transition becomes equitable.

TARGET AUDIENCE

This book is written for scholars, practitioners, policymakers, and educators who seek to understand and govern AI-driven logistics transformation in ways that are operationally credible and socially defensible. For researchers in logistics and supply chain management, operations, information systems, organisational studies, labour process research, and human resource development, the chapters offer mechanism-based explanations of how AI reconfigures roles, competence systems, and workplace governance. For industry professionals, consultants, and organisational leaders, the volume provides actionable insights into workforce planning, role classification, job redesign, learning pathway development, and responsible deployment strategies that can mitigate polarisation and intensification risks. For policymakers and institutional leaders, the chapters highlight where regulatory intervention, skill-system investment, and accountability design are required to align decarbonisation and productivity agendas with worker well-being and inclusion.

The volume also speaks directly to educators and graduate students as logistics curricula are reoriented toward AI-mediated work. Rather than treating "digital skills" as an undifferentiated requirement, the chapters specify the competence domains increasingly demanded in logistics settings: metric literacy, exception handling, system interpretation, coordination across interfaces, human–AI handoffs, and auditable judgement under algorithmic conditions. This specificity is intended to support more realistic workforce preparation and more empirically grounded debate about the distribution of reskilling opportunities.

IMPORTANCE OF THE CHAPTER SUBMISSIONS

Chapter 1, *AI, Sustainability Mandates, and the Intensification of Logistical Work*, develops a critical account of how AI-enabled green supply chain management can intensify labour and erode worker well-being when decarbonisation is operationalised through algorithmic management. Through a qualitative single-case study of a Southeast Asia-based logistics provider, it shows how carbon-efficiency targets compress temporal porosity and increase psychosocial stress by accelerating work pacing and diminishing autonomy, and it proposes a model of Green Digital Intensification that links sustainability governance to job redesign and skill bifurcation. The chapter's significance lies in demonstrating that "green" optimisation is not merely technical: it can legitimate tighter control and shift the burden of ecological efficiency onto workers unless counterbalanced by protective regulation and transition support.

Chapter 2, *AI and the Socio-Technical Transformation of Logistics: Warehousing, Transportation, and Inventory Management in the Context of Algorithmic Decision-Making*, offers an integrative socio-technical analysis that connects AI's operational capabilities to workforce transformation across three core logistics domains. By demonstrating how predictive planning, automated flow management, and routing optimisation redistribute decision work and revalue cognitive and digital competencies, the chapter clarifies that logistics performance depends on the balanced interaction between technological systems and human engagement. Its importance for the volume is to provide a function-spanning framework for responsible deployment that makes employment structure change and skill redefinition analytically central.

Chapter 3, *From Freight to Finance: AI-Enabled Supply Chain Finance and the Transformation of Skills and Employment in Integrated Logistics*, shows how AI-enabled supply chain finance reorganises logistics employment by embedding verification and risk assessment into trade execution. Using a single-case study of an anonymised global logistics provider, it demonstrates that routine checks are automated while exception regimes expand, shifting labour toward interpretive judgement, escalation coordination, and auditable accountability, and it traces how embedded finance re-bundles work across operations, finance, compliance, and data stewardship to produce hybrid roles and contested occupational boundaries. The chapter's contribution is to extend "employment impact" beyond substitution by revealing decision-work reorganisation and inclusion risks created by data-based liquidity gatekeeping.

Chapter 4, *Emerging Roles and Professional Identities in Smart Logistics Ecosystems*, conceptualises smart logistics as an ecosystem in which AI, automation, and platforms reshape occupations through new hybrid skill demands and identity reconstruction under algorithmic management. By examining how professional autonomy, transparency, and worker participation are reconfigured—and by highlighting disparities between developed and developing economies in AI readiness—the chapter situates employment transformation within broader governance and ethical arrangements. Its importance in the volume lies in explaining why identity and legitimacy issues are not peripheral: they are constitutive of how new roles become institutionalised and how skills are recognised and valued.

Chapter 5, *Governing Green Logistics through Algorithms: How AI-Driven Sustainability Targets Reshape Labour*, provides a comparative, theoretically generative account of how sustainability mandates become labour governance when operationalised through optimisation infrastructures and evidence regimes. Across four anonymised cases, it shows how algorithmic benchmarks shift from advisory instruments to normative reference points that compress temporal buffers, expand monitoring, and intensify accountability, while generating contestation where metrics fail to capture situated constraints; it theorises these dynamics through a green digital intensification model. The chapter's significance is to demonstrate that decarbonisation strategies are work-design strategies, and that ecological legitimacy can normalise intensification unless governance is redesigned to protect well-being.

Chapter 6, *AI, Sustainability, and Human Well-Being in Logistics Employment: Transforming Work, Efficiency, and Responsible Growth*, synthesises how AI-driven technologies reshape logistics efficiency and sustainability while transforming work conditions and skill requirements under human–AI collaboration. It highlights the duality of AI adoption—safety improvements and productivity gains alongside psychological impacts and inclusion risks—and it foregrounds governance and regulatory frameworks as prerequisites for responsible implementation. The chapter's contribution is to connect operational transformation to human well-being in a way that keeps employment and skills outcomes central to sustainable logistics development.

Chapter 7, *AI-Enabled Logistics Orchestration in EV Manufacturing: Employment Restructuring and Skill Reconfiguration Across Integrated Supply Networks*, examines AI-enabled orchestration as a socio-technical restructuring that transforms work organisation and skill demands across integrated EV supply networks. Through a four-pillar framework and a single-case study, it shows how shared interfaces integrate procurement, inbound logistics, planning, and distribution, shifting work from transactional expediting to structured escalation and anomaly resolution while increasing demand for hybrid skills that combine operational expertise, analytical literacy, and coordination capability. Its importance lies in demonstrating how industrial upgrading agendas in emerging sectors depend on inclusive workforce upgrading, not merely technical integration.

Chapter 8, *AI-Enabled Warehousing and the Changing Nature of Operational Skills in Logistics*, analyses AI-intensive fulfilment where autonomous mobile robots and decision systems reshape competence through task re-bundling, data-mediated performance, and exception handling. Drawing on an anonymised 3PL case, it shows how expertise increasingly involves interpreting system signals, coordinating human–machine handoffs, and managing exceptions under uncertainty, while stratified override rights and audit trails redistribute authority and intensify accountability. The chapter's contribution is to theorise skill transformation as a reconfiguration of task boundaries, governance structures, and learning pathways, making inclusive upgrading a central criterion of responsible automation.

Chapter 9, *Algorithmic Control and the Reconfiguration of Worker Autonomy in Logistics*, develops an autonomy regime framework to explain how dynamic routing and performance scoring reorganise discretion rather than simply diminishing it. Based on an anonymised parcel-delivery case, it shows that planning autonomy declines while execution relies on constrained judgement under high auditability, and it argues that legitimacy depends on the visibility and contestability of algorithmic decisions as workers' expertise shifts toward system-facing competence. The chapter is significant for showing that autonomy is a mechanism through which AI reshapes job design, skill formation, and employment governance.

Chapter 10, *Building a Digital Capability Pipeline for AI-Driven Workforce Transformation in Supply Chains*, proposes a multi-level capability pipeline that integrates digital literacy, AI oversight, structured reskilling, human–AI collaboration, and adaptive learning across individual, organisational, and ecosystem levels. Grounded in Human Capital Theory, it frames workforce readiness as a capability system requiring coordinated investment, leadership, and partnerships, supported by feedback mechanisms for iterative skill renewal and strategic adaptation. Its contribution is to translate workforce transformation into actionable capability design that can guide managers and policymakers under resource constraints.

Chapter 11, *Designing Just Reskilling Pathways for AI-Driven Logistics Transformation*, argues that reskilling is not a neutral technical solution but a socio-political process shaped by unequal learning support, organisational priorities, and differential access to opportunity. Using a case study, it shows how workload, education, supervisory support, scheduling flexibility, language ability, and assumptions about trainability produce uneven reskilling outcomes, enabling some workers to move into more secure analytical roles while excluding others. The chapter's importance lies in providing an equity-oriented reskilling model that reframes workforce transition as a distributive governance problem.

Chapter 12, *Reimagining Procurement and Logistics Transformation Through Artificial and Generative Intelligence: A Critical Review*, integrates fragmented scholarship on AI and GenAI adoption across procurement and logistics by examining adoption trends, role shifts, skill barriers, workforce implications, and performance outcomes. Using a literature-based approach underpinned by systematic review logic, it analyses how AI reshapes procurement roles and cross-functional collaboration while identifying capability constraints and research gaps that limit workforce transition. The chapter's contribution is to extend workforce analysis to procurement–logistics interfaces where decision authority and competence requirements are rapidly being reconfigured.

Chapter 13, *Skill Transitions in AI Augmented Road Freight Operations*, examines how AI applications in routing, maintenance analytics, and semi-autonomous control transform road freight work by shifting drivers from mechanical control toward system oversight requiring monitoring capacity, analytical judgement, and structured risk governance. Drawing on four anonymised cases, it shows how automation redistributes cognitive authority between human operators and algorithmic systems, reconfigures tacit knowledge, and renegotiates occupational identity, and it develops a hybrid stewardship model explaining how accountability and skill boundaries are reorganised rather than simply displaced. The chapter's significance is to provide a transport-specific account of employment and skills transformation that highlights stratification risks and governance demands in digitally augmented operations.

CONCLUSION - HOW OUR BOOK IMPACTS THE FIELD

Collectively, the chapters reposition employment and skills as the decisive analytical stakes of AI-enabled logistics transformation. They demonstrate that AI's labour consequences are best understood as reconfigurations of decision rights, competence systems, and accountability infrastructures, rather than as linear substitution of labour. Across contexts, the volume identifies recurring mechanisms—

exception expansion, metric-driven governance, auditability intensification, hybrid role formation, and the redistribution of cognitive authority—that shape job quality, mobility, and the distribution of learning opportunities.

The book contributes to scholarship by providing conceptual tools—such as green digital intensification, autonomy regimes, hybrid stewardship, capability pipelines, and equity-oriented reskilling—that clarify how AI transforms logistics work under sustainability and efficiency pressures. It contributes to practice by foregrounding design choices: how organisations build learning support, how they classify and reward hybrid roles, how they govern metrics and contestability, and how they prevent polarisation into system-facing elites and execution-focused residual labour. Above all, the volume argues for a forward-looking research and policy agenda in which responsible AI in logistics is treated as a work-design and capability-system challenge—one that must be addressed if the sector's promised gains in productivity, resilience, and sustainability are to be socially legitimate and institutionally sustainable.

Chapter 1
AI, Sustainability Mandates, and the Intensification of Logistical Work

Anh Ngoc Le
http://orcid.org/0009-0008-4003-4578
Ho Chi Minh City University of Economics and Finance, Vietnam

ABSTRACT

This research explores the evolving strategic tension between the imperatives of environmental sustainability and labour process intensification in the global logistics sector. While the integration of AI in GSCM is often described as a positive development, this paper contends that it is doomed into establishing a green panopticon that will inadvertently erode the well being of workers. Through a qualitative single case study, this study illuminates the process by which algorithmic management to meet carbon reduction targets reduces the temporal porosity, and increases the psychosocial stress. The findings propose a theoretical model of Green Digital Intensification which suggests that without regulatory intervention the cost of carbon neutrality is increasingly met by the human body in the form of accelerated work pacing and diminishes autonomy. This analysis obfuscates the current techno optimist narrative, through revealing the way in which the moral imperative of planetary preservation is being used to legitimate the subjugation of labour to rigid algorithmic control.

DOI: 10.4018/979-8-3373-7826-8.ch001

INTRODUCTION

The modern global logistics industry is experiencing a profound structural metamorphosis and this change has been defined by scholars as a dual transformation. This phenomenon is due to the combined acceleration of digitalization - which is largely embodied in the industry 4.0 paradigms - and the imperative to undertake the effort of achieving ecological decarbonization to arrange for net-zero operations. Bag et al. (2021) argue that regulatory frameworks are the major driver of this change, with the European Green Deal being the most prominent model that forces firms to massively reduce their carbon footprints. Moreover, Environmental, Social and Governance (ESG) standards of corporate governance have graduated from being voluntary guidelines to stringent compliance requirements that have subjected logistics providers to unprecedented pressure to report transparently and mitigate emission outputs according to the European Commission (2024). In response to these exigencies, enterprises are increasingly adopting Artificial Intelligence (AI) and advanced predictive analytics in their operational infrastructures to improve the sustainability performance.

Logistics organisations exploit these technologies to optimise the use of resources through the use of dynamic route planning and also to automate more complex warehouse operations. According to Dwivedi et al. (2021), an AI deployment is progressively being used in terms of reduced fuel use as well as material waste which is synchronized counter measure that addresses the issues of economic inefficiency and environmental degradation. For example, Ding et al. (2023) shows how smart production lines and IoT sensors are used to monitor energy usage in real time, allowing managers to make immediate, more ecologically favorable changes. This combination of digital applications and green goals is often framed in the literature as a win win process that guarantees the long term sustainability of the supply chain.

However, the intersection of these ecological and technological imperatives has produced a complex labour dynamic that is poorly theorized in mainstream management literature. Whilst the environmental gains of AI are often celebrated in reports about cutting empty miles and energy waste, the implications for the human workforce are often lost under a techno optimistic narrative. Agrawal et al. (2023) contest that this narrative assumes that technological progress will always bring benefits to all stakeholders, but this view often overlooks the immediate impact on worker autonomy. Recent critical scholarship challenges this assumption by suggesting that the elimination of operational inefficiencies for the sake of sustainability often correlates with the elimination of needed recovery time for workers.

Wood (2021) provides a critical foundation for this analysis by defining algorithmic management as a system where software algorithms assume the functions of direction and control. When these algorithms are set to achieve maximum energy efficiency, what they do is to systematically identify and eliminate porous time, which is the small and informal intervals of rest that exist within the working day. Parent-Rocheleau and Parker (2022) warn that if digital systems are instructing the pace of work for alignment with strict environmental measures, a phenomenon of work intensification occurs where the density of tasks being accomplished in a given hour increases significantly. This leads to a situation in which the physical and cognitive burden of the worker is being increased to achieve the sustainability targets set by the organization.

This research scrutinizes this intersection as an intersectional tension between ecological efficiency and social sustainability. Although the Triple Bottom Line framework is rooted in the principle that social and environmental goals should be of equal importance, research has shown that environmental measures tend to trump social measures based on their quantifiability and regulatory urgency. Fernandez Macias et al. (2023) suggest that this prioritization runs the risk of creating a green panopticon where the use of digital surveillance tools is not only justified by profit seeking but by the moral imperative of carbon reduction. In this context the granular surveillance of driver behavior or warehouse picker speed is recast under the guise of energy conservation, making resistance to such surveillance morally difficult for the workforce.

Therefore, the purpose of this study is to investigate the extent to which sustainability-driven AI-requirements may transform the labour process in the logistics sector and contribute to work intensification. In direct dialogue with the central theme of this edited volume, this research explicitly examines how the deployment of these "green" algorithms affects not only immediate working conditions, but structurally reshapes employment pathways and skills systems. By taking this view of green logistics through the lens of Labour Process Theory, this paper articulates a critique of the present assumption that green logistics is inherently socially sustainable. It argues that green algorithms can act as sophisticated mechanisms of control in which the goal of planetary preservation is employed to legitimize the intensification of human labour. Kellogg et al. (2020) and Delfanti (2021) previously identified similar control mechanisms in traditional digital settings, but this research adapts their logic for the particular area of sustainability mandates.

To clearly signal the contributions of this paper: First, it identifies the empirical mechanisms of algorithmic labour control utilized for decarbonization. Second, it extrapolates a broader conceptual model of Green Digital Intensification. Finally, it systematically maps the resulting skill shifts, specifically the devaluation of experiential logistics skills in favor of interface navigation and monitoring literacy. Consequently, this research addresses the broader themes of employment and skills by exploring not only the mechanisms of algorithmic labour control, but also the subsequent implications for work design, shifting skill demands, and the critical need for workforce transition support in the logistics sector. By analyzing these dynamics this research seeks to contribute to a more holistic understanding of the twin transition to ensure that the pursuit of environmental resilience does not jeopardize the fundamental standards of decent work as emphasized by Nguyen et al. (2025).

The remainder of this paper is organized as follows to systematically investigation these dynamics. Section 2 synthesizes the existing literature on green logistics and algorithmic management to establish the theoretical basis for the study. Section 3 describes the methodological approach which utilize a single case study designing to examines the operational changes within a logistics firm. Section 4 outlines the empirical results on the deployment of AI systems at the subject firm and the direct impact on their daily operation. Section 5 analyses these observations to develop the concept of Green Digital Intensification and discusses the theoretical implications for labour process theory. Finally Section 6 concludes the research by summarizing the implications for worker welfare and by suggesting avenues for future scholarship.

1. THEORETICAL BACKGROUND

This section sets the theoretical foundation of the research work through a synthesis of two different, but increasingly intersecting bodies of literature which are Green Supply Chain Management (GSCM) and the Labour Process Theory (LPT) in the context of Algorithmic Management. Whereas the literature on GSCM often approaches digitalization as a tool for ecological optimization and efficiency of operations, the literature on LPT takes a critical look to how these same technologies serve as instruments of control and intensification. By integrating these views, this research attempts to build a framework for understanding Green Digital Intensification which suggests that sustainability mandates have often been the site for justifying the elimination of porosity from the working day, potentially furthering the subordination of labour to the demands of capital under the pretext of environmental stewardship.

2.1. The Digitalization of Green Supply Chain Management

The contemporary logistics sector is in under the immense pressure of the twin transition which Vaseei et al. (2024) describes as the simultaneous need for digitizing operations and for decarbonizing supply chains. Green Supply Chain Management (GSCM) has emerged as the state-of-the-art paradigm on environmental dimension management. It involves the integration of environmental thinking into supply chain management including product design, material sourcing and selection, manufacturing processes, delivery of the final product to the consumers, and end of life management of the product. Recently, the focus of the literature has shifted to the role of Industry 4.0 technologies in helping to support these green objectives.

2.1.1. AI as an Enabler of Environmental Performance

A large amount of recent research points to the game-changing possibilities of Artificial Intelligence (AI) in reaching sustainability objectives. Dwivedi et al. (2021) and Bag et al. (2021) propose that current, manual means of management are limited in addressing the complexity of modern supply chains, where emission sources are diffused and hard to trace. AI technologies, such as machine learning and predictive analytics, enable businesses to go beyond simply crunching mountains of data and figure out where all the carbon is being squandered in inefficiencies. For example, Hryhorak et al. (2023) has discussed the benefit of AI tools that allow logistics companies to make demand predictions with an unprecedented degree of precision. By estimating accurate inventory needs, companies can keep overproduction to a minimum and avoid related warehousing energy costs. Furthermore, Albayrak et al. (2023) emphasise how large scale statistical analysis provides the ability to optimise logistics networks to minimise the overall distance travelled by goods. This application is critical in the transport sector where empty miles or less than ideal routing contributes significantly to greenhouse gas emissions. In this context, the algorithm is seen as a benevolent agent of ecological rationality, eradicating the waste and conserving resources.

2.1.2. The Logic of Optimization and Resource Efficiency

The major logic underlying artificial intelligence in GSCM is optimization. Seyedan and Mafakheri (2020) explain that optimization algorithms do work by continuously looking for the mathematical minimum or maximum for a certain function such as minimizing fuel consumption or maximizing container space utilization. This relentless effort to be efficient is compatible with economic interests for the firm and ecological interests for the society. Ding et al. (2023) give an example of this in the context of manufacturing, where smart production lines have IoT sensors to monitor energy usage in real-time and automatically switch off inactive machinery.

However, the literature tends to address the human element of the supply chain as a secondary factor or as one more variable to be optimized along with fuel and raw materials. As found in Li et al. (2024) and Masood et al. (2023) AI and Green Human Resource Management (GHRM) integration can create synergies for corporate sustainability however, there is a potential risk of the emphasis on environmental metric could overshadow the social considerations. The optimization logic assumes that any slack or idle time reduction is inherently positive because there is waste reduction. Yet, as the ensuing section describes, what the algorithm classifies as waste is frequently what the human worker perceives as recovery time.

Table 1. Theoretical divergence in logistics optimization

Feature	Green Supply Chain Management Perspective	Labour Process Theory Perspective
Primary Goal	Minimize Carbon and Cost The central objective is to simultaneously reduce environmental impact including carbon footprint and waste and operational costs through efficiency gains.	Control Labour Power and Effort The primary goal is to maximize the conversion of potential labour power into actual labour effort by overcoming worker resistance and minimizing idleness.
Role of AI	Tool for Efficiency and Visibility AI is viewed as a benevolent tool that processes vast datasets to identify inefficiencies optimize resource utilization in areas like route planning and inventory and provide real time visibility into supply chain operations.	Mechanism of Surveillance and Discipline AI is seen as a sophisticated mechanism of control that enables granular and real time surveillance of worker activity and automates discipline through algorithmic directives and performance tracking.
View on Slack or Idle Time	Waste to be Eliminated Any non-productive time such as waiting or empty travel is viewed as inefficiency or waste that must be systematically identified and eliminated to improve environmental and economic performance.	Porosity Essential for Human Health Porosity which refers to the small gaps of rest and recovery within the working day is considered physiologically and psychologically essential for preventing fatigue and burnout Its elimination is seen as detrimental to worker well being.
Worker Agency	Facilitated by Better Data The assumption is that AI provides better data and tools which can potentially enhance decision-making and facilitate worker tasks though the human element is often treated as a secondary variable to be optimized.	Diminished by Algorithmic Pacing Worker autonomy is significantly reduced as the pace and sequence of work are increasingly dictated by opaque algorithmic systems creating a digital panopticon that limits discretion and increases stress.
Key Outcome	Environmental and Economic Optimization The successful implementation of AI leads to reduced emissions lower energy consumption minimized waste and cost savings.	Work Intensification and Cybernetic Proletarianization The drive for optimization leads to a densification of work where workers are engaged in active labour for a greater proportion of their shift under constant digital pressure leading to new forms of subordination.

Source: Li et al. (2024); Masood et al. (2023)

2.2. Algorithmic Management and the Control of Labour

In contrast to the optimism of the GSCM literature, scholars of work and employment use Labour Process Theory (LPT) to unpack the darker implications of digital transformation. LPT, originating with the dissection of the process of capital, concerns the transformation of labour power (capacity to work) into actual labour (the effort expended). A central concern of LPT is how the management systems function to maximize this conversion by overcoming worker resistance and minimizing idleness.

2.2.1. Defining Algorithmic Management

Algorithmic Management (AM) refers to the use of software algorithms to assume functions traditionally performed by human supervisors including the allocation of tasks, the evaluation of performance and the administration of discipline. Wood (2021) presents a seminal definition which states that AM is distinct from previous forms of technical control because of its comprehensive nature and opacity. Unlike an assembly line which controls the pace of work through physical speed, AM controls the pace through digital commands and real time performance metrics.

The report that has been commissioned by the Organization for Economic Co-operation and Development (2025) on AM highlights how this form of management is no longer restricted to the gig economy but is common across more traditional employment sectors such as logistics and warehousing. In these environments, AM systems are a digital panopticon. Cheon (2023) and Dencik and Stevens (2023) say that the warehouse is now a site for this experimentation with workers wearing equipment that measures their location, movement rate and ability to accurately pick second by second.

2.2.2. The Elimination of Porosity

A key concept in LPT is the notion of porosity which refers to the gaps in the working day where labor is not being actively performed. These can be micro breaks, time spent walking between tasks, or moments of social interaction between colleagues. From a physiological and psychological perspective, porosity is fundamental to preventing fatigue and burnout. However, from the perspective of an optimization algorithm, porosity is synonymous with inefficiency.

Cini (2023) and Schaupp (2022) contend that AM is a form of cybernetic proletarianization in which the digital system attempts to fill these gaps completely. For example, in a traditional warehouse, a worker might have a brief rest while waiting for a new instruction. Under AM, the instruction appears instantaneously through a headset or scanner the moment the previous task is marked complete. This results in a densification of work where the worker is engaged in active labour for a much higher percentage of the shift. Omidi et al. (2023) describe this as a revitalization of Taylorism but with much more granular tools for measurement and enforcement.

2.2.3. Surveillance and Invisible Discipline

The enforcement mechanism in AM is often subtle but pervasive. Wood (2021) and Duggan et al. (2020) describe how discipline is often automated in algorithmic systems. If a driver strays from an AI prescribed route or a warehouse picker falls short of a required pick rate, the system might automatically send out a warning or flag the worker for review. This creates a state of constant anxiety known as the panoptic effect where workers regulate their own behaviour because they know they are being watched at all times.

Moreover, the opacity of the algorithm compounds this stress. Parent Rocheleau and Parker (2022), found workers often do not understand exactly how their performance scores are calculated. This lack of transparency means workers may push themselves beyond safe to make sure they are meeting the obscure standards of the machine. In the logistics sector, this dynamic is especially perilous as it incentivises swerving and unsafe physical exertion in order to beat the algorithm's time estimates.

2.3. The Intersection: Green Digital Intensification

The theoretical contribution of this study lies in identifying the convergence of these two regimes. While GSCM provides the *moral justification* for optimization (saving the planet), AM provides the *technical means* to achieve it (controlling the worker). This study terms this phenomenon Green Digital Intensification.

2.3.1. The Moralization of Speed

Green Digital Intensification works by reframing work intensification as an environmental virtue. In traditional capitalist relations, the demand to work faster is clearly understood as a demand for higher profit which workers might resist. However, when the pressure to work faster, or take a more efficient route is couched in terms of carbon emissions reduction, resistance becomes more complex.

Li et al. (2024) and Pham et al. (2020) address that Green HRM seeks to align employee behavior with organizational environmental goals. While often pitched as fostering engagement, such alignment may also be a way to silence grievance. For instance, if an AI system directs a driver down a complicated road to conserve fuel, the driver's complaint about fatigue could be refuted by the notion that the new route is part of the company's net zero commitment. The moral weight of sustainability gives rise to a hegemonic discourse that legitimizes the intensification of the labour process.

2.3.2. The Redistribution of Environmental Risk to the Body

The concept of Green Digital Intensification proposes a cost transfer. By employing AI to decrease the amount of fossil fuels and electricity used, the logistics company is, in effect, offloading the weight onto the biological energy of the workforce. Masood et al. (2023) point out that although there is potential for AI to amplify the effectiveness of green strategies, the human cost becomes externalized.

For example, a green algorithm could command a warehouse system to dim lighting down to minimum levels to conserve electricity (as mentioned in smart warehouse literature). While this makes the facility's carbon footprint better, it adds more cognitive load and eyestrain to human workers furrowing through the gloom. Similarly, reducing the number of delivery vehicles by dynamic routing (Albayrak et al., 2023) means that the rest of the drivers have to deal with heavier loads and stiffer schedules. The risk of environmental damage decreasing with more risk of physiological damage to the worker.

2.3.3. The Paradox of Sustainable Development Performance

This framework reveals a paradox in the measurement of sustainable development performance. Studies such as Li et al. (2024) often quantify sustainability based on indicators such as energy consumption, waste reduction, and adherence to environmental regulations. By these metrics, an AI-driven logistics firm looks very sustainable. However, if the social dimension of sustainability is considered - specifically the quality of work (SDG 8) - the same firm may show significant degradation. Lata et al. (2023) and Morales and Stecher (2023) argue that the precarity and intensity of digitalized work undermine the social fabric which is a core component of true sustainability. Therefore, a theoretical approach that only considers environmental outputs without labour process inputs is incomprehensively incomplete. This study addresses that gap by positing that true sustainability cannot be achieved through trade off between ecological health and worker health.

2.4. Boundary Conditions of Green Digital Intensification

It is critical to conceptualize that the labour intensification observed in algorithmic management is not an inevitable outcome of AI, but rather contingent on specific contextual boundaries. As Kellogg et al. (2020) emphasize, algorithms are not deterministic; their impact is deeply mediated by the institutional and organizational terrain in which they are deployed. The dynamics of Green Digital Intensification are likely most pronounced under conditions of high regulatory ESG pressure combined with an efficiency-first managerial orientation. In such environments, the “Environmental” (E) pillar of ESG frequently overshadows the “Social” (S) pillar, effectively weaponizing carbon metrics to justify hyper-surveillance and the systematic squeezing of labour porosity (Delfanti, 2021).

Furthermore, weak worker protections and top-down, opaque algorithmic implementations exacerbate these effects. When algorithms operate as black boxes, frontline workers are stripped of their agency and left unable to contest intensified workloads, as the pacing and routing decisions are obscured behind a veil of complex, proprietary environmental logic (Moore & Joyce, 2020). Without institutional pushback, management can effortlessly translate external decarbonization targets into draconian, individualized shop-floor quotas.

Conversely, if these technologies are deployed in environments featuring strong labor union traditions and institutionalized worker voice, the outcomes may differ significantly. Research on algorithmic governance demonstrates that robust collective bargaining can force management to negotiate the terms of digital deployment, preventing the unilateral imposition of algorithmic control (Doellgast & Wagner, 2022). In these settings, participatory AI design and transparent algorithms become feasible. When workers and their representatives are involved in co-designing the systems that govern their daily tasks, green metrics can be structurally balanced against occupational health and safety standards.

Finally, the presence of mandated 'human-in-the-loop' safeguards serves as a vital boundary condition. As Parent-Rocheleau and Parker (2022) argue, preserving human discretion within algorithmic workflows is essential for maintaining job quality and preventing psychosocial harm. Under such protective conditions, the intensifying effects of green algorithms could be mitigated, allowing for necessary worker rest and autonomy while still pursuing legitimate ecological goals. Recognizing these boundary conditions is essential for calibrating the conceptual scope of this phenomenon, moving the scholarly discourse away from technological determinism and toward a nuanced understanding of the political economy of green logistics.

2.5. Conceptual Framework

The proposed conceptual for this study combines the environmental imperative of GSCM with the control mechanisms of LPT. It suggests that:

1) **Driver:** External sustainability mandates (EU Green Deal, ESG) create the pressure for decarbonization.
2) **Mechanism:** AI and Algorithmic Management are deployed to achieve this decarbonization through hyper optimization.
3) **Process:** This optimization systematically targets and removes porosity from the labour process.

4) **Outcome:** The result is Green Digital Intensification where environmental gains are inextricably linked to increased labour intensity and reduced worker autonomy.

This framework serves to inform the further analysis of the case studies by giving attention not only to what technologies are implemented, but also how their specific configurations change the daily reality of the logistics workforce. It takes the debate away from the either/or of "technology is good" or "technology is bad" to a discussion of more nuanced ways in which particular "green" configurations of technology are altering power relations on the shop floor.

Figure 1. Conceptual framework of green digital intensification

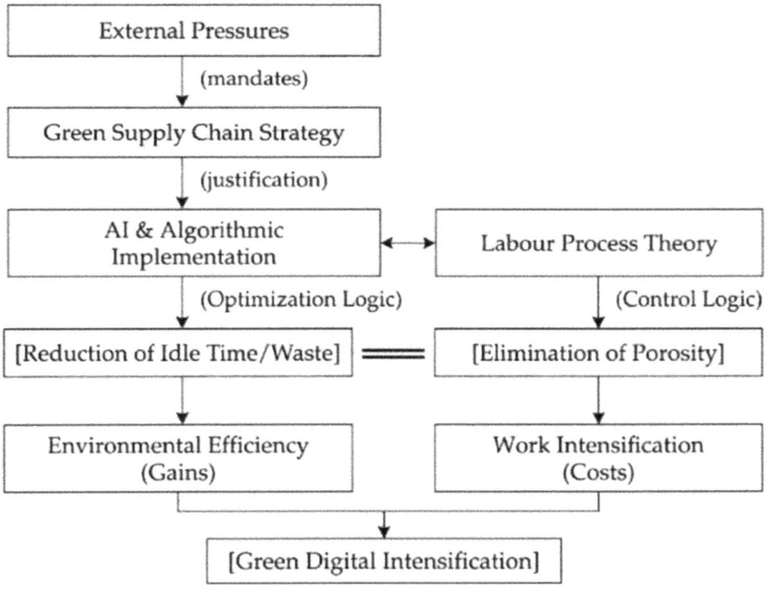

3. CASE STUDY

This research uses qualitative single case study research design to explore the operational and labour implications of sustainability driven artificial intelligence. The subject of this inquiry is a mid sized third party logistics provider in Southeast Asia that will be referred to by the pseudonym EcoLogistics to keep it anonymous. The choice of this particular firm relied on the recent and aggressive implementation of a thoroughgoing digitalization strategy explicitly focusing on carbon emission standards of the European Union. By concentrating on one organization, the study will enable a thick description of the mechanisms by which abstract mandates for sustainability are translated to concrete work routines on a daily basis. The main data sources for work on this analysis are internal strategic documents related to the Green Speed initiative, operational manuals for the new AI systems and non participant observation of the dispatch centre and warehouse floor over a period of fourteen days in late 2025.

3.1. Case Background

EcoLogistics operates a fleet of around two hundred heavy goods vehicles and have two major distribution centres which are used as regional centres for the export of goods to Western markets. In the financial year 2023, the firm was under increasing pressure from its transnational clients for granular data on Scope 3 emissions. These pressures were compounded by the enforcement of the European Corporate Sustainability Due Diligence Directive which requires that logistics partners make sure they adhere to strict environmental standards. In response, the executive management introduced a strategic overhaul called the Green Speed initiative. This program was not simply an update of the policy but was a fundamental revision of the operational architecture of the firm driven by acquisition of sophisticated algorithmic management tools.

The technological backbone of the Green Speed initiative is composed of two different but complementary artificial intelligence systems. The first one is called Eco Route AI which is a dynamic transport management platform. Unlike legacy systems that relied on static route planning Eco Route AI utilizes machine learning to process real time traffic data weather conditions and vehicle load weight to calculate the most fuel efficient path for delivery. The explicit objective of this system is to cut fuel consumption by fifteen percent and eliminate what the software developers call empty miles or non productive engine usage. The system communicates directly with an in cab tablet which provides turn by turn instructions to the driver and monitor driving behavior such as braking patterns and idle time.

The second system deployed is the Green Pick Smart Warehousing solution which automates the internal logistics of the distribution centres. This system combines Internet of Things (IoT) sensors and a central processing algorithm to optimize the movement of goods and energy consumption in the form of electricity. A key feature of Green Pick is control of the facility environment specifically the lighting and climate control systems. The AI automatically darkens sectors of the warehouse that are not in immediate use to conserve energy which goes hand in hand with the findings of Ding et al. (2023) with respect to smart production lines. Furthermore, the system guides human pickers with wrist mounted terminals to dictate the optimal order of the tasks in order to minimize the total walking distance. The management at EcoLogistics promoted these technologies inside the company in the name of a double win, which was at the same time to secure the ecological certification of the firm and to optimize the operation.

3.2. Case Analysis

The implementation of the Green Speed initiative at EcoLogistics suggests empirical support for the theoretical tension of institutional processes between ecological efficiency and quality of labour processes. The analysis helps uncover that the ambition of carbon neutrality by algorithmic means appears to have inadvertently led to a strict intensification of the labour process. This section looks at these dynamics through three thematic lenses, including the algorithmic displacement of porosity, the emergence of a green panopticon, and the moralization of compliance.

3.2.1. The Algorithmic Displacement of Porosity

The most immediate effect of the Eco Route AI system was the radical change in the temporal structure of the drivers work. In the past without AI implementation, the drivers were operated with some degree of temporal autonomy. The static route plans anticipated buffer periods to account for unpredictable traffic or administrative delays. These buffers acted as porosity in the working day to permit drivers to take informal micro breaks such as pausing to stretch or modifying their route to avoid stress. However, the optimization logic of the Eco Route AI sees this porosity as a source of carbon inefficiency. The algorithm calculates the theoretical minimum time needed to complete a delivery according to optimal fuel usage and sets this as rigid standard for performance.

The observation data shows the system considers a stationary car a critical failure in its sustainability performance. When a driver idles for more than 3 minutes the in cab tablet sends a visual and auditory alert notifying the driver that his/her current behavior is hurting the fleet's carbon score. This mechanism substantially restricts the opportunity for informal rest. The driver is forced to be constantly on the move to meet the algorithm's definition of green efficiency. This captures in the critique presented by Wood (2021) that algorithmic management squeezes the air out of work. At EcoLogistics, this removal is not based on profits alone but on the need to cut emissions urgently. Consequently, the drivers encounter a densification of labour in which the ratio of active driving time to total shift time is significantly increased. The cognitive load involved in following the ever-changing dynamic route further intensifies this load as the driver cannot simply rely on habit or familiarity with a fixed route but must keep a state of hyper vigilance to follow the AI instructions.

3.2.2. The Green Panopticon and Granular Control

In the distribution centres, the deployment of the Green Pick Smart Warehousing system created a regime of surveillance that is what Fernandez Macias et al. (2023) call a digital panopticon. The operational logic of the Green Pick system relies on the granular tracking of every energy consuming variable which includes the human worker. To optimise the lighting and climate control, the system has to know the exact location of every picker every second. The warehouse is divided into zones and the LED lighting is only activated when a worker comes into a certain zone to perform a task. As the worker leaves the lights are turned off immediately to save some electricity.

This energy saving mechanism becomes a strong tool of labour control. The lighting system serves as a bodily expression of the algorithmic gaze. A worker is unable to move into an unauthorized zone without being alerted because the lights will fail to activate. Furthermore, the pace of the worker is inextricably connected to the energy metrics. If a picker spends more time in an aisle than the algorithm predicts he needs to accomplish the task the system registers an energy anomaly where electricity is being used without corresponding increases in productivity. This puts a direct pressure on the worker to calibrate their physical speed to the energy targets of the systems. The observation showed that workers internalised this pressure frequently rushing their work to make sure they did not run beyond the allocated time of light. This validates the hypothesis of Parent Rocheleau and Parker (2022) that digital pacing produces a situation of work intensification fuelled by opaque metrics. The sustainability objective of energy conservation thus provides the justification for the level of surveillance that would be seen as intrusive in the traditional management situation.

3.2.3. The Moralization of Compliance and Erosion of Autonomy

The last dimension of the analysis is about the erosion of worker autonomy and the moral reframing of obedience. Under the previous management regime workers had some degree of tacit knowledge and discretion. A driver might take a slightly longer route to avoid a dangerous intersection or a warehouse picker might re-order tasks to save physical strain. However the introduction of AI has centralized decision making authority within the algorithm. The system takes over the function of the expert agent with better knowledge about the most sustainable course of action.

This implies a deskilling of the workforce with the human role being limited to the mechanical execution of digital commands.

Crucially, this loss of autonomy is reinforced by a moral discourse. Management at EcoLogistics often describes following the AI directives as an ethical obligation to the environment. During the observation period operational supervisors were noted to correct non compliant behaviour by referencing the company's carbon footprint rather than productivity targets. If a driver challenged a route that they were told by the AI as the best path to take to minimise emissions, they might be told this deviation would damage the firm's ESG rating. This moralizing makes resistance hard for the workforce. To question the intensification of work is de facto phrased as challenging the company environmental responsibility. This dynamic supports the argument of Li et al. (2024) that the integration of green objectives can take precedence over social considerations relative to worker well being. The workers at EcoLogistics thus find themselves in a position where keeping themselves well by resting or by allowing themselves autonomy becomes an act of environmental negligence.

3.2.4. Synthesis of Case Findings

The evidence of EcoLogistics shows that the integration of AI for sustainability purposes does not involve the mere optimization of resources but the fundamental restructuring of the relations of power in production. The elimination of empty miles in transport and energy waste in warehousing are achieved by systematic elimination of human recovery time. The technologies act as a transmission belt that transforms outside pressure in regulatory mandates into inside pressure on the shop floor. The result is a working environment in which the physical and psychological capacity of the worker is destroyed to preserve the ecological capacity of the supply chain. This empirical reality stands in stark contrast to the win win narrative often promoted in Green Supply Chain Management literature and validates the Critical Labour Process Theory perspective that views these technologies as engines of intensification.

Table 2. Synthesis of case study findings at ecologistics

AI System	Operational Mechanism	Environmental Goal	Labour Impact
Eco Route AI	Dynamic real time route optimization and elimination of static buffers	Reduction of fuel consumption and elimination of empty miles	Displacement of Porosity Drivers lose informal rest periods as idle time is flagged as an efficiency failure leading to continuous driving and cognitive fatigue.
Green Pick Smart Warehousing	IoT controlled lighting and algorithmic picking sequences based on energy usage	Minimization of electricity consumption in distribution centres	Green Panopticon Workers are subject to granular surveillance where their location and speed are tracked second by second to ensure alignment with energy saving protocols.
Management Discourse	Framing of algorithmic directives as ethical mandates for sustainability	Compliance with EU Green Deal and ESG reporting standards	Moralization of Compliance Resistance to work intensification is delegitimized by framing obedience to the algorithm as an environmental duty rather than a productivity target.

Figure 2. The operational process of green digital intensification at Ecologisti

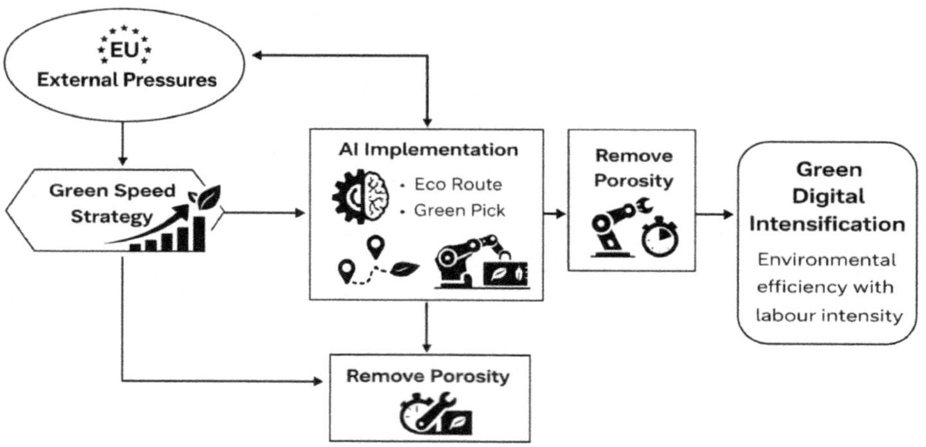

The figure above shows the sequential flow seen at EcoLogistics. The process starts with external regulatory pressures such as the EU Green Deal which requires reporting of Scope 3 emissions. This is the motivation behind the internal strategic decision to introduce the Green Speed initiative. The deployment of AI tools such as Eco Route and Green Pick specifically aims at operational porosity to make them carbon efficient. The end effect thus comes out as a dual condition in which environmental metrics are improving and worker well-being is worsening due to elimination of recovery time and imposition of rigid algorithmic control.

4. DISCUSSION

The empirical findings derived from the EcoLogistics case study constitute a critical vantage point for re-assessing the intersection of sustainability mandates and digital transformation. While the dominant academic discourse tends to present the integration of Artificial Intelligence into Green Supply Chain Management as a synergistic evolution, this research suggests a more contentious reality under certain managerial conditions. The rise of Green Digital intensification at EcoLogistics shows that the quest for ecological efficiency is structurally conjoined with the degradation of the labour process quality. This section discusses these observations by comparing and contrasting them with previous studies, paying particular attention to the paradox of optimization, the mechanism of the green panopticon, and the moralization of control.

4.1. Challenging the Win Win Narrative of Green AI

The basic difference between the result of this study and other literatures lies in the assessment of AI driven optimization. Recent scholarship by Bag et al. (2021) and Dwivedi et al. (2021) argues that the application of AI in logistics results in a mutually beneficial position where efficiency in operations benefits both having monetary gains and restoring the environment. Similarly, Ding et al. (2023) also argue that the decrease in waste from smart production lines can be attributed to precise energy monitoring, which implies that slack removal for waste removal is purely a resource saving measure. However, the EcoLogistics case challenges this perspective of techno optimist by showing that the slack being removed is not simply mechanical inefficiency but crucial human recovery time. The elimination of empty miles and the elimination of idle time by the Eco Route AI system relate directly to the elimination of the driver's ability to rest. This confirms the critical warning by Wood (2021) who argues that algorithmic management functions by stripping the porosity from the working day. While Bag et al. (2021) consider optimization an avenue to the Sustainable Development Goals, this research indicates that without certain safeguards, such optimization is actively dismantling SDG 8 on decent work.

4.2. The Green Panopticon and Invisible Discipline

This study further expands the theories of surveillance in the workplace. Fernandez Macias et al. (2023) and Cheon (2023) have previously characterized the ascendance of digital panopticon in logistics where wearable sensors monitor the movement of workers to enforce their productivity targets. The results at EcoLogistics illustrate this model clearly, but add an important dimension to it i.e. the environmental legitimacy for surveillance. At EcoLogistics, the granular tracking of warehouse pickers was not due to the need to ship more boxes but due to the need to save electricity and reduce the carbon footprint. This is consistent with the research of Parent Rocheleau and Parker (2022), which found that transparent algorithmic measures will often determine the pace of work in ways that are invisible to the worker but physically demanding. But, by connecting the lighting system to worker movement, EcoLogistics effectively operationalized the green panopticon in which the worker is disciplined not by a human manager but by the energy saving logic of the facility itself. This finding makes it more complex the point of view of Li et al. (2024) who affirm that AI improves the sustainable development performance of supply chains. This is something that, whereas the environmental metrics may improve as Li et al. (2024) predict, the social cost is a pervasive anxiety in the workforce which is perceived to constantly be monitored by the sustainability algorithm.

4.3. The Moralization of Speed and Erosion of Autonomy

A major contribution of this research is the identification of how the sustainability mandates are employed to neutralize the resistance of workers. Masood et al. (2023) and Pham et al. (2020) talk about Green Human Resource Management as the tool to align behavioral flow of employees with the organizational ecology. In the literature, such alignment is normally presented as leading to a sense of purpose and engagement. On the other hand, a coercive aspect of this alignment becomes apparent in the EcoLogistics case. The management discourse witnessed at the firm subjectified the notion of carbon reduction to delegitimize complaints against fatigue. This parallels the mechanism of control reported by Kellogg et al (2020) in which algorithms restrict worker discretion but adds a moral dimension to the issue, in which disobedience is enacted as environmental negligence. This moralizing makes intensification of work challenging to fight through traditional channels of industrial relations. Furthermore, the deskilling of drivers in the case supports the proposition suggested by Albayrak and Zeren (2023) whose main argument is that digitalization can lead to a decrease in human agency in the transport sector. As the algorithm takes over the role of the expert navigator in order to save fuel, the human driver becomes the mere follower of digital command execution, resulting in the situations of cognitive fatigue outlined by Adjekum and Tosun (2024) in their review of Industry 4.0 safety risks.

4.4. The Externalization of Environmental Risk

Finally, the redistribution of risk needs to be addressed in the discussion. The reduction of fuel and energy is an absolute good in the literature on Green Supply Chain Management. However, this study favors the critical perspective reported by Cini (2023) and Masood et al. (2023), stating that the costs of these reductions are often externalized on the workforce. By reducing the energy inputs of the fleet and facility, EcoLogistics maximized the biological energy expenditure of the workers. The high pick rates and constant driving schedules equate to a transfer of strain from the fossil fuel engine to the human body. This finding contradicts the argument by Nguyen et al. (2025) that green logistics has an inherent link to sustainable performance. Instead, it implies a trade off where sustainability of the environment is bought with the currency of worker well being. This adds to the need for a more holistic definition of sustainability, one that includes the preservation of human labour power as a renewable resource that must be protected from exhaustion.

4.5. Implications for Employment Design, Skills, and Workforce Transition

Moving from the empirical findings to broader conceptual implications, this study highlights critical challenges for the future of work in logistics amidst the "twin transition" of simultaneous digitalization and decarbonization (Vaseei & Paris, 2024). By analyzing the internal comparative dimensions of the EcoLogistics case, spanning both transport (Eco Route AI) and warehousing (Green Pick), we can synthesize how sustainability-oriented AI functions not merely as an operational tool, but actively acts as a work designer that restructures task allocation, imposes tighter pacing, and enforces granular performance monitoring (Parent-Rocheleau & Parker, 2022).

This restructuring triggers a profound transformation in job roles and task composition across the organizational hierarchy. For frontline workers, both drivers and warehouse pickers, decision authority is systematically transferred to the algorithm. Traditional skills face active suppression; experiential coordination, local problem-solving, and adaptive judgment (e.g., a driver assessing local road safety, or a picker pacing their physical exertion) are no longer valued. Instead, these competencies are structurally replaced by a strict requirement for interface navigation and the ability to seamlessly execute digital commands in real-time. Simultaneously, the research reveals the emergence of new skill tiers and role redesigns for middle management.

Supervisors, previously tasked with logistical problem-solving and team coordination, find their task composition dramatically altered. Their roles increasingly center on monitoring literacy, the ability to interpret AI dashboards, manage algorithmic alerts, and enforce ESG-aligned performance metrics. This represents the rise of digital compliance work and exception handling, where human intervention is only required when the algorithmic system encounters an anomaly it cannot optimize.

Consequently, this operational shift fundamentally alters the skills landscape, creating a stark bifurcation in logistical competencies (Agrawal et al., 2023). On one hand, there is an increased demand for new, compliance-driven technical competencies: workers must seamlessly navigate digital systems, respond to AI instructions in real-time, interpret data dashboards, and maintain high awareness of sustainability reporting requirements. On the other hand, traditional skills face obsolescence or active suppression (Albayrak & Zeren, 2023). Experiential coordination skills, tacit route judgment, local problem-solving autonomy, and self-paced task organization are no longer valued; instead, they are systematically flagged as operational inefficiencies or deviations by the algorithmic system (Wood, 2021).

To bridge these findings to practical workforce management, robust worker transition support is vital to prevent the ecological transition from generating a social crisis (Lata et al., 2023). Policymakers and logistics firms must prioritize comprehensive reskilling and upskilling programs to help workers adapt to these high-pressure environments. Crucially, as recognized by recent institutional frameworks, this must be paired with algorithmic transparency training and strict ergonomic and psychosocial protections to mitigate the severe occupational safety and health risks introduced by digital pacing (Adjekum & Tosun, 2024; OECD, 2025). Furthermore, transition support must involve institutionalizing worker voice. Implementing mandatory worker consultation during AI rollout, establishing clear grievance channels for algorithmic decisions, and mandating the protected right to override unsafe AI instructions are critical steps for resisting unilateral algorithmic control (Cini, 2023; Doellgast & Wagner, 2022). Alongside protected recovery time, these structural interventions are essential to ensure that the green transition does not achieve its environmental goals at the expense of human sustainability.

5. CONCLUSION AND IMPLICATIONS

5.1. Findings

This research investigated labour process implications of sustainability driven artificial intelligence in the logistics sector. By analyzing the Green Speed initiative at EcoLogistics and synthesizing the cross-functional impacts across both transport routing and smart warehousing operations, this research indicates that the intersection of ecological mandates and digital optimization can result in a particular phenomena, called Green Digital Intensification. The central finding suggests that the removal of operational waste that is necessary to meet carbon reduction aims by means of an algorithm often systematically removes the porosity of the working day. Specifically, the dynamic routing and smart warehousing systems achieved their environmental goals not merely through technological innovation, but through the intensification of human effort across different logistical domains. Consequently, the search for net zero may unwittingly accumulate a green panopticon in which worker surveillance is justified by the moral urgency of climate action.

However, it is crucial to acknowledge that mixed outcomes may occur depending on how these systems are governed and implemented. The findings suggest that achieving true sustainability requires a balanced approach. Without proactive regulatory intervention and human-centric design, the costs of the green transition may be externalized onto the workforce. True sustainability must pair environmental mandates with decent work safeguards, emphasizing the critical need for reskilling, work redesign, and comprehensive worker transition support to navigate this dual transformation effectively.

5.2. Theoretical Implications

Moving beyond the empirical boundaries of the specific case, this research proposes the broader theoretical model of Green Digital Intensification.The theoretical contribution of this paper is the integration of Green Supply Chain Management literature and Critical Labour Process Theory. Previous studies in GSCM such as those by Bag et al. (2021) have largely characterized AI as a neutral enabler of the Triple Bottom Line. This research challenges this consensus by producing empirical evidence of the tension between environmental efficiency and decent work. It expands on the idea of Algorithmic Management by calling out sustainability as a new mechanism of control. Where Kellogg et al. (2020) identified market pressure as the driver of digital control this study identifies regulatory pressure as a parallel driver. The concept of Green Digital Intensification offers a new theoretical framework to consider the question of the extent to which ESG mandates can be paradoxically counterproductive to social sustainability goals. It would suggest that future research will have to go beyond an analysis of environmental outputs, to the inputs of labour processes that will promote their achievement.

5.3. Managerial and Policy Implications

The findings have important implications for industry practitioners and policy makers. For managers, the study highlights the operational risks of implementing green technologies without comprehensive social impact assessments. While AI can optimise fuel usage, the human need for sufficient time for recovery can lead to burnout and high turnover of the workforce and ultimately impact the resilience of long-term operations. Managers should adopt a human-in-the-loop approach, one in which efficiency of algorithms is restrained by physiological constraints. This recommendation is in line with the position of Parent-Rocheleau and Parker (2022), who underline the need to maintain worker's agency in automatic contexts.

For policymakers, in particular those involved in the implementation of frameworks like the European Green Deal, this research highlights the need for a Just Transition that balances the need to protect the rights of workers in the digital age. Existing regulations put a strong emphasis on carbon reporting, but there are no specific provisions concerning intensity of work in automated environments. There is need for legislation that makes algorithmic audits mandatory to ensure sustainability software is not breaching occupational health standards. As recognized by the OECD (2025) the digital transformation must be regulated in order to avoid a loss in the quality of jobs. Policymakers should consider digital rights to porosity as rest preserving porosity of the working day regardless of algorithmic optimization.

5.4. Limitations and Suggestions for Future Research

This study has its limitations with the use of a single case study in context Southeast Asia. While such a design allowed for a deep qualitative analysis, the findings may not be universally generalizable to areas where labour union traditions are stronger, or to different regulatory landscapes. Future research should attempt to quantify the relation between green metrics and worker stress - levels across a for more broad sample of firms. Quantitative studies to quantify physiological indicators of stress for drivers with use of AI routing compared with drivers using traditional methods should be administered in the future. Moreover, additional research is encouraged to investigate the ways in which worker resistance is expressed in these green regimes, and the possibility for new forms of collective bargaining to subvert the moral authority of sustainability algorithms. Such inquiry would yield a finer understanding of how the twin transition remakes the global division of labour.

REFERENCES

Adjekum, D. K., & Tosun, O. (2024). Occupational safety and health implications of Industry 4.0: A review of literature. *Safety Science*, *172*, 106420.

Agrawal, A., Gans, J., & Goldfarb, A. (2023). The distributional effects of technology: AI and labor. *Brookings Papers on Economic Activity*, *2023*(1), 1–45.

Albayrak, Ö., & Zeren, F. (2023). The impact of digitalization on the carbon footprint in logistics: An empirical investigation. *Environmental Science and Pollution Research International*, *30*(15), 44642–44655.

Bag, S., Gupta, S., Kumar, A., & Sivarajah, U. (2021). An integrated artificial intelligence framework for achieving sustainable development goals. *Journal of Cleaner Production*, *292*, 126010.

Cheon, S. H. (2023). Data-driven automated management in logistics warehouse operations: The case of CJ Logistics in South Korea. *Geoforum*, *141*, 103737.

Cini, L. (2023). Resisting the algorithmic boss: Guessing, gaming, and grieving in the gig economy. [REMOVED HYPERLINK FIELD]. *New Technology, Work and Employment*, *38*(2), 278–294.

Delfanti, A. (2021). Machinic dispossession and augmented despotism: Digital work in an Amazon warehouse. *New Media & Society*, *23*(1), 49–67. DOI: 10.1177/1461444819891613

Dencik, L., & Stevens, A. (2023). Regimes of justification in the datafied workplace: The case of warehousing. *Work, Employment and Society*.

Ding, Y., Zhang, H., & Evans, S. (2023). Smart production lines and energy conservation in manufacturing. *Journal of Cleaner Production*, *386*, 135803.

Duggan, J., Sherman, U., Carbery, R., & McDonnell, A. (2020). Algorithmic management and app-work in the gig economy: A research agenda for employment relations and HRM. *International Journal of Human Resource Management*, *31*(1), 114–132.

Dwivedi, Y. K., Ismagilova, E., Hughes, D. L., Carlson, J., Filieri, R., Jacobson, J., Jain, V., Karjaluoto, H., Kefi, H., Krishen, A. S., Kumar, V., Rahman, M. M., Raman, R., Rauschnabel, P. A., Rowley, J., Salo, J., Tran, G. A., & Wang, Y. (2021). Setting the future of digital and social media marketing research: Perspectives and research propositions. *International Journal of Information Management*, *59*, 102168. DOI: 10.1016/j.ijinfomgt.2020.102168

European Commission. (2024). *Corporate sustainability due diligence directive*. EU Publications.

Fernández-Macías, E., Bisello, M., & Sarkar, S. (2023). The platformisation of work: Evidence from the JRC CODE survey. *European Economic Review, 158*, 104555.

Hryhorak, M., Kulak, N., & Galkin, A. (2023). Artificial intelligence in logistics and supply chain management of hazardous materials. *Transportation Research Procedia, 72*, 147–154.

Kellogg, K. C., Valentine, M. A., & Christin, A. (2020). Algorithms at work: The new contested terrain of control. *The Academy of Management Annals, 14*(1), 366–410. DOI: 10.5465/annals.2018.0174

Lata, A., Chandani, A., & Sharma, S. (2023). Sustainable development goals and gig economy: A bibliometric analysis and future research agenda. *International Journal of Innovation and Sustainable Development, 17*(1), 1–26.

Li, J., Wang, Z., & Li, X. (2024). The impact of artificial intelligence on sustainable development performance of public healthcare supply chain. *Frontiers in Public Health, 12*, 1368953.

Masood, A., Irshad, M., & Ahmad, F. (2023). Artificial Intelligence and Green Human Resource Management: A synergistic approach for environmental sustainability in the manufacturing industry. *Sustainability, 15*(18), 13838.

Morales, P., & Stecher, A. (2023). Algorithmic management and precarious labour in the platform economy: The case of riders in Chile. *Work Organisation, Labour & Globalisation, 17*(1), 68–87.

Nguyen, T. H., Le, D. A., & Pham, T. T. (2025). The impact of green logistics management and Industry 4.0 on sustainable performance in Vietnam. *Journal of Science and Technology - IUH, 77*(5), 89–102.

OECD. (2025). *Algorithmic management and the labour process in logistics*. OECD Publishing.

Omidi, F., & Zarei, A. (2023). The impact of algorithmic management on the labour process in the platform economy: A systematic review. *New Technology, Work and Employment*.

Parent-Rocheleau, X., & Parker, S. K. (2022). Algorithms as work designers: How algorithmic management influences the quality of jobs. *Human Resource Management Review, 32*(3), 100838. DOI: 10.1016/j.hrmr.2021.100838

Pham, N. T., Tučková, Z., & Jabbour, C. J. C. (2020). Greening the hospitality industry: How do green human resource management practices influence organizational citizenship behavior in hotels? A mixed-methods approach. *Tourism Management*, *78*, 104054.

Schaupp, S. (2022). Algorithmic governance in smart cities: The case of Barcelona. *Theory, Culture & Society*, *39*(4), 169–189.

Seyedan, M., & Mafakheri, F. (2020). Predictive big data analytics for supply chain demand forecasting: Methods, applications, and research opportunities. *Journal of Big Data*, *7*(1), 1–22. DOI: 10.1186/s40537-020-00329-2

Vaseei, M., & Paris, G. (2024). The twin transition in logistics: Balancing digitalisation and decarbonisation. *International Journal of Logistics Management*, *35*(1), 22–45.

Wood, A. J. (2021). *Algorithmic management: Consequences for work organisation and working conditions*. International Labour Organization.

Chapter 2
AI and the Socio-Technical Transformation of Logistics Warehousing, Transportation, and Inventory Management

Dorra Dridi
http://orcid.org/0000-0002-2825-5895
University of Sfax, Tunisia

Younes Boujelbene
University of Sfax, Tunisia

ABSTRACT

This chapter explores the socio-technical transformation of logistics driven by artificial intelligence (AI), focusing on inventory management, automated warehouses, and transport optimization. Beyond technological performance, it examines how AI reshapes employment structures, transforms skills, and redefines job roles within logistics systems. AI reconfigures tasks, redistributes decision-making activities, and increases the importance of cognitive and digital competencies required for algorithmic supervision and human–AI collaboration. It enables predictive inventory planning, intelligent flow management, and optimized routing, while raising managerial and ethical challenges related to workforce adaptation and organizational change. Logistics performance thus depends on the balanced interaction between technological capabilities and human engagement, providing a framework for the responsible and inclusive deployment of AI in logistics environments.

DOI: 10.4018/979-8-3373-7826-8.ch002

1. GENERAL INTRODUCTION

Contemporary logistics is undergoing a profound transformation due to the accelerated integration of artificial intelligence (AI) technologies. Traditionally focused on optimizing physical flows, reducing costs, and improving operational reliability, the logistics function is now evolving toward algorithmic management, where decisions are increasingly supported, and sometimes guided, by intelligent systems. This evolution is part of a broader trend of supply chain digitalization, driven by growing market complexity, demand volatility, and heightened requirements for responsiveness and overall performance (Ivanov & Dolgui, 2020). AI now plays a key role in areas such as demand forecasting, dynamic inventory management, transport route optimization, and warehouse automation, profoundly redefining traditional logistics practices (Baryannis et al., 2019).

However, while the operational benefits of AI in logistics—improved forecast accuracy, reduced lead times, optimized resource utilization, and error minimization—are widely emphasized in the literature, most existing studies adopt a predominantly techno-centric approach, focused on algorithmic performance and quantitative results (Choi et al., 2022). The human, organizational, and social implications of AI integration remain relatively underexplored, even though these technologies directly influence work methods, decision-making processes, and interactions between human actors and automated systems.

Beyond technological efficiency, the diffusion of artificial intelligence in logistics also raises important questions regarding workforce transformation and skill evolution. As algorithmic systems become increasingly integrated into logistics operations, employees are required to develop new competencies related to data interpretation, digital system supervision, and human–AI interaction. Rather than eliminating human roles, many logistics environments are witnessing a reconfiguration of tasks, where routine analytical activities are increasingly automated while human actors focus on monitoring, exception handling, and strategic decision-making. Understanding these changes is essential for organizations seeking to successfully integrate AI while maintaining effective coordination between technological capabilities and human expertise (Babashahi et al., 2024 ; Pradhan & Saxena, 2023).

Therefore, this chapter adopts a socio-technical approach, which considers that the performance of an organizational system arises from the combined interaction between technical and social components. Initially developed in the field of work systems and organizational studies, the socio-technical approach emphasizes the mutual adjustment between technology, work organization, and human skills (Trist & Bamforth, 1951; Baxter & Sommerville, 2011). Applied to AI-augmented logistics, this perspective allows the analysis not only of what algorithms do but also of how workers interact with, interpret, and integrate them into their daily practices.

Contrary to deterministic narratives that present AI as a substitute for human labor, recent studies highlight the emergence of hybrid configurations in which human intelligence and artificial intelligence cooperate and complement each other (Raisch & Krakowski, 2021). In these configurations, AI automates repetitive and computational tasks, while human workers retain a central role in supervision, result interpretation, exception management, and decision-making under uncertainty. However, this complementarity introduces new challenges related to cognitive load, algorithmic transparency, and the redistribution of decision-making responsibilities (Jarrahi, 2018).

The main objective of this chapter is to analyze the socio-technical transformations induced by AI in three major logistics domains: inventory management, warehousing, and transportation. In inventory management, machine learning-based predictive models enable more dynamic and accurate planning, altering the traditional role of planners (Baryannis et al., 2019). In warehouses, the introduction of autonomous robots and intelligent management systems transforms collaboration between human operators and automated technologies (Boysen et al., 2019). In transportation, algorithmic management of routes and resources redefines planning and driving professions (Crainic et al., 2011).

Through the analysis of these three areas, this chapter aims to address the following questions: How does AI transform logistics activities and decision-making processes? What skills are required to interact effectively with intelligent systems? How do roles, professional identities, and coordination mechanisms evolve in AI-driven logistics environments? And finally, what are the managerial, organizational, and ethical challenges associated with these transformations?

The contribution of this chapter is twofold, from a theoretical perspective, it enriches the supply chain management literature by proposing a socio-technical interpretation of artificial intelligence, which remains underdeveloped in a field largely dominated by quantitative and technological approaches. From a managerial and operational perspective, it offers insights into how logistics organizations can adapt employee roles, operational skills, and coordination mechanisms in environments where AI is increasingly pervasive. In this context, the chapter places particular emphasis on employment restructuring, skill transformation, and workforce implications, considering them as central dimensions of AI-driven logistics transformation rather than secondary consequences of technological change.

The chapter is structured as follows: Section 2 presents the conceptual framework and develops the socio-technical approach applied to logistics systems. Section 3 analyzes the main applications of artificial intelligence in logistics, examining in turn intelligent inventory management, AI-augmented warehouses, and algorithmic transport optimization. Section 4 provides a cross-sectional analysis of the socio-technical transformations induced by AI in logistics and production systems, highlighting the reconfiguration of operational processes, redistribution of decision-making activities, and evolution of the skills required for flow management. Finally, Section 5 discusses managerial, ethical, and organizational issues related to AI deployment in logistics systems, before the conclusion synthesizes the main contributions of the chapter and opens avenues for future research.

2. LITERATURE REVIEW AND CONCEPTUAL FRAMEWORK

2.1. Artificial Intelligence and the Transformation of Supply Chains

Artificial intelligence (AI) now occupies a central role in the transformation of supply chains and supply chain management. It refers to a set of techniques—machine learning, deep learning, expert systems, and algorithmic optimization—that enable computer systems to analyze large volumes of data, identify patterns, and support or even automate decision-making. In the logistics context, AI builds on traditional decision support systems while representing a significant shift due to its ability to learn, adapt, and operate in uncertain and dynamic environments (Baryannis et al., 2019).

Recent literature highlights that the rise of AI in logistics is closely linked to several concurrent developments: process digitalization, massive data availability (big data), increased complexity of logistics networks, and greater pressure on overall supply chain performance. In this context, AI is deployed to enhance demand forecasting, optimize planning, coordinate physical and informational flows, and increase responsiveness to disruptions. Ivanov and Dolgui (2020) notably show that intelligent technologies play a key role in the resilience and adaptability of supply chains facing unstable environments.

In logistics operations, AI is often presented as a major lever for performance improvement. Machine learning-based forecasting algorithms allow overcoming the limitations of traditional statistical methods by incorporating a large number of heterogeneous variables, such as seasonality, customer behavior, promotions, or exogenous factors (Choi et al., 2022). Similarly, intelligent optimization systems are used to enhance transport route planning, resource allocation, and synchronization of logistics activities, contributing to cost reduction, lead-time improvement, and a lower environmental footprint (Crainic et al., 2011).

In warehouses, AI is associated with advanced automation and the development of so-called "intelligent" systems. Warehouse management systems integrating AI modules optimize picking, reduce errors, and improve internal flow efficiency. The introduction of autonomous mobile robots coupled with real-time planning algorithms transforms work organization and coordination between human actors and technologies (Boysen et al., 2019). These developments illustrate a shift from rigid automation toward more flexible and adaptive systems.

Beyond operational efficiency, several recent studies highlight that the diffusion of artificial intelligence in logistics environments is accompanied by significant changes in workforce roles and required competencies. As AI-driven decision-support systems become increasingly embedded in logistics operations, employees are expected to develop new capabilities related to data interpretation, system monitoring, and collaborative interaction with algorithmic tools.

However, a detailed analysis of the literature reveals that most studies on AI in logistics adopt a primarily techno-economic perspective. Research focuses mainly on algorithmic performance, efficiency gains, and process optimization, paying limited attention to human and organizational dimensions. Workers are often considered mere users or executors of intelligent systems, without a detailed analysis of their interactions with technologies, the evolution of their skills, or the impact of AI on work organization.

This focus on the technical dimension leads to a partial view of the logistics transformation induced by AI. As Raisch and Krakowski (2021) note, AI systems do not mechanically replace human labor but redefine the boundaries between automation and human intervention. Supply chain performance thus depends not only on the quality of algorithms but also on the ability of organizations to integrate these technologies into coherent, acceptable, and effective work systems.

Consequently, recent literature calls for moving beyond purely technological approaches toward more integrative analytical frameworks that simultaneously consider the technical, human, and organizational dimensions of AI in logistics (Jarrahi, 2018). This shift paves the way for socio-technical approaches that analyze supply chains as complex systems in which technology, work, and organization co-evolve. It is within this perspective that this chapter situates itself, providing an analysis of AI-induced transformations not only in terms of operational performance but also in terms of the reconfiguration of roles, skills, and coordination mechanisms within supply chains.

2.2. Socio-Technical Approach to Logistics Systems

The socio-technical approach provides a central analytical framework for understanding the transformations induced by artificial intelligence in logistics systems. Originating from the seminal work of Trist and Bamforth (1951), this approach is based on the idea that the performance of an organizational system results from the joint alignment of two interdependent subsystems: the technical system, which includes technologies, tools, and processes, and the social system, which encompasses actors, skills, relationships, and work organization. This perspective has been progressively consolidated and extended to contemporary complex systems, particularly in the fields of information systems and digital organizations (Cherns, 1976; Baxter & Sommerville, 2011).

Applied to supply chains, the socio-technical approach allows moving beyond an instrumental view of technology, which remains dominant in part of the supply chain management literature. Logistics systems cannot be reduced to flows optimized by algorithms; they constitute complex socio-organizational entities, in which performance depends as much on human coordination as on technological efficiency. Recent studies emphasize that advanced digital technologies, such as AI, do not produce automatic effects but interact with existing practices, organizational structures, and professional logics (Leonardi, 2011; Sarker et al., 2019).

From this perspective, the introduction of AI into logistics systems should not be analyzed as a mere automation process but as a reconfiguration of work systems. Forecasting, planning, or optimization algorithms integrate into existing decision-making processes and modify the allocation of tasks between humans and technologies. Several studies highlight the emergence of hybrid decision-making systems, in which AI and human actors cooperate by leveraging complementary skills (Jarrahi, 2018; Raisch & Krakowski, 2021). AI excels at processing large volumes of data and identifying patterns, while humans retain a key role in interpreting results, considering contextual factors, and managing uncertainty.

This human–algorithm collaboration has major implications for the organization of logistics work, particularly in activities such as inventory planning, warehouse operations coordination, and transport optimization. The socio-technical approach highlights a gradual transformation of professional roles, characterized by a shift from execution functions toward supervision, management, and control functions. Operators, planners, and transport managers become actors of algorithmic supervision, responsible for validating recommendations from intelligent systems, detecting anomalies, and intervening in situations not anticipated by the models (Faraj et al., 2018). This evolution is accompanied by an increase in the complexity of required skills, particularly in digital literacy, algorithmic understanding, and critical assessment of automated decisions.

The socio-technical approach also enables the analysis of organizational and managerial challenges associated with AI integration into supply chains. Algorithmic decisions raise issues of transparency, trust, and accountability, especially when systems operate as "black boxes." Literature shows that human actors' trust in AI systems is a key factor in their acceptance and effective performance (Glikson & Woolley, 2020). Conversely, algorithmic aversion may arise when users perceive systems as opaque, restrictive, or disconnected from operational reality (Burton et al., 2020).

Also, the socio-technical approach offers a relevant framework for analyzing the conditions for sustainable performance in AI-augmented logistics systems. It emphasizes that expected gains in efficiency, responsiveness, and resilience cannot be achieved without alignment between technology, work organization, and human practices. In supply chain management, several studies demonstrate that the performance of intelligent systems strongly depends on organizations' ability to integrate human actors into the decision-making loop and establish appropriate governance of technologies and data (Ivanov & Dolgui, 2020).

In AI-enabled logistics environments, the socio-technical perspective highlights that technological performance alone cannot guarantee operational effectiveness. The successful deployment of intelligent logistics systems depends on the ability of organizations to redesign work processes, develop appropriate employee skills, and ensure effective coordination between human expertise and algorithmic decision-support systems. Consequently, the transformation of logistics systems involves not only technological innovation but also significant changes in organizational practices, workforce capabilities, and decision-making structures.

Thus, the socio-technical approach constitutes the theoretical framework structuring this chapter. It allows for the analysis of artificial intelligence in logistics not as an isolated technology but as a constitutive element of work systems and organizations. This perspective will serve as a guiding thread for the analysis of AI-induced transformations in inventory management, warehousing, and transportation, emphasizing the reconfiguration of roles, skills, and coordination mechanisms within supply chains.

Figure 1. Socio-technical framework for AI-augmented logistics systems

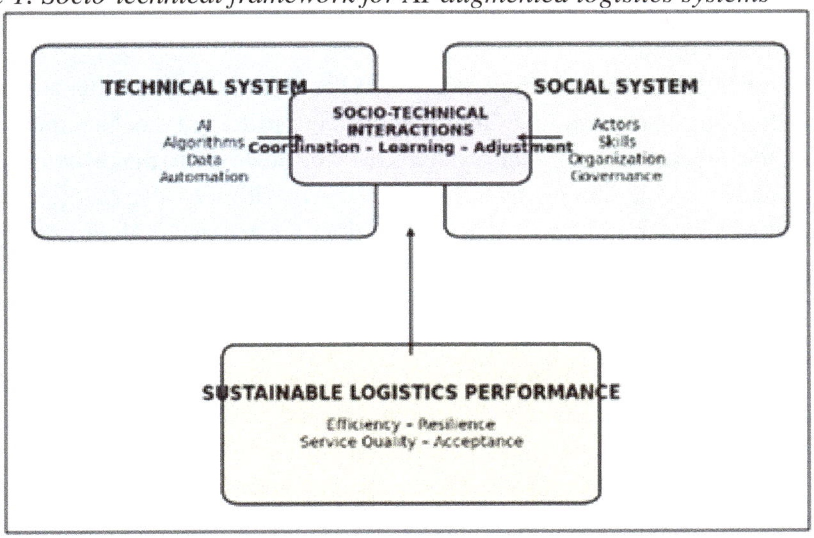

Figure 1 illustrates the socio-technical framework adopted in this chapter to analyze AI-augmented logistics systems. This framework highlights the interaction between the technical system, which encompasses AI technologies, algorithms, and data, and the social system, composed of actors, skills, work organization, and governance mechanisms. Sustainable logistics performance results from the alignment and coordination between these two subsystems, emphasizing that AI does not constitute a standalone solution but is an integrated element within socio-technical work systems.

2.3. Human–Algorithm Cooperation and Hybrid Systems

Cooperation between humans and algorithms constitutes one of the foundations of AI-augmented logistics systems. Contrary to deterministic visions of automation, which portray AI as a substitute for human labor, recent literature highlights the emergence of hybrid systems in which decision-making is distributed between human actors and intelligent technologies. These systems rely on complementary skills: algorithms excel at processing massive volumes of data and identifying patterns, while humans leverage their judgment, experience, and understanding of the operational context (Jarrahi, 2018; Raisch & Krakowski, 2021).

In logistics systems, this human–algorithm cooperation occurs at multiple decision-making levels. At the operational level, algorithms support inventory planning, warehouse task scheduling, and transport route optimization by producing real-time recommendations. Human actors intervene to interpret, validate, or adjust these recommendations according to local constraints, unforeseen events, or factors not modeled. This continuous interaction illustrates the concept of "augmented AI," where technology enhances human capabilities rather than replacing them (Raisch & Krakowski, 2021).

Socio-technical literature emphasizes that the effectiveness of this cooperation strongly depends on the quality of interfaces and coordination mechanisms between humans and algorithms. Intelligent systems must be designed to make their decisions understandable and actionable by human users. Algorithmic opacity, often referred to as the "black box" problem, constitutes a major barrier to technology adoption and can limit real performance in complex logistics environments (Faraj et al., 2018). The ability of actors to understand the general logic of AI systems, even without mastering technical details, thus appears as a key success factor.

Another central issue in human–algorithm cooperation concerns trust. Empirical studies show that users' trust in AI systems directly influences their willingness to follow or challenge algorithmic recommendations (Glikson & Woolley, 2020). Excessive trust can lead to overreliance on automated systems, whereas insufficient trust may result in rejection or algorithmic aversion, reducing the potential benefits of AI (Burton et al., 2020). In logistics systems, where decisions have immediate operational impacts, managing this balance between trust and vigilance is particularly critical.

Human–algorithm collaboration also has significant implications in terms of cognitive load and decision-making responsibility, as well as the evolution of professional skills. Logistics actors must progressively develop new competencies related to data interpretation, intelligent system supervision, and algorithm-assisted decision-making. Supervising intelligent systems requires human actors to continuously monitor algorithmic recommendations, detect anomalies, and intervene promptly in case of malfunctions. This increased cognitive load can generate stress and increase the risk of errors, especially when systems produce large volumes of information or operate without clear explanations of their decisions (Jarrahi, 2018). Moreover, the allocation of responsibilities between humans and algorithms raises organizational and ethical questions, particularly in the event of errors or system failures.

In logistics, these issues are particularly visible in highly automated environments, such as smart warehouses and AI-optimized transport systems. Operators and planners must work with systems that strongly guide their decisions while maintaining sufficient autonomy to handle non-standardized situations. Literature indicates that the most effective hybrid systems are those that explicitly allow for human intervention, recognizing the value of judgment and experience in managing complexity and uncertainty (Ivanov & Dolgui, 2020).

Furthermore, analyzing human–algorithm cooperation highlights the need for organizational design adapted to hybrid systems. The performance of AI-augmented supply chains depends not only on the technical capabilities of algorithms but also on how organizations define roles, processes, and governance mechanisms associated with these technologies. A socio-technical approach to human–algorithm cooperation thus enables understanding the conditions under which AI can contribute to a logistics transformation that is both effective, acceptable, and sustainable, consistent with organizational objectives and human actors' expectations.

In logistics environments increasingly supported by artificial intelligence, hybrid human–algorithm systems redefine how operational decisions are produced and validated. Rather than replacing human expertise, intelligent systems reshape the distribution of tasks between automated analysis and human judgment. Logistics professionals increasingly assume roles related to system supervision, exception management, and contextual interpretation of algorithmic recommendations. These transformations highlight the importance of designing logistics systems where technological capabilities and human expertise evolve in a coordinated and complementary manner.

In this perspective, Figure 2 summarizes the architecture of human–algorithm hybrid systems within supply chains, illustrating the complementarity of human and algorithmic capabilities, as well as the supervisory mechanisms necessary for their coordination.

Figure 2. Architecture of human–algorithm hybrid systems in supply chains

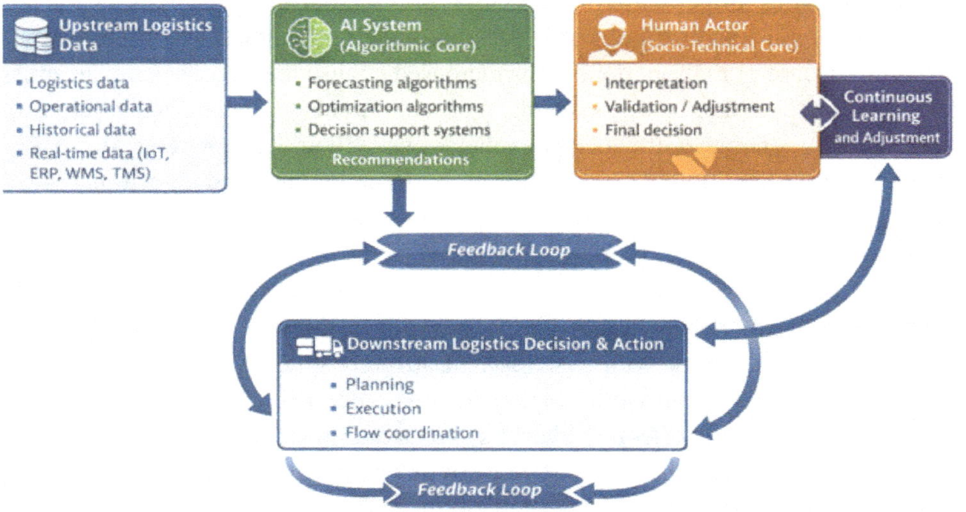

2.4. Transformations of Logistics Work in the Age of Artificial Intelligence

The integration of artificial intelligence into logistics systems goes beyond transforming technical processes; it induces a profound reconfiguration of work, skills, and professional identities. Contrary to narratives focused on replacing human labor through automation, recent literature shows that AI primarily transforms the nature of logistics activities by redistributing tasks between human actors and intelligent systems, while increasing the cognitive and organizational demands of work (Raisch & Krakowski, 2021).

One of the first effects of AI on logistics work concerns the redistribution of tasks across several key activities such as inventory planning, warehouse operations scheduling, and transport route optimization. Routine, repetitive, and highly standardized tasks—such as basic demand calculation, standard planning, or certain handling operations—are increasingly automated by algorithms and robotic systems. In contrast, tasks requiring judgment, coordination, and a nuanced understanding of the operational context are strengthened. This redistribution leads to a polarization of activities, where the added value of human work lies mainly in supervision, decision-making, and managing exceptional situations (Faraj et al., 2018).

This evolution is accompanied by an increase in the complexity of skills required in logistics professions. Workers must now master not only operational processes but also the intelligent systems that support them. Literature emphasizes the growing importance of skills such as digital literacy, the ability to interpret algorithmic recommendations, understanding the limitations of AI models, and exercising critical judgment over automated decisions (Jarrahi, 2018). In this context, cognitive and analytical skills increasingly outweigh purely physical skills, particularly in warehouses and planning activities.

AI also contributes to a reconfiguration of roles and professional identities in logistics. Operators gradually become supervisors of automated systems, planners evolve into data analysts, and transport managers assume roles in algorithmic management. This transformation can generate opportunities by valuing higher-skilled competencies, but it may also create identity tensions and resistance to change when workers perceive a loss of autonomy or meaning in their activities (Leonardi, 2011; Sarker et al., 2019).

At the organizational level, AI integration modifies the forms of coordination and control of logistics work. Intelligent systems enable real-time monitoring of activities, dynamic task allocation, and fine-grained flow coordination. However, this intensification of algorithmic control can increase workers' mental workload and exacerbate time pressures, especially when systems impose high work rates or difficult-to-achieve targets (Glikson & Woolley, 2020). The literature thus highlights the need to design organizational arrangements capable of regulating AI usage while preserving room for human actors to exercise judgment.

Transformations in logistics work in the AI era also raise major issues regarding training and skills management. Recent studies emphasize the key role of continuous training and change management in enabling workers to adopt intelligent technologies and fully leverage their potential (Burton et al., 2020). The absence of appropriate training measures can exacerbate professional inequalities and limit the overall effectiveness of AI-augmented logistics systems..

Therefore, analyzing transformations in logistics work in the age of AI shows that supply chain performance depends not only on the efficiency of deployed technologies but also on organizations' ability to rethink work, skills, and coordination mechanisms. In line with the socio-technical approach adopted in this chapter, these transformations should be analyzed as the result of coevolution between technology, organization, and human actors. Building on this conceptual understanding, the next section presents concrete applications of AI in logistics, highlighting how intelligent systems reshape inventory management, warehouse operations, and transport planning in practice.

3. APPLICATIONS OF AI IN LOGISTICS

3.1. AI and Intelligent Inventory Management: Towards Augmented Planning

Inventory management is one of the fundamental pillars of logistics performance due to its direct impact on costs, service levels, and flow efficiency. Traditionally, classical forecasting approaches, such as simple moving averages, exponential smoothing, and deterministic planning systems like MRP, have long structured inventory management. Although widely adopted, these approaches show their limits in the face of increasing demand volatility, market complexity, and the proliferation of data sources. In this context, artificial intelligence paves the way for so-called intelligent inventory management, based on data- and algorithm-driven augmented planning (Choi et al., 2022).

Recent advances in artificial intelligence, particularly in machine learning, allow the development of predictive models capable of simultaneously integrating a large number of explanatory variables. These models consider not only seasonality and sales history but also purchasing behavior, past stockouts, pricing and promotion effects, as well as exogenous factors related to the economic environment or supply chain disruptions. Several recent studies show that AI-based approaches significantly improve forecast accuracy compared to traditional methods, thereby reducing uncertainty in inventory planning (Carbonneau et al., 2008; Babai et al., 2019).

Beyond forecasting, AI profoundly transforms planning and replenishment mechanisms. Intelligent systems enable dynamic demand planning, where inventory management parameters—safety stock levels, reorder points, lot sizes—are continuously adjusted based on evolving data. This intelligent automation supports automatic replenishment and fine-grained item segmentation according to criticality, using multi-criteria approaches that consider item value, demand variability, and stockout risks. These developments contribute to reducing overstock, limiting stockouts, improving product turnover, and better allocating logistics resources (Babai et al., 2019).

However, the contribution of artificial intelligence to inventory management is not limited to measurable operational gains. As highlighted in Section 2, the introduction of intelligent systems is accompanied by a profound transformation of planning practices and professional roles. Traditionally repetitive tasks performed by planners—calculating safety stock, manual adjustments, operational order tracking—tend to be automated by algorithms. At the same time, new responsibilities emerge, focusing on analyzing algorithmic recommendations, detecting biases or anomalies, configuring models, and validating decisions proposed by AI systems.

This evolution marks the shift from rule-based planning to augmented planning, where AI functions as an advanced decision-support tool rather than a substitute for human judgment. Planners become analysts capable of understanding the overall functioning of intelligent systems, interpreting results, and adjusting parameters according to operational constraints. Dominant competence is no longer only the mastery of classical forecasting methods but also the ability to supervise and manage complex systems based on data and algorithms (Jarrahi, 2018; Raisch & Krakowski, 2021).

In addition to role transformation, AI adoption in inventory management leads to a profound redistribution of tasks between human actors and intelligent systems. Routine and data-intensive activities, such as demand forecasting, parameter calculation, and replenishment execution, are increasingly automated, while higher-value tasks are reassigned to human planners. These include exception management, scenario analysis, and cross-functional coordination with procurement, production, and distribution units. As a result, planners are progressively disengaged from operational micro-decisions and repositioned toward supervisory and strategic functions.

This redistribution of tasks is accompanied by a significant evolution in required competencies. Beyond traditional expertise in forecasting and inventory control, planners are now expected to develop data literacy skills, including the ability to interpret model outputs, understand algorithmic logic, and interact with decision-support systems. In addition, critical thinking and sensemaking capabilities become essential to assess the relevance of AI-generated recommendations, particularly in uncertain or disrupted environments. Recent studies also highlight the emergence of hybrid skill profiles combining domain knowledge in logistics with analytical and digital competencies, reinforcing the need for continuous training and organizational learning mechanisms (Raisch & Krakowski, 2021; Jarrahi, 2018).

However, this transformation also raises important challenges. The increasing reliance on AI systems may lead to risks of deskilling in certain operational tasks, as well as over-dependence on algorithmic outputs. Moreover, the opacity of some machine learning models can limit users' ability to fully understand decision processes, potentially affecting trust and adoption. Therefore, organizations must carefully design human–AI interaction frameworks that ensure transparency, maintain human oversight, and support skill development, in line with a socio-technical perspective.

In this context, the role of the inventory planner evolves into that of an "algorithmic supervisor," responsible for ensuring consistency between AI system recommendations and operational reality. This supervision is particularly critical in environments characterized by high uncertainty or events not anticipated by models, such as sudden demand fluctuations or supply disruptions. Recent studies emphasize that the performance of intelligent inventory management systems closely depends on the quality of interaction between human actors and technologies, confirming the importance of the socio-technical approach developed in Section 2 (Ivanov & Dolgui, 2020; Sarker et al., 2019).

Ultimately, artificial intelligence fundamentally renews inventory management by combining automation, advanced data analysis, and reconfiguration of planning practices. The performance of AI-augmented inventory systems relies not only on algorithm sophistication but also on organizations' ability to support skill development, structure decision-making processes, and keep humans at the center of planning. This analysis paves the way for examining other logistics domains impacted by AI, notably warehouses and transportation systems, which will be addressed in the following sections.

Figure 3. AI-enhanced inventory planning cycle

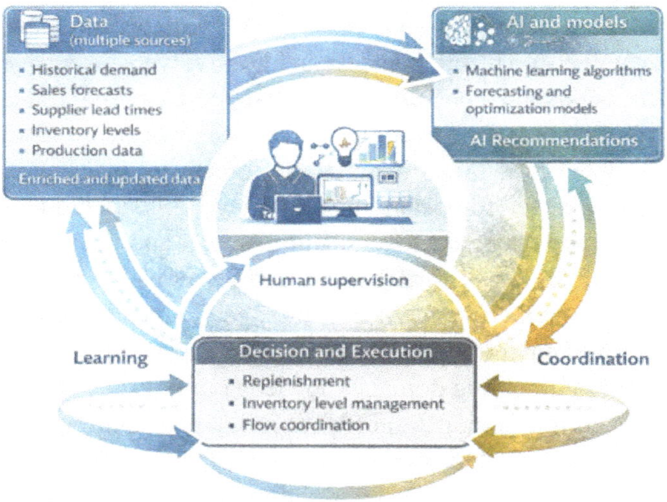

Figure 3 illustrates the AI-based augmented inventory planning cycle. It highlights a hybrid decision-making process in which AI models leverage multi-source data to generate planning recommendations, while planners ensure supervision, adjustment, and validation of decisions. The feedback loop emphasizes the dynamic nature of AI-augmented inventory management, based on continuous learning and ongoing adaptation to operational conditions.

3.2. AI and Smart Warehouses: Human–Algorithm Collaboration

Warehouses are among the logistics environments where the transformation induced by artificial intelligence is most visible and structuring. The development of smart warehouses relies on the integration of advanced technologies such as autonomous mobile robots (AMRs), robotic arms, computer vision, and warehouse management systems (WMS) enhanced with AI engines. These technologies primarily aim to reduce travel times, optimize picking sequences, decrease picking errors, and improve the flow of internal logistics, thereby contributing to increased operational performance (Boysen et al., 2019).

In these highly automated environments, AI plays a central role in operational control. Intelligent systems act as decision-making brains capable of coordinating human and robotic resources in real time, anticipating congestion, dynamically reconfiguring picking zones, and allocating tasks according to the system's current state. Algorithmic management of internal flows relies on continuous analysis of data from sensors, logistics information systems, and activity histories, enabling ongoing adaptation to operational conditions (Wurman et al., 2008; Azadeh et al., 2019).

However, this increasing automation does not lead to a complete replacement of human labor. On the contrary, the literature highlights the emergence of hybrid systems, in which AI serves as a tool to augment decision-making capabilities rather than as an autonomous decision agent (Raisch & Krakowski, 2021). In smart warehouses, human–algorithm collaboration thus becomes a structuring element of the logistics system. Recommendations generated by algorithms must be interpreted, validated, or adjusted by operators according to real-world context, local constraints, and unforeseen situations.

The role of warehouse operators undergoes a profound transformation. From primarily performing physical tasks, they evolve into supervisory technicians within complex socio-technical systems. Their responsibilities include intervening in cases of uncertainty or exceptions, managing operational contingencies (robotic failures, unexpected flows, delays), adjusting algorithmic decisions, and ensuring safety in automated environments. This evolution is accompanied by a shift in required skills, with cognitive competencies—rapid diagnosis, decision-making, problem-solving—becoming central (Dellermann et al., 2019).

Building on this transformation, the deployment of AI in smart warehouses entails a significant redistribution of tasks between human operators and intelligent systems. Repetitive and physically demanding activities, such as basic picking operations, routing, and inventory tracking, are increasingly automated or assisted by robots and AI-driven systems. In contrast, human operators are reassigned to higher-value tasks, including exception handling, system supervision, coordination between robotic and human resources, and real-time decision-making in uncertain situations. This shift reflects a transition from execution-oriented roles toward monitoring and control functions within highly automated environments.

This reallocation of tasks is accompanied by a profound evolution in required competencies. Beyond traditional manual and operational skills, warehouse workers must develop digital interaction capabilities, including the ability to work with interfaces, interpret system alerts, and collaborate effectively with robotic agents. Cognitive and behavioral skills, such as adaptability, situational awareness, and problem-solving under time constraints, become increasingly critical. Furthermore, the emergence of hybrid roles—combining technical, operational, and analytical expertise—highlights the need for continuous training and upskilling strategies within organizations (Klumpp, 2018; Dellermann et al., 2019).

Nevertheless, this transformation also raises important challenges related to workforce adaptation. The increasing complexity of human–algorithm interaction may lead to cognitive overload, while the standardization imposed by algorithmic systems can reduce operator autonomy. In addition, unequal access to training may create skill gaps within the workforce. These issues underline the importance of designing inclusive and adaptive socio-technical systems that balance automation benefits with human capabilities.

This human–algorithm collaboration also leads to a reconfiguration of organizational modes and professional identities within warehouses. Picking teams tend to become flow-management teams, while warehouse managers move towards data-driven management, coordination of technologies, and arbitration between performance, safety, and working conditions. Several studies emphasize that the success of these transformations strongly depends on the implementation of suitable training programs, enabling actors to understand the functioning of intelligent systems and develop effective interaction with them (Klumpp, 2018).

However, the introduction of AI in warehouses is not without tensions. The intensification of algorithmic control can increase operators' cognitive load and stress, particularly when systems impose high speeds or strict targets. Therefore, the performance of smart warehouses depends not only on the technological robustness of the deployed solutions but also on the organization's ability to design balanced socio-technical systems that integrate human, organizational, and technological dimensions (Ivanov et al., 2019).

Ultimately, smart warehouses exemplify the dynamics of human–algorithm collaboration in contemporary logistics systems. AI emerges as a powerful lever for flow management and operational optimization, whose effectiveness closely depends on the active integration of human actors into the decision-making loop. This approach enables a reconciliation of logistics performance gains, operational safety, and sustainable evolution of professions, in line with the socio-technical perspective developed in this chapter.

Figure 4. Smart warehouse as a hybrid socio-technical system

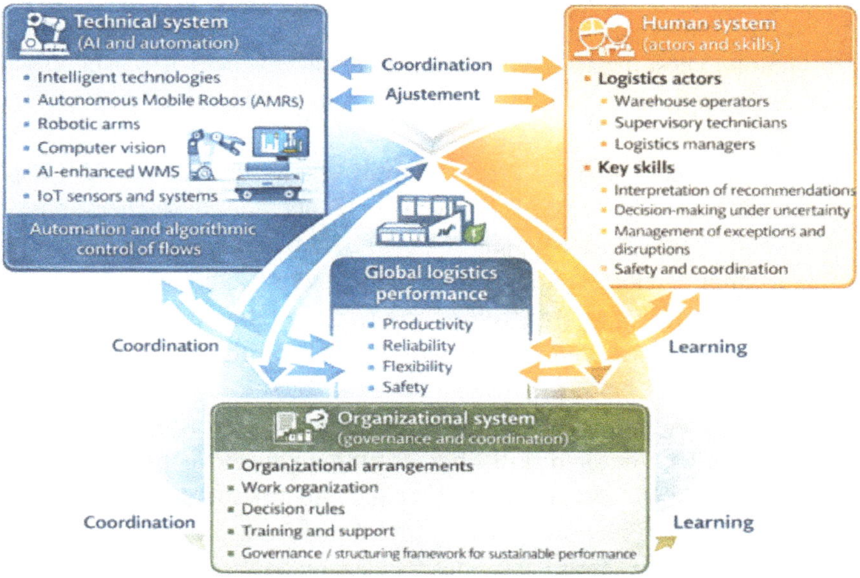

Figure 4 depicts the smart warehouse as a hybrid socio-technical system resulting from the interaction between artificial intelligence technologies, human actors, and organizational arrangements. It highlights the central role of human–algorithm collaboration in flow management and disruption handling, as well as the importance of coordination, learning, and regulation mechanisms in achieving sustainable logistics performance.

3.3. AI and Transport Optimization: Algorithmic Control and New Forms of Work Organization

Transport represents a central lever of logistics performance, both because of its economic weight and its environmental impact. The integration of artificial intelligence into transport systems now enables advanced route optimization, capable of simultaneously considering a complex set of constraints such as distances, traffic conditions, delivery time windows, vehicle types, customer priorities, and regulatory limitations. AI-supported planning systems leverage these data to generate shorter, more cost-efficient, and less polluting routes, thereby reducing unnecessary travel and improving service capacity (Crainic et al., 2011; Vidal et al., 2020).

Approaches based on machine learning and intelligent optimization allow for the dynamic reconfiguration of transport plans according to real-time operational conditions. AI systems can thus integrate unforeseen events—such as congestion, incidents, or last-minute requests—and propose rapid route adjustments to maintain service reliability. These capabilities enhance the responsiveness of transport systems and improve the robustness of logistics decisions in highly variable environments (Ivanov & Dolgui, 2020).

However, as in other segments of the supply chain, AI does not fully replace human actors in transport activities. Drivers, planners, and dispatchers must continuously interact with intelligent planning platforms to validate or adjust proposed routes, report anomalies, and incorporate local or contextual constraints that are not modeled by algorithms. AI therefore acts as an intelligent assistant providing decision-making recommendations, while final responsibility for decisions remains with human actors (Raisch & Krakowski, 2021).

This ongoing interaction with intelligent systems transforms the nature of work in transport activities. Required skills increasingly involve a deeper understanding of algorithmic planning mechanisms and the data underlying decisions. The roles of planners and dispatchers are redefined, shifting from predominantly manual operational management toward activities focused on data analysis, supervision of algorithmic recommendations, and exception handling. At the same time, drivers must adapt to digital guidance and control systems that shape their daily practices, reinforcing human–machine cooperation in operational execution (Klumpp, 2018).

Building on this transformation of roles, the integration of AI in transport systems leads to a significant redistribution of tasks between human actors and algorithmic systems. Routine planning activities, such as route calculation, schedule adjustments, and load optimization, are increasingly automated through intelligent optimization tools. In contrast, human actors—particularly planners and dispatchers—are reassigned to higher-value functions, including exception management, coordination across stakeholders, and real-time decision-making in complex or uncertain situations. This shift reflects a transition from execution-oriented roles toward supervisory and coordination-intensive activities.

This redistribution of tasks is accompanied by a substantial evolution in required competencies. In addition to traditional expertise in transport planning, professionals must develop data interpretation skills, understand algorithmic outputs, and interact effectively with digital platforms. For drivers, the increasing use of navigation and monitoring systems requires the ability to follow algorithmically generated instructions while maintaining situational awareness and adapting to real-world constraints. More broadly, cognitive skills such as critical thinking, adaptability, and rapid decision-making become essential in environments characterized by real-time data flows and dynamic reconfiguration.

However, this transformation also raises important challenges. The growing reliance on algorithmic systems may reduce human autonomy in decision-making and create risks of over-dependence on automated recommendations. In addition, discrepancies between algorithmic outputs and field realities may generate tensions for operators, particularly when performance pressures are high. These challenges highlight the need to design transport systems that preserve human agency, ensure transparency of algorithmic decisions, and support continuous skill development within a socio-technical framework.

Nevertheless, this evolution introduces new organizational and human challenges. Continuous supervision of intelligent systems can generate additional cognitive load, linked to the need to understand, monitor, and sometimes challenge algorithmic recommendations. The literature emphasizes that the effectiveness of AI-augmented transport systems depends as much on the performance of deployed technologies as on the ability of human actors to interact effectively with them within an appropriate organizational framework (Dellermann et al., 2019). Training, change management, and clear role definition thus become essential conditions for ensuring the acceptability and effectiveness of AI solutions in transport.

From this perspective, the socio-technical dimension is particularly salient in transport activities. Performance does not result solely from algorithmic route optimization, but from the successful articulation of intelligent technologies, human skills, and organizational arrangements. Smart transport therefore exemplifies the challenges of algorithmic control and new forms of work organization within contemporary logistics systems, in line with the socio-technical approach developed in this chapter.

These three logistics domains illustrate distinct patterns in the application of artificial intelligence. In inventory management, AI is primarily used for predictive analytics, supporting demand forecasting and replenishment decisions. In contrast, warehousing is characterized by a higher level of physical automation, where AI is embedded in robotics and material handling systems. Transportation, on the other hand, relies on AI for dynamic optimization, enabling real-time route planning and adaptive decision-making. These differences highlight that AI adoption in logistics is not homogeneous but varies significantly depending on operational contexts and technological requirements. This comparative overview sets the stage for Section 4, which examines the socio-technical implications of these AI applications on workforce roles, skills, and organizational practices.

Figure 5. Intelligent transport system as a socio-technical system based on algorithmic routing

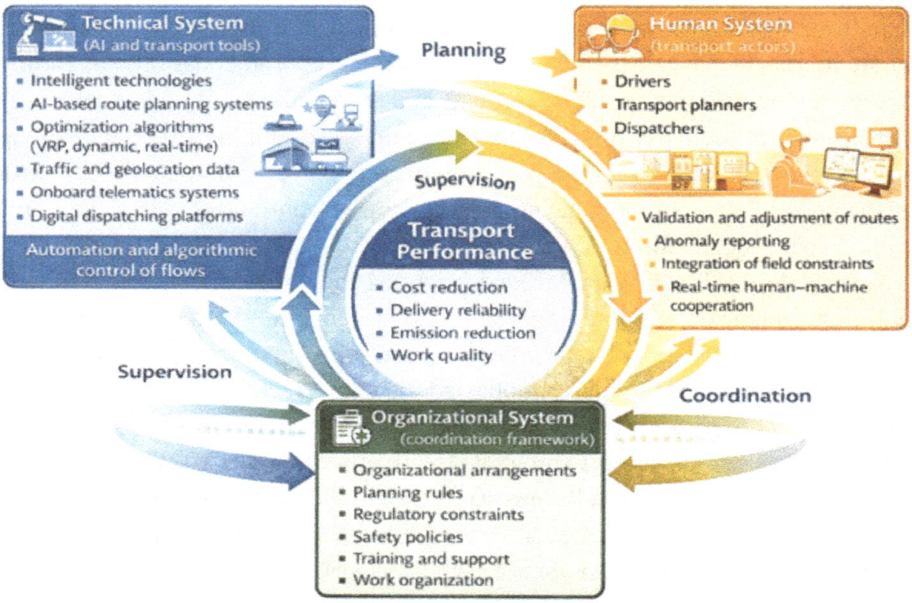

Figure 5 depicts the intelligent transport system as a socio-technical system based on algorithmic route control. It highlights the continuous cooperation between artificial intelligence technologies, human actors, and organizational arrangements, emphasizing that transport performance results from a balance between algorithmic optimization, human supervision, and organizational governance.

Building on the practical applications of AI in inventory management, warehousing, and transport, the next section explores the socio-technical transformations these technologies induce. Beyond operational efficiency, AI reshapes work organization, redefines roles and skills, and influences professional identities, highlighting the need to analyze logistics performance as a product of human–technology–organization interactions.

4. SOCIO-TECHNICAL TRANSFORMATIONS: REDISTRIBUTION OF WORK, SKILLS, AND IDENTITIES

One of the main contributions of this chapter lies in its analysis of the socio-technical transformations induced by the introduction of artificial intelligence into logistics systems. Contrary to media narratives that often focus on the substitution of human labor by intelligent technologies, the examination of AI applications in inventory management, warehousing, and transport reveals a more complex dynamic, characterized by a profound reconfiguration of work, skills, and professional identities. Logistics performance thus appears as the outcome of a socio-technical balance based on the articulation between technologies, human actors, and organizational arrangements (Raisch & Krakowski, 2021; Sarker et al., 2019).

4.1. Task Redistribution: From Execution to Supervision

The integration of AI into logistics systems leads to a gradual redistribution of tasks between humans and technologies. Repetitive, standardized, and low–value-added tasks—such as certain planning calculations, routine activity sequencing, or simple physical execution—tend to be automated. In contrast, complex, uncertain, and highly contextual tasks are reinforced and continue to rely on human judgment. Logistics actors are particularly involved in interpreting algorithmic recommendations, managing exceptions, arbitrating between conflicting objectives, and adapting decisions to local operational constraints (Boysen et al., 2019; Dellermann et al., 2019).

More specifically, the impact of AI varies across different logistics roles. Inventory managers increasingly rely on algorithmic recommendations for demand forecasting and replenishment decisions, shifting their tasks toward supervision and exception management. Warehouse operators transition from manual handling activities to the monitoring and coordination of automated systems and robots. In transportation, planners and dispatchers focus more on data analysis and real-time decision-making, while drivers interact with digital guidance systems that influence routing and delivery execution. These changes illustrate a clear evolution of tasks and highlight the growing importance of analytical, digital, and coordination skills in logistics jobs.

This task redistribution transforms the very nature of logistics work. AI acts as a mechanism of informational augmentation, producing decision-making recommendations that must be supervised, validated, and adjusted by human actors. Recent studies emphasize that this logic of algorithmic supervision constitutes one of the main value-creation levers in AI-augmented organizations, while simultaneously introducing new cognitive demands on workers (Sarker et al., 2019).

4.2. Increasing Skill Complexity and Knowledge Hybridization

Socio-technical transformations are accompanied by an increasing complexity of the skills required in logistics professions. Purely physical or procedural skills tend to lose relative importance, while cognitive skills become central. Workers are now required to understand the general functioning of intelligent systems, interpret the data they produce, identify biases or anomalies, and adjust algorithmic decisions according to real operational contexts (Klumpp, 2018).

This evolution affects all actors across the logistics chain. Planners develop algorithmic literacy that enables them to interact effectively with augmented planning tools. Warehouse operators become supervision technicians capable of diagnosing malfunctions and managing unforeseen situations. Transport actors, in turn, continuously cooperate with algorithmic control systems that influence their daily decisions. Recent research shows that this hybridization of skills is a key performance factor in AI-augmented work environments (Baptista et al., 2020).

Beyond these transformations, AI adoption in logistics also raises important challenges related to workforce planning. Organizations must anticipate future skill requirements, redesign job profiles, and align workforce capabilities with evolving technological systems. This requires a more strategic approach to human resource management, integrating long-term planning of competencies, continuous reskilling initiatives, and adaptive workforce allocation. As logistics systems become increasingly data-driven and automated, workforce planning emerges as a critical lever to ensure both operational performance and organizational resilience.

4.3. Work Reorganization and New Forms of Coordination

The introduction of AI also leads to a reorganization of logistics work, characterized by increased role transversalization and an intensification of coordination mechanisms. Traditional boundaries between planning, execution, and control tend to blur in favor of integrated, data-driven control systems. Human–machine communication becomes a structuring element of the daily functioning of logistics systems, requiring continuous interactions between actors and intelligent technologies (Ivanov et al., 2019).

This reorganization modifies collective coordination modes. Operational teams evolve into flow-control teams, in which coordination relies on a shared interpretation of information generated by intelligent systems. Managers assume an orchestration role, ensuring coherence between performance objectives, human constraints, and technological capabilities. Recent studies emphasize that the effectiveness of these new organizational forms depends strongly on the quality of the socio-technical coordination mechanisms implemented (Sarker et al., 2019).

4.4. Transformation of Professional Identities and Socio-Technical Balance

The integration of AI into logistics systems profoundly transforms professional identities. Operators are no longer defined solely by their capacity for physical execution, but by their roles in supervision, analysis, and decision-making. Planners become data analysts and guarantors of decision quality, while drivers operate within intelligent systems that continuously shape their operational practices. These identity transformations may create opportunities for work valorization, but also generate tensions related to increased cognitive load and the loss of traditional professional reference points (Klumpp, 2018; Baptista et al., 2020).

From this perspective, the performance of AI-augmented logistics systems cannot be assessed solely through techno-economic indicators. It fundamentally depends on socio-technical balance—that is, on how organizations restructure work, develop skills, and support identity transformations around intelligent technologies. This approach makes it possible to move beyond a techno-centric view of AI and to highlight the central role of human actors in the creation of sustainable logistics value.

Table 1 provides a synthesis of the main socio-technical transformations induced by the integration of AI into logistics systems, highlighting changes in work, skills, organization, and professional identities.

Table 1. Socio-technical transformations induced by AI in logistics systems

Dimension	Traditional Logistics	AI-Augmented Logistics	Socio-Technical Implications
Nature of tasks	Manual execution, repetitive tasks	Supervision, arbitration, and exception management	Redistribution of human–technology work
Decision-making processes	Local and reactive decisions	Decisions assisted by predictive algorithms	Hybrid human–machine management
Dominant skills	Physical and procedural	Cognitive, analytical, and digital	Increased skill complexity
Work organization	Functional and siloed structuring	Cross-functional, data-driven coordination	Strengthening socio-technical cooperation
Professional roles	Operational worker, technical planner	Algorithmic supervisor, logistics analyst	Transformation of professional identities
Relationship to technology	Support tool	Decision-making partner	Managed dependency and conditional trust
Logistics performance	Operational efficiency	Overall and sustainable performance	Socio-technical balance as a key factor

This synthesis highlights that logistics performance in the AI era relies less on technological sophistication alone than on organizations' ability to build a sustainable socio-technical balance.

While Section 4 has highlighted the socio-technical transformations reshaping work, skills, and professional identities, these changes also generate a set of managerial, ethical, and organizational challenges. Understanding how organizations can support skill development, ensure fair redistribution of tasks, maintain social acceptance of AI, and govern data responsibly is crucial to realizing the full potential of AI-augmented logistics systems. The next section examines these challenges in detail.

5. MANAGERIAL, ETHICAL, AND ORGANIZATIONAL CHALLENGES OF AI IN LOGISTICS

The adoption of artificial intelligence in logistics systems is not limited to a technological transformation of processes. It raises a set of managerial, ethical, and organizational challenges that strongly condition the success of AI projects and the sustainability of the performance achieved. These challenges concern the development of skills, the social acceptability of technologies, data governance, and organizational fairness. Recent studies emphasize that the benefits of AI depend less on the sophistication of algorithms than on organizations' ability to support the associated human and organizational transformations (Raisch & Krakowski, 2021; Sarker et al., 2019).

5.1. Training, Reskilling, and Skills Development

One of the primary managerial challenges associated with the introduction of AI concerns the training and reskilling of logistics actors. As shown in the previous sections, jobs are evolving toward roles focused on supervision, analysis, and the steering of intelligent systems. This evolution makes the development of digital, analytical, and cognitive skills essential, as well as a basic understanding of how the algorithms used operate. Continuous training thus appears as a central lever for reducing skills gaps and securing professional career paths in AI-augmented logistics organizations (Klumpp, 2018; Baptista et al., 2020).

Beyond training and reskilling, organizations must also reconsider career progression and job design in AI-augmented logistics environments. As traditional roles evolve, new career paths emerge, requiring hybrid profiles that combine operational expertise with analytical and digital skills. Redesigning jobs to integrate human–AI collaboration and offering clear career development opportunities become essential to attract, retain, and motivate employees in increasingly digitalized logistics systems.

5.2. Social Acceptability and Technology Appropriation

Social acceptability represents a major challenge in the AI-driven transformation of logistics. The introduction of automated decision-making systems may generate resistance when actors perceive these technologies as tools of control, substitution, or deskilling. Conversely, research shows that the appropriation of AI is facilitated when workers understand the objectives pursued, the limitations of algorithms, and their complementary role in the decision-making process. Transparency, communication, and the involvement of end users during deployment phases therefore appear as essential conditions for the social acceptability of intelligent systems (Dellermann et al., 2019; Sarker et al., 2019).

5.3. Mental Workload, Cognitive Ergonomics, and Working Conditions

While AI can reduce certain forms of physical strain, it may also lead to an increase in mental workload related to algorithmic supervision. Logistics actors are required to continuously monitor the recommendations of intelligent systems, manage complex information flows, and intervene rapidly in the event of anomalies or exceptions. This cognitive intensification may generate stress, particularly when algorithms operate as opaque "black boxes" that are difficult to interpret. Addressing cognitive ergonomics and working conditions thus becomes a central issue to avoid negative effects of digital transformation on workers' health and performance (Parasuraman et al., 2000; Klumpp, 2018).

5.4. Organizational Justice and Fairness in Work Redistribution

The partial automation of logistics activities also raises questions of organizational justice. The way automated and non-automated tasks are allocated can either reinforce or, conversely, mitigate internal inequalities among different categories of workers. Managerial decisions regarding AI deployment directly influence perceptions of fairness, motivation, and employee engagement. Recent studies emphasize that organizations must ensure a balanced redistribution of responsibilities and a clear recognition of the new skills mobilized in AI-augmented environments (Raisch & Krakowski, 2021).

5.5. Data Governance and Reliability of Intelligent Logistics Systems

AI-based logistics systems rely on intensive use of operational data generated from production, storage, and transportation processes. The quality, consistency, and security of this data directly determine the reliability of algorithmic decisions and, consequently, the performance of intelligent logistics systems. Data governance should be understood here as a set of operational mechanisms aimed at ensuring data traceability, clarity of responsibilities, and robustness of decision-making processes.

Explicit data management rules, combined with control and validation procedures, help limit algorithmic biases and ensure effective interaction between human actors and intelligent systems. Poor governance can undermine the continuity of logistics operations and reduce organizations' ability to manage their flows in uncertain environments (Ivanov et al., 2019; Sarker et al., 2019).

5.6. Toward a Controlled Human and Organizational Transformation

All of these challenges show that the introduction of AI in logistics cannot be reduced to a purely technological project. It represents a socio-organizational transformation that requires a holistic approach, simultaneously integrating human, organizational, and ethical dimensions. Organizations' ability to manage these challenges conditions the construction of a sustainable socio-technical balance, in which AI acts as a factor augmenting human work rather than as a mere automation tool.

CONCLUSION

This chapter has provided a comprehensive analysis of the impact of artificial intelligence on logistics systems by focusing on three key areas of the supply chain: intelligent inventory management, AI-augmented warehouses, and algorithmically optimized transport. By adopting a socio-technical approach, it highlights that the performance gains associated with AI do not stem solely from technological sophistication, but rather depend closely on the way organizations articulate technologies, human actors, and organizational structures.

The analysis shows that AI does not replace workers but profoundly transforms the nature of logistics work. It leads to a redistribution of tasks, an increase in the complexity of required skills, and a reconfiguration of roles and professional identities. These transformations highlight that employment restructuring and skill evolution constitute central dimensions of AI-driven logistics systems rather than secondary effects of technological change. Human actors remain at the core of decision-making processes as supervisors, analysts, and guarantors of the quality of algorithmic decisions, thus emphasizing the fundamentally hybrid nature of AI-augmented logistics systems.

This chapter contributes to the literature by providing a socio-technical analytical perspective on AI-driven logistics systems and by highlighting the central role of workforce transformation, skill evolution, and human–AI collaboration in shaping logistics performance. It also identifies the organizational conditions required for the effective and responsible integration of AI, including the development of skills, the support of organizational change, the social acceptability of technologies, and the establishment of robust data governance mechanisms.

This chapter contributes to the literature by providing a socio-technical analytical perspective on AI-driven logistics systems and by highlighting the central role of workforce transformation, skill evolution, and human–AI collaboration in shaping logistics performance. It also identifies the organizational conditions required for the effective and responsible integration of AI, including the development of skills, the support of organizational change, the social acceptability of technologies, and the establishment of robust data governance mechanisms.

REFERENCES

Azadeh, K., de Koster, R., & Roy, D. (2019). Robotized and automated warehouse systems: Review and recent developments. *Transportation Science*, *53*(4), 917–945. DOI: 10.1287/trsc.2018.0873

Babai, M. Z., Dallery, Y., Boubaker, S., & Kalai, R. (2019). A new method to forecast intermittent demand in the presence of inventory obsolescence. *International Journal of Production Economics*, *209*, 30–41. DOI: 10.1016/j.ijpe.2018.01.026

Babashahi, L., Barbosa, C. E., Lima, Y., Lyra, A., Salazar, H., Argôlo, M., Almeida, M. A., & Souza, J. M. (2024). AI in the workplace: A systematic review of skill transformation in the industry. *Administrative Sciences*, *14*(6), 127. Advance online publication. DOI: 10.3390/admsci14060127

Baptista, J., Stein, M.-K., Klein, S., Watson-Manheim, M. B., & Lee, J. (2020). Digital work and organisational transformation: Emergent Digital/Human work configurations in modern organisations. *The Journal of Strategic Information Systems*, *29*(2), 101618. DOI: 10.1016/j.jsis.2020.101618

Baryannis, G., Dani, S., & Antoniou, G. (2019). Predictive analytics and artificial intelligence in supply chain management: Review and implications for the future. *Computers & Industrial Engineering*, *137*, 106024.

Baxter, G., & Sommerville, I. (2011). Socio-technical systems: From design methods to systems engineering. *Interacting with Computers*, *23*(1), 4–17. DOI: 10.1016/j.intcom.2010.07.003

Boysen, N., de Koster, R., & Weidinger, F. (2019). Warehousing in the e-commerce era: A survey. *European Journal of Operational Research*, *277*(2), 396–411. DOI: 10.1016/j.ejor.2018.08.023

Burton, J. W., Stein, M.-K., & Jensen, T. B. (2020). A systematic review of algorithm aversion in augmented decision making. *Journal of Behavioral Decision Making*, *29*(6), 543–565. DOI: 10.1002/bdm.2155

Carbonneau, R., Laframboise, K., & Vahidov, R. (2008). Application of machine learning techniques for supply chain demand forecasting. *European Journal of Operational Research*, *184*(3), 1140–1154. DOI: 10.1016/j.ejor.2006.12.004

Cherns, A. (1976). The principles of socio-technical design. *Human Relations*, *29*(8), 783–792. DOI: 10.1177/001872677602900806

Choi, T.-M., Kumar, S., Yue, X., & Chan, H.-L. (2022). Disruptive Technologies and Operations Management in the Industry 4.0 Era and Beyond. *Production and Operations Management*, *31*(1), 9–31. DOI: 10.1111/poms.13622

Crainic, T. G., Fu, X., Gendreau, M., Rei, W., & Wallace, S. W. (2011). Progressive hedging-based metaheuristics for stochastic network design. *Networks*, *58*(2), 114–124. DOI: 10.1002/net.20456

Dellermann, D., Ebel, P., Söllner, M., & Leimeister, J. M. (2019). Hybrid intelligence. *Business & Information Systems Engineering*, *61*(5), 637–643. DOI: 10.1007/s12599-019-00595-2

Faraj, S., Pachidi, S., & Sayegh, K. (2018). Working and organizing in the age of the learning algorithm. *Information and Organization*, *28*(1), 62–70. DOI: 10.1016/j.infoandorg.2018.02.005

Glikson, E., & Woolley, A. W. (2020). Human trust in artificial intelligence: Review of empirical research. *The Academy of Management Annals*, *14*(2), 627–660. DOI: 10.5465/annals.2018.0057

Ivanov, D., & Dolgui, A. (2020). A digital supply chain twin for managing the disruption risks and resilience in the era of Industry 4.0. *Production Planning and Control*, *32*(9), 775–788. DOI: 10.1080/09537287.2020.1768450

Ivanov, D., Dolgui, A., & Sokolov, B. (2019). The impact of digital technology and Industry 4.0 on the ripple effect and supply chain risk analytics. *International Journal of Production Research*, *57*(3), 829–846. DOI: 10.1080/00207543.2018.1488086

Jarrahi, M. H. (2018). Artificial intelligence and the future of work: Human–AI symbiosis in organizational decision making. *Business Horizons*, *61*(4), 577–586. DOI: 10.1016/j.bushor.2018.03.007

Klumpp, M. (2018). Automation and artificial intelligence in business logistics systems: Human reactions and collaboration requirements. *International Journal of Logistics*, *21*(3), 224–242. DOI: 10.1080/13675567.2017.1384451

Leonardi, P. M. (2011). When flexible routines meet flexible technologies: Affordance, constraint, and the imbrication of human and material agencies. *Management Information Systems Quarterly*, *35*(1), 147–167. DOI: 10.2307/23043493

Parasuraman, R., Sheridan, T. B., & Wickens, C. D. (2000). A model for types and levels of human interaction with automation. *IEEE Transactions on Systems, Man, and Cybernetics. Part A, Systems and Humans*, *30*(3), 286–297. DOI: 10.1109/3468.844354 PMID: 11760769

Pradhan, I. P., & Saxena, P. (2023). Reskilling workforce for the artificial intelligence age: Challenges and the way forward. In Tyagi, P., Chilamkurti, N., Grima, S., Sood, K., & Balusamy, B. (Eds.), *The adoption and effect of artificial intelligence on human resources management, Part B* (pp. 181–197). Emerald Publishing Limited., DOI: 10.1108/978-1-80455-662-720230011

Raisch, S., & Krakowski, S. (2021). Artificial intelligence and management: The automation–augmentation paradox. *Academy of Management Review*, *46*(1), 192–210. DOI: 10.5465/amr.2018.0072

Sarker, S., Chatterjee, S., Xiao, X., & Elbanna, A. (2019). The sociotechnical axis of cohesion for the IS discipline: Its historical legacy and its continued relevance. *Management Information Systems Quarterly*, *43*(3), 695–719. DOI: 10.25300/MISQ/2019/13747

Trist, E. L., & Bamforth, K. W. (1951). Some social and psychological consequences of the longwall method of coal-getting. *Human Relations*, *4*(1), 3–38. DOI: 10.1177/001872675100400101

Vidal, T., Laporte, G., & Matl, P. (2020). A concise guide to existing and emerging vehicle routing problem variants. *European Journal of Operational Research*, *286*(2), 401–416. DOI: 10.1016/j.ejor.2019.10.010

Wurman, P. R., D'Andrea, R., & Mountz, M. (2008). Coordinating hundreds of cooperative, autonomous vehicles in warehouses. *AI Magazine*, *29*(1), 9–20.

Chapter 3
From Freight to Finance:
AI-Enabled Supply Chain Finance and the Transformation of Skills and Employment

Phan Nguyet Anh Do
http://orcid.org/0009-0005-4738-6873
Northumbria University, UK

Hoang Anh Nguyen
VNU Economics and Business, Vietnam

ABSTRACT

This chapter examines how AI-enabled supply chain finance (SCF) transforms skills and employment within integrated logistics by embedding financing decisions into trade execution. Drawing on an in-depth single-case study of an anonymised global logistics provider, the analysis shows that AI-driven verification and risk assessment do not primarily eliminate work but redesign decision architectures: routine checks are automated while exception regimes expand, shifting labour toward interpretive judgement, escalation coordination, and auditable accountability. The chapter further demonstrates how embedded finance re-bundles work across operations, finance, data stewardship, and compliance, producing hybrid roles and contested occupational boundaries. Beyond the firm, AI-enabled SCF introduces data-based gatekeeping that unevenly shapes access to liquidity, particularly for smaller suppliers with limited traceability, requiring employees to perform supplier enablement and legitimacy maintenance.

DOI: 10.4018/979-8-3373-7826-8.ch003

1. INTRODUCTION

Artificial intelligence (AI) is increasingly reshaping logistics not only through visible operational automation—such as smart warehousing, routing optimisation, and predictive demand planning—but also through less visible transformations in how logistics firms manage cash, risk, and trade execution across multi-tier networks. In parallel with digital logistics integration, supply chain finance (SCF) has evolved from a specialist financial service into a strategic operating layer that can stabilise trade flows, reduce working capital pressure, and protect continuity in uncertain environments. This convergence matters because AI-enabled SCF increasingly relies on operational data streams (shipment status, documentation, supplier performance signals, exception patterns) to automate credit decisions, accelerate payment flows, and distribute risk across global supply networks. As a result, the logistics sector is witnessing not merely the automation of tasks, but a reconfiguration of work systems in which financing becomes embedded in supply chain execution, and labour is reorganised around new roles of verification, oversight, orchestration, and data-driven governance.

Despite growing practitioner attention to digital SCF platforms and embedded finance models, the academic discussion remains fragmented across logistics innovation, financial technology, and the future of work. Existing studies often treat SCF as a financial instrument and AI as a technological enabler, but fewer accounts examine how the integration of AI and SCF restructures employment inside logistics organisations and their wider ecosystems. This gap is increasingly consequential because AI-enabled financing redistributes decision authority and informational power across buyers, suppliers, financial institutions, and logistics intermediaries. It also alters the skill composition of logistics work by shifting value creation away from routine transaction handling toward cross-functional coordination, compliance assurance, customer enablement, and exception management. In developing economies, these shifts may produce uneven labour outcomes: while AI-enabled SCF can widen access to liquidity for SMEs and reduce friction in trade execution, it can also create new exclusion risks through data-based credit scoring and platform gatekeeping, a concern that resonates with broader debates on AI, development, and productivity in developing countries (Aly, 2022) as well as the distributional politics of automation (Boyd & Holton, 2018).

This chapter aims to explain how and why AI-enabled SCF transforms employment structures and skill requirements within integrated logistics firms, and why these changes matter for the governance and sustainability of AI-driven logistics ecosystems. Rather than focusing on automation as displacement alone, the chapter analyses AI-enabled SCF as a form of organisational and inter-organisational redesign that shifts human work toward higher-accountability functions—such as human-in-the-loop risk governance, cross-border compliance interpretation, data quality stewardship, supplier onboarding and relationship enablement, and operational–financial exception resolution. The chapter argues that AI-enabled SCF expands the strategic significance of labour in logistics: workers increasingly operate at the intersection of trade execution, financial decision-making, and digital oversight, where failures are not only operational disruptions but also financial and reputational risks. By unpacking this shift through a comparative multiple-case analysis in integrated logistics, the chapter contributes to scholarship on AI-enabled SCF innovation (Olan et al., 2022a; Olan et al., 2022b; Ronchini et al., 2024) and digital SCF platforms (Tanveer et al., 2025), while advancing future-of-work debates by specifying how skills and employment are reconfigured through decision-architecture redesign and ecosystem governance (Tschang & Almirall, 2021; Arranz Lahuerta et al., 2026).

2. LITERATURE REVIEW

2.1 Core concepts

This chapter is anchored in three interrelated concept clusters: integrated logistics, supply chain finance, and AI-enabled organisational transformation. Integrated logistics refers to the bundling of freight transport, warehousing, customs brokerage, and end-to-end coordination into a single service architecture that seeks to manage physical flows, information flows, and increasingly the financial conditions under which trade is executed. In such settings, operational performance is inseparable from documentation integrity, compliance routines, partner coordination, and risk management. Supply chain finance, in turn, describes the set of financing solutions that optimise working capital and liquidity across supply networks by aligning payment terms and financing instruments with trade transactions and supply chain milestones. While SCF has historically been associated with bank-led trade finance and buyer-driven programmes (e.g., reverse factoring), recent developments foreground digital SCF platforms and data-driven integration with operational systems, pushing SCF from a financial adjunct toward an embedded operational capability (Tanveer et al., 2025).

The integration of AI intensifies this shift by enabling real-time evaluation of trade risks, automated verification and anomaly detection, and faster decision-making in financing approval and execution. Research on sustainable supply chain finance emphasises that AI can improve transparency, risk assessment, and sustainability alignment across supply networks (Olan et al., 2022a; Olan et al., 2022b). Work on SCF innovation processes further suggests that AI is not only an efficiency enhancer but also a driver of organisational reconfiguration because it changes how actors search for solutions, recombine resources, and institutionalise new routines (Ronchini et al., 2024). At the same time, the broader AI and analytics literature highlights that AI-enabled decision-making increasingly relies on big data and business analytics infrastructures, raising questions of data quality, interpretability, and governance (Khan, 2025).

The chapter's problem is therefore not merely whether AI substitutes labour, but how AI-enabled SCF reorganises decision rights, work bundles, and accountability across logistics ecosystems. This focus aligns with scholarship that conceptualises AI as "augmenting automation"—a technology that reallocates tasks and reshapes roles rather than producing a linear substitution of human work (Tschang & Almirall, 2021). It also connects to evidence that AI adoption affects employment structure and skill composition, often favouring higher-skill task content while increasing insecurity and adoption tensions when organisational capabilities lag behind technological change (Ma et al., 2022; Liang et al., 2025; Arranz Lahuerta et al., 2026). Accordingly, this chapter develops a theoretical framework that integrates three lenses—decision architectures and algorithmic governance, skill hybridisation and work re-bundling, and ecosystem power/inclusion dynamics—to explain employment transformation in AI-enabled SCF within integrated logistics.

2.2 Decision architectures and algorithmic governance in AI-enabled SCF

The first pillar of the framework conceptualises AI-enabled SCF as a redesign of decision architectures. In integrated logistics, financing decisions are increasingly linked to operational milestones—such as shipment departure, customs clearance, proof of delivery, documentation verification, and exception resolution—creating a tighter coupling between trade execution and liquidity release. AI accelerates this coupling by automating aspects of risk assessment and verification using operational data signals. Studies in sustainable supply chain finance argue that AI enables new forms of network-level decision-making by processing multi-source data, improving visibility, and supporting more adaptive allocation of financial resources across supply networks (Olan et al., 2022a). In sector-specific contexts, AI networks can enable sustainable SCF by linking performance signals to financing and thereby aligning incentives for compliance, transparency, and risk reduction (Olan et al., 2022b).

However, the organisational consequences of such automation are not limited to speed. AI-enabled financing changes who has authority to decide, which criteria are legitimised, and how decisions are monitored and contested. Ronchini et al. (2024) highlight that AI's role in SCF innovation extends across stages of the innovation process, shaping search, design, validation, and scaling of SCF solutions. This implies that algorithmic decision-making is co-produced with organisational routines and governance choices. Bag et al. (2025) further show that generative AI and data-driven decision systems can alter financial decision-making in operations and supply chain contexts, with performance outcomes shaped by organisational conditions and decision processes rather than technology alone. For integrated logistics firms, this suggests that AI-enabled SCF is best analysed as algorithmic governance: the creation of rule-like decision infrastructures that embed risk logics into workflows, define escalation pathways, and redistribute accountability for financial outcomes.

This chapter uses the concept of decision architecture to emphasise three mechanisms. First, routinisation occurs when AI automates repetitive verification and scoring tasks (e.g., document checks, invoice matching, anomaly detection), compressing cycle time but also creating dependence on data quality and model validity. Second, exception regimes emerge when AI systems flag anomalies or borderline cases that require human interpretation, negotiation, and override decisions. Third, accountability layering becomes salient when firms implement human-in-the-loop governance to manage reputational and regulatory risks associated with automated financing decisions. These mechanisms provide a structured way to analyse how employment shifts toward oversight, justification, and exception handling.

2.3 Hybridisation of skills and re-bundling of work across operations, finance, and compliance

The second pillar of the framework focuses on skills and role transformation. AI adoption has been widely associated with changes in the composition of labour demand, with evidence that AI development shifts employment skill structures and increases the premium on analytical, digital, and complex problem-solving capabilities (Ma et al., 2022). Macro-level studies further suggest that AI and technological innovation can drive employment transformation in ways that support sustainable development, though effects vary by sectoral structure and complementary capabilities (Liang et al., 2025; Shen & Zhang, 2024; Zhang, 2023). At the organisational level, AI adoption is also associated with technical skill upgrading, heightened job insecurity, and uneven adoption outcomes depending on change management and workforce readiness (Arranz Lahuerta et al., 2026).

Within integrated logistics, AI-enabled SCF re-bundles work in a distinctive way because it brings financial reasoning and governance demands into operational roles. This results in hybrid skill bundles that combine logistics process expertise with financial literacy (e.g., working capital logic, risk pricing intuition), data literacy (e.g., interpreting dashboards and anomaly signals), compliance awareness (e.g., KYC/AML, trade documentation rules), and customer-facing negotiation capabilities. Such hybridisation aligns with scholarship that identifies "indispensable" human skills in AI-enabled workplaces, including judgement under uncertainty, ethical reasoning, social communication, and integrative problem-solving (Chuang, 2024). It also resonates with the view that AI augments work by shifting task content toward complementary human capabilities rather than fully substituting labour (Tschang & Almirall, 2021).

The framework therefore treats skill change as re-bundling rather than generic upskilling. As SCF becomes embedded, workers are expected to coordinate across operational, financial, and compliance domains, translating AI-mediated risk signals into actionable decisions and relationship management. This process also produces new professional identities and contested boundaries around "who owns" risk, customers, and decisions. The chapter uses this lens to interpret emerging roles such as finance-enabled operations coordinators, risk-monitoring specialists, supplier enablement advisors, and AI workflow supervisors, while critically assessing whether these roles represent genuine upgrading or intensified responsibility without commensurate authority.

2.4 Power, inclusion, and data-based gatekeeping in platformised SCF ecosystems

The third pillar foregrounds ecosystem governance and distributional outcomes. Digital SCF platforms are increasingly described as reshaping trade finance ecosystems by connecting buyers, suppliers, logistics intermediaries, and financiers through data infrastructures that enable faster decisions and broader reach (Tanveer et al., 2025). This platformisation can widen access to liquidity, particularly for SMEs in developing economies, as documented in multiple-case insights on sustainability-oriented SCF in Vietnam (Nguyen et al., 2023). Yet the same data-driven architectures can also intensify exclusion through opaque scoring criteria, uneven data availability, and gatekeeping by powerful ecosystem actors.

From a critical perspective, the political economy of AI and robotics suggests that technological change does not automatically translate into social transformation; rather, employment and power outcomes depend on institutional arrangements, bargaining structures, and how control is exercised through technology (Boyd & Holton, 2018). In developing countries, AI-led digital transformation may produce productivity gains while also amplifying dependency and uneven value capture when governance is weak or when platform intermediaries consolidate control (Aly, 2022). Within AI-enabled SCF, these concerns become concrete: suppliers with limited digital traceability, incomplete documentation histories, or weaker bargaining positions may face higher financing costs or exclusion, even when financing is formally "available."

This chapter conceptualises these dynamics as data-based gatekeeping and legitimacy work. Data-based gatekeeping refers to the way access to financing becomes contingent on the ability to produce "credible" operational data and comply with platform rules. Legitimacy work refers to the organisational labour devoted to maintaining trust and accountability when decisions are automated and distributed across partners. Importantly, this labour often falls on employees in hybrid operational-financial roles, who must manage disputes, explain decisions, assist onboarding, and mitigate reputational risks. The framework thus links ecosystem power directly to skill and employment transformation.

3. CASE SETTING AND RESEARCH DESIGN

This chapter is developed through an in-depth qualitative *single-case* study of an anonymised global integrated logistics provider, referred to as *Orion Logistics*. Orion offers ocean freight, inland transport, warehousing, customs brokerage, and end-to-end supply chain coordination, and has strategically expanded into digital trade enablement and working-capital support services for customers managing complex cross-border flows. The chapter examines Orion's implementation of an *AI-enabled supply chain finance (SCF)* capability designed to accelerate financing decisions by integrating operational visibility signals with automated verification and risk assessment routines.

Orion's AI-enabled SCF capability is analytically important because it is embedded in day-to-day execution rather than positioned as an auxiliary financial product. Financing eligibility and timing are connected to operational events (for example, documentation completion, shipment milestones, and exception resolution), meaning that the system does not merely "support" logistics; it becomes part of the operating logic through which trade is enacted. This integration creates a particularly revealing setting for investigating how AI-enabled SCF transforms work in three interlinked domains that organise the chapter's theoretical framework: first, the redesign of decision architectures and the emergence of algorithmic governance (Olan et al., 2022a; Ronchini et al., 2024); second, the hybridisation of skills and the re-bundling of work across operations, finance, and compliance (Tschang & Almirall, 2021; Chuang, 2024; Arranz Lahuerta et al., 2026); and third, the reconfiguration of power and inclusion dynamics in the ecosystem through data-based gatekeeping and platform rules (Tanveer et al., 2025; Nguyen et al., 2023; Aly, 2022).

The unit of analysis is the *work system* surrounding embedded finance: the interconnected routines through which operational data are converted into financing signals, decisions are produced and escalated, and accountability is enacted through human-in-the-loop oversight. This includes how employees coordinate documentation flows, interpret AI-generated risk flags, manage exceptions, communicate financing conditions to customers and suppliers, and maintain auditable decision trails. The case therefore allows the chapter to move beyond generic statements about "digital upskilling" and to specify how labour is reorganised when financing becomes inseparable from execution.

The selection of Orion Logistics follows a *theory-building logic* in which a single case is used to illuminate mechanisms that are difficult to observe through abstract macro indicators of AI adoption and employment change. The case is information-rich and mechanism-revealing for three reasons. First, Orion's AI-enabled SCF is deeply embedded in execution, enabling close observation of how operational data streams become decisive inputs into credit and payment decisions. This is central to the chapter's argument that AI-enabled SCF constitutes a redesign of decision architectures rather than a narrow technological upgrade. In the language of SCF research, this setting makes visible how AI-supported visibility, verification, and scoring routines reshape the innovation process by changing how decisions are produced, validated, and stabilised in organisational practice (Olan et al., 2022a; Ronchini et al., 2024).

Second, the integration of financing into execution produces strong conditions for role hybridisation and governance labour. When financing eligibility depends on documentation integrity, milestone validity, and exception resolution, operational staff cannot remain confined to execution in a narrow sense; they become implicated in financial reasoning, evidence management, and compliance interpretation. This is precisely the organisational pathway implied by "augmenting automation" arguments—AI reallocates task content and expands complementary human work in judgement, coordination, and explanation—yet it requires empirical demonstration in context (Tschang & Almirall, 2021; Chuang, 2024). A single-case approach permits careful tracing of how these hybrid responsibilities are enacted, experienced, and contested.

Third, Orion operates within an ecosystem that includes heterogeneous customers and suppliers, making visible the distributional consequences of data-based financing. Digital SCF platform research emphasises that platform rules and data infrastructures can reshape trade finance ecosystems and value capture (Tanveer et al., 2025). At the same time, developing-economy evidence highlights both the promise of SCF for inclusion and the practical constraints that create uneven participation (Nguyen et al., 2023). Orion's case provides a grounded context in which these tensions are enacted through day-to-day onboarding, remediation, and dispute work performed by employees.

Accordingly, the chapter aims for analytic generalisation. It does not claim statistical representativeness; instead, it develops transferable insights about how AI-enabled SCF reorganises work through exception regimes, accountability layering, and ecosystem mediation. This complements existing literature that frequently highlights AI as an enabler of sustainable SCF and data-driven decision-making

(Olan et al., 2022a; Olan et al., 2022b; Bag et al., 2025) while leaving the labour process and organisational redesign under-specified.

4. CASE FINDINGS

The findings are organised to mirror the theoretical framework developed in Section 2. The logic is cumulative: decision-architecture redesign (Section 4.1) establishes the structural conditions under which hybrid work emerges (Section 4.2); this hybrid work, in turn, makes accountability and governance labour central rather than peripheral (Section 4.3). Building on these internal transformations, the chapter then shows how ecosystem-facing inclusion and gatekeeping tensions become enacted through employee practices (Section 4.4). Finally, the analysis consolidates how these dynamics translate into workforce restructuring and capability bottlenecks (Section 4.5), clarifying why reskilling is inseparable from organisational governance design.

4.1 Reconfiguring decision architectures - from manual verification to AI-mediated approvals and exception regimes

Orion introduced AI-enabled SCF to address routine bottlenecks that slowed financing approval and raised transaction costs, particularly in invoice checks, document completeness validation, milestone confirmation, and early risk screening. The system automated rule-based verification and generated risk flags from operational visibility data, compressing cycle time for transactions that aligned with expected patterns. This initial "efficiency" framing, however, obscures the deeper organisational shift that followed. Rather than removing decision work, AI-mediated verification *reallocated* it.

As automated routines expanded, employees described a marked change in the temporal organisation of work. Instead of work being triggered primarily by customer requests or scheduled documentation steps, daily activity increasingly began with system-generated anomaly queues. These queues included mismatches between shipment events and documentation timestamps, missing or inconsistent trade documents, unusual supplier patterns, and borderline risk scores that required human assessment. In practical terms, Orion's AI-enabled SCF created a bifurcated environment: "standard" cases moved quickly through automated checks, while "non-standard" cases accumulated in exception streams that demanded interpretive judgement and cross-functional coordination.

This redesign altered Orion's decision architecture in three interconnected ways. First, routine approvals became increasingly system-produced, reducing discretionary interpretation in standard cases and shifting performance attention toward managing exceptions rather than processing volume. Second, exception handling became the primary site of human discretion, with employees expected to interpret uncertainty, negotiate clarifications with customers and partners, and decide whether and how to justify overrides. Third, accountability moved both upward and outward. Because automated approvals can scale errors quickly, employees had to document rationales for exceptions and coordinate escalation pathways across operations, risk, and compliance. In effect, Orion's system embedded a governance logic: the organisation became more sensitive to the integrity of data signals, the legitimacy of decision criteria, and the auditable justification of interventions.

The importance of this shift is not merely procedural. It reshapes what "skill" means in AI-enabled SCF. When decision work concentrates in exception regimes, competence is measured less by routine throughput and more by the capacity to interpret ambiguous signals, mobilise evidence, and maintain decision legitimacy under time pressure. This is the mechanism through which the chapter's broader claims about hybridisation and governance labour begin to take organisational form.

4.2 Hybrid roles and skill re-bundling - the emergence of finance-enabled operations work

The reconfiguration of decision architectures in Orion created direct implications for role design. Because financing eligibility depended on operational milestones and documentation integrity, employees could not treat financing as an external event handled elsewhere. Instead, work became oriented toward *finance readiness* within execution. This orientation produced a re-bundling of tasks that integrated operational coordination, documentation management, customer operations, and financing eligibility in ways that challenged legacy job families.

Operational staff who previously focused on shipment execution and document processing were now required to understand the logic of working capital timing, the evidentiary thresholds demanded by financiers, and the pathways through which AI-generated flags would delay eligibility. Orion did not resolve this shift by establishing a separate "finance unit" that would absorb these responsibilities. Rather, it developed intermediary roles and informal expansions that sat between customer operations, risk/compliance functions, and analytics teams. These employees combined process knowledge—how milestones are produced, what constitutes valid documentation, and how exceptions propagate—with the ability to interpret risk outputs and translate them into action.

Over time, employees described a gradual emergence of a finance-enabled operations identity. Logistics competence remained necessary but became insufficient unless paired with financial reasoning, data literacy, and compliance awareness.

Customer-facing roles became more consultative: staff were expected to explain why an AI-mediated decision resulted in a delay, what evidence would resolve the exception, and how customers and suppliers might adjust practices to reduce future friction. Importantly, this hybridisation redefined the locus of professional value. Workers increasingly created value not by moving transactions through a pipeline, but by stabilising the interface between operational execution and financial decision-making.

This transformation also introduced boundary tensions. When embedded finance becomes part of execution, questions of ownership intensify: who "owns" the customer when financing outcomes are embedded in service delivery; who is accountable for risk classification; and who has authority to negotiate evidentiary standards with external partners. In Orion, these tensions were not simply managerial inconveniences; they shaped employees' experience of role clarity, career progression, and perceived fairness. The shift toward hybrid work therefore had an ambivalent character: it created opportunities for skill broadening while also increasing role load and, in some instances, responsibility without commensurate authority.

4.3 Human-in-the-loop governance - accountability work, data stewardship, and trust maintenance

As Orion's hybrid roles expanded, human-in-the-loop governance moved from a safeguard to an operational necessity. AI-enabled SCF increased the speed and volume of decisions, but it also increased the organisational consequences of data integrity failures and interpretability deficits. In this environment, governance is not an abstract ethical principle; it is enacted through everyday work that sustains legitimacy and prevents error amplification. Employees described three governance work streams that became more salient after deployment. The first was *data stewardship*. Workers spent substantial time reconciling inconsistent documentation, correcting milestone discrepancies, and coordinating with external parties—carriers, brokers, customers, and suppliers—to confirm event validity so that financing could proceed. Data, in this sense, was not a passive resource consumed by AI. It was an organisational product that required continuous maintenance, and this maintenance became labour.

The second stream was *override governance and auditability*. Employees were expected to justify manual interventions, document evidence trails, and maintain decision records that could withstand internal scrutiny and external audit demands. This requirement changed the texture of work: interventions had to be defensible, consistent with agreed criteria, and recorded in ways that made accountability traceable. The third stream was *trust maintenance*. When automated decisions delayed financing or demanded additional evidence, employees needed to translate outcomes to customers and internal stakeholders, particularly where stakeholders expected immediate liquidity release based on operational events.

Orion institutionalised review routines in which recurring exception patterns were examined to adjust rules, improve data pipelines, and refine escalation thresholds. These routines reveal an important point: governance labour is not merely reactive. It becomes part of organisational learning around AI-enabled SCF. The firm learns not only from operational disruptions, but from legitimacy disruptions—moments when stakeholders contest decisions, question fairness, or lose confidence in the system's outputs. Through these processes, employees become central to maintaining the credibility of algorithmic governance, reinforcing the chapter's argument that AI's employment impact is best understood as a reorganisation of decision work and accountability, not simply the automation of clerical tasks.

4.4 Power, inclusion, and data-based gatekeeping - who gains access to embedded finance?

The internal reorganisation of work in Orion was inseparable from ecosystem dynamics. As financing became embedded in execution, access and speed became contingent on data availability, documentation integrity, and compliance readiness. This conditionality produced uneven outcomes across Orion's customer and supplier landscape. Orion's AI-enabled SCF expanded financing availability for customers by accelerating approval where data were complete and milestones were traceable. Yet participation was not evenly distributed. Large buyers typically possessed mature digital infrastructures that produced standardised data and documentation. Smaller suppliers often lacked stable data histories, consistent formats, or the organisational capacity to produce evidence at the required pace. Consequently, suppliers with weaker traceability experienced more delays and more frequent requests for evidence. Employees framed this as a "preparedness gap," in which differential digital capability translated into differential financing conditions even when programmes were nominally open.

This dynamic repositioned employees as ecosystem mediators. Staff became responsible for supplier onboarding support, data remediation, and the negotiation of acceptable evidence standards. At the same time, they encountered tensions around perceived fairness. Suppliers often experienced requirements as opaque or imposed, especially when they interpreted data demands as a mechanism of control rather than a neutral risk practice. Buyers, conversely, benefited from improved working-capital control and faster financing flows. Orion therefore confronted an inclusion dilemma: embedded finance can support broader participation through liquidity provision, yet the same data-based architecture that enables speed can reproduce exclusion through gatekeeping.

The implications for skills and employment are direct. Inclusion work—onboarding, explanation, remediation, and dispute handling—becomes part of the labour process. Employees require relational and interpretive capacities to sustain participation, particularly in contexts where data capability is uneven and where power asymmetries shape what counts as "acceptable" evidence. This reinforces the chapter's critical stance: AI-enabled SCF does not merely optimise flows; it reorganises governance and power in ways that are experienced through work.

4.5 Workforce restructuring and capability building - reskilling pathways, new career ladders, and organisational bottlenecks

The preceding sections show how decision-architecture redesign, hybridisation, governance labour, and ecosystem mediation collectively transform work. Orion's workforce redesign did not manifest as immediate job elimination; instead, it emerged as a structural shift in role composition and performance expectations. Routine transaction handling and basic verification declined in relative importance as automation expanded, while governance-oriented work grew: exception management, auditability, data stewardship, and partner enablement. Orion attempted to institutionalise reskilling through blended learning pathways that combined process knowledge with risk governance, analytics interpretation, and compliance reasoning. The firm's internal logic implicitly recognised that AI-enabled SCF cannot be sustained through technology alone; it requires human capability to manage uncertainty, maintain legitimacy, and stabilise partner participation.

Nevertheless, capability bottlenecks emerged. Employees with hybrid competence became scarce internal resources, often carrying both operational workload and informal mentoring responsibilities. This created role strain and, in some units, contributed to perceptions of heightened surveillance and intensified performance pressure. A further bottleneck concerned boundary clarity. As embedded finance blurred the separation between operations and finance, employees reported ambiguity about who owned customer decisions, who managed disputes, and who had final authority to override system outcomes. Where these boundaries were unclear, employees experienced accountability without authority, especially when service metrics remained anchored to speed while responsibilities expanded to include risk outcomes and legitimacy maintenance.

Taken together, Orion's experience suggests that capability building for AI-enabled SCF is inseparable from organisational design choices. Reskilling must be paired with explicit role architectures, escalation rights, and recognition of governance labour as value-creating work. Without such redesign, firms risk amplifying exception overload, intensifying role ambiguity, and weakening system legitimacy—outcomes that ultimately undermine both the operational promises and the inclusive aspirations often attached to AI-enabled SCF.

5. FINAL REMARKS

This chapter examined AI-enabled supply chain finance as a distinctive mechanism through which AI transforms skills and employment in integrated logistics. Across four anonymised cases, the findings show that AI-enabled SCF does not primarily eliminate work; rather, it redesigns decision architectures by routinising verification while expanding exception regimes, thereby shifting labour toward oversight, interpretation, and accountability. The transformation produces hybrid skill bundles that integrate operations, finance, data literacy, and compliance, while intensifying the importance of human-in-the-loop governance for legitimacy and trust. At the ecosystem level, embedded finance both expands liquidity potential and increases data-based gatekeeping, producing uneven inclusion outcomes that must be managed through supplier enablement and relational mediation.

5.1 Theoretical contributions

The chapter contributes to SCF and operations scholarship by positioning AI-enabled SCF as an organisational and inter-organisational redesign of decision architectures rather than a narrow technological upgrade. While prior studies highlight AI's role in enabling sustainable SCF and improving network-level transparency (Olan et al., 2022a; Olan et al., 2022b), and describe AI's contribution to SCF innovation processes (Ronchini et al., 2024), this chapter specifies how such innovation is enacted through exception regimes and accountability layering that materially reconstitute work. The chapter extends emerging research on digital SCF platforms and ecosystem transformation (Tanveer et al., 2025) by demonstrating that platformisation is also a labour process: employees become the operational carriers of ecosystem governance through onboarding, data stewardship, decision explanation, and dispute resolution.

In addition, the chapter advances future-of-work theory by providing a grounded account of how AI functions as augmenting automation in logistics-finance integration (Tschang & Almirall, 2021). Rather than treating skills as generically upgraded, the chapter theorises skill hybridisation as re-bundling that reshapes occupational identities and authority relations. This enriches macro-level debates on AI and employment structure change (Ma et al., 2022; Zhang, 2023; Shen & Zhang, 2024; Liang et al., 2025) by identifying the micro-level mechanisms—decision-architecture redesign, governance labour expansion, and ecosystem gatekeeping—through which employment outcomes are produced and contested. Finally, by foregrounding power and inclusion tensions, the chapter aligns with critical accounts that caution against assuming technologically driven social transformation and instead emphasise governance and power as boundary conditions (Boyd & Holton, 2018; Aly, 2022).

5.2 Practical implications

For integrated logistics firms, the findings imply that successful AI-enabled SCF requires deliberate organisational design, not only platform deployment. Firms should formalise exception-handling and escalation protocols, invest in auditability and data provenance capabilities, and recognise governance work as a core operational function rather than a compliance afterthought. Workforce strategies should prioritise hybrid capability pathways that integrate logistics process expertise with financial reasoning, data stewardship, and compliance interpretation, while establishing clear role ownership so that employees are not held accountable for outcomes without decision authority.

For policymakers and industry bodies, the chapter highlights that AI-enabled SCF can support SME liquidity and trade continuity, but only if exclusion risks created by data-based gatekeeping are addressed. Support mechanisms that improve SME data readiness, documentation capacity, and digital interoperability can reduce structural disadvantages, especially in developing economies where digital infrastructure is uneven. Governance guidance for transparency and contestability in data-driven credit decisions can also mitigate legitimacy risks and help prevent the concentration of decision power in platform intermediaries.

For educators and training providers, the results indicate that reskilling programmes should move beyond generic "digital skills" toward cross-functional competence development for embedded finance operations. Curricula should emphasise interpretive judgement under uncertainty, ethical and compliance reasoning, data quality management, and stakeholder communication, preparing graduates for roles where operational disruptions translate into financial and reputational risks. In doing so, training systems can better support inclusive and sustainable transitions in AI-enabled logistics ecosystems.

REFERENCES

Aly, H. (2022). Digital transformation, development and productivity in developing countries: Is artificial intelligence a curse or a blessing? *Review of Economics and Political Science*, *7*(4), 238–256. DOI: 10.1108/REPS-11-2019-0145

Arranz Lahuerta, L., López Ramajo, M. R., & Gandía, A. (2026). Artificial intelligence and organisational transformation: Technical skills, job insecurity and adoption. *Management Decision*, •••, 1–16. DOI: 10.1108/MD-05-2025-1462

Bag, S., Routray, S., Saikouk, T., & Roubaud, D. (2025). Generative AI-Powered Innovation on Data-Driven Financial Decision-Making in Operations and Supply Chain Management: A Moderated Mediation Analysis. *Information Systems Frontiers*, •••, 1–30. DOI: 10.1007/s10796-025-10662-7

Boyd, R., & Holton, R. J. (2018). Technology, innovation, employment and power: Does robotics and artificial intelligence really mean social transformation? *Journal of Sociology (Melbourne, Vic.)*, *54*(3), 331–345. DOI: 10.1177/1440783317726591

Chuang, S. (2024). Indispensable skills for human employees in the age of robots and AI. *European Journal of Training and Development*, *48*(1/2), 179–195. DOI: 10.1108/EJTD-06-2022-0062

Khan, M. N. M.Md Nazmuddin Moin Khan. (2025). Artificial intelligence driven big data and business analytics: A comprehensive review of multi-sectoral applications in healthcare, finance, supply chain, and organizational innovation. *Pacific Journal of Business Innovation and Strategy*, *2*(4), 122–137. DOI: 10.70818/pjbis.v02i04.0130

Liang, H., Fan, J., & Wang, Y. (2025). Artificial intelligence, technological innovation, and employment transformation for sustainable development: Evidence from China. *Sustainability (Basel)*, *17*(9), 3842. DOI: 10.3390/su17093842

Ma, H., Gao, Q., Li, X., & Zhang, Y. (2022). AI development and employment skill structure: A case study of China. *Economic Analysis and Policy*, *73*, 242–254. DOI: 10.1016/j.eap.2021.11.007

Nguyen, A. H., Hoang, T. G., Ngo, V. M., Nguyen, L. Q. T., & Nguyen, H. H. (2023). Sustainability-oriented supply chain finance in Vietnam: Insights from multiple case studies. *Operations Management Research : Advancing Practice Through Research*, *16*(1), 259–279. DOI: 10.1007/s12063-022-00303-6

Olan, F., Arakpogun, E. O., Jayawickrama, U., Suklan, J., & Liu, S. (2022a). Sustainable supply chain finance and supply networks: The role of artificial intelligence. *IEEE Transactions on Engineering Management*, *71*, 13296–13311. DOI: 10.1109/TEM.2021.3133104

Olan, F., Liu, S., Suklan, J., Jayawickrama, U., & Arakpogun, E. O. (2022b). The role of Artificial Intelligence networks in sustainable supply chain finance for food and drink industry. *International Journal of Production Research*, *60*(14), 4418–4433. DOI: 10.1080/00207543.2021.1915510

Ronchini, A., Guida, M., Moretto, A., & Caniato, F. (2024). The role of artificial intelligence in the supply chain finance innovation process. *Operations Management Research*, 1-31.

Shen, Y., & Zhang, X. (2024). The impact of artificial intelligence on employment: The role of virtual agglomeration. *Humanities & Social Sciences Communications*, *11*(1), 122. DOI: 10.1057/s41599-024-02647-9

Tanveer, U., Hoang, T. G., & Ishaq, S. (2025). Reshaping global trade finance and supply chains through digital supply chain finance platforms. *Journal of Business Logistics*, *46*(3), e70022. DOI: 10.1111/jbl.70022

Tschang, F. T., & Almirall, E. (2021). Artificial intelligence as augmenting automation: Implications for employment. *The Academy of Management Perspectives*, *35*(4), 642–659. DOI: 10.5465/amp.2019.0062

Zhang, Z. (2023). The impact of the artificial intelligence industry on the number and structure of employments in the digital economy environment. *Technological Forecasting and Social Change*, *197*, 122881. DOI: 10.1016/j.techfore.2023.122881

Chapter 4
Emerging Roles and Professional Identities in Smart Logistics Ecosystems

Faiz Izaz Fathoni
http://orcid.org/0009-0004-2203-4073
Universitas Esa Unggul, Indonesia

Binastya Anggara Sekti
http://orcid.org/0000-0001-5489-4888
Universitas Esa Unggul, Indonesia

ABSTRACT

This chapter per the authors examines the transformation of logistics work, professional roles, and identities within smart logistics ecosystems shaped by artificial intelligence, automation, and digital platforms. The chapter aims to conceptualize smart logistics as a socio-technical ecosystem in which technological innovation interacts with human agency, organizational structures, ethical considerations, and governance arrangements. It analyzes the shift from traditional logistics roles to AI-augmented occupations, the emergence of hybrid skills, and the reconstruction of professional identity under algorithmic management. Organizational, ethical, and governance dimensions are explored to highlight challenges related to autonomy, transparency, and worker participation. A global comparative perspective illustrates disparities between developed and developing economies in AI readiness and workforce transformation. The chapter concludes by outlining policy and organizational implications for human-centered and socially sustainable smart logistics ecosystems.

DOI: 10.4018/979-8-3373-7826-8.ch004

1. INTRODUCTION: AI AND THE TRANSFORMATION OF EMPLOYMENT IN LOGISTICS

The logistics sector is undergoing a profound transformation driven by the rapid integration of artificial intelligence (AI), automation technologies, and digital platforms. AI-enabled forecasting systems, robotic warehouse operations, algorithmic route optimization, and predictive inventory management are reshaping how logistics organizations plan, coordinate, and execute operations. While these technologies are often discussed in terms of efficiency gains and operational optimization, their implications extend beyond productivity by fundamentally restructuring employment patterns, task allocation, and skill requirements within logistics systems. An adaptive, flexible, resilient, and reliable inventory management system ensures a stable supply of cross-border e-commerce products, facilitates efficient product flow among supply chain members, meets rapidly changing customer demands, and supports the automation of e-commerce services (Tang, Chau, Lau, & Zheng, 2023).

Traditionally, logistics work relied heavily on manual coordination, physical handling of goods, and rule-based planning supported by conventional information systems. Decision-making processes were largely reactive and dependent on human experience, often constrained by limited data visibility across supply chain operations. The emergence of AI-driven logistics environments has altered this operational logic by embedding predictive analytics, automated decision-making, and real-time monitoring into everyday logistics activities. In the global market, increasingly complex supply chains require agile and sustainable management strategies that traditional analytical methods often fail to address effectively (Pasupuleti, Thuraka, Kodete, & Malisetty, 2024). Figure 1 shows the Transition from traditional logistics to smart logistics ecosystems with human-AI collaboration.

Figure 1. Transforming logistics with smart ecosystems

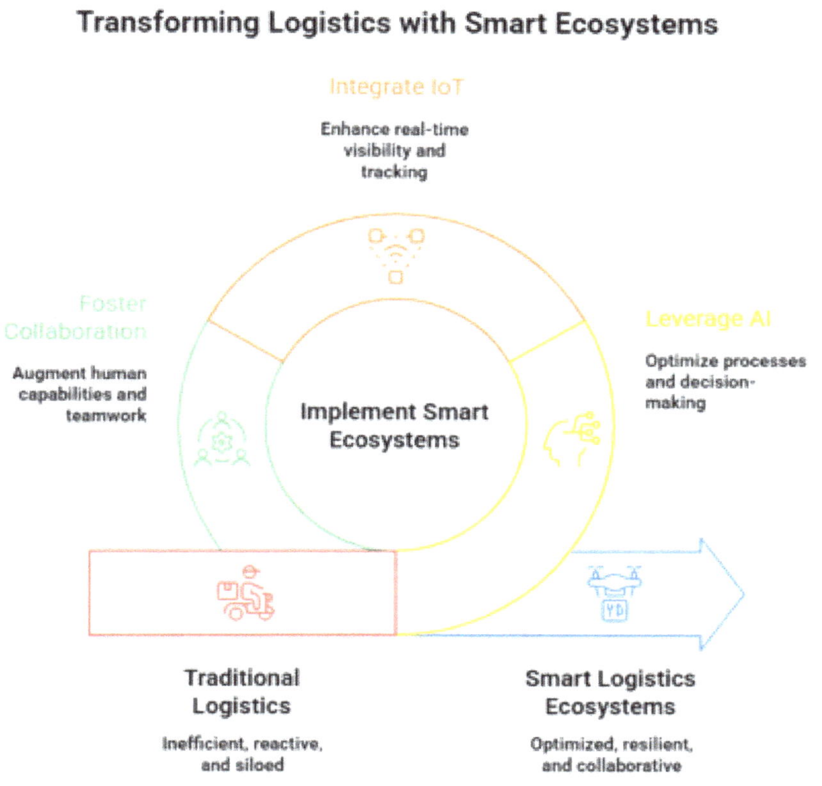

Importantly, the transformation of logistics work does not simply involve replacing human labor with automated systems. Instead, AI technologies redistribute tasks between humans and machines, creating new forms of collaboration, oversight, and analytical work. Routine and data-intensive tasks increasingly shift toward algorithmic systems, while human professionals focus on supervision, contextual interpretation, exception management, and strategic decision-making.

These developments raise critical questions about the future of employment and skills in logistics. Which jobs are changing as AI becomes embedded in logistics operations? How are task structures reorganized between humans and intelligent systems? What new competencies are required for logistics professionals to operate effectively in AI-mediated environments?

This chapter addresses these questions by examining how AI adoption reshapes employment roles, task allocation, and skill requirements within smart logistics ecosystems. It argues that AI does not eliminate logistics work but reorganizes it through the emergence of AI-augmented roles, hybrid skill systems, and new forms of human–AI collaboration. Professional identity transformation and governance challenges emerge as consequences of these structural changes.

1.1 Background and Rationale

The rapid integration of AI and automation technologies has transformed logistics systems into data-intensive and highly interconnected operational environments. Contemporary logistics increasingly relies on real-time information flows, predictive analytics, and algorithmic optimization to manage demand forecasting, warehouse operations, and transportation planning. Technologies such as robotics-assisted picking, digital twins, and intelligent routing platforms enable organizations to anticipate disruptions, allocate resources dynamically, and improve supply chain coordination.

However, the significance of these technologies extends beyond operational efficiency. Scholars emphasize that automation in logistics should not be understood merely as a tool for productivity improvement but as a catalyst for structural transformation in how logistics systems are designed, managed, and experienced by workers (Ferreira & Reis, 2023). AI systems increasingly perform tasks traditionally executed by humans, including forecasting, scheduling, and operational optimization.

As these systems assume analytical and decision-support functions, the boundaries between operational, analytical, and managerial work become increasingly blurred. Digital transformation therefore generates demand for hybrid competencies that integrate technical expertise, data literacy, and interpersonal skills (Koh & Yuen, 2022). Logistics professionals are increasingly valued not for their ability to perform routine tasks but for their capacity to interpret data, interact with intelligent systems, and exercise judgment in complex or uncertain operational contexts.

From a sociotechnical perspective, AI integration also introduces new forms of work mediation that influence power relations within organizations. Algorithmic systems can shape task allocation, performance measurement, and operational decision-making processes while remaining partially opaque to workers. These dynamics raise important questions regarding autonomy, accountability, and professional authority within AI-mediated logistics environments.

1.2 Smart Logistics Ecosystems and the Evolution of Work

Smart logistics ecosystems can be understood as interconnected socio-technical systems in which AI, Internet of Things (IoT) devices, robotics, digital platforms, and human actors interact across supply chain activities. Unlike traditional logistics models characterized by linear processes and hierarchical coordination, smart ecosystems emphasize continuous data exchange, predictive intelligence, and adaptive decision-making.

Within these ecosystems, logistics activities such as demand planning, inventory management, transportation routing, and warehouse operations are increasingly orchestrated through AI-enabled platforms. Automation technologies embedded in logistics infrastructures reconfigure how coordination and control are distributed across supply chains, enabling more anticipatory and data-driven decision-making processes (Ferreira & Reis, 2023).

The integration of AI in logistics information systems also reshapes the role of human labor. Intelligent systems increasingly support or partially execute planning, monitoring, and optimization tasks, while human professionals focus on supervision, analytical interpretation, and system validation. As a result, human work becomes oriented toward managing complex interactions between digital infrastructures, organizational processes, and physical logistics operations.

This evolution also transforms occupational structures within the sector. Traditional roles such as warehouse supervisors, logistics planners, and fleet managers are increasingly augmented by AI capabilities that reshape task boundaries. At the same time, new professional roles are emerging, including logistics data analysts, automation coordinators, digital twin specialists, and human–robot interaction managers.

These developments illustrate the hybrid nature of work in smart logistics ecosystems. Workers must navigate both technical infrastructures and organizational dynamics, balancing efficiency objectives with ethical and human considerations. Logistics work therefore evolves into an ecosystem of professional practices shaped by continuous interaction between humans and intelligent technologies.

1.3 Professional Identity in the Age of Intelligent Automation

The transformation of logistics work also influences how professionals understand their roles and identities within organizations. Professional identity refers to how individuals define themselves in relation to their work roles, competencies, values, and social recognition. In AI-driven logistics environments, these identities become increasingly dynamic as intelligent systems reshape both tasks and decision-making processes.

Research suggests that AI technologies simultaneously enable and challenge professional identity formation (Mirbabaie, Brünker, Möllmann Frick, & Stieglitz, 2022). On one hand, AI augmentation allows workers to engage in more analytical and strategically meaningful activities by reducing routine operational burdens.

On the other hand, the automation of core decision-support functions can weaken traditional sources of expertise and authority, creating tensions regarding professional relevance.

Logistics professionals operating within smart ecosystems therefore navigate multiple identity dimensions. They act as operators of digital technologies, collaborators with intelligent systems, and interpreters of algorithmic outputs. For many workers, this transformation provides opportunities for professional growth as AI enhances analytical capabilities and decision-making support. For others, the rise of algorithmic monitoring and automated performance evaluation may create concerns about deskilling, reduced autonomy, or loss of professional control.

Addressing these identity dynamics is essential for ensuring sustainable workforce transformation. Scholars argue that organizations must actively support identity adaptation through training, participatory governance mechanisms, and transparent AI systems (Koh & Yuen, 2022). When identity transformation is managed proactively, smart logistics ecosystems can become environments that empower professionals rather than displace them.

Despite the growing literature on smart logistics and automation, existing studies often emphasize technological efficiency and operational optimization, while providing limited understanding of how AI adoption restructures employment roles, task allocation, and skill requirements within logistics work systems.

2. AI-DRIVEN RESTRUCTURING OF LOGISTICS WORK

The integration of artificial intelligence (AI) and automation technologies is fundamentally transforming the structure of work in the logistics sector. Historically, logistics operations were organized around stable and clearly defined roles such as inventory handling, transportation coordination, warehouse supervision, and demand planning. These roles relied heavily on human experience, procedural knowledge, and sequential decision-making supported by conventional information systems. Artificial intelligence (AI) has garnered significant attention within the modular construction industry, emerging as a prominent frontier development trend (Liu et al., 2024).

The emergence of AI-driven logistics systems alters this traditional arrangement by embedding intelligent capabilities directly into operational processes. Technologies such as machine learning–based demand forecasting, algorithmic route optimization, automated warehouse allocation, and predictive inventory control increasingly perform tasks that were previously managed manually. As a result, logistics work is no longer defined primarily by routine operational execution but by interactions between human expertise and intelligent systems. AI Technology

Management focuses on strategically integrating AI into organizations to enhance innovation and value creation (Sekti, 2025a).

This transformation does not simply eliminate human roles. Instead, AI adoption redistributes responsibilities between humans and machines, leading to the emergence of new forms of work organization. Routine and data-intensive tasks are increasingly executed by algorithms, while human professionals focus on system supervision, contextual interpretation, and strategic coordination. The restructuring of logistics work therefore reflects a broader shift toward human–AI collaboration within smart logistics ecosystems.

2.1 From Traditional Roles to AI-Augmented Work

Traditionally, logistics work was organized around task-oriented operational roles such as inventory control, transportation scheduling, and warehouse coordination. These roles were typically performed through manual planning and rule-based decision-making supported by conventional information systems. Professional expertise in logistics was therefore closely associated with procedural knowledge, operational efficiency, and the ability to manage complex physical flows of goods (Joosten, Bilgram, Hahn, & Totzek, 2024).

The integration of AI-driven automation significantly disrupts this traditional structure by embedding predictive and analytical capabilities into logistics processes. AI systems increasingly perform functions such as demand forecasting, routing optimization, warehouse slotting, and inventory prediction. Rather than eliminating human involvement entirely, these technologies redistribute decision-making authority between humans and intelligent systems.

As AI systems assume responsibility for routine and data-intensive tasks, human roles shift toward supervisory and analytical functions. Logistics professionals increasingly act as interpreters of algorithmic recommendations, validating AI outputs and intervening when operational disruptions or contextual uncertainties arise. This transition reflects the emergence of AI-augmented work, in which intelligent systems perform computational optimization while human workers contribute contextual knowledge, ethical judgment, and strategic oversight. Figure 2 shows the Transformation of logistics work roles in smart logistics ecosystems.

Figure 2. Evolution of job roles in AI-driven logistics (Mohsen, 2024)

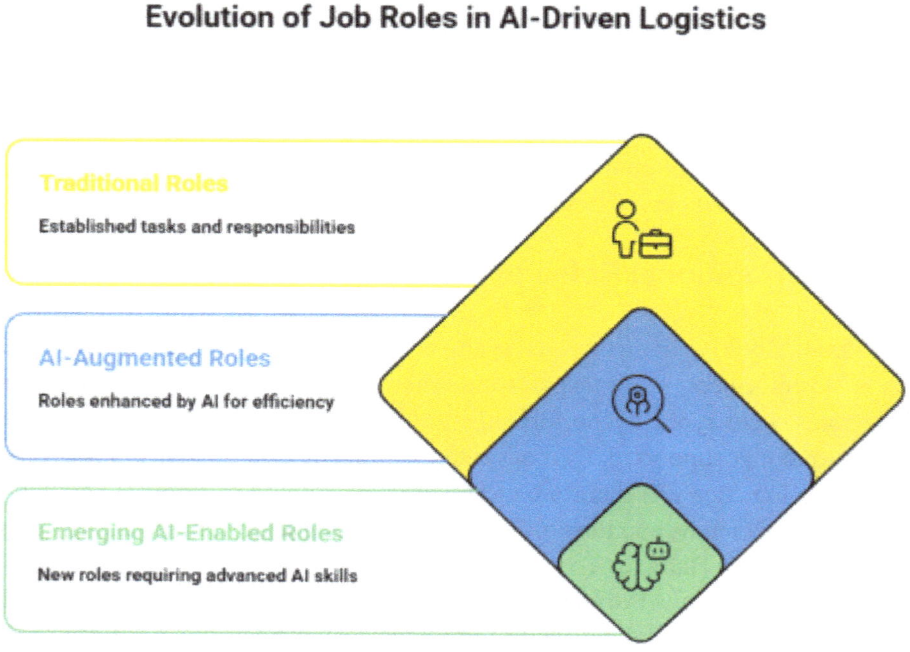

In practice, logistics planners and operations managers increasingly evaluate algorithmic forecasts, adjust automated decisions based on real-world conditions, and coordinate responses to unexpected disruptions. Human judgment therefore remains essential, but it is repositioned at higher levels of decision-making where it complements machine intelligence rather than replacing it.

2.2 Emerging AI-Enabled Roles in Logistics

The transformation of logistics work has also led to the emergence of new occupational categories that were largely absent in traditional logistics structures. These emerging roles reflect the growing importance of data analytics, automation management, and digital infrastructure within logistics operations. The Smart Logistics Node benefits from data sharing, supporting infrastructure, and Connected and Automated Transport (CAT) technologies (Brunetti, Mes, & Lalla-Ruiz, 2024).

One prominent example is the Logistics Data Scientist, whose responsibilities include analyzing large-scale operational datasets and developing predictive models for demand forecasting, inventory optimization, and transportation planning. As logistics organizations increasingly rely on data-driven decision-making, analytical expertise becomes a central professional capability.

Another emerging role is the Automation and Robotics Coordinator, responsible for managing interactions between human workers and automated warehouse systems such as robotic picking solutions, autonomous vehicles, and intelligent sorting systems. This role requires both technical understanding and strong coordination skills to ensure that automated systems operate effectively within complex organizational environments.

The growing use of simulation technologies has also created demand for Digital Twin Analysts, who develop virtual representations of logistics systems to test operational scenarios, anticipate disruptions, and improve system resilience. Through simulation-based experimentation, digital twin technologies enable organizations to evaluate strategic decisions without disrupting real-world operations. Logistics distribution plays a crucial role in smart logistics systems, with delivery time prediction being a key issue (Zhu et al., 2025). Table 1 shows the Evolution of Work Roles in Smart Logistics Ecosystems.

Table 1. Evolution of work roles in smart logistics ecosystems

Traditional Logistics Roles	AI-Augmented Roles	Emerging AI-Enabled Roles
Inventory handler	Inventory system supervisor	Logistics Data Scientist
Transportation coordinator	AI-assisted route planner	Automation and Robotics Coordinator
Manual demand planner	AI forecast validator	Digital Twin Analyst
Warehouse operator	Human-robot collaboration operator	Human-Robot Interaction Specialist
Operations supervisor	Algorithm-guided operations manager	AI Ethics and Governance Officer
Inventory controller	Data interpreter and exception handler	AI Governance and Compliance Specialist

In addition, the increasing influence of algorithmic decision-making has led to the emergence of roles related to AI governance and oversight, including professionals responsible for ensuring transparency, accountability, and fairness in AI-enabled logistics systems.

Together, these new roles illustrate how logistics employment is shifting from predominantly manual and routine work toward more analytical, interdisciplinary, and technologically integrated forms of professional practice.

2.3 Reconfiguration of Task Boundaries and Decision Authority

Beyond the emergence of new roles, AI adoption fundamentally reshapes task boundaries and decision authority within logistics organizations. In traditional logistics environments, decision-making authority was largely hierarchical, with planners, supervisors, and managers exercising direct control over operational processes.

In smart logistics ecosystems, however, many operational decisions are increasingly generated or supported by algorithmic systems. AI applications perform tasks requiring rapid data processing, such as demand prediction, route optimization, and inventory replenishment planning. This redistribution of tasks reduces cognitive workload for human workers but simultaneously shifts their responsibilities toward supervising and validating automated decisions.

As a result, the boundaries between operational and strategic work become increasingly fluid. Tasks once considered routine now require contextual judgment when algorithmic outputs conflict with real-world conditions or organizational priorities. Human professionals must therefore combine domain knowledge with the ability to critically evaluate AI-generated insights.

This redistribution of responsibilities creates a new form of human–AI collaboration in which logistics professionals function as supervisors and interpreters of intelligent systems rather than direct executors of logistics processes.

2.4 Human–AI Collaboration as a Core Work Practice

Within smart logistics ecosystems, human–AI collaboration becomes a central feature of everyday work practices. Intelligent systems rarely operate in isolation; their effectiveness depends on continuous human interaction, interpretation, and oversight. Employees can achieve AI-augmented creativity, but this desirable outcome is skill-biased by favoring experts with greater job skills (Jia, Luo, Fang, & Liao, 2024).

In warehouse environments, workers increasingly collaborate with robotic systems to coordinate picking, sorting, and replenishment processes. In logistics planning functions, professionals interact with AI-generated forecasts and optimization models to support operational decision-making. These interactions require workers to understand both the capabilities and limitations of algorithmic systems.

Human–AI collaboration therefore involves more than simply using digital tools. It requires professionals to develop competencies that enable effective interaction with intelligent technologies, including data interpretation skills, critical reasoning, and digital communication capabilities. The ability to translate algorithmic outputs into actionable operational decisions becomes a central component of logistics expertise.

This collaborative model also reshapes accountability structures. Although AI systems generate recommendations, human professionals remain responsible for evaluating and implementing decisions. Maintaining this balance between automation and human oversight is essential for ensuring trust, transparency, and operational reliability in AI-driven logistics systems.

2.5 Implications for Career Pathways and Workforce Development

The restructuring of logistics work has significant implications for career pathways and workforce development. Traditional career trajectories based primarily on operational experience and hierarchical promotion are becoming less relevant as digital competencies and interdisciplinary skills gain importance.

Emerging AI-enabled roles often require expertise that combines logistics knowledge with data analytics, automation management, and digital systems understanding. Consequently, logistics professionals must engage in continuous learning to remain effective in rapidly evolving technological environments.

Organizations therefore play a critical role in supporting workforce adaptation through reskilling and upskilling initiatives. Training programs that integrate technical skills, operational knowledge, and ethical awareness are essential for enabling workers to participate effectively in AI-driven logistics environments.

From a strategic perspective, organizations that successfully align technological innovation with workforce capability development are more likely to achieve sustainable competitive advantage. Workforce development thus becomes a central component of smart logistics strategy rather than a peripheral organizational activity.

3. SKILL TRANSFORMATION IN AI-DRIVEN LOGISTICS

The restructuring of logistics work through artificial intelligence (AI), automation, and data-driven technologies has fundamentally reshaped the competency landscape of logistics professionals. As intelligent systems become embedded within planning, monitoring, and decision-making processes, effective participation in logistics operations increasingly requires capabilities that extend beyond traditional operational expertise. Workers are expected not only to understand logistics processes but also to interpret algorithmic outputs, manage digital infrastructures, and collaborate with automated systems. Deep Learning and AI perform well in fitting local extreme values and forecasting volatility (Li, Yang, Zhao, Ni, & Zhang, 2024).

These developments redefine professional competence in logistics as a multidimensional construct combining technical, analytical, and human-centered capabilities. AI-driven logistics environments require workers to navigate complex interactions between technological infrastructures, organizational processes, and supply chain networks. Consequently, the transformation of logistics work is accompanied by a parallel transformation in the skills required to perform that work effectively.

Rather than replacing human expertise, AI systems reposition it. Routine tasks are increasingly automated, while human professionals assume responsibilities involving interpretation, oversight, and contextual decision-making. This shift places growing emphasis on hybrid competencies that integrate digital literacy, analytical reasoning, ethical awareness, and collaborative skills.

Understanding how these skills evolve is therefore essential for examining the broader impact of AI on employment and workforce development in logistics systems.

3.1 The Emergence of Hybrid Skill Sets

The integration of AI into logistics systems has given rise to hybrid skill sets that combine technical expertise with higher-order cognitive and interpersonal capabilities. In traditional logistics environments, professional competence was often defined by operational experience, procedural knowledge, and the ability to manage physical flows of goods. In AI-driven environments, however, workers must interact with intelligent systems that continuously generate predictive insights and automated recommendations. Table 2 shows the Key Dimensions of Hybrid Skills Required in Smart Logistics Ecosystems.

Table 2. Key dimensions of hybrid skills required in smart logistics ecosystems

Skill Dimension	Core Capabilities	Role in Smart Logistics Ecosystems
Digital and Data Skills	Data interpretation, AI output validation, system interaction	Enables supervision of AI-driven planning and operational systems
Analytical and Systems Thinking	Systems integration, critical evaluation, scenario reasoning	Supports decision-making in complex and interconnected logistics processes
Human-Centered Skills	Collaboration, adaptability, communication	Facilitates effective human-AI interaction and cross-functional coordination
Ethical and Reflective Skills	Bias awareness, accountability, ethical judgment	Ensures responsible AI use and trust in automated logistics decisions

Hybrid skills emerge from the need to integrate several complementary competencies. Digital and data-related capabilities allow professionals to interpret algorithmic outputs, validate AI-generated forecasts, and interact with automated decision-support systems. Analytical and systems-thinking skills enable workers to understand interdependencies across supply chain networks and evaluate complex operational scenarios. Human-centered capabilities such as communication, collaboration, and adaptability remain critical for coordinating decisions across organizational boundaries and interacting with cross-functional teams.

In addition, ethical and reflective skills are increasingly important as algorithmic systems influence operational decisions. Logistics professionals must recognize potential biases in automated recommendations, evaluate the implications of algorithmic outputs, and maintain accountability in situations where AI systems affect resource allocation or performance evaluation.

These competencies collectively form hybrid skill sets that combine technological insight with human judgment and organizational awareness. Rather than replacing traditional expertise, hybrid skills expand the scope of logistics professionalism by enabling workers to operate effectively within AI-mediated environments.

3.2 Lifelong Learning and Organizational Support

The emergence of hybrid skill requirements makes lifelong learning a structural necessity for logistics professionals. Because AI technologies evolve rapidly, one-time training interventions are insufficient to maintain workforce competence. Continuous skill development allows workers to adapt to changing technological environments and maintain professional relevance within AI-driven logistics systems (Sekti, 2025c).

Organizations play a critical role in enabling this transition by establishing learning infrastructures that support workforce adaptation. Structured reskilling and upskilling initiatives help employees transition into AI-augmented roles, while AI literacy programs improve understanding of algorithmic systems and reduce uncertainty associated with technological change. Collaborative learning environments such as cross-functional teams, mentoring programs, and communities of practice further facilitate the exchange of knowledge and experiential learning. Table 3 shows the Organizational Mechanisms Supporting Hybrid Skill Development in Smart Logistics.

Table 3. Organizational mechanisms supporting hybrid skill development in smart logistics

Organizational Mechanism	Skill Outcome	Workforce Impact
Upskilling & reskilling programs	Hybrid technical-analytical skills	Role adaptability
AI literacy training	System understanding	Reduced resistance
Collaborative learning	Social & communication skills	Knowledge sharing
Inclusive access	Skill equity	Workforce sustainability

Equally important is the inclusiveness of training opportunities. When access to learning resources is uneven, technological transformation may exacerbate skill inequalities within the workforce. Inclusive training policies ensure that employees across different occupational levels can participate in the development of new competencies.

Through these mechanisms, lifelong learning becomes a key mediator between technological innovation and workforce sustainability. Organizations that institutionalize learning as an ongoing process are better positioned to support workforce adaptability and maintain employee engagement in AI-driven logistics environments.

3.3 Hybrid Skills and Professional Identity Reconstruction

The transformation of logistics skills also has important implications for professional identity. As AI systems increasingly perform tasks that were once associated with professional expertise, workers must redefine how they understand their roles, contributions, and value within the organization. Recent artificial intelligence (AI) tools have demonstrated the ability to produce outputs traditionally considered creative (Zhou & Lee, 2024).

Hybrid competencies enable logistics professionals to reposition themselves as interpreters and coordinators of intelligent systems rather than solely operational specialists. Workers who develop the ability to interpret algorithmic outputs, evaluate system performance, and integrate digital insights into operational decisions are more likely to maintain professional legitimacy and agency.

However, identity reconstruction does not occur uniformly. Some professionals experience the transition toward AI-augmented roles as an opportunity for career development and intellectual growth. Others may perceive automation as a threat to established expertise, particularly when algorithmic systems appear to replace decision-making authority previously exercised by human workers.

The extent to which organizations recognize and reward hybrid skills therefore plays a decisive role in shaping identity transformation. When hybrid competencies are institutionally valued and supported through training and career pathways, workers are more likely to view technological change as a source of empowerment rather than displacement.

3.4 Ethical Competence and Responsible Skill Formation

As AI systems increasingly influence logistics decision-making, ethical competence becomes an essential component of professional capability. Smart logistics environments expose workers to ethical challenges related to algorithmic bias, transparency, accountability, and the distribution of responsibility between humans and automated systems.

Addressing these challenges requires more than technical proficiency. Logistics professionals must develop reflective capacities that allow them to critically evaluate algorithmic outputs and recognize potential risks associated with automated decision-making. Ethical competence therefore includes the ability to identify biases in predictive models, understand the limitations of algorithmic recommendations, and determine when human judgment should override automated outputs.

Furthermore, professionals must be capable of balancing efficiency objectives with broader organizational and social considerations. Decisions influenced by AI systems may affect employee performance evaluations, resource allocation, and operational priorities. Ethical reasoning helps ensure that these decisions remain aligned with principles of fairness, transparency, and accountability.

Embedding ethical competence within skill development frameworks strengthens responsible AI adoption and supports trust in automated logistics systems.

3.5 From Skill Development to Governance Readiness

The cumulative development of hybrid skills, lifelong learning practices, and ethical competence contributes to what can be described as governance readiness within smart logistics ecosystems. Professionals equipped with interdisciplinary capabilities are better positioned to engage with organizational policies, monitor algorithmic systems, and participate in oversight processes related to AI deployment.

When workforce development integrates technical, ethical, and organizational dimensions, governance responsibilities can be distributed more effectively across the organization. Employees are able not only to operate AI systems but also to question their outputs, evaluate their implications, and contribute to responsible decision-making practices.

In this sense, skill transformation extends beyond individual competence to influence organizational governance structures. Workforce capabilities and governance mechanisms become mutually reinforcing components of AI-driven logistics systems. The development of hybrid skills therefore represents not only a response to technological change but also a foundation for responsible and sustainable implementation of intelligent logistics infrastructures.

4. PROFESSIONAL IDENTITY, ORGANIZATIONAL GOVERNANCE, AND HUMAN–AI COLLABORATION

The integration of artificial intelligence into logistics operations reshapes not only work roles and skill requirements but also professional identity and organizational governance structures. As intelligent systems increasingly perform analytical and operational tasks that were traditionally associated with human expertise, logistics professionals must renegotiate their roles within organizational contexts.

In AI-driven logistics environments, professional identity becomes increasingly dynamic. Workers are no longer defined solely by operational expertise but by their ability to interact with intelligent systems, interpret algorithmic outputs, and ensure that automated decisions align with operational realities. This transformation positions logistics professionals as intermediaries between technological infrastructures and organizational objectives.

For some professionals, AI adoption is experienced as empowerment. Automated systems reduce routine tasks and enable workers to focus on higher-level analytical, supervisory, and strategic responsibilities. For others, however, automation can create uncertainty regarding professional relevance and autonomy. These contrasting experiences illustrate how technological transformation simultaneously expands opportunities for professional development while also generating tensions related to control, authority, and accountability.

Consequently, the restructuring of logistics work cannot be understood solely as a technological process. It must also be analyzed through organizational, ethical, and governance dimensions that shape how intelligent systems are implemented and how workers interact with them.

4.1 Algorithmic Management and Professional Autonomy

AI-driven logistics increasingly relies on algorithmic management systems that allocate tasks, monitor performance, and coordinate workflows across supply chain activities. These systems function as digital coordinators that translate organizational objectives into operational directives in real time. By processing large volumes of data, algorithmic systems can optimize routing decisions, inventory allocation, and warehouse operations with a level of speed and precision that is difficult to achieve through manual planning.

While algorithmic management enhances operational efficiency and scalability, it also reconfigures how authority and control are exercised within logistics organizations. Task allocation, performance monitoring, and scheduling decisions that were previously made by supervisors or planners may now be generated automatically through algorithmic processes.

Research suggests that such systems can significantly affect professional autonomy. When decision-making processes are governed by opaque algorithms, workers may experience reduced discretion and diminished influence over operational decisions. In logistics environments where planning expertise historically formed the basis of professional authority, algorithmic management can challenge established hierarchies and redefine decision rights.

Transparency therefore becomes a critical factor in determining whether algorithmic systems are perceived as supportive tools or restrictive controls. When professionals can understand how algorithms operate and influence outcomes, they are more likely to maintain a sense of agency within AI-mediated environments.

4.2 Ethical Implications of Automation in Logistics

The increasing use of AI and automation in logistics operations raises several ethical concerns that extend beyond efficiency considerations. Although intelligent systems can enhance productivity and improve operational accuracy, they also introduce new forms of monitoring, standardization, and data-driven evaluation that affect worker autonomy and well-being (Sekti, 2025b). Table 4 shows the Ethical challenges of AI-driven automation in logistics.

Table 4. Ethical challenges of AI-driven automation in logistics

Ethical Issue	Description	Impact on Workers	Organizational Implications
Surveillance and performance monitoring	Continuous data collection and algorithmic evaluation of worker activities	Increased stress, reduced perceived autonomy, and erosion of trust	Need for transparency policies and limits on monitoring practices
Deskilling and erosion of expertise	Automation absorbs routine and decision-making tasks traditionally performed by humans	Loss of professional confidence and reduced opportunities for judgment	Necessity of reskilling programs and role redesign
Unequal access to reskilling opportunities	Disparities in training availability across roles or employment status	Marginalization of certain worker groups and career stagnation	Risk of widening inequality and reduced workforce cohesion
Algorithmic opacity	Limited explainability of AI-driven decisions	Difficulty contesting decisions and unclear accountability	Demand for explainable AI and procedural fairness mechanisms

One prominent concern relates to surveillance and performance monitoring. Algorithmic systems continuously collect data on worker activities, productivity levels, and compliance with operational procedures. While such monitoring can improve operational visibility, it may also create environments characterized by constant evaluation and increased psychological pressure.

Another concern involves the risk of deskilling. As automated systems assume tasks that previously required human expertise, workers may lose opportunities to exercise judgment and develop professional competencies. Over time, this shift may reduce professional confidence and weaken the knowledge base associated with logistics expertise.

Inequality in access to reskilling opportunities represents a further ethical challenge. When training resources are distributed unevenly, certain groups of workers may benefit from technological transformation while others face marginalization or career stagnation.

These ethical challenges highlight the importance of responsible AI adoption. Automation should be implemented in ways that preserve professional dignity, support skill development, and maintain meaningful human oversight rather than simply replacing human labor.

4.3 Governance Mechanisms for Responsible AI Adoption

Addressing the ethical and organizational challenges associated with AI-driven logistics requires robust governance mechanisms. Governance frameworks define how intelligent systems are introduced, monitored, and adjusted over time, shaping the relationship between organizations, workers, and technological infrastructures.

Artificial intelligence (AI) has become a disruptive force that has revolutionized industries and changed business practices (Kumar, Ashraf, & Nadeem, 2024). Table 5 shows the Governance mechanisms for responsible AI adoption in smart logistics.

Table 5. Governance mechanisms for responsible AI adoption in smart logistics

Governance Dimension	Key Mechanisms	Primary Actors Involved	Relation to Autonomy and Ethics
Algorithmic transparency	Documentation, explainability tools, system audits	Management, IT teams, AI vendors	Enhances trust and enables informed human oversight
Accountability structures	Clear role definition and escalation procedures	Managers, supervisors, governance committees	Clarifies responsibility for automated decisions
Worker participation	Feedback channels, participatory system design	Logistics professionals, unions, HR	Supports professional autonomy and voice
Ethical oversight	Ethics committees, ethical impact assessments	Governance bodies, compliance units	Aligns AI use with organizational and societal values
Continuous monitoring and review	Performance reviews, bias detection, system updates	Management, data analysts	Ensures adaptability and long-term responsibility

Effective governance typically involves several interrelated mechanisms. Algorithmic transparency ensures that system objectives, decision rules, and limitations are clearly documented and communicated to relevant stakeholders. Accountability structures define who is responsible for automated decisions and establish procedures for resolving conflicts between algorithmic outputs and human judgment.

In addition, governance frameworks often incorporate ethical oversight mechanisms, such as review committees or impact assessments, that evaluate the broader implications of AI deployment. Continuous monitoring and evaluation processes allow organizations to identify unintended consequences and adjust systems accordingly.

By establishing these mechanisms, logistics organizations can ensure that AI systems remain aligned with operational objectives while respecting ethical principles and workforce sustainability.

4.4 Worker Participation and Voice in Algorithmic Systems

Worker participation is a critical element in mitigating the risks associated with algorithmic management. When intelligent systems are introduced without mechanisms for employee input, operational processes may become rigid and disconnected from practical experience.

Participatory approaches allow workers to contribute insights regarding system functionality, operational constraints, and contextual factors that may not be fully captured in algorithmic models. Involving employees in system design and implementation processes can therefore improve both technical performance and organizational acceptance.

Feedback channels and appeal mechanisms further enable workers to question algorithmic decisions when they conflict with situational realities. Such mechanisms help maintain a balance between automated efficiency and human expertise.

Transparency initiatives also play an important role. When organizations provide clear explanations of how algorithms operate and how decisions are generated, workers are better able to understand and engage with automated systems. These practices reinforce professional agency and encourage constructive interaction with intelligent technologies.

4.5 Integrating Ethics, Identity, and Governance in Smart Logistics

The organizational, ethical, and governance dimensions of AI-driven logistics are closely interconnected. Algorithmic management reshapes professional autonomy, ethical concerns arise from the ways intelligent systems are deployed, and governance structures determine whether these transformations are managed responsibly.

When organizations treat workers merely as system operators, technological transformation may weaken professional identity and reduce employee engagement. In contrast, when governance frameworks recognize workers as knowledgeable contributors to AI-enabled processes, technological change can reinforce professional legitimacy and organizational trust.

Integrating ethical reasoning, participatory governance, and professional identity considerations therefore provides a foundation for sustainable smart logistics ecosystems. This integration ensures that technological innovation supports both operational efficiency and the social structures that sustain logistics organizations.

4.6 Algorithmic Accountability and Explainable AI in Smart Logistics

As AI systems increasingly influence logistics decision-making, algorithmic accountability and explainable AI become essential components of organizational governance. Algorithmic accountability refers to the ability of organizations to trace, evaluate, and justify decisions produced by automated systems. Figure 3 shows the Achieving Algorithmic Accountability in Smart Logistics.

Figure 3. Achieving algorithmic accountability in smart logistics

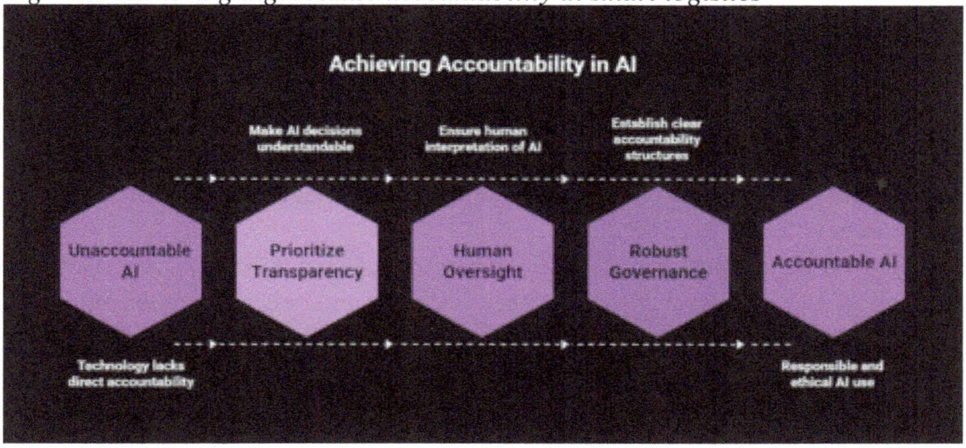

In logistics environments, accountability mechanisms ensure that algorithmic outputs can be audited, challenged, and revised when necessary. Without such mechanisms, automated systems risk functioning as opaque authorities whose decisions cannot be meaningfully questioned.

Explainable AI supports accountability by enabling professionals to understand how algorithmic decisions are generated. When workers can interpret the reasoning behind automated recommendations, they are better equipped to evaluate system reliability and apply contextual judgment when necessary.

From an organizational perspective, explainability strengthens trust and reinforces professional agency. Logistics professionals remain responsible for operational outcomes, and their ability to interpret algorithmic outputs allows them to integrate technological insights with practical experience.

Ultimately, integrating algorithmic accountability and explainable AI into governance frameworks ensures that intelligent logistics systems remain transparent, contestable, and aligned with human values. Such mechanisms enable organizations to balance technological efficiency with professional autonomy and ethical responsibility in smart logistics ecosystems.

5. GOVERNANCE AND GLOBAL PERSPECTIVES ON AI-DRIVEN LOGISTICS WORK

The integration of artificial intelligence into logistics operations introduces significant governance challenges related to transparency, accountability, and worker autonomy. As intelligent systems increasingly guide operational decisions such as routing, inventory allocation, and performance monitoring, the relationship between technological efficiency and human oversight becomes a central concern for organizations. Artificial Intelligence (AI) has become an influential force shaping modern society, raising urgent ethical questions about responsibility, fairness, transparency (Sekti, 2025b).

Algorithmic management systems can influence task allocation, workflow coordination, and performance evaluation, sometimes reducing worker discretion and altering traditional forms of professional authority. Without adequate transparency and institutional oversight, such systems may generate ethical concerns related to excessive monitoring, deskilling, and unequal access to reskilling opportunities.

Responsible AI adoption therefore requires governance mechanisms that ensure both operational effectiveness and workforce sustainability. Key governance principles include algorithmic transparency and explainability, clear accountability for automated decisions, worker participation in system design and evaluation, and sustained organizational investment in workforce training. When these mechanisms are implemented effectively, AI-driven logistics systems can support innovation while maintaining trust and professional agency within the workforce.

At the same time, the transformation of logistics work does not occur uniformly across regions. Differences in infrastructure, institutional capacity, and workforce skills produce diverse trajectories of AI adoption, highlighting the importance of global and comparative perspectives on smart logistics ecosystems.

5.1 Developed and Developing Economies

The evolution of logistics roles under AI-driven transformation varies significantly across regions. In advanced economies, the adoption of smart logistics technologies is typically supported by mature digital infrastructures, strong innovation ecosystems, and well-established educational systems. These conditions facilitate the emergence of high-skill AI-enabled roles such as logistics data analysts, system integrators, and digital operations managers. Table 6 shows the Smart logistics transformation in developed and developing economies.

Table 6. Smart logistics transformation in developed and developing economies

Dimension	Developed Economies	Developing Economies
Digital infrastructure	Advanced digital networks, high connectivity, and integrated data platforms	Limited or uneven connectivity and fragmented digital infrastructure
AI readiness	High AI readiness supported by strong research capacity and public-private investment	Lower AI readiness due to constrained research capacity and limited public investment
Dominant logistics roles	High-skill AI-enabled roles (e.g., data analysts, system integrators, digital operations managers)	Mixed roles combining manual work with partial automation and basic digital coordination
Workforce skills	Strong emphasis on advanced analytics, systems thinking, and AI supervision	Predominant skill gaps in data literacy and AI-related competencies
Mode of AI adoption	Large-scale and integrated deployment across logistics processes	Isolated, pilot-based, or incremental implementation
Workforce risks	Risk of work intensification and algorithmic control	Higher risk of skill mismatch, labor displacement, and inequality
Institutional support	Well-established governance frameworks and training ecosystems	Limited institutional support and evolving regulatory frameworks

In contrast, many developing economies face structural constraints that shape a different trajectory of transformation. Limited digital infrastructure, restricted research capacity, and lower levels of public investment in technological development can slow the adoption of AI technologies. As a result, AI deployment in logistics often occurs through isolated pilot projects rather than integrated large-scale systems.

These structural differences influence the nature of logistics employment. In developed economies, logistics professionals increasingly perform analytical and supervisory roles within highly automated systems. In developing regions, logistics work may remain partially manual while incorporating selective digital tools, creating hybrid work environments characterized by uneven technological integration.

Consequently, logistics workers in resource-constrained contexts may face challenges such as skill mismatches, limited training opportunities, and greater vulnerability to labor displacement. Without targeted institutional support, technological transformation may reinforce existing global inequalities in logistics capability and workforce development.

5.2 Structural Barriers to AI-Driven Logistics Transformation

Several structural barriers systematically influence the adoption of AI in logistics systems, particularly in emerging and developing economies. One of the most significant challenges is the limitation of digital infrastructure. Inadequate connectivity, fragmented data systems, and limited integration between logistics platforms restrict the ability of organizations to implement real-time optimization and AI-driven coordination.

A second major barrier involves shortages of skilled human resources. The effective operation of AI-enabled logistics systems requires expertise in data analytics, machine learning, and digital supply chain management. In regions where educational and training systems have not yet adapted to these emerging skill requirements, organizations may struggle to recruit professionals capable of managing intelligent logistics infrastructures. Artificial Intelligence (AI) and Machine Learning (ML) are transformative technologies reshaping industries (Sekti, 2025d).

Financial constraints also play an important role. Implementing and maintaining AI-driven logistics systems often requires substantial investments in technology, data management, and system integration. For many small and medium-sized enterprises, these costs may exceed available resources, slowing the pace of technological transformation.

Finally, institutional and regulatory gaps can hinder adoption. In the absence of clear governance frameworks or supportive policy environments, organizations may hesitate to invest in AI-enabled logistics solutions. These structural barriers demonstrate that technological diffusion alone is insufficient; broader institutional and economic conditions must also support workforce transformation.

5.3 Global Knowledge Transfer and Capability Building

Addressing regional disparities in smart logistics development requires deliberate strategies for knowledge transfer and capability building. Rather than simply replicating models developed in technologically advanced regions, AI adoption must be adapted to local institutional and socio-economic contexts.

Collaborative initiatives involving governments, educational institutions, and industry actors play a crucial role in strengthening foundational capabilities. Educational programs that integrate logistics expertise with data analytics and digital technologies can prepare professionals to participate effectively in AI-driven logistics systems. At the same time, organizational training programs can support workforce transitions toward more analytical and supervisory roles.

International partnerships and research collaborations also contribute to global learning. By sharing technical knowledge, governance frameworks, and operational practices, organizations across different regions can collectively improve their capacity to manage intelligent logistics systems. Such collaborative efforts help reduce disparities in technological capability and promote more balanced global development of smart logistics ecosystems.

5.4 Toward Inclusive Global Smart Logistics Ecosystems

The development of inclusive smart logistics ecosystems requires approaches that combine technological innovation with social and institutional inclusion. As AI systems become central to logistics operations, ensuring equitable access to skills, training, and career opportunities becomes essential for sustainable workforce development.

One key principle involves context-sensitive AI deployment. Technologies must be aligned with local infrastructure capabilities, workforce competencies, and regulatory environments rather than applied uniformly across diverse contexts. Another principle concerns equitable access to skill development, ensuring that training opportunities extend beyond highly specialized roles and are accessible to a broad range of workers.

Adaptive governance frameworks are equally important. Regulatory and organizational systems must evolve to address emerging ethical and operational challenges associated with AI-driven logistics, including transparency, fairness, and accountability. Finally, shared ethical standards can help align global logistics practices around common values while allowing flexibility in implementation across different regions.

Through these approaches, global logistics systems can move toward more inclusive forms of technological transformation in which AI-driven innovation supports both economic performance and workforce sustainability.

6. IMPLICATIONS FOR POLICY AND WORKFORCE DEVELOPMENT IN LOGISTICS

The transformation of logistics employment through artificial intelligence carries important implications for both policymakers and organizational leaders. AI-driven logistics systems reshape labor structures, skill requirements, and governance arrangements, requiring coordinated responses that integrate workforce development, ethical safeguards, and institutional support. Rather than treating technological innovation and workforce adaptation as separate processes, effective smart logistics strategies must align technological capability with human capital development (Sekti, 2025c).

Education and training systems therefore play a central role in preparing logistics professionals for AI-mediated work environments. Traditional logistics education focused primarily on operational coordination and efficiency, but future curricula must incorporate competencies such as data literacy, systems thinking, digital platform interaction, and ethical reasoning. These competencies enable professionals to interpret algorithmic outputs, manage intelligent systems, and participate in responsible decision-making processes within AI-enabled logistics environments.

At the organizational level, leaders must adopt human-centered AI strategies that treat employees as collaborators rather than substitutes for intelligent systems. Investments in reskilling, participatory technology design, and transparent algorithmic practices can strengthen workforce engagement, professional identity, and long-term organizational trust. Aligning technological adoption with workforce capability development is therefore essential for sustaining both operational performance and human well-being in smart logistics ecosystems.

6.1 Policy Implications for Workforce Transition and Education Reform

From a policy perspective, the transformation of logistics work requires significant adjustments in education systems, labor market policies, and workforce governance frameworks. AI-driven economic transformation increasingly demands interdisciplinary competencies that combine digital capability, systems thinking, and ethical awareness. Governments and educational institutions therefore need to update logistics and supply chain curricula to reflect the realities of AI-mediated work environments.

Educational reform should move beyond traditional logistics management training and incorporate data analytics, digital platform management, and human–AI collaboration. Such reforms help prepare future professionals to operate in environments where decision-making is distributed between human judgment and intelligent systems.

In addition to educational reform, active labor market policies are crucial for supporting workforce transition. Automation-driven occupational shifts may create uncertainty or displacement if workers lack access to retraining opportunities. Policy initiatives that provide reskilling programs, vocational transitions, and social protection mechanisms can help workers adapt to emerging AI-augmented roles without long-term exclusion from the labor market. These measures are particularly important in regions where institutional support for workforce adaptation remains limited.

6.2 Organizational Leadership and Human-Centered AI Implementation

While public policy establishes the broader institutional framework, organizational leadership determines how AI transformation is experienced within everyday work practices. Smart logistics adoption represents not only a technological shift but also a socio-organizational transformation that affects professional identity, trust, and employee engagement (Kuaites & Thungwha, 2025). Table 7 shows the Policy and Organizational Implications for Human-Centered AI in Smart Logistics.

Table 7. Policy and organizational implications for human-centered AI in smart logistics

Dimension	Policy-Level Implications	Organizational-Level Implications
Education and skills development	Reform logistics and supply chain curricula to integrate AI literacy, systems thinking, and ethical reasoning	Invest in continuous upskilling and reskilling programs aligned with AI-augmented roles
Workforce transition	Implement active labor market policies and social protection mechanisms to support occupational mobility	Design internal career pathways that enable role transition without loss of professional identity
AI governance and regulation	Establish regulatory frameworks emphasizing transparency, accountability, and human oversight	Develop internal AI governance guidelines clarifying responsibilities and escalation mechanisms
Ethical safeguards	Promote fairness, inclusion, and worker participation in AI policy design	Embed ethical principles into algorithmic practices and performance evaluation systems
Organizational culture	Encourage cross-sector collaboration and knowledge sharing	Foster cultures of learning, participation, and human-technology collaboration

Organizations that frame AI primarily as a replacement for human labor are more likely to encounter resistance, reduced morale, and ethical tensions. In contrast, organizations that emphasize collaboration between humans and intelligent systems can foster more sustainable technological adoption. Human-centered AI strategies therefore focus on empowering employees to work alongside intelligent systems rather than being displaced by them.

Key organizational practices that support human-centered AI implementation include investment in continuous upskilling and reskilling programs, participatory system design processes that incorporate worker expertise, and transparent algorithmic practices that clarify how automated decisions are generated. When these practices are embedded within organizational culture, employees are more likely to perceive AI systems as enabling tools that enhance professional capabilities rather than threats to job security.

6.3 Inclusive Innovation and Global Capability Alignment

The uneven global adoption of AI-driven logistics systems highlights the need for inclusive innovation strategies. Differences in digital infrastructure, institutional capacity, and workforce skills create varied pathways of technological transformation across countries and regions. As a result, AI implementation strategies must be adapted to local socio-economic and institutional conditions rather than applied uniformly.

Inclusive innovation requires collaboration between governments, educational institutions, and industry actors to strengthen foundational capabilities. Educational initiatives can expand access to digital logistics skills, while industry partnerships can provide practical training and knowledge exchange opportunities. International collaborations and research partnerships also contribute to global capability building by facilitating the transfer of technological expertise and governance practices.

For multinational logistics organizations, aligning technological strategies with regional workforce capabilities is particularly important. AI implementation must account for differences in infrastructure readiness, training systems, and regulatory environments to ensure that technological transformation produces shared benefits rather than reinforcing existing inequalities.

6.4 Toward Socially Sustainable Smart Logistics Ecosystems

Taken together, the policy and organizational implications of AI-driven logistics transformation underscore the importance of social sustainability as a guiding principle. Smart logistics ecosystems are not sustainable solely because they improve operational efficiency or technological sophistication. They must also support meaningful work, continuous learning, and ethical responsibility within the workforce. An integrated smart framework could be enhance logistics performance in the fast-moving consumer goods (FMCG) sector (GhanavatiNejad, Tavakoli, Sheikhalishahi, Aydın, & Aria, 2025).

When workforce development, governance frameworks, and organizational leadership are aligned, AI adoption can enhance both economic performance and human capability development. Workers remain active contributors to intelligent logistics systems, providing contextual knowledge, ethical judgment, and strategic oversight that complement machine intelligence.

Ultimately, the long-term success of smart logistics ecosystems depends on recognizing workers as central participants in technological transformation. By integrating human-centered policies, inclusive skill development, and responsible AI governance, logistics organizations and policymakers can ensure that AI-driven innovation contributes to both productivity and workforce resilience.

CONCLUSION

Artificial intelligence is reshaping logistics employment by reorganizing work roles, task allocation, and skill requirements across smart logistics ecosystems.

Rather than simply replacing human labor, AI redistributes responsibilities between intelligent systems and logistics professionals. Routine and data-intensive tasks increasingly shift toward automated systems, while human workers move toward supervisory, analytical, and interpretive roles. This transition has led to the emergence of AI-augmented occupations and the growing importance of hybrid skills that combine digital literacy, systems thinking, and human-centered competencies.

The chapter shows that AI-driven transformation requires logistics professionals to adapt to new forms of human–AI collaboration. As algorithmic systems influence operational decisions, workers are expected to interpret predictive outputs, manage exceptions, and maintain oversight of automated processes. These changes reshape professional identities while emphasizing the importance of continuous learning and workforce development. Organizations must therefore invest in reskilling initiatives and training programs that enable employees to operate effectively within AI-mediated logistics environments.

At the same time, the integration of AI raises governance and ethical challenges related to transparency, accountability, and worker autonomy. Responsible AI adoption requires organizational and policy frameworks that balance technological efficiency with human agency and fair labor practices. When technological innovation is aligned with workforce development, ethical oversight, and participatory governance, AI-driven logistics systems can enhance both operational performance and long-term workforce sustainability.

REFERENCES

Brunetti, M., Mes, M., & Lalla-Ruiz, E. (2024). Smart logistics nodes: Concept and classification. *International Journal of Logistics, 27*(11), 1984–2020. DOI: 10.1080/13675567.2024.2327394

Ferreira, B., & Reis, J. (2023). A Systematic Literature Review on the Application of Automation in Logistics. *Logistics (Basel), 7*(4), 80. Advance online publication. DOI: 10.3390/logistics7040080

GhanavatiNejad, M., Tavakoli, M., Sheikhalishahi, M., Aydın, N., & Aria, S. S. (2025). An integrated smart framework for fast-moving consumer goods online market logistics: A digital twin framework. *Journal of Industrial and Production Engineering, 42*(5), 533–549. DOI: 10.1080/21681015.2025.2470244

Jia, N., Luo, X., Fang, Z., & Liao, C. (2024). WHEN AND HOW ARTIFICIAL INTELLIGENCE AUGMENTS EMPLOYEE CREATIVITY. *Academy of Management Journal, 67*(1), 5–32. DOI: 10.5465/amj.2022.0426

Joosten, J., Bilgram, V., Hahn, A., & Totzek, D. (2024). Comparing the Ideation Quality of Humans with Generative Artificial Intelligence. *IEEE Engineering Management Review, 52*(2), 153–164. DOI: 10.1109/EMR.2024.3353338

Koh, L. Y., & Yuen, K. F. (2022). Emerging competencies for logistics professionals in the digital era: A literature review. *Frontiers in Psychology, 13*, 965748. Advance online publication. DOI: 10.3389/fpsyg.2022.965748 PMID: 36389597

Kuaites, T., & Thungwha, S. (2025). Enabling Smart Cold Chain Logistics Through Standardization and Digital Transformation: A Structural Model for Reducing Food Loss in Thailand's Agri-Food Sector. *Sustainability (Basel), 17*(13), 6085. Advance online publication. DOI: 10.3390/su17136085

Kumar, V., Ashraf, A. R., & Nadeem, W. (2024). AI-powered marketing: What, where, and how? *International Journal of Information Management, 77*, 102783. Advance online publication. DOI: 10.1016/j.ijinfomgt.2024.102783

Li, B., Yang, Y., Zhao, Z., Ni, X., & Zhang, D. (2024). A Novel Ensemble Learning Approach for Intelligent Logistics Demand Management. *Wangji Wanglu Jishu Xuekan, 25*(4), 507–515. DOI: 10.70003/160792642024072504002

Liu, Q., Ma, Y., Chen, L., Pedrycz, W., Skibniewski, M. J., & Chen, Z.-S. (2024). Artificial intelligence for production, operations and logistics management in modular construction industry: A systematic literature review. *Information Fusion, 109*, 102423. Advance online publication. DOI: 10.1016/j.inffus.2024.102423

Mirbabaie, M., Brünker, F., Möllmann Frick, N. R. J., & Stieglitz, S. (2022). The rise of artificial intelligence – understanding the AI identity threat at the workplace. *Electronic Markets*, *32*(1), 73–99. DOI: 10.1007/s12525-021-00496-x

Mohsen, B. M. (2024). AI-Driven Optimization of Urban Logistics in Smart Cities: Integrating Autonomous Vehicles and IoT for Efficient Delivery Systems. *Sustainability (Basel)*, *16*(24), 11265. Advance online publication. DOI: 10.3390/su162411265

Pasupuleti, V., Thuraka, B., Kodete, C. S., & Malisetty, S. (2024). Enhancing Supply Chain Agility and Sustainability through Machine Learning: Optimization Techniques for Logistics and Inventory Management. *Logistics (Basel)*, *8*(3), 73. Advance online publication. DOI: 10.3390/logistics8030073

Sekti, B. A. (2025a). AI Technology Management Concepts and Strategies. In *AI Technology Management and Value Creation* (pp. 1–32). DOI: 10.4018/979-8-3373-2497-5.ch001

Sekti, B. A. (2025b). Foundations of Artificial Intelligence Ethics. In *Navigating Social Trust in the AI Era* (pp. 23–47). DOI: 10.4018/979-8-3373-7011-8.ch002

Sekti, B. A. (2025c). Machine learning and artificial intelligence (AI) in manufacturing. In *Integrating Digital Innovation and Integrated Frameworks in Manufacturing* (pp. 255–292). DOI: 10.4018/979-8-3373-1082-4.ch011

Sekti, B. A. (2025d). Machine Learning vs. AI: Key Concepts. In *Implementing Enterprise Cybersecurity With AI* (pp. 1–27). DOI: 10.4018/979-8-3373-2252-0.ch001

Tang, Y. M., Chau, K. Y., Lau, Y.-Y., & Zheng, Z. (2023). Data-Intensive Inventory Forecasting with Artificial Intelligence Models for Cross-Border E-Commerce Service Automation. *Applied Sciences (Basel, Switzerland)*, *13*(5), 3051. Advance online publication. DOI: 10.3390/app13053051

Zhou, E., & Lee, D. (2024). Generative artificial intelligence, human creativity, and art. *PNAS Nexus*, *3*(3), pgae052. Advance online publication. DOI: 10.1093/pnasnexus/pgae052 PMID: 38444602

Zhu, D., Han, Z., Du, X., Zuo, D., Cai, L., & Xue, C. (2025). Hybrid Model Integrating Fuzzy Systems and Convolutional Factorization Machine for Delivery Time Prediction in Intelligent Logistics. *IEEE Transactions on Fuzzy Systems*, *33*(1), 406–417. DOI: 10.1109/TFUZZ.2024.3472043

Chapter 5
Governing Green Logistics Through Algorithms:
How AI-Driven Sustainability Targets Reshape Labor

Ngo Tinh Giang Nguyen
http://orcid.org/0000-0001-6838-8951
Ho Chi Minh City University of Economics and Finance, Vietnam

ABSTRACT

This chapter examines how sustainability mandates in logistics are transformed into modes of labour governance when embedded in AI-enabled systems. Drawing on four anonymized cases, the analysis identifies a recurrent mechanism through which policy mandates are converted into standardised targets and evidentiary obligations. Algorithmic benchmarks progressively shift from advisory tools to de facto normative standards. Across the cases, these dynamics intensify work by accelerating operational cycles, thickening task architectures, increasing cognitive demands, and amplifying individual accountability, while simultaneously provoking disputes over metrics that obscure local constraints. The chapter advances green digital intensification to theorise how mandates, optimisation logics, and evidence regimes co-produce a normalised form of labour intensification that is rendered environmentally legitimate. It concludes by outlining design implications for decarbonisation initiatives to reconcile climate objectives with the protection of worker well-being in datafied logistics environments.

DOI: 10.4018/979-8-3373-7826-8.ch005

1. INTRODUCTION

AI systems are increasingly mobilised as pragmatic instruments for meeting sustainability mandates in logistics, notably through carbon reduction, route optimisation, and higher asset utilisation. In many logistics-intensive sectors, environmental performance is no longer treated as a discretionary add-on to corporate responsibility narratives. Instead, it is progressively translated into auditable obligations shaped by regulatory disclosure regimes, customer procurement requirements, and internal ESG governance architectures. This shift matters because it changes the organisational meaning of "being green": sustainability becomes measurable, comparable, and accountable, thereby creating a demand for operational technologies capable of producing traceable evidence of progress. Within this context, AI becomes attractive not only because it can optimise routes or predict demand, but because it can render sustainability actionable—by converting broad environmental objectives into calculable targets, routinised decision rules, and continuous measurement infrastructures.

However, translating sustainability into a mandate also changes the labour politics of logistics. When environmental objectives are embedded in optimisation systems and monitoring dashboards, they do not remain at the level of organisational intention; they are enacted through daily work arrangements. In road freight and last-mile delivery, operational variability is persistent, service levels are time-sensitive, and feasibility is routinely achieved through situated judgement by planners, supervisors, and frontline workers. Under these conditions, AI-enabled "green" optimisation can generate a distinctive reconfiguration of work: buffers are reduced in the name of efficiency and emissions reduction; task cycles accelerate; exception handling becomes more frequent; and monitoring expands into new domains of performance, including "green" indicators that are increasingly treated as discipline and proof.

Research on AI in logistics and supply chain management has mapped the breadth of AI applications and clarified the promise of intelligent optimisation, predictive analytics, and digitised coordination (Richey Jr et al., 2023; Sanders et al., 2019; Chen et al., 2024). At the same time, logistics scholarship has cautioned that technological innovation can produce social sustainability risks, including the emergence of an "artificial divide" in human–computer interaction and uneven distributions of burdens and benefits (Klumpp & Zijm, 2019). These debates have matured, but they have not yet fully captured how sustainability mandates themselves—rather than generic efficiency imperatives—can intensify logistical work when pursued through AI. This chapter addresses that gap by examining sustainability and AI not as separate agendas, but as mutually reinforcing governance logics with consequential implications for labour.

Empirically, the chapter develops a comparative analysis using four anonymised cases. Three cases correspond to prominent corporate exemplars with articulated

AI-enabled sustainability narratives: Case A reflects a parcel logistics operator deploying ORION/UPSNav-style routing and navigation optimisation; Case B reflects a large platform retailer and logistics operator deploying AI-driven routing and transportation optimisation; and Case C reflects a global logistics provider institutionalising sustainability through GoGreen-style carbon transparency and optimisation services. A fourth case (Case D) is included to strengthen cross-case reasoning by representing a telematics-centric "green performance governance" configuration that is increasingly visible in the sector. The cases are treated as analytic devices rather than exhaustive organisational histories, enabling the chapter to surface recurring mechanisms and to identify boundary conditions.

The chapter's central theoretical contribution is the green digital intensification model, which explains how sustainability mandates and AI optimisation jointly reshape labour conditions in logistics, producing new tensions between ecological efficiency and worker well-being. Conceptually, the model extends the sustainability–digitalisation debates by treating labour conditions as a constitutive outcome of green transitions, rather than merely an externality to be managed after the fact. Practically, it clarifies why firms pursuing decarbonisation through AI must evaluate workload and well-being effects alongside carbon and utilisation outcomes if they are to build socially sustainable logistics systems.

2. LITERATURE REVIEW AND THEORETICAL FRAMEWORK

2.1 Chapter background and core concepts

The conceptual backdrop of this chapter is the rapid convergence of digital transformation and sustainability governance in logistics. AI is now routinely framed as central to "smart logistics" and sustainable supply chain management, enabling route optimisation, predictive maintenance, dynamic scheduling, and data-intensive decision-making that can reduce waste, energy use, and emissions (Sanders et al., 2019; Chen et al., 2024; Lin, 2025). Reviews and research roadmaps emphasise that AI capabilities in logistics are expanding from isolated optimisation tasks toward integrated socio-technical systems in which data, algorithms, and organisational routines jointly shape performance and organisational outcomes (Richey Jr et al., 2023). Parallel to this digital trajectory, sustainability has become increasingly mandatory: carbon accounting, customer-led emissions reporting, and institutionalised ESG expectations require verifiable evidence rather than general commitments. This reorientation matters because the operationalisation of sustainability depends on infrastructures that can measure, attribute, and explain performance—functions that AI and analytics promise to deliver.

Three core concepts anchor the chapter. First, sustainability mandates refer to enforceable or semi-enforceable requirements for environmental performance, such as emissions reporting, carbon reduction targets, and customer procurement standards. Second, AI-enabled operational governance refers to the ways AI systems shape decision rights, define normative baselines for "good" performance, and create infrastructures of accountability through optimisation and measurement (Richey Jr et al., 2023; Sanders et al., 2019). Third, work intensification refers to increases in work pace, density, and cognitive load, including compressed buffers, heightened time discipline, and expanded responsibilities without commensurate resources. While these concepts are often studied separately, this chapter examines their intersection: how sustainability mandates—implemented through AI-enabled governance—can intensify logistical work.

The literature provides several starting points for this integration. AI in logistics is widely acknowledged as a source of efficiency and agility, enabling coordination under uncertainty and supporting sustainable competitiveness (Richey Jr et al., 2023; Tan et al., 2025). Sustainability and digitisation are increasingly treated as mutually reinforcing, with AI and analytics enabling smarter, greener supply chains (Sanders et al., 2019; Mohsen & Mohsen, 2025). At the same time, scholars emphasise the need to avoid social sustainability divides and to scrutinise how human–computer interaction, metric design, and performance governance shape worker experiences (Klumpp & Zijm, 2019). Building on these foundations, the following subsections develop a theoretical framework that links sustainability mandates (as compliance infrastructure), AI-enabled optimisation (as operational governance), and labour intensification (as a patterned outcome of green digital transitions).

2.2 Sustainability mandates as compliance infrastructure

Sustainability mandates reshape logistics by converting environmental objectives into enforceable performance expectations. Although mandates vary across institutional settings, they commonly take the form of carbon disclosure requirements, emissions-reduction commitments embedded in contracts, supplier standards, and customer procurement criteria that require proof of progress rather than symbolic compliance. In logistics, mandates often focus on measurable levers: reducing distance travelled, increasing route density, minimising idling, improving load factors, and enhancing asset utilisation. Such levers appear operationally straightforward, but their governance implication is significant: they invite a shift from periodic reporting toward continuous measurement and iterative performance improvement.

This compliance orientation reorganises organisational attention and elevates measurement infrastructures from supportive tools to strategic necessities. Where sustainability is auditable, firms have incentives to standardise data capture, define comparable metrics, and build routines that can demonstrate causality between operational decisions and environmental outcomes. Research on AI capabilities and sustainable competitiveness in logistics suggests that such dynamics are not only technologically driven; they also interact with resilience and institutional arrangements, including government support and intervention, which can accelerate diffusion and shape the goals that AI systems are tasked with achieving (Tan et al., 2025). Likewise, studies of AI-enabled digital transformation in circular logistics highlight that organisational, technological, and environmental drivers jointly influence adoption and the direction of change (Oncioiu et al., 2025). These findings imply that sustainability mandates do not simply impose costs; they constitute a governance environment that can catalyse digital transformation and reshape operational routines.

Importantly, sustainability mandates operate as *compliance infrastructure* because they are enacted through organisational systems of responsibility and proof. The mandate is realised when targets are embedded in dashboards, when reporting cycles become organisational rhythms, and when accountability chains translate aggregate goals into role-specific expectations. This chapter uses that insight as a theoretical bridge. If sustainability is increasingly organised through continuous targets and proof mechanisms, then the deployment of AI for sustainability compliance is likely to alter not only operational efficiency but also labour demands and managerial surveillance.

2.3 AI-enabled environmental optimisation as operational governance

AI applications in logistics include optimisation, prediction, classification, and decision support across routing, warehousing, transport planning, and reverse logistics. The literature consistently underlines the efficiency and sustainability potential of these applications, particularly where optimisation incorporates sustainable criteria such as emissions, energy use, and waste reduction (Chen et al., 2024). AI-driven energy optimisation in urban logistics further illustrates how data-intensive systems can reduce fuel consumption and align logistics operations with smart city and smart supply chain agendas (Mohsen & Mohsen, 2025). Moreover, use-case-oriented scholarship documents a widening portfolio of AI applications in freight logistics, suggesting that AI is becoming integral to strategic operations rather than a peripheral experiment (du Plessis et al., 2025).

However, the analytical significance of AI for this chapter is not confined to computational performance. Optimisation systems operate as governance mechanisms because they (i) translate strategic objectives—here, sustainability mandates—into routinised decision rules; (ii) embed assumptions about what constitutes efficient and acceptable performance; and (iii) reorganise discretion and responsibility across planners, supervisors, and frontline workers. AI-enabled optimisation can therefore create new "normative baselines": outputs become expectations, and deviations become accountable events. This is particularly consequential where sustainability is tied to auditability. Under a compliance orientation, the question is not only whether operations are efficient, but also whether decisions are justified as consistent with sustainability targets and reporting claims.

Recent scholarship explicitly recognises that AI in logistics can have a dual role: it can drive sustainability and energy consciousness while also producing organisational and social consequences that exceed simple efficiency narratives (AlSheikh et al., 2025). This duality resonates with broader calls in sustainable supply chain research to examine governance, accountability, and the unintended consequences of digitised coordination (Sanders et al., 2019). Building on these debates, the chapter conceptualises AI-enabled environmental optimisation as *operational governance*: a socio-technical arrangement through which sustainability mandates are enacted, monitored, and enforced.

2.4 Work intensification under green digital transitions

Work intensification refers to the increasing density, pace, and cognitive load of work. It often manifests through compressed time buffers, heightened performance expectations, and an expansion of responsibilities without commensurate resources. In logistics, intensification is particularly salient because time discipline and service reliability are central to competitiveness, while variability in traffic, customer constraints, and asset conditions remains persistent. The driver and frontline worker have long been recognised as pivotal actors in sustainable transportation outcomes, shaping emissions and operational efficiency through behaviour and decision-making (Dubey & Gunasekaran, 2015). The introduction of AI does not remove this human centrality; instead, it reconfigures it.

When sustainability mandates are operationalised through AI systems, intensification can emerge through two interrelated pathways. First, optimisation can compress slack and buffer time in the name of efficiency and emissions reduction. Reduced idling, fewer empty miles, and higher utilisation are environmentally beneficial, yet they also reduce the margins workers use to absorb variability, recover from delays, and manage safety. Second, AI-enabled governance can increase workers' cognitive burden as they reconcile algorithmic plans with situational contingencies. When systems specify "optimal" routes and schedules, workers become responsible for feasibility work: adapting plans, handling exceptions, and maintaining service levels while remaining accountable to system-defined baselines.

This intensification pathway connects directly to social sustainability concerns. Klumpp and Zijm (2019) warn that logistics innovation may create an "artificial divide" in human–computer interaction, whereby workers are expected to comply with systems that do not fully capture on-the-ground complexity, potentially generating stress, conflict, and perceived unfairness. The chapter, therefore, treats intensification as a patterned outcome of green digital transitions, rather than as an incidental side effect.

The pathway is not deterministic. Research on sustainable human resource management practices suggests that HRM design can shape how AI is experienced in logistics and can mediate performance outcomes such as agility (Jahangir et al., 2025). This matters because it indicates that organisations possess levers—training, job redesign, support routines, workload governance—through which intensification can be mitigated or amplified. The chapter builds on this insight by showing how intensification is produced through governance configurations, and by clarifying where managerial interventions can alter the trajectory.

2.5 Monitoring, accountability, and the well-being–sustainability tension

Monitoring is not new in logistics; however, AI-enabled sustainability compliance expands what is monitored and how it is interpreted. Where sustainability becomes a performance domain, monitoring extends into "green performance" indicators: idling time, eco-driving behaviours, route adherence tied to emissions targets, energy-use proxies, and utilisation-based measures of carbon intensity. In organisations that treat sustainability as a compliance infrastructure, such measurement is not optional. It is central to organisational claims of credibility and progress. The governance consequence is that accountability expands: workers are evaluated not only on service and productivity but also on behavioural and operational indicators framed as environmental responsibilities.

This expansion can produce accountability escalation. Workers become responsible for metrics that are partly shaped by system parameters and external constraints. In practical terms, the system's baseline can harden into an evaluative standard even when feasibility depends on local judgement. The literature on AI-driven sustainable logistics increasingly recognises that AI's sustainability contributions are accompanied by governance and ethical questions, including the risk that efficiency and energy consciousness become disciplinary logics (AlSheikh et al., 2025; Sanders et al., 2019). The result is a tension between well-being and ecological efficiency: ecological efficiency is pursued through mechanisms that can intensify work, while worker well-being is often treated as a secondary consideration because it is less visible in sustainability reporting.

A broader implication is that sustainability transitions are not purely technical, but socially organised and governance-dependent. Research on circular transitions and procurement highlights that organisational change involves negotiation, relational governance, and capacity building across actors (Tanveer et al., 2024), while digital integration can reshape innovation capabilities through relational mechanisms (Tanveer et al., 2026). Although these studies are not centred on labour intensification, they reinforce a central premise: the outcomes of sustainability transitions depend on how responsibilities, incentives, and accountability are organised. Extending this premise to logistics work, the chapter argues that green digital transitions should be evaluated as socio-technical and socio-organisational transformations in which labour outcomes are analytically central.

3. CASE DESIGN, SETTINGS, AND JUSTIFICATION

3.1 Multiple-case logic and selection rationale

The chapter employs a multiple-case design to theorise how sustainability mandates and AI systems jointly reshape labour conditions in logistics. A multiple-case approach is appropriate because the green digital intensification model concerns mechanisms that may recur across organisational contexts but manifest differently depending on business model, operational domain, and governance arrangements. Comparative analysis supports analytical generalisation by enabling the identification of cross-case patterns, the separation of idiosyncratic practices from recurring mechanisms, and the clarification of boundary conditions. In addition, a multiple-case design is consistent with the need, emphasised in the AI-in-logistics research roadmap, to complement technical accounts of AI with organisational and social analyses that examine governance, adoption consequences, and performance trade-offs (Richey Jr et al., 2023).

The cases are selected for theoretical relevance rather than representativeness. Each case displays a visible coupling between AI-enabled optimisation and sustainability objectives, and each case exhibits performance governance arrangements that plausibly intensify work. Together, the cases allow the chapter to examine the framework's internal logic: mandates become targets; AI operationalises targets through optimisation and measurement; optimisation compresses buffers and accelerates cycles;

and monitoring expands into "green performance," escalating accountability. The design is therefore oriented to mechanism tracing: the analytic aim is not to claim that every logistics firm experiences intensification in identical ways, but to identify the conditions under which "green" optimisation becomes a channel through which intensified tempo and heightened accountability are normalised.

3.2 Case contexts and analytic abstraction

The cases are anonymised as Case A–D to focus analytic attention on mechanisms rather than brand-specific performance claims. The anonymisation also reflects the chapter's purpose: it uses widely discussed adoption exemplars as theoretically generative cases rather than as benchmarking exercises. While each case corresponds to a recognisable organisational context, the analysis deliberately abstracts to the level of work organisation and socio-technical governance. This abstraction is necessary because the chapter's concern is not whether one firm performs "better" than another, but how sustainability mandates are translated into operational logics and how those logics are enacted through AI systems that reorder discretion, pace, and accountability. In this sense, each case is treated as a configuration of mandate, optimisation, and proof: sustainability objectives are rendered actionable through algorithmic decision architectures, and the resulting coordination infrastructure reshapes the practical conditions of work.

Case A represents AI-enabled route optimisation and dynamic routing in a large-scale carrier context, conceptualised as a sustainability-aligned recalibration of planning authority and execution discipline. Algorithmic routing becomes the default organiser of daily work, and it is legitimised not only as an efficiency tool but also as a carbon-reduction instrument insofar as it promises fewer miles, less fuel consumption, and less idling. The case is theoretically valuable because it makes visible how environmental objectives become embedded in what counts as the "normal" route and, by extension, as "normal" work. When routing is treated as an optimisation output rather than a product of local planning, frontline discretion is not removed but re-specified as exception management: workers increasingly decide when, how, and whether to deviate, and they must then absorb the interpretive and justificatory labour of explaining deviation in a language that remains legible to the system. This produces a distinctive governance effect in which the algorithm supplies the baseline, and the workforce supplies feasibility under uncertainty.

Case B represents AI-driven routing and transportation optimisation in a high-volume, high-variability delivery network, conceptualised as continuous optimisation and tempo governance under sustainability-compatible efficiency imperatives. In this case, optimisation is infrastructural rather than episodic. Task allocation and route sequencing are recalibrated as conditions change, which reduces the temporal and organisational distance between planning and execution. The case is theoretically valuable because it concentrates the intensification dynamic that sits at the heart of the chapter: continuous optimisation tends to reclassify slack as inefficiency, tighten cycle times, and amplify time discipline. At the same time, the system's capacity to continuously re-optimise can increase the volume and volatility of exception work—because algorithmic baselines are repeatedly updated, and the workforce must repeatedly translate those baselines into workable conduct amid situational constraints. The sustainability dimension is consequential here because waste minimisation (miles, time, idle capacity) is easily framed as both operational excellence and ecological responsibility, thereby strengthening the legitimacy of accelerated tempo.

Case C represents carbon transparency and optimisation services in a global logistics provider, conceptualised as mandate-driven proof work and the institutionalisation of sustainability as compliance infrastructure. This case foregrounds the external-facing and audit-oriented dimension of sustainability governance. Carbon accounting routines, customer-facing reporting, and recurring disclosure cycles convert environmental commitments into organisational rhythms. The case is theoretically valuable because it shows how mandates become durable governance structures: reporting and assurance demands require consistent data capture, stable metric definitions, and demonstrable progress over time. In this setting, optimisation becomes tightly coupled to proof obligations. Operational interventions are not only pursued for internal efficiency or environmental improvement; they are also pursued because the organisation must be able to demonstrate that improvement is real, attributable, and repeatable. The practical consequence is that measurement infrastructures acquire heightened organisational authority, since they are the vehicle through which sustainability credibility is maintained.

Case D represents telematics-enabled "green performance" governance, conceptualised as behavioural optimisation, evidentiary regimes, and accountability escalation. This case captures a configuration that is increasingly common across the sector: AI-enabled dashboards and in-motion analytics construct evidence about idling, eco-driving, route adherence, and utilisation proxies, and those indicators are used to steer conduct and interpret performance. Case D is theoretically valuable because it makes the monitoring and legitimacy dimension explicit. In contrast to cases where sustainability is enacted primarily through routing or reporting, this configuration brings sustainability into direct contact with everyday behaviour by turning "green" into an evaluative vocabulary for work. Because telematics indicators often function simultaneously as coaching signals and as evaluative metrics, they can intensify work in two ways: they compress buffers by discouraging behaviours categorised as wasteful (such as idling), and they expand accountability by treating data traces as evidence of responsibility. The analytic rationale for including Case

D is therefore to demonstrate that the chapter's mechanisms are not restricted to high-profile exemplars but are structurally plausible in more typical logistics settings where dashboard-based governance is central.

Across the four cases, the unit of analysis is the green digital intensification configuration: the patterned ways in which sustainability mandates, algorithmic optimisation, time discipline, and monitoring infrastructures jointly reorganise cognitive authority, accountability, and the lived experience of work. This unit of analysis aligns with the literature's emphasis that AI adoption is embedded within organisational routines and governance arrangements rather than being a mere technological overlay (Richey Jr et al., 2023). The analysis proceeds by presenting findings in four sections aligned with the theoretical framework developed in Section 2. Each findings section first provides within-case discussion across Cases A–D and then develops a cross-case synthesis that identifies common mechanisms and salient variations, thereby clarifying both the general logic of intensification and the context-specific ways it is enacted.

4. FINDINGS: GREEN DIGITAL INTENSIFICATION ACROSS CASES

4.1 Mandates become internal targets: sustainability as routinised performance obligation

In Case A, sustainability is operationalised by translating environmental objectives into route-level efficiency targets embedded in optimisation outputs. Reductions in miles travelled, fuel use, and idle time are treated as measurable outcomes of "better routing," and the optimisation sequence becomes the practical site where sustainability is enacted. The reorganisation begins upstream in planning: dispatch and routing routines stabilise around algorithmic baselines, and those baselines acquire normative status because they are framed as simultaneously cost-efficient and environmentally responsible. The legitimacy effect is important. When a route is justified as the "green" option, deviation becomes more than an operational preference; it becomes a potential departure from an environmental promise. Consequently, daily execution is increasingly judged through the lens of adherence to the optimisation logic, and the sustainability mandate becomes a background condition that strengthens the authority of the plan.

In Case B, sustainability-compatible efficiency imperatives are internalised through a metrics regime that demands continuous improvement in time, distance, and utilisation outcomes. Sustainability does not always appear as a separate operational category; it is frequently folded into a broader logic of waste minimisation that treats slack as a problem to be engineered out. The mandate effect, therefore, appears as a persistent pressure to tighten cycles and raise utilisation, with continuous re-optimisation establishing rolling baselines that convert "improvement" into a standing organisational expectation. The key point is that when performance targets are continuously recalibrated, the organisation effectively installs a moving definition of adequacy, and sustainability rationales can be used to legitimate this moving target by framing tighter cycles as environmentally responsible.

In Case C, sustainability is most explicitly institutionalised as compliance infrastructure. Carbon transparency, accounting routines, and customer-facing reporting cycles convert environmental commitments into organisational rhythms and into recurring moments of accountability. Sustainability becomes a proof obligation: the organisation must demonstrate progress, attribute gains to operational interventions, and sustain the credibility of reporting claims. This compliance orientation draws sustainability into the everyday governance of operations because measurable improvement becomes routine rather than exceptional. In practice, the mandate does not merely request "better outcomes"; it requests stable evidence-making practices. As a result, data capture, metric consistency, and demonstrable action become organisational disciplines that shape how operations are planned and reviewed.

In Case D, sustainability becomes lived as a daily target system through telematics dashboards that structure evaluation and conversation. Indicators such as idling reduction, eco-driving measures, and utilisation proxies render environmental performance visible at fine granularity. Visibility, in turn, reshapes governance: supervisors and workers can discuss performance using an environmentalised vocabulary, and the dashboard anchors accountability around green-coded indicators. Because these indicators operate at high frequency, they tend to pull sustainability governance into the temporal grain of everyday work, making the pursuit of "green" improvements a continuous rather than episodic practice.

Cross-case, sustainability shifts from value statement to target infrastructure. Mandates are enacted through routinised indicators, reporting cycles, and performance baselines, thereby intensifying organisational attention and strengthening the authority of optimisation and measurement. This pattern supports the theoretical claim that sustainability mandates function as compliance infrastructures (Section 2.2) and resonates with evidence that AI capabilities and institutional environments jointly shape sustainable competitiveness and adoption trajectories (Tan et al., 2025; Oncioiu et al., 2025). The critical implication for the green digital intensification model is that once sustainability becomes measurable and auditable, it becomes organisationally consequential in ways that cascade into how work is planned, paced, and judged. Put differently, mandates do not intensify work directly; they intensify it by making tighter baselines legitimate and by expanding the organisational demand for proof.

4.2 Environmental optimisation as operational governance: reshaping decision rights and feasibility work

In Case A, AI-enabled route optimisation reconfigures decision rights by making the algorithmic sequence the default organiser of daily work. Drivers and supervisors encounter the route less as an expression of local planning autonomy and more as an authoritative baseline that solves a multi-constraint problem, now including sustainability-relevant objectives. Discretion is not eliminated; it is relocated into boundary work. Workers decide when a deviation is warranted, how to execute the deviation without undermining service reliability, and how to account for the deviation in ways that remain legible to the system. This transformation expands interpretive labour: workers monitor feasibility, detect local misfits such as access constraints and customer-specific realities, and judge whether the optimisation remains robust under changing conditions. Over time, expertise is expressed through boundary recognition and exception stewardship rather than through continuous route ownership.

In Case B, operational governance is intensified by the continuous nature of optimisation. Routing and task allocation are recalibrated in near real time, collapsing the distance between planning and execution and converting adjustment into an everyday condition of work. The system governs the plan, while workers and supervisors govern feasibility, absorbing the cognitive and temporal labour required to reconcile algorithmic intent with local volatility. Because the baseline can change repeatedly, feasibility work becomes more demanding: workers must not only cope with variability but do so under conditions where the target state is continuously redefined. The governance consequence is subtle but powerful: the organisation can treat the optimisation output as a constantly refreshed "best possible plan," thereby narrowing the space within which deviation is regarded as legitimate.

In Case C, optimisation is bound to carbon transparency and reporting credibility. Environmental optimisation is therefore not only an internal efficiency exercise but a compliance-relevant practice that supports externally visible sustainability claims. Operational governance becomes entangled with proof obligations: adherence to optimisation routines, disciplined data capture, and stable metric definitions become part of what makes carbon accounting credible. Deviations and exceptions thus carry added significance because they can be framed as risks to reporting integrity or as obstacles to demonstrable improvement. In this setting, governance is enacted through the coupling of optimisation with documentation, and documentation becomes a form of operational discipline.

In Case D, telematics extends operational governance into behavioural domains. Environmental optimisation is enacted through prompts, alerts, and evaluative indicators that steer conduct toward idling reduction, eco-driving patterns, and route adherence. Governance operates through a dual mechanism: forward-looking behavioural shaping (through coaching signals) and retrospective judgement (through data-trace evaluation). Feasibility work is therefore reconfigured: workers must manage practical constraints while being accountable to behavioural metrics that represent a stylised model of "efficient and green" work. Because these metrics are continuous and fine-grained, they can make the boundary between acceptable adaptation and non-compliance more contested.

Cross-case, AI-enabled optimisation operates as operational governance rather than neutral assistance, consistent with the argument that AI in logistics reorganises decision architectures and routines (Richey Jr et al., 2023; Sanders et al., 2019). Across planning, execution, and evaluation, optimisation systems produce normative baselines and relocate discretion into exception handling and interpretive labour. The sustainability mandate strengthens this governance effect by rendering the baseline morally and organisationally authoritative: "optimal" is not only efficient but also environmentally justified. This coupling clarifies a central mechanism in the green digital intensification model: governance tightens not simply because algorithms exist, but because mandates make algorithmic baselines difficult to contest.

4.3 Green acceleration and work intensification: compressed buffers, denser cycles, and cognitive load

In Case A, optimisation supports environmental performance by reducing distance travelled and idle time, but the gains are achieved partly through buffer compression. Tighter sequencing and higher route density reduce the temporal margins workers use to absorb variability, recover from disruptions, and maintain safety. Intensification therefore appears as denser cycles and fewer recovery spaces, alongside heightened pressure to maintain adherence to the route logic. The sustainability narrative strengthens the legitimacy of acceleration by framing reduced slack as environmentally virtuous: less idle time and fewer detours are presented as responsible outcomes. The practical consequence is that what once functioned as a buffer becomes recoded as waste, and the labour process tightens accordingly.

In Case B, intensification is visible in the temporal dynamics of continuous optimisation. Real-time re-optimisation reduces slack and demands rapid adaptation, converting responsiveness into a defining feature of work. Intensification is both temporal and cognitive: workers must reconcile algorithmic updates with situated constraints, manage exceptions, and sustain service levels under tight time discipline. Because plans are frequently recalibrated, the worker's day becomes structured by a succession of micro-adjustments rather than by a stable route. This can increase cognitive load, as sensemaking must be continuous and errors become more consequential when buffers are thin.

In Case C, intensification is sustained through the organisational requirement to demonstrate measurable progress across reporting cycles. When environmental improvement is institutionalised as a proof obligation, efficiency gains are not treated as a one-off project outcome but as a continuing expectation. The result is a longer-horizon intensification dynamic: operations are subject to repeated rounds of optimisation, standardisation, and performance tightening so that improvement remains demonstrable and reportable. Here, intensification is not only experienced in the tempo of a single shift but also in the organisational cadence of continuous improvement, where the removal of slack becomes a recurring governance project.

In Case D, eco-driving and idling reduction regimes intensify work by redefining "non-productive" time as environmentally undesirable. Behavioural optimisation can contribute to emissions reduction, yet it also compresses the practical margins workers use to manage variability and safety trade-offs. Intensification is experienced as tempo tightening and increased self-monitoring, because workers must sustain performance while aligning conduct with green-coded indicators and coping with external constraints such as congestion and customer access limitations. The continuous evaluative presence of telematics can also encourage workers to internalise monitoring, increasing attentional labour and reducing perceived autonomy.

Cross-case, sustainability narratives legitimate acceleration by equating reduced slack with ecological efficiency. The result is a distinctive intensification pathway: ecological gains are pursued through the compression of time buffers and the densification of cycles, while feasibility work expands to manage the friction between algorithmic baselines and situated constraints. This finding extends concerns about the social sustainability implications of logistics innovation and the risk of an artificial human–computer divide (Klumpp & Zijm, 2019) by specifying how the mandate–optimisation coupling can make intensification appear both operationally necessary and environmentally virtuous. It also reinforces the argument that research on optimisation with sustainable criteria should examine organisational consequences alongside technical performance outcomes (Chen et al., 2024; Sanders et al., 2019).

4.4 Green performance monitoring and accountability escalation: evidence, contestability, and well-being tension

In Case A, the optimisation baseline becomes a monitoring reference point. Performance evaluation increasingly includes adherence to the route logic, and deviations become visible because they can be compared against an algorithmic sequence framed as the efficient and environmentally responsible default. Monitoring therefore expands from outcome-based assessment (deliveries completed) toward process-based assessment (how the route was executed). This expansion intensifies accountability because it increases the number of measurable points at which performance can be judged, and it can reduce the organisational legitimacy of situated adaptations when the system is treated as the preferred explanation of what should have happened.

In Case B, granular measurement and continuous tracking support coordination but also transform evaluation into an always-on regime. Micro-deviations become visible, comparable, and potentially sanctionable, tightening the accountability environment in which work is performed. Sustainability-compatible narratives can further strengthen this regime by linking adherence and efficiency to broader claims of responsible operations. The result is a justificatory shift: tight measurement is easier to defend when it is framed not only as managerial control but also as a mechanism for reducing waste and emissions.

In Case C, carbon transparency tools extend auditability and create proof work. Data must be captured, stabilised, and made comparable so that reporting remains credible. Monitoring is directed outward for legitimacy and inward for continuous improvement, widening what counts as accountable performance. Because the organisation is invested in the credibility of sustainability claims, measurement infrastructures can acquire heightened authority internally, and accountability negotiations become more intense when operational realities disrupt target achievement. Here, the governance question becomes not only whether targets were met, but whether the organisation can convincingly explain how and why outcomes occurred.

In Case D, monitoring becomes explicitly behavioural through eco-driving scores, idling indicators, route adherence metrics, and utilisation proxies. Accountability escalates because workers are evaluated on indicators partially shaped by situational constraints and by system design choices. This creates contestability: workers may experience metrics as misaligned with on-the-ground realities, while organisations may treat metrics as objective evidence of responsibility. Contestability is analytically consequential because it can erode legitimacy, intensify stress, and generate coping practices that preserve feasibility but conflict with compliance narratives. In turn, coping practices can produce an organisational paradox: the system is used to stabilise governance and proof, yet practical work often requires forms of adaptation that the metrics interpret as deviation.

Cross-case, AI enables an expansion of monitoring into "green performance," converting sustainability into an evaluative domain in which data traces are treated as evidence of responsible conduct. This monitoring expansion is central to green digital intensification (Section 2.5): mandates require proof and AI provides proof infrastructures, but the same infrastructures can escalate accountability and intensify work. The resulting well-being tension is theoretically significant because worker strain, fatigue risk, and contestability are weakly represented in sustainability accounting, while carbon and utilisation indicators are strongly represented. This asymmetry reinforces the need to treat social sustainability as a core dimension of

AI-enabled green transitions, consistent with the call to prevent social divides in human–computer interaction (Klumpp & Zijm, 2019) and to scrutinise unintended consequences of AI-driven sustainable supply chain management (Sanders et al., 2019; AlSheikh et al., 2025). The model therefore encourages organisations and scholars to evaluate sustainability not only as an emissions outcome but also as a governance configuration that shapes the lived conditions of logistical work.

5. CONCLUSION AND CONTRIBUTIONS

The chapter has theorised and illustrated how sustainability mandates and AI optimisation can co-produce a distinctive form of work intensification in logistics. Across four cases, sustainability becomes embedded as internal targets and compliance routines; AI operationalises these targets through optimisation and measurement; optimisation compresses buffers and accelerates cycles; and monitoring expands into "green performance," escalating accountability. The combined effect is an intensification dynamic that can remain obscured when sustainability success is evaluated primarily through carbon and utilisation metrics. By reframing green digital transitions as socio-technical transformations with labour consequences, the chapter clarifies why ecological efficiency and worker well-being should be treated as jointly governed outcomes.

5.1 Theoretical contributions

The chapter advances logistics and sustainability scholarship by proposing the green digital intensification model, which integrates sustainability mandates, AI-enabled operational governance, intensification through acceleration, and monitoring expansion into a unified explanatory account. This contribution extends AI-in-logistics debates that emphasise capability building and performance gains (Richey Jr et al., 2023; Tan et al., 2025) by specifying labour-process consequences as theoretically central rather than peripheral. It also extends sustainable supply chain scholarship by demonstrating how AI-driven sustainability can produce social sustainability tensions, reinforcing the need to prevent an "artificial divide" in human–computer interaction and to foreground worker experience in the evaluation of logistics innovation (Klumpp & Zijm, 2019).

A second theoretical contribution is the model's articulation of mandates as compliance infrastructures that intensify organisational attention and reshape operational routines. This is consistent with scholarship emphasising that AI-enabled transformation is shaped by organisational, technological, and environmental drivers (Oncioiu et al., 2025) and that HRM practices can mediate how AI contributes to agility and performance (Jahangir et al., 2025). In the chapter's account, mandates matter because they provide a legitimating rationale for optimisation and measurement; the pursuit of sustainability proof strengthens the authority of algorithmic baselines and expands monitoring into "green performance."

Finally, the chapter contributes to forward-looking debates on sustainable logistics by connecting optimisation research with social sustainability concerns. While AI optimisation with sustainable criteria is widely studied as a technical opportunity (Chen et al., 2024), the green digital intensification model specifies the organisational pathway through which such optimisation can intensify work, thereby inviting future research to examine the conditions under which ecological gains can be achieved without normalising intensification as the hidden cost of sustainability.

5.2 Practical implications

For managers, the findings underscore that AI-enabled decarbonisation initiatives can unintentionally transfer sustainability burdens onto workers through accelerated cycles and expanded monitoring. Firms should therefore treat workload, fatigue risk, and metric contestability as operational design issues rather than HR side concerns. Practically, this implies building explicit buffers and exception protocols into optimisation systems, clarifying the boundaries of accountable performance, and adopting participatory KPI design to improve legitimacy. Importantly, sustainability dashboards should include indicators that reflect worker well-being and workload stability alongside carbon and utilisation metrics, so that trade-offs become visible rather than implicit.

For policymakers and industry bodies promoting green logistics, the chapter suggests that sustainability standards and reporting regimes should incorporate expectations for social sustainability governance, encouraging organisations to demonstrate not only emissions reductions but also fair and safe work conditions under AI-enabled compliance. For HR and capability development, sustainability-oriented digital transformation should be accompanied by training, support, and job redesign that protects workers from cognitive overload and from being held solely accountable for system-generated targets. In this regard, sustainable HRM practices can function as mitigation mechanisms that enable agility without normalising intensification as the routine price of "green" logistics performance.

REFERENCES

AlSheikh, M., Morshed, A., Alkhodary, D., Khrais, L. T., & Altarawneh, R. (2025). Beyond efficiency: Unpacking AI's dual role in driving sustainable and energy-conscious logistics in North Africa. *Technological Sustainability*, *4*(3), 293–310. DOI: 10.1108/TECHS-05-2025-0101

Chen, W., Men, Y., Fuster, N., Osorio, C., & Juan, A. A. (2024). Artificial intelligence in logistics optimization with sustainable criteria: A review. *Sustainability (Basel)*, *16*(21), 9145. DOI: 10.3390/su16219145

du Plessis, M. J., Gerber, R., Goedhals-Gerber, L. L., & van Eeden, J. (2025). Shaping the Future of Freight Logistics: Use Cases of Artificial Intelligence. *Sustainability (Basel)*, *17*(4), 1355. DOI: 10.3390/su17041355

Dubey, R., & Gunasekaran, A. (2015). The role of the truck driver in sustainable transportation and logistics. *Industrial and Commercial Training*, *47*(3), 127–134. DOI: 10.1108/ICT-08-2014-0053

Jahangir, S., Xie, R., Iqbal, A., & Hussain, M. (2025). The influence of sustainable human resource management practices on logistics agility: The mediating role of artificial intelligence. *Sustainability (Basel)*, *17*(7), 3099. DOI: 10.3390/su17073099

Klumpp, M., & Zijm, H. (2019). Logistics innovation and social sustainability: How to prevent an artificial divide in human–computer interaction. *Journal of Business Logistics*, *40*(3), 265–278. DOI: 10.1111/jbl.12198

Lin, K. Y. (2025). Generative artificial intelligence–driven sustainable supply chain management: a UNISONE framework for smart logistics and predictive analytics under Industry 5.0. *International Journal of Logistics Research and Applications*, 1-32.

Mohsen, B. M., & Mohsen, M. (2025). AI-Driven Energy Optimization in Urban Logistics: Implications for Smart SCM in Dubai. *Sustainability (Basel)*, *17*(18), 8301. DOI: 10.3390/su17188301

Oncioiu, I., Mândricel, D. A., & Hojda, M. H. (2025). Artificial intelligence-enabled digital transformation in circular logistics: A structural equation model of organizational, technological, and environmental drivers. *Logistics (Basel)*, *9*(3), 102. DOI: 10.3390/logistics9030102

Richey, R. G.Jr, Chowdhury, S., Davis-Sramek, B., Giannakis, M., & Dwivedi, Y. K. (2023). Artificial intelligence in logistics and supply chain management: A primer and roadmap for research. *Journal of Business Logistics*, *44*(4), 532–549. DOI: 10.1111/jbl.12364

Sanders, N. R., Boone, T., Ganeshan, R., & Wood, J. D. (2019). Sustainable supply chains in the age of AI and digitization: Research challenges and opportunities. *Journal of Business Logistics*, *40*(3), 229–240. DOI: 10.1111/jbl.12224

Tan, C. N. L., Liu, D., Dou, J., & Chung, H. F. (2025). AI capabilities and sustainable competitiveness in logistics: A mediated moderation model of resilience, government support, and intervention. *Journal of Enterprise Information Management*, •••, 1–36. DOI: 10.1108/JEIM-06-2025-0494

Tanveer, U., Hoang, T. G., Ishaq, S., Kamal, M. M., & Attri, R. (2026). Enhancing supplier innovation capabilities through digital technology integration: A relational perspective. *Technological Forecasting and Social Change*, *223*, 124426. DOI: 10.1016/j.techfore.2025.124426

Tanveer, U., Hoang, T. G., Truong, H. Q., Ishaq, S., & Gong, Y. (2024). The critical role of procurement in the emergence of circular business models: Insights from multiple cases of Vietnamese manufacturers. *Business Strategy and the Environment*, *33*(8), 7689–7707. DOI: 10.1002/bse.3888

Chapter 6
AI, Sustainability, and Human Well-Being in Logistics Employment:
Transforming Work, Efficiency, and Responsible Growth

S. Anbu
Vel Tech Multi Tech Dr. Rangarajan Dr. Sakunthala Engineering College, India

P. Jayabharathi
St. Joseph's College of Engineering, India

T. Thilagam
http://orcid.org/0000-0002-7657-0726
Vel Tech Rangarajan Dr. Sangunthala R&D Institute of Science and Technology, India

R. Vinoth
http://orcid.org/0000-0001-5866-1395
R.M.K. College of Engineering and Technology, India

G. Manisha
R.M.D. Engineering College, India

M. G. Dinesh
http://orcid.org/0009-0009-7643-5338
Easa College of Engineering and Technology, India

ABSTRACT

This chapter explores the transformative role of Artificial Intelligence (AI) in modern logistics, emphasizing its influence on operational efficiency, sustainability, and human well-being. It explores how AI-driven technologies including automation, predictive analytics, and intelligent decision systems enhance productivity while supporting environmental goals through optimized energy use and reduced emissions. The chapter highlights the evolving nature of logistics employment, detailing skill transitions, safety improvements, and psychological impacts associated with human AI collaboration. Ethical considerations, regulatory frameworks, and gover-

DOI: 10.4018/979-8-3373-7826-8.ch006

nance models are analyzed to ensure responsible and equitable AI deployment. Key challenges and future research directions are identified, focusing on sustainable AI development, workforce inclusion, data security, and policy innovation. The chapter underscores the need for balanced, human-centric adoption to achieve resilient and sustainable logistics ecosystems.

1. INTRODUCTION

1.1 Background and Context of AI in Logistics Employment

The logistics industry has become an intricate, and highly technological ecosystem that has been transformed into a digitalized, automated, and interconnected global industry (Nicoletti, 2025a). In the past, logistics used to be manual, physical, paper-based with human decision-making. Nevertheless, the fast development of Artificial Intelligence (AI), along with the evolution of robotics, the Internet of Things (IoT), machine learning, self-driving vehicles, and intelligent optimization systems have completely changed the way of how logistics processes are performed. AI has become remarkable in route planning, inventory, warehouse automation, predictive maintenance, demand forecasting, and optimization of transportation. This change has not only increased the efficiency of the logistics systems but has also transformed the qualities of the employment, changed the task demands, job roles and competency levels. Although the benefits of AI are enormous: more accuracy, more real-time decisions, fewer inefficiencies, and safer, it also brings the topic of the future of work, human role, and responsible adoption.

Simultaneously with the development of technologies, there is a pressure on global industries to become sustainable because of the environmental issue, increasing energy consumption, greenhouse gas emissions, and the necessity of a circular economic system. Logistics would be very instrumental in this sustainability agenda since transportation, warehousing, and distribution processes are some of the significant sources of carbon emissions. Artificial intelligence-driven optimization systems and automation tools have become strong facilitators of green logistics that enable to minimize fuel usage, optimize routes, increase load utilization, and assist in the introduction of renewable energy sources into the operations of warehouses (Nicoletti, 2025b). But sustainability is not only about environmental performance, it also includes economic sustainability and social welfare. Therefore, logistics organizations should pay attention to the impact of AI-led transitions on employees, localities, and employment ecosystems on the long-term (Ulle, R. S et al., 2024).

1.2 The Intersection of AI, Sustainability, and Human Well-Being

With the increasing implementation of AI solutions by logistics companies, there is an increasing desire to learn how technological efficiency can be combined with the idea of sustainability and human-oriented principles. AI allows organizations to become greener and waste-reduced, streamline energy consumption, but sustainable development also requires organizations to improve workforce welfare and inclusivity and to enhance the quality of jobs. Human well-being in logistic work involves physical security, psychological stability, adequate treatment, availability of skills development, and the possibility of engaging in work meaningfully in the process of work change. The AI systems can assist with the following factors by automatizing the high-risk tasks, improving the ergonomic conditions, and empowering informed decision-making with augmented intelligence. Nevertheless, there are also threats to the same technologies, including surveillance, fear of job displacement, and skill gap expansion when they are not responsibly introduced. One of the new approaches, which abandons the productivity measures, is the nexus of AI, sustainability and human wellbeing. It underlines the tension between the technological change and the moral development - that the application of AI will not harm the responsibility towards the environment and the respect towards the workforce. This cross division reflects the importance of total strategies that involve operational efficiency, environmental management and social protection. This multidimensional relationship is supposed to be viewed in such a way that the logistics systems in the future can be people-centric and performance-centric.

1.3 Motivation for the Chapter

Though there is abundant literature on AI-based optimization of logistics, sustainability in supply chains, and human features of automation no scholarly literature has united these three perspectives into one perspective. This chapter has been inspired by the increasing realization that the technological advances cannot be seen outside of the frames of the social and environmental context. Governments, stakeholders and the world policies (including the UN Sustainable Development Goals) are putting pressure on the logistics companies to ensure that they embrace responsible growth models. Besides, the rate of AI adoption is changing the labor market faster than the systems of training the workforce are abreast with it, and there is an urgent need to plan the systematic knowledge about the consequences of AI on the employees of different levels. The chapter is expected to fill this gap in knowledge by conducting a comprehensive review of literature on the applications of AI in the logistics industry and changes related to sustainability and what the technologies are supposed to mean to the human well-being. It is geared towards offering a systematic review in which the scholars, policymakers and leaders in the industry can assist them in understanding the current trends, evaluating the impacts, and identifying the challenges and future research directions on how to achieve a balanced and equitable growth.

1.4 Objectives and Scope of the Chapter

This chapter has several objectives. Firstly, it is talking about the notable AI technologies, which are already affecting the logistics sector and how they are transforming the organization of the processes of operations. Second, it looks at how the technologies contribute towards environmental, economic and social sustainability within international supply chains. Third, it examines the impact of AI-based transformations on human well-being, such as employment, occupational health, workplace competencies, and the corporate culture. Fourth, it measures the ethical, regulatory, and governance standards required to make AI responsible deployment in the logistics. Lastly, the chapter outlines research gaps, challenges and opportunities to develop future logistics systems that would balance automation with human-centric values.

The chapter has an expanse of several areas in the field of logistics such as transportation, warehouse, inventory, freight forwarding, and last-mile delivery. It combines AI research literature, sustainability science literature, labor literature, and human-computer interaction literature to give a multidisciplinary perspective. Although the emphasis is on the global level, particular emphasis is made on the emerging economies where the transformation in logistics is influential in terms of employment and development.

1.5 Structure of the Chapter

In order to have the logical flow, the chapter is divided into six major sections with a conclusion afterward. Section 2 discusses the topic of AI technologies in logistics and highlights the ways how it can transform logistics and introduce efficiency. The third section is the discussion of sustainability principles in logistics systems and the overview of how AI can be used to be environmentally and economically responsible. Part 4 discuss the human welfare such as the workforce changes, safety, skills and socio-psychological impacts of AI. Section 5 is focused on responsible development and is accompanied by references to the ethical concerns, regulatory norms, and approaches to the AI implementation. Section 6 outlines issues, constraints, and research opportunities and outlines key gaps and opportunities in the future. Finally, Section 7 also makes a concluding statement on the interaction of

AI, sustainability and workforce well-being to affirm the case of balanced and responsible innovation in logistics.

2. AI IN LOGISTICS

2.1 Evolution and Role of AI Technologies in Logistics

Artificial Intelligence (AI) use in logistics has grown at an unprecedented scale due to the necessity to be efficient, transparent, and able to make decisions in real-time in more complex global supply chains(Bentalha, B. 2023). The classic logistics systems used to be based on manual coordination, linear processes, and reactive problem resolution, and thus, these led to delays, inefficiencies, and lack of scalability. The introduction of intelligent automation and predictive functions at all levels of the logistics process has changed this picture radically, and AI is the one that has enabled such a shift. Machine Learning (ML), Deep Learning (DL), Natural Language Processing (NLP), robotics, and AI systems that use IoTs have now become very important in processing large amounts of data, optimizing resource distribution, and increasing the accuracy of operations(Prasath, R et al., 2025). The technologies have also helped the logistic companies to transform to proactive and predictive models that minimize disruption and increase customer satisfaction compared to reactive. An AI is not only capable of assisting in enhancing the efficiency of operations, but it is also capable of assisting in making strategic decisions, which allows organizations to be able to predict demand trends, reduce uncertainties, as well as streamline supply chain networks in real-time(Dhamija, P et al., 2021). With the logistics sector becoming increasingly digitally integrated in the future AI is an underlying technology that allows automation, resilience and constant innovation.

2.2 AI-Driven Optimization in Transportation and Routing

One of the most resource-consuming and time-sensitive parts of logistics is transportation, and AI has changed it greatly with intelligent routing, predictive analytics, and automating the fleet. AI-driven algorithms process the conditions of the traffic, weather, fuel consumption, the performance of vehicles, and the customer delivery windows to prescribe the most preferable routing plans. The systems assist in cutting on the traveling time, reducing emissions, and enhancing the degree of reliability in delivery. As an example, reinforcement learning is applied in dynamic route optimization platforms to adapt routes to current circumstances in order to be as efficient as possible. Another important field of use is predictive maintenance, in which AI models track the health of vehicles by monitoring them with IoT sensors and predicting the failure of the components before they happen(Padmavathi, V., & Saminathan, R. 2023). This will avoid expensive breakdowns, increase the fleet life, and increase safety. AI is also useful in optimization of loads, which is the optimal method of ensuring that the shipments are consolidated and the vehicles used. Also, autonomous trucks and drones will be the next stage of AI-powered transportation, which promises to make transportation safer, more efficient, and around-the-clock. Even though the full autonomous logistics vehicle mass deployment is still in its early stages, the implementation of AI into the logistics game is still transforming the opportunities and sustainability performance of operations.

2.3 AI-Enabled Warehouse Automation and Smart Inventory Systems

The increasing customer demands, the booming e-commerce, and the requirement to fulfil the demands quickly and precisely, have complicated warehousing operations. The automation of warehouses through artificial intelligence has altered the ecosystem of warehouses by removing manual and repetitive processes in favor of smart robotic systems and the use of data to make decisions. Autonomous mobile robots (AMRs), automated guided vehicles (AGVs), and robotic picking systems apply AI algorithms in navigation, object recognition, and task prioritization, making them much more accurate and shorter in operational delays. Another role of AI in inventory management is its ability to predict the stock level and minimize over-stocking or stock-outs and allow automatic replenishment. Machine learning models compare past sales information, seasonal dynamics, customer behavior, and supply chain interrupts in order to predict future demand with a high degree of accuracy(Gracious, L. A et al., 2023). IoT devices and smart sensors installed in storage systems can constantly check the state of the inventory, the movement of the products, and storage conditions, which allow viewing the warehouse in real-time(Jaffrin, L. C et al., 2025). Quality control, detection of damaged goods, checking product size and adherence to packaging regulations are also important aspects of AI. Collectively, these technologies can produce smarter and more efficient warehouses that can address the needs of the current logistics and save on costs and human error.

2.4 AI in Supply Chain Visibility and Predictive Analytics

Among the most radical effects of AI in the logistics sector, there is the improvement of supply chains visibility and predicting issues before they go out of control. In the past, invisibility between suppliers, distributors and transport networks resulted in delays, bottlenecks and uncertainty(Moorthy, K. S et al., 2024).

AI facilitates end-to-end transparency, combining the data provided by numerous sources, such as enterprise systems, IoT devices, shipment tracking systems, and digital twins(Rose, R. M et al., 2025; Sathya, U et al., 2024). These combined systems enable the logistics organizations to track the real-time position of goods, assess the performance metrics, and identify aberrations in real-time. The predictive analytics models recognize possible risks like delivery delays, lack of supplies, congestion at ports, geopolitical disturbances or fluctuating demand. Through the simulation of various ways, the AI assists businesses in selecting the most resilient and cost-effective strategies. One of the biggest developments of AI-enabled visibility is digital twin technology, which generates virtual copies of physical supply chains, so that decision-makers can test solutions and evaluate effects of operations without risk of the world. Such predictive and simulation tools can give organizations practical information that enables them to be resilient, agile, and long-term in an ever-shifting global market.

Figure 1. AI in logistics

2.5 AI in Customer Service, Last-Mile Delivery, and Experience Enhancement

The logistics customer expectations have shifted radically, particularly the emergence of e-commerce and delivery within a day offering. The AI technologies have enhanced customer-facing logistics functions by providing real-time tracking, quicker customer support, and more dependable last-mile delivery. The NLP-based chatbots and virtual assistants address the questions of customers, deliveries, and support procedures, making them quicker and more user-friendly. AI will also be important in streamlining the final-mile delivery that is the most costly and complicated phase of the logistics. Machine learning models decide how to deliver the best windows, cluster deliveries based on the location, and allocate the tasks to a driver or autonomous delivery robots. Micro-fulfilment centers, small-scale warehouses that are automated and located near consumers, further increase the efficiency of the last-mile and lead to a decrease in the time of delivery. Also, AI is useful in enabling logistics companies to personalize their customer experience based on previous interactions, preferences, and order patterns, which allows them to communicate with customers in a personalized manner and enhance the quality of service. Such developments make AI one of the primary tools in fulfilling the needs of contemporary consumers and lowering the workload.

2.6 Overall Transformation and Strategic Impact of AI in Logistics

The adoption of AI in logistics is a paradigm change between the conventional operation models to smart, data-driven ecosystems to be constantly improved. The AI makes the logistics networks faster, more accurate, more transparent, and more sustainable, enabling organizations to scale their operations successfully and adapt flexibly to the changes in the markets. Besides automation, AI also changes labour relations, strategic decisions and corporate culture. It enables the logistics firms to divert to long-term optimization, which is supported by predictive intelligence and scenario-oriented analysis rather than short-term planning. Moreover, AI creates innovation due to the ability to apply the new logistics models, such as autonomous delivery networks, hyper-optimized supply chains, and decentralized warehouses (Movahed, A. B et al., 2024). Though the economic benefits including cost reduction, increased efficiency and profitability are impressive, the strategic impact is evident in the global competitiveness and sustainability. Environmental objectives can also be attained with the help of AI by consuming less fuel, improving route optimization and waste minimization, and will harmonize logistics operations with broader sustainability objectives. Lastly, the disruptive ability of AI lies not only in the technology capabilities but in the ability to create more robust, efficient, and sustainable logistics systems that will be beneficial to the organizations and the society.

3. SUSTAINABILITY IN AI-INTEGRATED LOGISTICS SYSTEMS

3.1 Understanding Sustainability in the Logistics Context

The issue of logistics sustainability has gained momentum in the endeavour by the industries across the world to solve the environmental, economic and social challenges that accompany the growth of global supply chains. Traditionally, logistics activities, such as transportation, warehousing, packaging and last mile delivery have contributed greatly to carbon emissions, resource consumption and waste generation. These effects have been sustained by the rapidly expanding trend of e-commerce and international trade and have provided doubt to the sustainability of the existing logistics paradigms. The concept of sustainability here includes the harmonious approach to the protection of the environment, economic effectiveness, and social responsibility. AI has a disruptive role in that it allows the use of data in smart ways, streamlines the use of resources, and incorporates intelligent automation, which leads to more sustainable and ethical logistics processes. With the help of AI, logistics firms cannot just minimize their environmental footprint but also increase their economic stability and improve the conditions of the employees and communities impacted by the logistics operations.

3.2 Environmental Sustainability

Logistics organizations have environmental sustainability as a priority due to the high percentage of global emissions comprised of transportation and warehousing. AI helps to make the processes environmentally responsible, as it allows using more energy, fuel, and materials efficiently. In transportation systems, AI-based route optimization systems also help to greatly decrease fuel usage by choosing the shortest, least congested, or energy-efficient routes. Predictive models can also assist logistics companies to predict when they will be in need of services that require maintenance to avoid wasting fuel due to the inefficiency of vehicles that are not well maintained. The AI-based load optimization tools will make sure that trucks and cargo containers will work to their full capacity and will need fewer trips to be made, as well as carbon emissions will be reduced.

AI in warehousing assists in energy management systems that control the lighting, heating, cooling, and ventilation systems according to real-time demand. These intelligent systems are able to check occupancy, change in temperature, and performance of equipment in order to reduce the use of electricity. Also, AI can be used to improve waste reduction by improving inventory turnover forecasting to prevent unnecessary overstocking or spoilage of goods. In the packaging sector, AI-based designing software assists in determining materials that are eco-friendly and do not cause waste to products without affecting their safety. Combined, these technologies are crucial to decreasing the ecological footprint of logistics activities as well as to assist in global climate efforts, including the Paris Agreement and the Sustainable Development Goals (SDGs).

3.3 Economic Sustainability

Logistics economic sustainability is oriented towards ensuring profitability, enhancing operational effectiveness and resilience to disruptions in the supply chain including supply chain shocks, market variability and material inadequacy. As the global logistics networks get increasingly complicated, the managerial approach of human-based decision-making is unlikely to be able to sustain the operations of significant scale. AI enhances the sustainability of the economy, ensuring that economic resources are used to the full extent, decreasing the operational expenses and facilitating more precise forecasting.

As an example, predictive analytics can improve demand forecasting and enable companies to match inventory levels with the needs of customers and minimize financial losses due to stockouts or overstocks. AI-controlled robotics used in smart warehousing save labor costs and increase fulfilment operations in speed and accuracy. Transportation management systems created with the help of AI allow companies to save on fuel, minimize vehicle downtime, and increase the percentage of fleet utilization. Also, AI allows managing risks through detecting vulnerabilities in supply chains, including supplier instability, transportation risks, or geopolitical uncertainties. AI aids more robust long-term planning with early warning signals and alternative scenarios simulation.

The economic sustainability is also pegged on the capability of an organization to be innovative and competitive. AI assists logistics companies in the establishment of flexible business models, experimentation with new delivery models, and adjustment to market changes. Finally, AI will help the logistics organizations to work effectively and developing financial and adaptability that will help to survive in the world that becomes more unpredictable than ever before.

3.4 Social Sustainability

Social sustainability is an indispensable aspect of the contemporary logistics that focuses on fairness in labor, safety of workers, the effect on the community, and their well-being, in general. As an element in social sustainability, AI can be used to automate hazardous, physically demanding, or repetitive processes and, as a result, minimize the risk of injuries and ensure the safety of the workplace. As an example, robots and other automated vehicles that can be controlled by AI can be used to perform heavy lifting, transportation of hazardous materials, and repetitive work, allowing the employees to devote more time to more skilled tasks. Wearable AI machines are also capable of tracking employee health, fatigue, and notifying the supervisor about possible safety risks.

Artificial intelligence (AI) systems also contribute to social sustainability by enhancing transparency in labor relations, as well as fair treatment of employees. As an example, AI-assisted monitoring systems will be able to detect injustice in scheduling, overworking, or discrimination in hiring or promotion. Also, AI can improve the development of the workforce by detecting skills gaps and prescribing specific training. The use of AI in transforming the workforce should, however, be handled with care in order to prevent bad social effects. The issues related to job displacement, heightened surveillance, algorithm bias, and less human autonomy should be mentioned to make implementation ethical.

Social sustainability also incorporates the wider social effect of logistics operations, e.g. alleviating traffic congestion, enhancing air quality and decreasing disruptions in residential zones. The AI would assist businesses in creating more efficient urban delivery systems, which would make communities healthier and more livable by minimizing noise, pollution and road congestion. By doing so, AI does not only contribute to the welfare of the internal workforce but the welfare of society at a bigger scale as well.

3.5 AI as a Driver of Circular Logistics and Resource Recovery

Circular logistics is an emerging trend that seeks to prolong material lifecycle by reusing, recycling, remanufacturing and recovery of waste. AI is also essential in facilitating the implementation of circular economy models by enhancing the movement of materials through the supply chain and their monitoring. Intelligent reverse logistics systems are assisting businesses in controlling the returns of their products more proactively by forecasting the level of returns, analyzing the condition of the product, and sending the products to be repaired, recycled, or discarded. Machine vision and robotics allow the automated sorting of returned products enhancing the accuracy and speed of recycling activities.

Product lifecycle management is also supported by AI in the form of predictive analytics that show the health of products and usage patterns. This enables manufactures and logistics companies to provide repair services earlier than products fail or come to end-of-life. Also, AI design tools help businesses to design products that can be easier to repair, disassemble or recycle. Finally, AI-driven circular logistics lowers environmental effects, minimizes resource use, and generates new economic values in the logistics networks.

3.6 Challenges and Limitations in Achieving Sustainable AI-Driven Logistics

Although AI has a great contribution to long-term sustainability, there are also some challenges that organizations should carefully overcome when implementing AI. A big issue is the environmental footprint of AI per se. The process of training the more complicated AI models consumes a lot of computation power and thus consumes more energy and emits more carbon. Unless AI is regulated or supported by renewable energy, it will unintentionally lead to environmental degradation. Also, automation through AI can remove some occupational positions, and that is why the question of unemployment, income inequality, and job security will be increased.

It also has ethical issues associated with data privacy, employee monitoring, and algorithm prejudice. The biased datasets used to train AI systems may be used to propagate inequitous treatment or discriminatory behavior within the workforce management. The second constraint is that the implementation of AI technologies is very expensive, and it might not be able to enable small and medium-sized logistics firms to adopt sustainable innovations. The integration problem is also caused by interoperability between the old systems and the new AI solutions.

Lastly, to realize sustainable, AI-based logistics, effective governance mechanisms, open algorithms, and industry, government, and society cooperation are needed. In the absence of explicit instructions and protective measures, the advantages of AI will not necessarily result in any meaningful sustainability impacts.

4. HUMAN WELL-BEING AND WORKFORCE TRANSFORMATION IN LOGISTICS

4.1 Changing Nature of Work in AI-Enabled Logistics Environments

The introduction of Artificial Intelligence (AI) into the logistics industry has radically changed the essence of the work in this field. In the past, logistics was a manual task that involved physical repetitive activities and human decision making especially in sorting, picking, packing, routing and inventory. As AI-enabled systems (autonomous mobile robots (AMRs), robotic picking arms, intelligent warehouse management systems, and predictive analytics platforms) become more popular, they are becoming more automated, making the need to rely on manual labor less important and placing more emphasis on oversight, supervision, and exception handling. The human functions in logistics environments are, therefore, being re-configured into more technical, cognitive and decision making functions. Instead of having to work on repetitive tasks, employees are now expected to interface with the automated systems, digest on the digital insights and operate with intelligent machines. Such transformation presupposes the emergence of new skills, i.e., digital literacy, data interpretation skills, and the opportunity to work with more advanced equipment. Although AI increases the productivity and accuracy of operations, it also breaks the conventional job functions, forcing the employees to adjust to the new functions, systems and workflows. This is a big cultural change to most organizations, and there should be dynamic approaches that can help workers through the change without interruption in operations and motivation.

4.2 Skill Shifts, Training Needs, and Workforce Upskilling

With the further penetration of AI into logistics processes, the skills of the working population change significantly. The employees are now required to have a blend of technical, analytical and soft skills in order to operate in digitally enhanced environments. Physically demanding or manual skills are being augmented and replaced by jobs that involve understanding of robotics, automation, data analytics, machine surveillance and machine troubleshooting. To give an example, warehouse employees should know how to operate and maintain automated picking robots, and transportation workers might also be required to train on AI-based route planning systems or fleet management systems based on telematics. This change underscores the increased significance of upskilling and reskilling programs in logistics organizations. Organized training programs with an emphasis on digital skills, robotics service, human-machines safety, and decision-making with AI help to guarantee the flexibility of the workforce. Organizations that invest in life-long learning develop stronger and adaptable teams that can adapt to new changes in technology instead of opposing them. Nevertheless, restricted availability to good training programs, particularly in developing areas or smaller logistics companies is still a hindrance. In this regard, industry-academia-government partnerships will be essential in offering high volume, low-cost, and pertinent upskilling opportunities to protect the well-being of workforce and marketability.

4.3 Improving Workplace Safety and Ergonomics through AI

AI can be used to improve safety in the workplace, especially in areas where logistics employees are at risk, such as heavy lifting, machine operation, work in a confined area, or that of dangerous substances. Artificial intelligence and automated technology can help decrease the amount of accidents by tracking the functioning of equipment, detecting hazardous behavior, and anticipating possible failure before they happen. Smart helmets, gloves and exoskeletons are wearable AI technologies that can be used to prevent injuries by correcting posture, detecting fatigue and alerting workers when they reach unsafe physical limits. Moreover, collaborative robots (cobots) will be designed to operate in a safe environment with humans and carry out hazardous or tedious work, taking into account the low likelihood of collisions due to vision sensors and proximity sensors. The AI-based safety analytics systems are also capable of analyzing incident reports, environmental factors, and behavioral trends to determine the root causes of accidents and prescribe prevention strategies. AI can not only decrease the frequency of accidents, physical burden, and the risk of injuries but also improve the physical and emotional health of employees by reducing their fatigue. Consequently, logistics organizations have a higher chance to develop safer and more humane working conditions that encourage the long-term employee satisfaction and retention.

4.4 Psychological and Social Impacts of AI-Driven Workplace Changes

Although AI enhances efficiency and safety, its adoption in the workplace of the logistics sector may also lead to psychological and social difficulties. The majority of workers are anxious or stressed or unsure of what will happen to their jobs and are concerned that they will lose them due to automation. Such insecurity can lead to poor morale, lack of commitment or resistance to digital transformation initiatives. Moreover, the introduction of AI-based surveillance devices, which may be productivity trackers, surveillance cameras, or performance analytics tools, may result in the creation of perceptions of over-surveillance, which reduce trust and autonomy. The workers may be forced to make sure that they work at maximum rates, which may lead to psychological exhaustion and burnout. Social dynamics of teams can also change according to the increasing human-machine co-operation that can alter human-human relations and patterns of communication. Organizations must hence adopt humanistic strategies in adopting AI solutions. The psychological support systems, ethical data management, and involvement of employees in technology adoption processes can reduce the negative effects by ensuring there is clear communication, ethical data governance, and involvement of employees. By making sure that AI is employed to support human abilities as opposed to substituting them, it is possible to create a favorable organizational culture where employees feel appreciated, encouraged, and empowered.

4.5 Human-Machine Collaboration and Augmented Intelligence

The future of logistics work does not lie in the substitution of humans with the machines but in the development of mutual ecosystems where human intelligence and AI abilities do not oppose each other. AI is best at high-speed performance, accuracy, pattern matching and processing of data, whereas human beings are creative, think critically, adapt, empathic and judging of the context. In these types of collaborative systems, AI is a helper and not a replacement. To illustrate, AI-based decision support systems are used to assist logistics managers to make well-informed decisions in terms of inventory planning, risk management, or network optimization. Workers in warehouses are working together with robots, which collect items, organize inventory, or deliver materials so that humans can deal with quality, problem-solving, and customer-specific work. AI-based navigation systems allow drivers to reduce travel time and increase fuel efficiency and predictive analytics is used by dispatch teams to optimize workload distribution. Such synergy fosters productivity and job satisfaction through the reduction of stress, errors, and allows workers to do jobs with higher value. It is important to design working processes that focus on collaboration more than domination of automated systems so that the introduction of AI will help instead of harm human well-being.

4.6 Inclusion, Equity, and Workforce Diversity in an AI-Driven Era

With the use of AI technologies in logistics organizations, the problems of inclusion, equity, and diversity become more significant. Artificial Intelligence can expand the opportunities of various groups of people by decreasing the physical job burden, allowing flexible working hours, and helping to hire employees based on skills. To explain this, automation would open the opportunities to the physically challenged individuals to get employment in the logistics sector, which they were not able to access. AI-based analytic systems also help companies detect discrimination in the employment, scheduling, or promotion processes and promote equity and equal opportunity. However, when not implemented in a responsible manner, AI systems may reinforce the status quo of inequality because they have biased algorithms that discriminate specific population groups. The necessity to make the AI development teams diverse, apply representative datasets and conduct periodic audits of the algorithm are all essential benefits towards having a fair implementation. In addition, the AI-based workforce modifications must ensure that the vulnerable groups receive adequate coaching and education to adopt technological changes. The acceptance of AI is more resilient with inclusivity and also allows establishing a more socially sustainable ecosystem of logistics.

4.7 Organizational Culture and Leadership for Human-Centric AI Adoption

Leadership commitment and organizational culture are the main success factors of successful implementation of AI in the logistics industry. The use of AI in the human environment also needs leaders to focus on transparency, communication and empathy. Firms must create a learning, experimental, and adaptable atmosphere and make employees believe that AI is a powerful tool and not a menace. The leadership will play a pivotal role in planning the change management plans, a response to the staff issues, and the development of the desirable attitude towards the technological application. The policies which focus on the application of ethical AI, data privacy, autonomy of workers, and psychological security may reinforce the trust and the acceptance among the employees. Along with that, the creation of the teams of AI specialists, operations managers, human resource specialists, and front-line workers will become the key to the fact that the system design is premised on the real needs of the workspace. Inclusive governance, open communication, and supportive leadership can help the logistics organizations to attain the AI-driven change without subjecting human beings to the risks.

5. RESPONSIBLE GROWTH: ETHICAL, REGULATORY, AND GOVERNANCE CONSIDERATIONS

5.1 Importance of Responsible AI Adoption in Logistics

With AI becoming an unavoidable component of the logistic process, involving automated warehousing and smart transportation services, predictive analytics and human resource management software, the role of responsible AI implementation is acquiring even more importance. The logistics industry is one of the most important spheres of the world trade, economy, and social welfare, thus, the choices undertaken in the mentioned sphere carry the long-term effects. Responsible growth also highlights the necessity of the compromise of technological effectiveness and ethical righteousness, sustainability, and humanistic values. AI adoption in the logistics operations will be implemented fairly, transparently, accountably, and inclusively to guarantee that the innovation will not become a danger to the rights, safety, or dignity of stakeholders. The dangers of AI abuse like information abuse, biased choices, or volatile automation may destroy the faith and reduce the prospects of the implementation in the long-term. It is, therefore, not only a moral obligation but a competitive necessity to remain in the digitalized world, which is acceptable in society. This section will look into the ethical frameworks, regulatory provisions, regulatory mechanisms and functional safeguards that are necessary to ensure AI driven logistics systems do not suppress fair, robust, and sustainable development.

5.2 Ethical AI Principles

Responsible AI implementation in logistics is based on ethical principles. Fairness makes AI systems not biased, but it treats employees, customers, and all other stakeholders fairly. AI should be constructed to avoid any discrimination in workforce management applications (hiring, performance evaluation, scheduling, etc.) on the basis of gender, age, ethnicity, or socioeconomic status. It is also imperative that the AI-generated decisions are explainable and understandable, which is achieved through transparency. Employees and executives should be in a position to have faith in the logic of AI proposals, be it in route optimization, personnel, or predictive maintenance. In the absence of explainability, the use of AI can cause confusion, mistrust, or abuse. Accountability will help to keep the organizations accountable to the results of AI systems even in cases where automation contributes significantly to the decision-making. There should be clear lines of responsibility to ensure that failures, e.g. accidents caused by autonomous vehicles or mistakes in AI-based supply chain predictions, can be properly dealt with. In order to have ethical AI, one will have to carry out regular audits, feedback mechanisms, and rigorous testing to ensure that algorithms are consistent and do not lead to malicious consequences. With fairness, transparency, and accountability as the primary values, the logistics organizations create the trustful eco system where technology can improve the human judgment but not overpower the rights of the stakeholders.

5.3 Regulatory Frameworks and Legal Compliance in AI-Driven Logistics

The rapid implementation of AI in the logistics area is a major concern to the policymakers who must strike the right balance between innovation and community security. Strict policies are necessary to control safe AI systems and especially in the transportation robotization sector, personal data security, labor and environmental sustainability. The laws are to be directed at the responsibility of algorithms, whereby organizations are called to account and disclose the dangers of their AI applications. As an example, the autonomous trucks developed by AI need to be of high safety, performance, and liability, which would specify responsibility in case of accidents. The institutions implementing AI-driven surveillance and monitoring tools in logistic environments must ensure that the privacy policies are adhered to not to expose the staff to intrusive or unreasonable surveillance practices. The results of the sustainability can also be influenced by the regulatory frameworks, the environmental policies can force the logistics companies to reduce the emissions, apply the green technologies, and report about the environmental impacts. The governments should communicate with the industry players and technology gurus to agree on adaptive and progressive regulations that comply with the technological change. This is the only manner in which deployment of AI can be safe, ethical and within the needs of the society.

5.4 Worker Rights, Data Protection, and Ethical Surveillance

One of the most debatable questions in the context of introducing AI to the logistic industry is the issue of monitoring and data of employees in the workplace. The AI solutions are able to monitor the productivity and define the movement patterns, detect fatigue, and assess the performance in real-time. Even though these tools can assist in making the work safe and more efficient, they also introduce the issue of ethical surveillance, intrusion of privacy and autonomy among the workers. Sound governance is also that the firms have a clear line of what data is collected, the use and the people to whom the data is released. The employees will be made aware of the purpose and intention of the monitoring technologies and have the option of not being in agreement with or objecting to AI-generated evaluation. In addition to this, the information should be anonymous where possible; it should be kept in a safe place and not stored in the hands of the unauthorized personnel. Over and punitive surveillance by employers, which leads to the destruction of trust and unhealthy work environment should not be practiced. Rather, AI-based monitoring should be positioned as a system of safety and improving the work process and not as a system of control over the employees. Effective communication, voluntary collection of data and sound data management activities will play a significant role in protecting the rights of employees and guaranteeing the integrity of AI use.

5.5 Governance Models for Safe and Inclusive AI Deployment

One of the key factors to ensuring responsible development of AI-enabled logistics systems is good governance. Governance models put in place the design, implementation, monitoring, and improvement structures, policies, and processes of AI tools design, implementation, monitoring, and improvement. The model of responsible governance includes the participation of the broadest possible group of stakeholders, including technology professionals, operations managers, legal teams, ethicists, labor unions, and policymakers to ensure that the introduction of AI is something that is aligned with ethical and organizational goals. Good systems of governance possess risk evaluation mechanisms, algorithm audits, bias detectors and acceptable reporting. There are also provisions of human supervision in them and this is to ensure that human beings make crucial decisions particularly those that touch on the area of safety, the welfare of the workers or the strategic planners. The systems of governance should also offer retraining and transition of workforce processes that ensure that the victimized employees of automation are duly assisted. With efficient governance structures, the logistics entities will be in a position to mitigate the risks involved in its operations, promote ethical behaviors, and ensure that the AI-driven change would be useful to all the stakeholders.

5.6 Addressing Bias, Safety Risks, and Algorithmic Limitations

The quality of an AI system will be as reliable as the quality of the underlying data and assumptions. Unfair algorithms in logistics can lead to unequal recruiting, job distribution, false performance data or discrimination in schedules. To act upon these threats, institutions must integrate the best auditing mechanisms that evaluate AI performance across different population groups and under different work circumstances. Mistakes in the algorithm are identified and corrected through regular testing to ensure that AI tools are not unfair, unsafe, and ineffective. There is also the risk of safety when AI systems make independent decisions in the high-stakes setting like the warehouse robotics or the autonomous cars. Accidents or property damage or injuries can occur due to malfunctions or unpredictable behavior of algorithms. Therefore, any AI application must necessarily be supported by safety, like redundancy, emergency overriding, real-time monitoring, and severe validation testing. The other challenge is the nature of the algorithms that may be incapable of handling the complicated human cases or those that are highly fast or highly dynamic. Even these limitations should be managed by humans to ensure that AI replaces human knowledge but not replaces it. When logistics firms learn how to handle these concerns and manage them directly, they will be capable of building more believable and reliable AI.

5.7 The Role of Collaboration and Multi-Stakeholder Partnerships

The individual organizations cannot play a role in ensuring the development of AI in the logistics field. The necessity to establish multi-stakeholder relationships with governments, technology vendors, academic institutions, industry groups and labor unions becomes significant in the process of best practices development and common standards development. The **Collaboration** allows them to share information, design interoperable systems, and create open source tools that would achieve fairness and accessibility. The inter-industry collaborations will be in a position to assist it in creation of ethical principles, safety certification framework, and AI maturity models that will make it adopt responsibly. Academic institutions are carrying out research on the issue of the interaction between humans and AI, the sustainability phenomenon, and the transparency of algorithms. It is possible that employees and labor unions make sure that the concerns of the employees are represented and addressed. The role of policymakers in coordinating matters related to the essentiality of ethical innovations and its promotion and the creation of the frameworks that facilitate sustainability and human-centered development of AI is critical. Finally, collaborative governance also enhances trust, mitigates risks and promotes responsible technological transformation in the logistics ecosystem.

6. CHALLENGES, OPEN ISSUES, AND FUTURE RESEARCH DIRECTIONS

6.1 Technical Challenges in AI Integration and System Interoperability

Irrespective of how revolutionary AI will be in the logistics industry, it has several technical obstacles that deter easy integration and mass adoption. The modern logistics operations presuppose a colossal amount of interdependent systems (transport management systems, warehouse management systems, IoT-based tracking devices, and cloud-based analytics applications) that must be linked to each other in a manner that will guarantee the stable operation of AI models. Nevertheless, it remains a serious problem of how to interoperate between the old systems and new AI apps. Most logistics companies are using hardware that is either old or not connected with digital databases, which cannot process the computational capability of AI. The problem of the data fragmentation also makes it even more difficult since the logistics data is frequently spread across several platforms, suppliers, and geographical locations. The AI systems can be applied to quality and real-time data to give relevant insights, and the lack of consistency or gaps in the data reduces their efficiency. Additionally, AI models may experience challenges with adapting to changing and unstructured environment, which is characteristic of logistics, such as unforeseeable traffic flows, demand fluctuations, or last-minute supply chain disruptions. The technical remedies to these issues include investing in digital infrastructure, standardization of data formats, and the development of modular AI systems, which can be integrated into a variety of systems of operation.

6.2 Ethical and Social Challenges in Workforce Transition

The use of AI in the logistics field is sure to trigger workforce migration processes, which are ethically and socially problematic and are to be taken into account. Automation will also remove the services that were once performed by humans particularly in sorting, packing and information processing departments. Despite the fact that AI also creates new forms of work vacations, such as robotics maintenance specialists or data analysts, not all displaced workers are capable of moving to the new industry. Such labor demand and workforce capability mismatch may result in unemployment and increased inequality, and social instability. Moreover, the feeling of threat posed by AI can cause the resistance of the employees, which will slow the implementation of new solutions. There is also an ethical issue regarding AI-based monitoring systems that are implemented to monitor the productivity, movement, and behavior of workers. Too much surveillance may affect the autonomy of workers, cause stress and lack of trust. Logistics companies should therefore institute moral standards that provide adequate balance between efficiency of operations to human dignity. To reduce the social risks of transitions based on AI, one can invest in large-scale reskilling, joint change management, and inclusive decision-making processes to facilitate a more equitable technological evolution.

6.3 Environmental Limitations and Sustainability Considerations

Although AI results in a more sustainable approach due to more efficient routes, reduced emission, and more efficient use of resources, it has its own environmental problems. The design, deployment, and maintenance of AI systems require a high level of computational energy, which can lead to power-intensive operations and carbon emissions, particularly in information centres. Deep learning networks and other advanced AI systems require large data sets, and considerable processing capabilities and this aspect has caused the environmental footprint of AI systems to be an issue of concern(Sundari, V. M et al., 2024). Besides, AI-driven logistics automatization can be described by highly advanced hardware, such as robots, sensors, IoT devices, etc., which generate electronic waste at the end of the life cycle. This waste has caused degradation of the environment since there are no effective means of recycling. The other challenge is that AI has not been incorporated into the renewable energy systems as yet, even though AI can be applied to optimize energy use, energy supply in some regions might be erratic, and it might have an adverse impact on the processes managed by AI. In order to resolve these environmental issues, one needs to transition to the practices of Green AI, which is concerned with energy efficiency, low-carbon computing, and eco-friendly hardware design. More research should be carried out to develop light AI algorithms, renewable energy-powered data centers, and circular hardware lifecycle management in an attempt to ensure ecological sustainability in the long run.

6.4 Limitations in Data Quality, Security, and Privacy Protection

The artificially intelligent logistics systems rely on the extensive data gathered on the vehicles, warehouses, employees, and consumers. It is important to assure data quality and integrity because incorrect or unfinished data may result in incorrect predictions, flawed optimization, and malfunction. Nevertheless, the logistics ecosystems can also have multiple stakeholders, such as suppliers, transport partners, retailers, and customers, and it can be challenging to ensure that the data remains consistent throughout the supply chain(Shobhana, N. 2024). Another important issue is data security, and the logistics operations are a nice target of cyberattacks, such as ransomware, information breaches, and manipulation of the system. These attacks may interfere with the global supply chains, sensitive information, and financial losses. Besides the security threats, there is the issue of privacy in cases where AI-based systems gather extensive personal information about an employee or a client. Surveillance to keep an eye on the productivity of workers or information to track their locations can infringe on the presumed privacy unless it is under strict regulation. Future studies need to focus on how to make AI work privacy friendly - e.g. federated learning, homomorphic encryption and differential privacy - to enable organizations to use data understanding and retain sensitive data. Enhancing cybersecurity measures and developing cross-industry data governance principles are also important to provide the safe and ethical use of AI in the logistics.

6.5 Challenges in Regulatory Adaptation and Global Standardization

The AI regulation in logistics is underdeveloped and fragmented. Despite certain regions of the world developing AI ethics policies, data protection and autonomy of autonomous automobiles, there exists no universal policy which governs AI-driven logistics operations. Multinational logistics firms that pursue the implementation of AI solutions in a homogenous manner are hampered by the barriers in the form of differences in the legal requirements, safety standards, and compliance processes across the countries. Indicatively, the use of autonomous trucks across borders is restricted by the existence of higher laws on autonomous trucks in various jurisdictions. Furthermore, the rapid advancement of the AI technology is likely to overtake the ability of the regulators to keep up with the speed, and the absence of regulation will lead to the uncontrollability and the potential of its abuse or inadequate use.

Global laws regarding the safety of AI, environmental friendliness, and the visibility of data would assist in developing more reliable and compatible logistics. Business giants, world organizations and government officials must liaise to devise rules and regulations that will not compromise the safety of the people and ethical conduct. The future research should be conducted on the question of how the regulations are able to maintain the new trends of the AI, such as the decentralized logistics networks, autonomous delivery systems, and AI-based decision-making platforms.

6.6 Open Issues in Human–AI Collaboration and Organizational Integration

Despite the fact that AI is an effective productivity and decision-making tool, the question of how humans and AI can work together is still an unsolved research question. Human and AI systems tend to perceive situations in different ways; hence, to combine the advantages of the two, one has to develop dedicated interaction interfaces, easy-to-use control systems and common decision-making models. The engagement with complex AI systems can leave workers overwhelmed or marginalized, especially when they are not properly trained or they do not clearly understand how AI works. Moreover, the logistic environments are volatile and unpredictable and it is hard to have AI effective in such situations unless humans monitor it. Companies have to find the best balance between human decision making and AI automation in order to prevent the over-reliance on algorithms and abusive human oversight. The other open question is connected with the organization being ready to adopt AI. The majority of companies are not as digital, visionary, and culturally open to the integration of AI. To explore the models of enhancing human-AI cooperation, building user trust, and organizational flexibility, future research is required. The future of AI systems should be to design them to be explainable, flexible, and empowering of the user in order to achieve harmonious and productive human-machines.

6.7 Future Research Directions for Sustainable and Human-Centric AI in Logistics

The interdisciplinary studies can be applied to solve the problem of AI development in logistics; they concern technological, environmental, and human aspects. Another possible direction is the development of Green AI that would make AI models less carbon-intensive through the development of energy-efficient algorithms, data processing techniques, and the development of hardware development that would be more sustainable. The other significant way is exploration of hybrid AI systems, which combine machine learning and symbolic reasoning, and allow decisions in complex logistics cases to be stronger and easier to understand. The study of the decentralized AI systems, including edge computing and federated learning, will be able to improve the privacy of data, decrease latency, and increase the resilience of the operations. The second point, which will be discussed in the future study, is the creation of AI models that are fair to make the use of AI models in the workforce management or a customer service less biased. In addition, the necessity to investigate the policy frameworks permitting the equitable transition of the workforce, the ethical surveillance, and the safeguarding of the labor rights in the AI-enabled conditions is increasing. The supportive workplace policies would be useful to introduce by considering the longitudinal study of the psychological and social implications of the introduction of AI into the logistics industry. Lastly, digital literacy and inclusive training courses will be necessary so that the prospects of the AI implementation are not exclusive and unreachable to all categories of the logistics workforce so that the sustainable, equitable, and responsible innovation could be achieved.

7. CONCLUSION

The implementation of AI in logistics and the functioning of logistics systems as a whole is a transformative approach that significantly influences process efficiency, sustainability, and individual welfare. The chapter shows that innovations in AI, such as autonomous warehousing, intelligent routing, predictive analytics, and human–machine collaboration, are transforming the logistics sector by providing opportunities to enhance productivity, reduce environmental impact, and improve safety. However, the widespread adoption of AI is also associated with complex challenges such as the risk of labor displacement, privacy, ethical, and regulatory issues, and the need to establish transparent and responsible governance. To achieve responsible growth, these challenges should be addressed carefully, taking into account the interdependence between technological innovation and human-centric values. Logistics organizations must implement AI systems that reduce carbon footprints, enhance circularity and resilience to disruptions, and focus on employee rights, equal opportunities, and inclusive training to ensure long-term sustainability. In addition, algorithmic biases must be minimized, and multi-stakeholder collaboration along with effective governance frameworks must be established to ensure system interoperability and the development of globally uniform standards. Whether organizations, policymakers, and societies can integrate ethical, environmental, and human factors into every stage of technological advancement will not only define the future of logistics but also depend on the advancement of AI technologies. With the evolution of AI, energy-efficient algorithms, privacy-preserving analytics, fairness-oriented models, and human-centered design principles should be emphasized in future research, as they can safeguard dignity and enhance worker flexibility. Finally, the implementation of AI in sustainable and responsible logistics should aim to create a balance between efficiency and equity, innovation and responsibility, as well as automation and the protection of human well-being.

REFERENCES

Bentalha, B. (2023). A Framework for Exploring the Global Performance of Service Supply Chain Management: A Qualitative Study. *Government Impact on Sustainable and Responsible Supply Chain Management*, 106-129.

Dhamija, P., Bedi, M., & Gupta, M. L. (2021). Industry 4.0 and supply chain management: A methodological review. *Research Anthology on Cross-Industry Challenges of Industry*, *4*(0), 192–217. DOI: 10.4018/978-1-7998-8548-1.ch011

Gracious, L. A., Jasmine, R. M., Pooja, E., Anish, T. P., Johncy, G., & Subramanian, R. S. (2023, October). Machine Learning and Deep Learning Transforming Healthcare: An Extensive Exploration of Applications, Algorithms, and Prospects. In *2023 4th IEEE Global Conference for Advancement in Technology (GCAT)* (pp. 1-6). IEEE.

Jaffrin, L. C., Nithya, T., & Divya, J. (2025, April). IoT for Sustainable Development: Enhancing Environmental Efficiency and Resource Optimization. In *2025 5th International Conference on Trends in Material Science and Inventive Materials (ICTMIM)* (pp. 1224-1230). IEEE.

Moorthy, K. S., Balakrishnan, G., Kumar, S. S., Raja, L., & Vijayalakshmi, A. (2024). Embracing circular economy principles for sustainable green supply chain management in manufacturing industries. In *Convergence of Human Resources Technologies and Industry 5.0* (pp. 85–110). IGI Global Scientific Publishing. DOI: 10.4018/979-8-3693-1343-5.ch005

Movahed, A. B., Movahed, A. B., & Nozari, H. (2024). Opportunities and challenges of smart supply chain in Industry 5.0. *Information Logistics for Organizational Empowerment and Effective Supply Chain Management*, 108-138.

Nicoletti, B. (2025a). AI transformation of logistics. In *Artificial Intelligence for Logistics 5.0: From Foundation Models to Agentic AI* (pp. 107–131). Springer Nature Switzerland. DOI: 10.1007/978-3-031-94046-0_4

Nicoletti, B. (2025b). Future of AI-Driven Logistics. In *Artificial Intelligence for Logistics 5.0: From Foundation Models to Agentic AI* (pp. 267–299). Springer Nature Switzerland. DOI: 10.1007/978-3-031-94046-0_10

Padmavathi, V., & Saminathan, R. (2023). Fundamentals of IOT, artificial intelligence, and blockchain approaches for applications in Supply Chain Management. In *Blockchain, IoT, and AI Technologies for Supply Chain Management* (pp. 1-18). CRC Press. DOI: 10.1201/9781003264521-1

Prasath, R., Kumar, V. V., Jaisankari, V., & Sivasubramani, R. (2025). Semantic Search for IoT-Based Object Recognition Using Clustering and Classification. In *Utilizing AI in Network and Mobile Security for Threat Detection and Prevention* (pp. 151–172). IGI Global Scientific Publishing. DOI: 10.4018/979-8-3693-9919-4.ch009

Rose, R. M., Varun, C. M., Sivasakthi, K., Kennady, R., & Lekha, D. (2025, May). Leveraging AI and IoT Data for Predictive Modelling and Preventive Healthcare. In *2025 Third International Conference on Augmented Intelligence and Sustainable Systems (ICAISS)* (pp. 628-633). IEEE. DOI: 10.1109/ICAISS61471.2025.11041733

Sathya, U., Hashini, S., Lakshmipriya, C., Varun, C. M., & Nalini, M. (2024, December). Emerging Trends and Future Prospects in Internet of Things (IoT) Technology. In *2024 International Conference on Sustainable Communication Networks and Application (ICSCNA)* (pp. 79-85). IEEE.

Shobhana, N. (2024). AI-powered supply chains towards greater efficiency. In *Complex AI dynamics and interactions in management* (pp. 229–249). IGI Global Scientific Publishing. DOI: 10.4018/979-8-3693-0712-0.ch011

Sundari, V. M., Rose, R. M., Sassirekha, S. M., Nalini, M., & Girija, P. (2024, November). Deep Learning: Techniques, Taxonomy, Applications, and Future Directions. In *2024 International Conference on Smart Technologies for Sustainable Development Goals (ICSTSDG)* (pp. 1-5). IEEE.

Ulle, R. S., Yogananthan, S., Kumar, V. V., & Reddy, T. (2024). A review on the adoption of AI-powered supply chain and logistics management for effective organizational performance in smes in India. *Cross-Industry AI Applications*, 60-72.

Chapter 7
AI-Enabled Logistics Orchestration in EV Manufacturing:
Employment Restructuring and Skill Reconfiguration Across Integrated Supply Networks

Nam Hai Vu
http://orcid.org/0000-0003-3725-2597
Institute of International Training and Cooperation, Baria Vungtau University, Vietnam

Jihad Mohammad
Graduate Business School, UCSI University, Malaysia

ABSTRACT

This chapter examines AI-enabled logistics orchestration in electric vehicle (EV) manufacturing as a socio-technical transformation that reshapes work organization and skill requirements across integrated supply networks. Based on an in-depth single-case study, it applies a four-pillar framework encompassing coordination architecture redesign, exception governance, hybrid skill formation, and human-in-the-loop accountability. The findings show that AI-enabled orchestration integrates procurement, inbound logistics, production planning, and distribution through shared interfaces, reducing fragmented coordination while intensifying cross-functional alignment. Work shifts from transactional expediting toward structured escalation and anomaly resolution, accompanied by rising demand for hybrid skills that com-

DOI: 10.4018/979-8-3373-7826-8.ch007

bine operational expertise, analytical literacy, and coordination capabilities. The chapter contributes to theories of work reconfiguration in EV supply networks and provides implications for inclusive workforce upgrading.

1. INTRODUCTION

The transition to electric vehicles (EVs) is frequently presented as a technological discontinuity in mobility, centred on electrified drivetrains and battery innovation. Yet, at the level of industrial organisation, it is equally a structural transformation of supply networks and their governance. EV manufacturing reorders upstream dependence around batteries, critical minerals, and specialised electronics, while simultaneously elevating expectations for traceability, compliance, and responsiveness across multi-tier sourcing and distribution. These dynamics render EV production systems unusually sensitive to logistics disruption and demand volatility, not simply because inputs are scarce or costly, but because the temporal coupling between inbound flows, production sequencing, and outbound allocation becomes tighter as firms scale (Kalaitzi et al., 2019; Busch et al., 2024). In this environment, logistics can no longer be treated as an operational support function that follows production decisions; rather, logistics becomes a constitutive component of production feasibility, shaping whether manufacturing plans can be executed and whether customer commitments remain credible under constraint.

This heightened sensitivity has been reinforced by the changing architecture of the EV supply chain ecosystem. As supplier roles shift some gaining influence through proprietary battery technologies, standards, and embedded software—lead firms confront new forms of information asymmetry and coordination dependence (Jagani et al., 2024). Moreover, global trade configurations, capacity concentration, and geopolitical uncertainties condition EV production and battery requirements, creating structural exposure to cross-border frictions that can cascade into manufacturing instability (Busch et al., 2024). The EV transition therefore intensifies the practical requirement for decision systems that can sense disruptions early, update plans rapidly, and coordinate execution across procurement, logistics, and manufacturing. These requirements are not adequately met by conventional planning routines alone, which often rely on periodic updates and function-specific visibility.

In response, EV manufacturers are increasingly adopting AI-enabled logistics orchestration solutions—predictive supply-risk analytics, real-time inventory visibility, intelligent material routing, and digitally integrated planning systems—to stabilise inbound flows, synchronise production logistics, and optimise outbound distribution. The appeal of orchestration is typically justified through performance outcomes such as cost, speed, and reliability. However, the deeper and underexplored consequences of orchestration lie in the restructuring of work. AI-enabled orchestration changes how decisions are produced, validated, and escalated across procurement, production logistics, supplier management, and distribution planning. It reorganises the "coordination architecture" through which interdependent actors align actions under uncertainty, thereby reshaping job boundaries, accountability arrangements, and skill hierarchies.

This labour-centred perspective is particularly important because much of the future-of-work literature in logistics has concentrated on visible automation settings warehouse robotics, autonomous transport, or route optimisation where displacement is comparatively observable. In EV manufacturing, by contrast, the most consequential transformation may occur through what can be described as the "invisible" redesign of coordination work: AI systems mediate how feasibility is assessed, how exceptions are defined, and how responsibility is distributed when disruptions threaten production continuity. The social and organisational stakes of this shift are amplified in EV ecosystems because the cost of disruption is high and because firms increasingly pursue end-to-end integration through digitally mediated control structures. Yet, empirical work remains limited on how AI-enabled orchestration reconfigures employment structures and skill requirements within logistics-intensive manufacturing environments.

This chapter addresses that gap by examining AI-enabled logistics orchestration in EV manufacturing not merely as an automation technology, but as a socio-technical restructuring of coordination and governance. The chapter aims to explain how AI-enabled orchestration restructures logistics employment and reconfigures skill requirements across integrated supply networks, and why these shifts matter for both organisational performance and employment sustainability. The argument advanced is threefold. First, AI-enabled orchestration does not simply reduce labour demand; it redistributes labour toward higher-accountability activities including exception governance, cross-functional decision coordination, digital oversight, and supplier signal interpretation. Second, the workforce consequences of orchestration are shaped less by technology "presence" than by organisational choices about human-in-the-loop governance, the allocation of decision rights, and the institutionalisation of escalation routines. Third, while orchestration can professionalise some logistics roles through hybrid competence development, it can also generate segmentation between analytics-mediated governance roles and increasingly workflow-bound operational roles, with implications for equity and job quality.

The chapter proceeds as follows. Section 2 reviews the literature and develops a theoretical framework organised around four pillars: coordination architecture redesign, exception governance, hybrid skill formation, and accountability and trust-building in human-in-the-loop governance. Section 3 introduces the single-case setting (EV-X), an anonymised label for an enterprise-wide deployment of AI driven supply chain solution in a major EV manufacturing group, and justifies the use of a single case for mechanism elucidation. Section 4 presents the empirical findings through the four-pillar framework, showing how orchestration reshapes work routines and skill demands in EV-X. Section 5 summarises the argument and articulates theoretical contributions and practical implications for EV manufacturers, logistics leaders, and broader debates on employment sustainability in the EV transition.

This chapter makes three contributions. First, it reconceptualises AI-enabled logistics orchestration as a coordination architecture that restructures how decisions are produced and aligned across supply networks, rather than as a discrete automation tool. Second, it develops a labour-centred explanation of orchestration by showing how work is redistributed toward exception governance, cross-functional coordination, and accountability practices. Third, it demonstrates that orchestration produces a dual employment dynamic, simultaneously enabling professionalisation through hybrid skill formation and generating segmentation through uneven access to decision authority and capability development. Together, these contributions advance understanding of how AI reshapes work, skills, and employment sustainability in logistics-intensive manufacturing contex

2. LITERATURE REVIEW AND THEORETICAL FRAMEWORK

2.1 Core concepts and background: EV supply networks, AI-enabled orchestration, and work reconfiguration

EV manufacturing is embedded within an evolving supply chain ecosystem characterised by shifting supplier roles, intensified coordination requirements, and heightened exposure to multi-tier risks. Multi-tier research highlights that EV supply chains concentrate resource dependence around batteries, critical minerals, and specialised component technologies, producing vulnerability to upstream constraints and the strategic behaviour of powerful suppliers (Kalaitzi et al., 2019). At the same time, the EV ecosystem is reshaping the division of labour among automotive suppliers, with changing roles and bargaining positions as firms compete over proprietary technologies, standards, and integration capabilities (Jagani et al., 2024). At the macro level, global trade dynamics and geographic concentration of inputs influence EV production and battery requirements, shaping systemic exposure to policy shocks, border frictions, and logistical disruptions (Busch et al., 2024). These forces generate an environment where volatility is not episodic but structural, and where coordination must be continuous rather than periodic.

Within this context, the concept of "logistics orchestration" refers to the coordinated design and governance of flows, decisions, and exception responses across integrated supply networks. Orchestration is analytically distinct from discrete logistics automation because its unit of intervention is the coordination architecture itself: the information infrastructures, decision rights, routines, and interfaces through which actors align actions across functions and organisations. AI-enabled orchestration extends this by embedding predictive and prescriptive analytics into decision loops, integrating heterogeneous data streams, and enabling near real-time planning interfaces that connect procurement, production logistics, and distribution. The wider logistics AI literature includes applications such as trajectory optimisation in smart-city logistics systems (Du et al., 2024), and broad reviews synthesising AI use across sustainable supply chain activities (Abyaneh et al., 2025). However, the distinctive organisational promise of orchestration is not simply better optimisation, but the re-coupling of decision-making across silos and time horizons.

Orchestration is increasingly entangled with sustainability and circularity expectations in EV supply networks. Green and sustainable supply chain practices in EV manufacturing require visibility into environmental performance, supplier practices, and compliance obligations, which motivates investment in digital infrastructures that can support traceability and governance (Althaqafi, 2023). AI-enabled digital transformation in circular logistics has been linked to organisational, technological, and environmental drivers, suggesting that AI adoption is conditioned by capability readiness and institutional pressures rather than technical opportunity alone (Oncioiu et al., 2025). In EV contexts, traceability obligations may extend into product lifecycle considerations, and distributed ledger approaches have been proposed to strengthen transparency and verification across EV supply chains (Subramanian & Thampy, 2021). Importantly, these infrastructures reshape work by changing who produces information, who validates it, and how accountability is assigned when inconsistencies or disruptions occur.

To theorise workforce implications, the chapter draws on literatures on organisational restructuring and employment in networked production systems. Organisational restructuring and emerging service value chains demonstrate that work is reconfigured through reassignment of activities, standardisation of interfaces, and redistribution of control across organisational boundaries (Flecker & Meil, 2010). Competence-based strategies in global production networks emphasise that firms' competitive positioning depends on which competences are developed and retained, with consequential implications for employment structure and skill stratification (Palpacuer, 2000). Employment relations theory further argues that as production becomes increasingly organised through global value chains, employment outcomes are shaped by network governance and inter-firm coordination architectures rather than firm-level choices alone (Lakhani et al., 2013). In lead companies, restructuring can place distinct demands on high-skilled employees by expanding responsibility for integration and adaptation, even as other roles become more standardised (Hansen, 2016).

Finally, the chapter aligns with manufacturing workforce research that conceptualises workforce reconfiguration as a strategic response to changing technology and demand environments. State-of-the-art reviews emphasise that manufacturers pursue workforce reconfiguration strategies to maintain flexibility, redeploy skills, and sustain performance under change (Hashemi-Petroodi et al., 2021). At the same time, automation and digitalisation have generated contested labour outcomes, including ambiguous effects on job quantity and job quality in reshoring and restructuring contexts (Bárcia de Mattos et al., 2021). Taken together, these perspectives motivate a labour-centred reading of AI-enabled orchestration: the technology is not merely a tool applied to logistics tasks, but a restructuring device that reorganises coordination work and thereby redistributes skill value and accountability across the supply network.

2.2 Orchestration as a coordination architecture in integrated EV supply networks

The first pillar of the framework conceptualises AI-enabled logistics orchestration as a reconfiguration of coordination architecture. AI-enabled orchestration refers to the use of artificial intelligence technologies such as machine learning, predictive analytics, and algorithmic decision systems to coordinate and synchronize interdependent activities, resources, and actors across complex organizational or supply network environments. By processing large volumes of real-time data, AI systems support dynamic decision-making, optimize workflows, and facilitate integration across previously fragmented functions. In this sense, AI-enabled orchestration extends traditional resource and network orchestration by introducing adaptive, data-driven coordination mechanisms that enhance operational responsiveness and cross-functional alignment (Charles Dhanaraj & Parkhe, 2006, Dmitry Ivanov et al., 2018, Raisch & Krakowski, 2020).

Coordination architecture refers to the patterned arrangement of information infrastructures, decision rights, routines, and interfaces through which interdependent actors align actions across procurement, logistics, manufacturing, and distribution. In EV supply networks, coordination architectures are under acute stress because feasibility is contingent on upstream resource dependence, multi-tier risk propagation, and shifting supplier roles. EV supply chains are not only complex in breadth, but also sensitive in coupling: a constrained battery input, a delayed inbound shipment, or a compliance anomaly can rapidly translate into production disruption or delivery failure (Kalaitzi et al., 2019; Busch et al., 2024).

AI-enabled orchestration alters coordination architecture by integrating heterogeneous signals—supplier availability, logistics capacity, inventory positions, production constraints, and customer allocation priorities—into a shared planning and execution environment. This integration produces decision coupling: the capacity to align re-planning and execution across functions in shorter cycles. The impetus for such coupling is intensified by volatility in EV demand and by the strategic requirement to sustain service levels in logistics-intensive contexts (Sun et al., 2025). Moreover, strategic adaptation in EV supply chains increasingly requires firms to navigate transformative trends by building information-rich decision infrastructures that enable reconfiguration under uncertainty (Rehman & Jajja, 2025). Supply chain finance risks provide an additional coordination challenge because supplier liquidity constraints and payment risks can undermine reliability and propagate disruptions, strengthening the case for integrated risk sensing and coordinated response AI-enabled logistics orchestrationThe coordination architecture pillar therefore frames orchestration as a socio-technical intervention with labour consequences. It directs attention to where coordination is centralised or distributed, how decision rights are allocated, and how interfaces between functions are standardised. These design features condition the subsequent pillars—exception governance, hybrid skill formation, and accountability—because they shape what counts as an exception, who is responsible for escalation, and which roles must integrate knowledge across domains.

2.3 Work reconfiguration through exception governance and escalation regimes

The second pillar theorises that AI-enabled orchestration reconfigures logistics work by shifting it from transactional coordination toward exception governance. Transactional coordination involves routine reconciliation tasks—tracking shipments, chasing confirmations, rebooking capacity, and aligning purchase orders with inbound deliveries—that stabilise operations when visibility is fragmented and plans are periodically updated. Orchestration platforms seek to reduce the need for repeated reconciliation by standardising workflows and by enabling earlier detection of constraints. Yet the pivotal transformation is the systematic production of "exceptions" as work objects.

Through predictive analytics, alerting systems, and integrated constraint logic, orchestration converts volatility into continuous streams of anomalies, risk classifications, and constraint flags. These signals do not eliminate uncertainty; they reformat it. The organisational response is an escalation regime: a patterned process in which exceptions are surfaced, prioritised, assigned, and resolved through cross-functional coordination and trade-off decisions. In EV manufacturing, the salience of exception governance is amplified because resource dependence around batteries and critical components increases the probability that upstream constraints will translate into immediate production feasibility issues (Kalaitzi et al., 2019). Trade and capacity configurations can further magnify exception frequency by exposing supply networks to border disruptions and transit variability (Busch et al., 2024). Demand volatility and service expectations in logistics contexts similarly intensify the requirement to respond quickly to disruptions in availability and allocation (Sun et al., 2025).

Exception governance is not merely operational; it is also organisational restructuring in practice. Restructuring research argues that new service value chains and coordination infrastructures change work by redefining interfaces, standardising procedures, and intensifying performance discipline through visibility and comparability (Flecker & Meil, 2010). In orchestration contexts, exceptions become measurable objects that can be counted, timed, and attributed, which increases the visibility of response performance and can heighten monitoring pressures. Competence-based strategies in global production networks suggest that when firms compete on responsiveness and reliability, exception handling competences become strategically valuable, while routine work becomes more standardised and subject to tighter control (Palpacuer, 2000). Manufacturing workforce research likewise notes that reconfiguration strategies increasingly prioritise flexibility, rapid redeployment, and capability to respond under change, which aligns closely with the organisational demands of exception governance (Hashemi-Petroodi et al., 2021).

The exception governance pillar therefore anticipates a redistribution of labour. Orchestration may reduce some forms of ad hoc expediting, but it can increase the intensity of structured escalation work, especially in disruption-sensitive EV environments where the "cost of delay" is high. This redistribution changes job boundaries because work shifts toward interpretation, prioritisation, and cross-functional mobilisation, and it changes accountability because decisions about which exceptions matter and which responses are legitimate become central to organisational performance.

2.4 Skill reconfiguration and hybrid professional identities under AI-enabled orchestration

The third pillar focuses on how orchestration revalues skills and reshapes professional identities in logistics-intensive manufacturing. EV supply networks require logistics professionals to manage not only physical flows but also the integrity of information related to traceability, compliance, and sustainability performance (Althaqafi, 2023; Oncioiu et al., 2025). AI-enabled orchestration intensifies this informational dimension by embedding analytics within decision loops. Workers must interpret model outputs, understand constraint logic, and communicate implications across procurement, production, and distribution under time pressure. Consequently, competence shifts from familiarity with local routines to the capacity to work through integrated systems and to translate between multiple functional languages.

The concept of hybrid skill is central. Hybrid skills are not simply "digital skills" appended to operational knowledge; rather, they combine operational domain understanding with analytical literacy, system interaction competence, and cross-functional communication capability. Toth et al. (2025) argue that AI integration in fundamental logistics components can be understood through a hybridisation of knowledge process capabilities and dynamic capabilities, emphasising sensing, seizing, and reconfiguring alongside knowledge creation and integration. Applied to EV logistics, this implies that valuable competence includes the ability to sense early signals of disruption, to interpret their operational meaning, and to reconfigure plans and routines accordingly. Hybrid competence is therefore inherently relational: it is expressed in the ability to coordinate across functions and to mobilise organisational responses.

However, the labour implications of hybridisation are uneven. Competence-based strategies in global production networks highlight that firms may concentrate high-value competences within certain nodes—often those responsible for integration and governance—while routinising and standardising other roles (Palpacuer, 2000). Employment relations perspectives similarly emphasise that network governance reshapes who bears the burden of skill development and who gains access to career-enhancing competences (Lakhani et al., 2013). Restructuring in lead companies can also increase demands placed on high-skilled employees by expanding responsibility for integration and adaptation, even as other roles experience reduced discretion (Hansen, 2016). In EV manufacturing logistics, orchestration may therefore create new professional identities—such as control-tower analysts, traceability coordinators, and supplier-risk interface specialists—while simultaneously narrowing the scope of progression for employees whose roles become workflow-bound.

This pillar consequently anticipates a dual movement. On one hand, orchestration professionalises certain roles by combining operational and analytical work and by elevating cross-functional coordination competence. On the other hand, it risks occupational segmentation by differentiating employees according to their proximity to orchestration decision loops and their access to hybrid skill development opportunities.

2.5 Accountability, trust, and governance in human-in-the-loop orchestration

The fourth pillar theorises that AI-enabled orchestration can increase reliance on human accountability and trust-building work rather than removing it. Orchestration systems depend on data quality, model validity, and the legitimacy of algorithmic recommendations. In EV manufacturing, these requirements are heightened because traceability and compliance expectations are amplified for high-value and safety-critical components, particularly batteries. Sustainable supply chain practices in EV manufacturing require governance systems capable of demonstrating provenance and responsible handling, which makes data integrity an operational necessity as well as an ethical and regulatory concern (Althaqafi, 2023).

Digital infrastructures are often presented as remedies for transparency and verification challenges. For example, hybrid blockchain architectures have been proposed for EV supply chains to strengthen provenance and trust through distributed verification mechanisms (Subramanian & Thampy, 2021). Yet transparency infrastructures do not eliminate verification work; they re-specify it. They generate new routines of exception reconciliation, evidentiary documentation, and dispute resolution when records conflict or when partners contest responsibility. Similarly, the AI literature on sustainable supply chains suggests that AI applications can enhance decision-making, but also underscores that outcomes are shaped by organisational and environmental conditions, including governance readiness and institutional pressures (Abyaneh et al., 2025; Oncioiu et al., 2025). In orchestration settings, these conditions manifest as labour: workers must validate outputs, negotiate trade-offs between efficiency and resilience, and ensure that decisions are explainable and auditable.

From an employment perspective, accountability and trust are not abstract attributes; they are work demands distributed across roles. Human-in-the-loop governance involves who is authorised to override system recommendations, who is accountable when models err, and who bears responsibility for maintaining data quality and compliance. As production governance becomes more networked, accountability can become distributed yet contested, aligning with employment relations accounts that emphasise how value chain governance structures shape employment outcomes (Lakhani et al., 2013). Moreover, restructuring research indicates that increased visibility and performance comparability can intensify responsibility and monitoring, particularly for high-skilled employees tasked with integration and decision justification (Flecker & Meil, 2010; Hansen, 2016).

This pillar also foregrounds the distributional stakes of orchestration. Automation and digitalisation can produce ambiguous outcomes for job quality and inequality even when productivity improves, as evidenced in debates around automation, reshoring, and employment restructuring (Bárcia de Mattos et al., 2021). In EV logistics, orchestration may intensify accountability burdens for some roles while standardising and narrowing discretion for others, producing segmentation within logistics employment. The framework therefore treats governance design as central to employment sustainability: it is the organisational configuration of human-in-the-loop accountability, rather than the technology alone, that shapes whether orchestration contributes to inclusive upgrading or to new forms of labour stratification.

3. CASE SETTING, RESEARCH DESIGN, AND JUSTIFICATION FOR EV-X

This chapter adopts a qualitative single-case study design centered on mechanism elucidation within EV-X, an anonymized global electric vehicle manufacturing group. The case serves as a critical empirical referent, representing the contemporary transition from fragmented, siloed planning tools toward integrated, enterprise-wide orchestration layers. By deploying an industrial data and AI platform across multiple brands and functions, EV-X exemplifies a strategic response to the structural vulnerabilities inherent in EV supply networks—specifically upstream constraints and the necessity for real-time traceability. To achieve analytical depth, the study utilizes data triangulation across three primary streams: internal documentation, system-generated operational metrics, and qualitative insights derived from organizational practices observed within the EV-X environment. The analysis followed an iterative, theory-informed trajectory, blending the inductive identification of emerging patterns with a deductive interpretation anchored in the four-pillar framework.

Through a process of constant comparison between empirical observations and theoretical constructs, this approach ensures a robust, coherent explanation of how AI-enabled orchestration reconfigures labor and decision-making within compressed operational cycles.

EV-X functions as a high-scale, geographically dispersed electric vehicle manufacturing group characterized by high-volume production and intricate inbound supply architectures. Positioned within a volatile EV ecosystem, the group navigates a landscape of multi-tier resource dependencies and rapidly evolving supplier dynamics. To address these systemic pressures, the orchestration system analyzed herein was implemented at an enterprise-wide level, effectively collapsing the traditional boundaries between procurement, logistics, production planning, and distribution. This integrated deployment serves as the focal point for examining how cross-functional synchronization is achieved within such a complex, resource-dependent manufacturing environment. Upstream constraints, particularly around batteries and critical components, create feasibility uncertainty that cannot be resolved through conventional planning routines alone (Kalaitzi et al., 2019). The evolving EV supply chain ecosystem further redistributes influence among suppliers, altering information control and coordination dependence for lead firms (Jagani et al., 2024). At a broader level, global trade configurations and geographic concentration of inputs influence EV production and battery requirements, creating systemic exposure to border frictions and capacity shocks that can cascade into manufacturing instability (Busch et al., 2024). These conditions increase the value of orchestration capabilities that can sense risk, align decisions across functions, and mobilise coordinated responses.

EV-X's orchestration capability centred on a digitally integrated planning and execution environment that consolidated heterogeneous operational data streams and enabled near real-time coordination across organisational units. In operational terms, the system combined predictive analytics for material availability and supply risk, exception detection for disruption exposures, and integrated interfaces that connected procurement signals to production scheduling and outbound allocation. The strategic intent was to reduce reliance on manual expediting and fragmented spreadsheets by institutionalising data-driven coordination and faster escalation routines under uncertainty. This logic aligns with broader accounts of AI-enabled digital transformation in logistics and sustainable supply chains, which emphasise that AI value is contingent on organisational embedding, governance arrangements, and capability development rather than technical deployment alone (Abyaneh et al., 2025; Oncioiu et al., 2025).

A single-case design is appropriate for this chapter because the research objective is mechanism elucidation rather than population estimation. The chapter seeks to explain how AI-enabled orchestration reshapes coordination architectures and, through those architectures, restructures employment and reconfigures skills. These mechanisms are frequently difficult to capture through large-sample analyses because they are embedded in everyday decision loops, escalation practices, and cross-functional governance routines. EV-X provides unusually strong process visibility into these dynamics due to the enterprise-wide scope of the orchestration programme and its embedding across multiple functions and sites. The case also enables careful theorisation of how governance design choices shape workforce outcomes: who gains authority in escalation routines, how accountability is distributed when model outputs inform trade-offs, and how hybrid competences are cultivated or constrained across roles.

The case is therefore used as an analytically intensive setting that allows the chapter to trace the socio-technical reconfiguration of work. Rather than treating orchestration as a uniform technological intervention, the analysis attends to how orchestration is enacted through organisational routines and how those enactments revalue skills and restructure employment. This orientation is consistent with employment relations and restructuring perspectives that emphasise how network governance and organisational design mediate the employment consequences of technological and structural change (Flecker & Meil, 2010; Palpacuer, 2000)

4. FINDINGS: EMPLOYMENT RESTRUCTURING AND SKILL RECONFIGURATION IN EV-X

4.1 Coordination architecture redesign and the redistribution of coordination work

EV-X's enterprise orchestration initiative altered the coordination architecture through which procurement, inbound logistics, production planning, and distribution aligned decisions. Prior to orchestration, coordination work was distributed across functional silos and stabilised through repeated reconciliation of partial data. Procurement teams tracked supplier confirmations and negotiated availability; logistics units monitored inbound movement and capacity; and production planners managed feasibility based on internal constraints and periodically updated schedules. These arrangements functioned under conditions of relative stability, but they became increasingly strained as EV-specific dependencies and volatility intensified. The result was a form of coordination overload in which time was consumed by reconciling competing versions of operational reality rather than by governing trade-offs strategically.

Orchestration reshaped this landscape by coupling signals and constraints into a shared planning interface and by integrating decision logic across functions. In practice, the system consolidated heterogeneous operational data streams—supplier status, inventory positions, transport capacity, plant constraints, and customer allocations—into a common environment that enabled faster replanning cycles. This integration reduced some forms of transactional reconciliation while simultaneously making cross-functional interdependence more explicit. When constraints emerged, the orchestration layer did not merely "show" problems; it specified how problems were connected. This increased the salience of integrative coordination at precisely the points where priorities collided, such as when material shortages required trade-offs between production continuity, premium customer fulfilment, and outbound allocation fairness.

The coordination redesign is best interpreted as a response to EV supply-network conditions. Multi-tier resource dependence—especially around batteries and critical components—creates feasibility uncertainty that cannot be fully neutralised through conventional buffering (Kalaitzi et al., 2019). Ecosystem change redistributes information control and standard-setting power across suppliers, elevating the value of integrated visibility and the ability to interpret supplier signals strategically (Jagani et al., 2024). Global trade dynamics further condition transit reliability and input availability, amplifying the cost of misalignment across production sites and distribution commitments (Busch et al., 2024). In this setting, orchestration operates as a coordination architecture intervention that aims to stabilise feasibility through decision coupling.

From an employment perspective, EV-X's orchestration reconfigured job content through a partial standardisation of routine coordination and an expansion of coordination-at-the-boundaries. Routine activities increasingly flowed through system workflows, which narrowed discretion in some transactional tasks and shifted emphasis toward compliance with process discipline. At the same time, integrative coordination work grew in scope: employees spent more time translating constraint logic across functions, anticipating second-order effects of replanning decisions, and negotiating prioritisation when supply and capacity constraints collided. In other words, orchestration redistributed labour away from the repeated production of "updates" and toward the governance of interdependence.

This redistribution aligns with restructuring accounts that emphasise how new coordination infrastructures reassign work, intensify interface management, and reshape control through standardised procedures and heightened visibility (Flecker & Meil, 2010). It is also consistent with employment relations perspectives that locate employment outcomes within networked governance arrangements: as coordination becomes more central to operational feasibility, authority and responsibility shift toward those roles that manage interdependence across organisational boundaries (Lakhani et al., 2013). EV-X thus illustrates that coordination architecture is not merely a technical blueprint but a labour structure that reallocates discretion and skill value across roles.

4.2 Exception governance and the shift from transactional expediting to escalation work

A central workforce effect of orchestration at EV-X was the reallocation of labour from routine expediting toward exception governance. Predictive analytics and exception detection converted volatility into structured alerts and constraint flags, which reshaped the temporal organisation of work. Rather than reacting primarily to late shipments or last-minute shortages, logistics professionals increasingly worked on interpreting exception signals, validating whether anomalies reflected real constraints or data artefacts, and coordinating rapid cross-functional responses. This does not imply that expediting disappeared; rather, it became subordinated to a more formalised escalation regime in which exceptions were surfaced earlier and routed through defined decision pathways.

This exception orientation reflects the structural properties of EV supply networks. Resource dependence around batteries and critical components raises the likelihood that upstream constraints translate into immediate production feasibility issues (Kalaitzi et al., 2019). Global trade and capacity configurations further magnify exception frequency by exposing supply networks to border disruptions and transit variability (Busch et al., 2024). Demand volatility and service expectations in logistics contexts intensify the requirement to respond quickly to disruptions in availability and allocation (Sun et al., 2025). In addition, supply chain finance risks can undermine reliability and propagate disruptions when suppliers face liquidity constraints, reinforcing the need for early risk detection and coordinated response (Bui et al., 2025). EV-X's orchestration initiative operationalised these pressures by institutionalising a continuous cycle of exception detection, prioritisation, and resolution.

Exception governance, however, is not merely an operational improvement; it is a reconfiguration of work that reshapes authority and accountability. Orchestration increased the visibility of anomalies and made response performance more measurable, which intensified performance discipline. Employees had to prioritise which exceptions mattered most, determine the legitimacy of system signals, and mobilise cross-functional responses under time pressure. This elevated the strategic value of judgement and cross-functional coordination competences, consistent with competence-based perspectives that anticipate a migration of skill value toward problem-solving and governance roles when routine coordination is standardised (Palpacuer, 2000). It also aligns with manufacturing workforce research that frames reconfiguration strategies around flexibility and rapid redeployment under change (Hashemi-Petroodi et al., 2021).

Yet the shift also carried risks of segmentation. As exceptions became routable objects, some roles gained proximity to decision-making and trade-off governance, while other roles became more workflow-bound, responsible for executing prescribed responses and feeding local information into escalation channels. This is precisely the kind of restructuring dynamic highlighted in accounts of emerging service value chains, where standardised interfaces can intensify monitoring and narrow discretion even as higher-level roles expand in scope (Flecker & Meil, 2010). In EV-X, orchestration thus produced a redistribution of labour toward escalation work, with implications for career trajectories and perceived job quality depending on role location within the escalation regime.

4.3 Hybrid skills and emerging professional identities under orchestration

EV-X's orchestration initiative reconfigured skill requirements by increasing demand for hybrid competences that combine operational knowledge with analytical literacy and system interaction capability. In orchestration environments, it is insufficient to know how logistics processes work in isolation; employees must also understand how integrated constraint logic is produced, how predictive signals should be interpreted, and how decisions propagate across the system. Consequently, orchestration elevated the value of employees who could bridge functional boundaries—translating between procurement risk, production constraints, transport capacity, and distribution priorities—while engaging with analytics-mediated decision tools.

In EV-X, hybrid skills were expressed in several interlinked role families. Planning and logistics professionals increasingly performed work analogous to control-tower analysis, monitoring constraint signals and prioritising interventions. A parallel set of roles emerged around digital inventory and traceability coordination, particularly where compliance expectations required reliable recordkeeping and rapid reconciliation of discrepancies. Production logistics planning also evolved toward AI-supported sequencing and feasibility governance, where employees worked with predictive availability signals to anticipate bottlenecks and to coordinate adjustments with manufacturing teams. Although these role labels vary across organisations, the underlying competence shift was consistent: orchestration increases the premium on interpretive, integrative, and communicative skills that enable rapid coordination under uncertainty.

This hybridisation can be interpreted through theoretical accounts of AI integration in logistics. Toth et al. (2025) conceptualise AI integration as a hybridisation of knowledge process capabilities and dynamic capabilities, which emphasises the capacity to sense conditions, integrate knowledge, and reconfigure routines. Applied to EV-X, this suggests that hybrid competence involves not only technical interaction with AI systems, but also the organisational ability to translate signals into coordinated action. The EV context further intensifies these demands because sustainability and circularity expectations elevate the importance of traceability governance and data integrity, linking operational competence to compliance and legitimacy concerns (Althaqafi, 2023; Oncioiu et al., 2025).

However, the workforce implications of hybridisation are not uniformly positive. Competence-based strategies in global production networks suggest that when firms compete on responsiveness and reliability, they may concentrate high-value competences within roles closest to integration and governance, while routinising other roles through standardised interfaces (Palpacuer, 2000). Employment relations theory similarly cautions that network governance can redistribute responsibility for skill development unevenly, potentially creating segmented labour markets within and across firms (Lakhani et al., 2013). In EV-X, orchestration created professionalisation opportunities for some employees to move into analytics-mediated coordination roles, but it also risked limiting mobility for those whose tasks became tightly specified by workflow discipline unless deliberate reskilling pathways and progression routes were instituted.

The emergence of hybrid identities therefore represents both an organisational capability shift and an employment sustainability challenge. If orchestration is framed narrowly as a technology programme, training may be targeted primarily at central analytics roles, reinforcing segmentation. If it is framed as a socio-technical redesign of coordination work, hybrid competence development becomes a broader workforce development agenda that can support more inclusive upgrading.

4.4 Accountability, trust-building work, and the politics of human-in-the-loop governance

The emergence of hybrid roles also raises an important distinction between role enrichment and responsibility intensification. Role enrichment occurs when expanded responsibilities are accompanied by increased authority, skill development, and access to decision-making processes. In such cases, orchestration contributes to professionalisation and upward mobility. By contrast, responsibility intensification refers to situations in which employees face greater coordination demands, time pressure, and performance expectations without a corresponding increase in discretion or recognition. In EV-X, elements of both dynamics are observable, suggesting that orchestration can simultaneously enhance and constrain job quality depending on how authority and capability development are distributed across role

Orchestration at EV-X intensified accountability and expanded trust-building work, demonstrating that AI-enabled coordination can increase reliance on human judgement rather than simply replacing it. Integrated planning interfaces and predictive signals were used to justify allocation and sequencing decisions, which required employees to validate data quality, scrutinise model outputs, and explain decisions to cross-functional stakeholders. These demands were amplified in traceability-sensitive flows—particularly batteries and high-value components—where provenance and handling integrity are central to compliance and sustainability expectations (Althaqafi, 2023). Consequently, human-in-the-loop governance became a sustained operational practice rather than an implementation stage.

This accountability intensification is rooted in the organisational conditions of AI-enabled transformation. Reviews of AI applications in sustainable supply chains emphasise that AI value depends on governance readiness and organisational embedding, including the capacity to manage data, legitimacy, and decision accountability (Abyaneh et al., 2025). Empirical work on AI-enabled digital transformation in circular logistics similarly underscores the role of organisational, technological, and environmental drivers, implying that adoption outcomes are shaped by institutional pressures and capability development rather than technical possibility (Oncioiu et al., 2025). In EV-X, these drivers materialised as labour: employees invested time and expertise in ensuring data reliability, reconciling discrepancies, and maintaining confidence in the orchestration layer as a legitimate basis for operational trade-offs.

The case also illustrates why transparency infrastructures do not automatically reduce labour. Hybrid blockchain designs have been proposed to enhance provenance and transparency in EV supply chains (Subramanian & Thampy, 2021), but such infrastructures typically generate new verification routines and exception reconciliation work when records conflict, when partners contest responsibility, or when compliance requirements shift. EV-X's orchestration environment similarly required evidentiary work: documenting why allocations were changed, how exceptions were resolved, and what assumptions underpinned decisions. This evidentiary work is central to trust because it stabilises cross-functional acceptance of decisions, particularly when those decisions create perceived winners and losers in allocation.

Accountability, however, is not evenly distributed. As orchestration increases auditability and makes decision pathways more visible, it can intensify exposure to blame and justification pressures for employees positioned close to decision-making. At the same time, workflow-bound roles may experience increased monitoring and reduced discretion. This distributional dynamic echoes restructuring research, which shows that standardised interfaces and heightened visibility can intensify responsibility for some roles and performance discipline for others (Flecker & Meil, 2010; Hansen, 2016). It also resonates with debates on automation and restructuring that emphasise ambiguous effects on job quality and inequality even when productivity improves (Bárcia de Mattos et al., 2021).

EV-X therefore demonstrates that human-in-the-loop governance is a decisive organisational design choice. The politics of orchestration lies in who is authorised to override system recommendations, who bears responsibility for model and data errors, and how trade-offs are legitimised across functions and partners. These choices shape not only operational performance but also employment sustainability: they influence whether orchestration contributes to inclusive skill upgrading or reproduces segmentation by concentrating authority and hybrid competence in a narrow set of roles.

4.5 Employment restructuring outcomes under AI-enabled orchestration

Bringing together the four pillars, AI-enabled logistics orchestration at EV-X produces a systematic restructuring of employment across logistics-related functions. These outcomes can be understood along four interrelated dimensions.

First, role composition shifts from transaction-oriented coordination toward integrative coordination and exception governance. Routine expediting and reconciliation activities are partially standardised through system workflows, while a greater share of work is concentrated in roles that interpret constraints, prioritise responses, and coordinate cross-functional decisions under uncertainty.

Second, orchestration generates role stratification. Roles located close to orchestration decision loops—such as control-tower analysts, planning coordinators, and supplier-risk interface roles—gain increased influence over prioritisation and trade-offs. In contrast, roles embedded in workflow execution become more standardised and process-bound, with narrower discretion. This differentiation reflects uneven proximity to decision authority and access to hybrid skill development.

Third, mobility pathways become increasingly dependent on access to hybrid competences. Employees who develop the ability to interpret analytics, engage with integrated systems, and translate across functional domains are more likely to move into higher-value coordination roles. Conversely, employees whose roles remain workflow-bound may face constrained progression unless deliberate reskilling pathways are provided.

Fourth, authority distribution is reconfigured through human-in-the-loop governance. While orchestration systems structure decision-making, authority is not eliminated but redistributed. Certain roles gain the capacity to validate, override, or legitimise system outputs, while others are positioned primarily as contributors of local data and executors of predefined responses.

Taken together, these patterns indicate that AI-enabled orchestration does not simply reduce labour demand, but reorganises labour across differentiated roles with varying levels of discretion, authority, and skill intensity.

5. CONCLUSION AND IMPLICATIONS

This chapter examined AI-enabled logistics orchestration in EV manufacturing as a socio-technical restructuring of coordination and governance that reshapes employment structures and reconfigures skills across integrated supply networks. Building on prior research on EV supply chain vulnerability, ecosystem transformation, and global production dependencies (Kalaitzi et al., 2019; Jagani et al., 2024; Busch et al., 2024), the chapter argued that orchestration should be understood not merely as a performance-enhancing digital tool but as a coordination architecture that redistributes work across organisational interfaces. To analyse this transformation, the chapter developed a four-pillar interpretive framework comprising coordination architecture redesign, exception governance, hybrid skill formation, and accountability and trust-building work, which was applied to the anonymised case of EV-X—an enterprise-wide orchestration system enabled through a large-scale industrial AI platform.

The findings show that orchestration at EV-X fundamentally reconfigured coordination practices. Shared planning interfaces coupled signals and constraints across procurement, logistics, and production planning, reducing fragmented reconciliation while increasing the need for integrative coordination where cross-functional priorities intersect. At the same time, work was redistributed toward structured exception governance, as operational volatility became routable anomalies requiring prioritisation, validation, and coordinated response. Orchestration also reshaped skill valuation by elevating hybrid competences that combine operational expertise, analytical literacy, and cross-functional translation, producing emerging role identities around control-tower analysis, traceability coordination, and AI-supported planning. Finally, the case demonstrates that accountability and trust-building labour expands rather than diminishes in AI-mediated systems: human-in-the-loop governance remains central for validating algorithmic outputs and maintaining reliability in traceability-sensitive EV component flows.

Taken together, the chapter contributes a conceptual reframing of AI-enabled orchestration as a form of socio-technical work reconfiguration. Rather than simply automating logistics coordination, orchestration restructures how decisions are integrated, how disruptions are governed, and how expertise is organised across supply networks. This perspective highlights orchestration as a transformation of coordination architecture that redistributes labour, generates hybrid skill demands, and embeds accountability practices within AI-mediated operational systems.

5.1 Theoretical contributions

The chapter makes three interrelated theoretical contributions. First, it advances EV supply chain research by conceptualising AI-enabled orchestration as a coordination architecture mechanism through which firms attempt to govern structural vulnerability. Studies have documented multi-tier dependencies and resource constraints in EV supply networks (Kalaitzi et al., 2019) and have highlighted changing supplier roles and ecosystem restructuring (Jagani et al., 2024). By tracing how an enterprise orchestration layer re-couples procurement, logistics, production planning, and distribution decisions, the chapter shows how lead firms translate systemic volatility—shaped by trade configurations and input concentration (Busch et al., 2024)—into organisational routines of decision coupling and escalation. This reframes vulnerability management as a work-restructuring process rather than a purely structural condition.

Second, the chapter extends AI-in-logistics and sustainable supply chain debates by specifying a labour-centred mechanism of value creation that complements existing adoption and driver explanations. Reviews and empirical studies highlight AI-enabled transformation drivers and the promise of AI applications in sustainable supply chains (Abyaneh et al., 2025; Oncioiu et al., 2025), while capability-oriented frameworks theorise AI integration through hybridisation of knowledge process and dynamic capabilities (Toth et al., 2025). The present analysis contributes by showing that orchestration's operational value is mediated by exception governance and accountability work: predictive signals become actionable only through human interpretation, prioritisation, and legitimised trade-off governance. This shifts theorisation away from a substitution logic and toward an understanding of orchestration as socio-technical reconfiguration of coordination and judgement.

Third, the chapter contributes to restructuring and employment theory by demonstrating how digital coordination infrastructures operate as restructuring devices within networked production systems. Restructuring accounts emphasise that new coordination infrastructures reassign work and intensify governance through standardised interfaces and heightened visibility (Flecker & Meil, 2010). Competence-based perspectives anticipate that such changes can polarise employment by concentrating high-value competences in certain roles while standardising others (Palpacuer, 2000). Employment relations theory further suggests that network governance shapes employment outcomes as production shifts from firm-centric to value-chain coordination architectures (Lakhani et al., 2013). EV-X illustrates how orchestration redistributes discretion and responsibility, potentially concentrating authority and hybrid competence in roles close to decision loops, while narrowing discretion and increasing monitoring in workflow-bound roles. In doing so, it provides a mechanism-based account of how AI-enabled coordination can simultaneously professionalise and segment logistics employment.

5.2 Practical implications

A key implication of the findings is that AI-enabled orchestration does not produce uniform employment outcomes; rather, its effects depend on organisational conditions. Inclusive upgrading is more likely when access to hybrid skill development is broadly distributed, when employees are given opportunities to engage with orchestration systems, and when internal mobility pathways enable progression into integrative coordination roles. In contrast, segmentation is more likely when hybrid competences are concentrated within a narrow group of roles, when decision authority is centralised, and when workflow-bound roles are tightly standardised without corresponding opportunities for skill development. These conditions suggest that employment outcomes are shaped less by the presence of AI systems than by organisational choices regarding governance design, capability development, and access to decision-making processes

For EV manufacturers and logistics leaders, the findings imply that orchestration success depends on organisational design and workforce capability investment as much as on analytics sophistication. First, firms should treat exception governance as a core operational capability, not an incidental by-product of digital tools. This requires clear escalation protocols, role clarity for exception ownership, and cross-functional decision forums that can adjudicate trade-offs between cost, speed, resilience, and compliance under constraint. Second, because orchestration elevates the importance of data integrity and auditability, organisations should invest in data stewardship and traceability governance routines that specify responsibilities for verification, reconciliation, and evidentiary documentation, especially for battery-related components where compliance stakes are high. Third, orchestration should be accompanied by deliberate workforce development strategies that support hybrid competence across both central and operational roles. Training should extend beyond tool usage to include analytical literacy, system reasoning, and cross-functional communication, thereby enabling employees to interpret signals and coordinate responses rather than merely execute workflows. Fourth, leaders should monitor distributional effects and job quality outcomes. Orchestration can generate segmentation if hybrid skill opportunities and decision authority are concentrated in a narrow set of roles, while other roles become increasingly workflow-bound and monitored. Inclusive role redesign, internal mobility pathways, and reskilling programmes can mitigate this risk and align AI-enabled upgrading with employment sustainability.

Finally, EV manufacturers should recognise that orchestration efficacy is shaped by supply network relationships. Partner data credibility and incentive alignment influence signal reliability and response feasibility. Firms should therefore develop governance arrangements—shared standards, joint exception response routines, and transparent performance dialogues—that stabilise trust and reduce adversarial blame dynamics. In the broader societal context, the EV transition is promoted as a pathway to sustainable industrial development; the analysis here suggests that employment sustainability must be treated as a design objective of orchestration. Without deliberate investment in reskilling and inclusive progression routes, AI-enabled logistics upgrading may reproduce new inequalities even as it improves operational performance.

REFERENCES

Abyaneh, A. G., Ghanbari, H., Mohammadi, E., Amirsahami, A., & Khakbazan, M. (2025). An analytical review of artificial intelligence applications in sustainable supply chains. *Supply Chain Analytics*, 100173.

Althaqafi, T. (2023). Cultivating sustainable supply chain practises in electric vehicle manufacturing: A MCDM approach to assessing GSCM performance. *World Electric Vehicle Journal*, *14*(10), 290. DOI: 10.3390/wevj14100290

Bárcia de Mattos, F., Eisenbraun, J., Kucera, D., & Rossi, A. (2021). Disruption in the apparel industry? Automation, employment and reshoring. *International Labour Review*, *160*(4), 519–536. DOI: 10.1111/ilr.12213

Bui, T. D., Chan, F. T., Kumpimpa, T., Tan, K., Sethanan, K., & Tseng, M. L. (2025). A supply chain finance risk management model for the electric vehicle supply chain: A data-driven analysis. *International Journal of Logistics*, *28*(12), 1422–1453. DOI: 10.1080/13675567.2024.2351561

Busch, P., Pares, F., Chandra, M., Kendall, A., & Tal, G. (2024). Future of global electric vehicle supply chain: Exploring the impact of global trade on electric vehicle production and battery requirements. *Transportation Research Record: Journal of the Transportation Research Board*, *2678*(11), 1468–1482. DOI: 10.1177/03611981241244797

Dhanaraj, C., & Parkhe, A. (2006). Orchestrating Innovation Networks. *Academy of Management Review*, *31*(3), 659–669. DOI: 10.5465/amr.2006.21318923

Du, P., Shi, Y., Cao, H., Garg, S., Alrashoud, M., & Shukla, P. K. (2024). AI-enabled trajectory optimization of logistics UAVs with wind impacts in smart cities. *IEEE Transactions on Consumer Electronics*, *70*(1), 3885–3897. DOI: 10.1109/TCE.2024.3355061

Flecker, J., & Meil, P. (2010). Organisational restructuring and emerging service value chains: Implications for work and employment. *Work, Employment and Society*, *24*(4), 680–698. DOI: 10.1177/0950017010380635

Hansen, N. W. (2016). International company restructuring and the effects on high-skilled employees in lead companies. *Competition & Change*, *20*(4), 237–254. DOI: 10.1177/1024529416646695

Hashemi-Petroodi, S. E., Dolgui, A., Kovalev, S., Kovalyov, M. Y., & Thevenin, S. (2021). Workforce reconfiguration strategies in manufacturing systems: A state of the art. *International Journal of Production Research, 59*(22), 6721–6744. DOI: 10.1080/00207543.2020.1823028

Ivanov, D., Dolgui, A., & Sokolov, B. (2018). The impact of digital technology and Industry 4.0 on the ripple effect and supply chain risk analytics. *International Journal of Production Research, 57*(3), 1–18. DOI: 10.1080/00207543.2018.1488086

Jagani, S., Marsillac, E., & Hong, P. (2024). The electric vehicle supply chain ecosystem: Changing roles of automotive suppliers. *Sustainability (Basel), 16*(4), 1570. DOI: 10.3390/su16041570

Kalaitzi, D., Matopoulos, A., & Clegg, B. (2019). Managing resource dependencies in electric vehicle supply chains: A multi-tier case study. *Supply Chain Management, 24*(2), 256–270. DOI: 10.1108/SCM-03-2018-0116

Lakhani, T., Kuruvilla, S., & Avgar, A. (2013). From the firm to the network: Global value chains and employment relations theory. *British Journal of Industrial Relations, 51*(3), 440–472. DOI: 10.1111/bjir.12015

Oncioiu, I., Mândricel, D. A., & Hojda, M. H. (2025). Artificial intelligence-enabled digital transformation in circular logistics: A structural equation model of organizational, technological, and environmental drivers. *Logistics (Basel), 9*(3), 102. DOI: 10.3390/logistics9030102

Palpacuer, F. (2000). Competence-based strategies and global production networks a discussion of current changes and their implications for employment. *Competition & Change, 4*(4), 353–400. DOI: 10.1177/102452940000400401

Raisch, S., & Krakowski, S. (2021). Artificial intelligence and management: The automation–augmentation paradox. *Academy of Management Review, 46*(1), 192–210. DOI: 10.5465/2018.0072

Rehman, A. U., & Shakeel Sadiq Jajja, M. (2025). Strategic adaptation in the electric vehicle supply chain: Navigating transformative trends in the automobile industry. *Journal of Enterprise Information Management, 38*(3), 745–767. DOI: 10.1108/JEIM-10-2024-0554

Subramanian, G., & Thampy, A. S. (2021). Implementation of hybrid blockchain in a pre-owned electric vehicle supply chain. *IEEE Access : Practical Innovations, Open Solutions, 9*, 82435–82454. DOI: 10.1109/ACCESS.2021.3084942

Sun, Y., Zhu, Q., & Li, X. (2025). Electric vehicle adoption in logistics supply chain. *International Journal of Production Research*, •••, 1–20.

Toth, Z., Goga, A. S., & Bo coianu, M. (2025). AI Integration in Fundamental Logistics Components: Advanced Theoretical Framework for Knowledge Process Capabilities and Dynamic Capabilities Hybridization. *Logistics (Basel)*, *9*(4), 140. DOI: 10.3390/logistics9040140

Chapter 8
AI-Enabled Warehousing and the Changing Nature of Operational Skills in Logistics

Ngan Tuyet Truong
http://orcid.org/0000-0002-8925-6226
Ho Chi Minh City University of Economics and Finance, Vietnam

Vikas Kumar
University of Portsmouth, UK

ABSTRACT

This chapter examines how AI-intensive warehousing reshapes operational skills as autonomous mobile robots (AMRs) and AI-driven decision systems become embedded in high-throughput fulfilment. Moving beyond substitution narratives, it conceptualises automation as task re-bundling that creates hybrid roles and redefines competence through data-mediated performance. Drawing on an anonymised case of a large 3PL centre scaling AMRs over several years, the analysis shows that expertise now centres on interpreting system signals, coordinating human–machine handoffs, and managing exceptions to sustain flow under uncertainty. Algorithmic orchestration redistributes authority via stratified override rights and audit trails, reshaping accountability and learning incentives. The chapter theorises skill transformation as a reconfiguration of task boundaries, governance structures, and learning pathways, with implications for inclusive upgrading and responsible automation in logistics.

DOI: 10.4018/979-8-3373-7826-8.ch008

1. INTRODUCTION

Artificial intelligence (AI) and advanced automation are increasingly reshaping warehousing, a core operational node of contemporary logistics systems. Across many fulfilment environments, autonomous mobile robots (AMRs), robotic picking solutions, and AI-enabled decision-support tools are deployed to increase throughput, accuracy, and scalability, while enabling more responsive orchestration of inventory and order flows (Lam et al., 2024; Ekren et al., 2026). Yet the most consequential implications of these technologies are not confined to technical performance. They materialise in the labour process: how tasks are decomposed and recombined, how competence is defined and evaluated, and how decision-making authority is redistributed in day-to-day operations. Despite extensive discussion of "automation replacing jobs," evidence from the broader technology–employment literature indicates that employment and skill effects are uneven and contingent, shaped by task content and organisational redesign rather than by technology adoption per se (Montobbio et al., 2024a; Montobbio et al., 2024b). Warehousing is therefore a strategically important setting for re-examining how AI alters work, because it is simultaneously labour-intensive, measurement-driven, and increasingly governed through digital infrastructures.

The chapter's rationale is grounded in a gap between how AI-enabled warehousing is commonly framed and how it is experienced organisationally. In industry and policy discourse, warehouse automation is often presented as a relatively direct substitution of manual labour, implying that the central workforce challenge is displacement. However, research on smart warehousing readiness suggests that outcomes hinge on organisational conditions such as trust, acceptance, and preparedness for new work arrangements, implying that workforce transition is a governance and learning problem as much as a technical one (Mahroof, 2019; Gupta et al., 2022). In parallel, scholarship on decision support and knowledge infrastructures anticipates operational contexts in which work is increasingly enacted through data systems, dashboards, and algorithmic recommendations, thereby redefining what "competence" means at the point of execution (Nemati et al., 2002; Hamilton et al., 2024). Finally, logistics digital transformation and ecosystem perspectives indicate that warehousing is becoming more tightly integrated into platform-mediated operating models, where performance is governed through visibility, traceability, and auditability across organisational boundaries (Nicoletti & Appolloni, 2025; Saqib & Qin, 2024). Taken together, these strands motivate a more critical question: not whether automation removes work, but how it recomposes work—shifting the centre of operational expertise toward system-facing coordination, exception handling, and new accountability regimes.

Accordingly, the aim of this chapter is to explain how AI-intensive warehousing transforms operational skills through the recomposition of tasks, competence criteria, and authority relations. Using an anonymised case of a high-throughput fulfilment centre within a large global 3PL network that scaled AMR deployments over multiple years, the chapter examines five interrelated dynamics: task reconfiguration into hybrid roles, data-mediated operational competence, exception handling as a central locus of judgement, redistribution of authority and accountability through algorithmically mediated governance, and the learning and occupational identity transitions that condition whether skill upgrading is inclusive or polarised (Wu & Tai, 2024; Lopes et al., 2025; Montobbio et al., 2024a). By connecting these dynamics, the chapter contributes to debates on human–machine complementarity by showing that skill transformation is not merely additive; it is a reconstitution of task boundaries, oversight structures, and learning pathways.

The remainder of the chapter is organised as follows. Section 2 develops the conceptual background and positions AI-intensive warehousing within task-based automation, digital transformation, and capability-oriented perspectives. Section 3 introduces the research setting and then presents the case findings, each aligned with the core mechanisms developed in Section 2 and interpreted through the literature. Section 4 concludes by synthesising the chapter's theoretical implications for understanding skill recomposition and by outlining practical implications for managing AI-intensive warehousing transitions responsibly and effectively.

2. LITERATURE BACKGROUND

This section develops an integrated conceptual lens for examining how AI-intensive warehousing reshapes employment and skills through skill recomposition rather than straightforward labour substitution. The review is organised as a cumulative argument: it first positions AI-intensive warehousing within broader logistics digital transformation and future-of-work debates, then elaborates five mechanisms through which work is reconstituted—task re-bundling, data-mediated competence, exception-centred expertise, redistributed authority/accountability, and learning and identity transitions. The intent is not to treat these mechanisms as separate themes, but as interdependent dynamics that unfold together as automation scales and becomes embedded in operational governance.

2.1. Background and positioning of the study

This chapter is positioned at the intersection of three literatures that have often advanced in parallel: research on technology–employment dynamics and occupational change, scholarship on logistics digital transformation and smart warehousing, and capability-oriented work in supply chains that explains how firms learn, coordinate, and manage risk during major transitions. First, task-based evidence on labour-saving automation suggests that the employment effects of new technologies should be traced through how tasks are reorganised within occupations rather than inferred from job titles alone (Montobbio et al., 2024a), while broader syntheses caution that impacts on employment and skills vary across settings because they are mediated by organisational redesign, complementary investments, and institutional conditions (Montobbio et al., 2024b). Second, logistics digital transformation research depicts the sector's performance frontier as increasingly data-driven, with warehousing a focal operational site where digital tools reshape coordination, decision-making, and measurement (Lam et al., 2024). Within this transformation, smart warehousing readiness studies emphasise that workforce preparedness, acceptance, and human-centric organisational conditions are decisive for whether technology becomes enabling or destabilising (Mahroof, 2019), an argument amplified by the emerging "Warehousing 5.0" agenda that foregrounds human-centred, sustainable, and resilient design principles in future warehousing systems (Ekren et al., 2026). Third, ecosystem-level accounts of digital transformation suggest that warehousing is increasingly embedded in integrated operating models that connect actors, platforms, and standards across logistics networks, with implications for governance, visibility, and skill requirements (Nicoletti & Appolloni, 2025). The practical relevance of these shifts is sharpened by empirical work linking digital innovations to sustainable logistics operations (Saqib & Qin, 2024) and by applied studies demonstrating how AI-enabled warehousing management changes operational routines and decision environments in specific contexts (Hamilton et al., 2024; Wu & Tai, 2024).

At the same time, a capability lens highlights that sustaining AI-intensive operations requires more than technology deployment; it depends on how organisations develop relational and organisational capabilities to integrate digital technologies, coordinate across functions and partners, and avoid defensive reasoning that can block learning under pressure. Evidence on digital technology integration and relational capability building points to the importance of coordination and shared routines in realising performance outcomes (Tanveer et al., 2026), while research on circular transitions underscores that learning can be constrained by defensive reasoning even when formal change initiatives exist (Ishaq et al., 2025). Related work on procurement's role in enabling circular business models and on the moderating role of dynamic supply chain management practices in sustainability-related risks further reinforces that transitions are shaped by governance routines and adaptive practices that condition both performance and the distribution of burdens across roles (Tanveer et al., 2024; Ngo et al., 2024). Finally, competency-focused studies in adjacent logistics domains show that digitisation pressures are already reshaping what is defined as "essential competence," particularly around digital, analytic, and coordination capabilities (Lopes et al., 2025). Anchoring the chapter in these combined strands allows the case analysis to treat skill change as an organisationally produced recomposition of tasks, data practices, authority relations, and learning pathways—rather than as an inevitable, linear consequence of automation.

2.2. Task reconfiguration under AI-intensive warehousing

AI-intensive warehousing transforms work most consequentially through the rebundling of tasks rather than the wholesale removal of jobs. Task-based research on labour-saving automation stresses that exposure to automation is best understood by examining which task components within occupations are susceptible to codification and mechanisation, and which components remain dependent on situated judgement or coordination (Montobbio et al., 2024a). This insight is directly applicable to warehouses, where operational roles commonly combine physical execution with local coordination, informal problem solving, and quality vigilance. When autonomous mobile robots, robotic picking systems, and AI-enabled allocation tools are introduced, they typically target routinised fragments—such as repetitive transport, standardised picking sequences, or deterministic routing—while leaving intact, or even amplifying, the complementary work needed to sustain flow. Consequently, work is not simply "reduced"; it is reorganised into new task constellations in which some activities are automated, others are residualised, and others newly emerge.

The empirics of technology, employment, and occupations further caution that outcomes depend on how organisations redesign jobs and restructure operational processes, not merely on the technical properties of the technology itself (Montobbio et al., 2024b). In warehousing, this organisational mediation is especially pronounced because performance is produced by tightly coupled flows. A change in one segment (e.g., automated picking) reverberates across replenishment, slotting, staging, quality checks, and dispatch. Automation therefore generates additional coordination work: maintaining alignment between physical stock and system records, resolving mismatches between automated instructions and real constraints, and synchronising human labour around automated "cells" or robot pathways. Warehousing 5.0 discussions reinforce this systems logic by framing the future warehouse as a socio-technical configuration in which technologies, processes, and human roles co-evolve, and where human-centric design is part of operational architecture rather than a peripheral concern (Ekren et al., 2026).

Digital transformation scholarship in logistics similarly portrays performance improvement as a process redesign project rather than a tool replacement exercise (Lam et al., 2024). For AI-intensive warehouses, the key analytical issue is how task boundaries are redrawn: which elements become system-driven, which become supervisory, which become exception-oriented, and which remain manual due to variability, cost, or risk. Competency work in other logistics domains indicates that digitalisation pressures can reshape role expectations and widen differentiation between digitally proximate and digitally peripheral work (Lopes et al., 2025). This task recomposition also occurs within broader ecosystem architectures where operating models and platform interfaces shape what is automated, what is standardised, and what remains locally contingent (Nicoletti & Appolloni, 2025). In short, task reconfiguration should be read as intertwined with the data infrastructures and governance arrangements that accompany AI adoption (Nemati et al., 2002; Hamilton et al., 2024), and with the organisational capabilities required to coordinate change without reinforcing defensive responses or risk amplification (Tanveer et al., 2026; Ishaq et al., 2025; Tanveer et al., 2024; Ngo et al., 2024; Saqib & Qin, 2024; Wu & Tai, 2024).

2.3. Data-mediated operational competence

As warehouses become AI-intensive, operational competence is increasingly enacted through data-mediated performance rather than solely through physical speed or manual accuracy. Early foundations in the integration of decision support, AI, knowledge management, and data warehousing anticipated organisational settings in which work is organised through codified information infrastructures and analytic routines (Nemati et al., 2002). In contemporary warehousing, such infrastructures are materialised in dashboards, dynamic allocation engines, exception alerts, predictive signals, and real-time metrics that translate operational flows into digital representations. This translation embeds decision logics and prioritisation rules, shaping what is visible, what is actionable, and what is judged as competent.

Logistics digital transformation research emphasises that performance improvements increasingly rely on data-driven coordination and analytic decision-making (Lam et al., 2024). In warehouses, this implies that competence increasingly entails the capacity to interpret system outputs, understand what the metrics are actually measuring, and act appropriately under algorithmic constraints. Workers and supervisors must navigate a practical dilemma: the system offers standardisation, yet operational reality contains variability and ambiguity. Data-mediated competence therefore includes recognising when the system is reliable, when inputs (e.g., scanning, labelling, data capture) have degraded, and when escalation is required. The integration of external AI into firm-wide warehousing solutions heightens this requirement, because it introduces additional layers of model-driven logic, integration complexity, and governance obligations that operational actors must accommodate even when the system's internal reasoning is opaque (Hamilton et al., 2024). Ecosystem-level operating models further intensify these demands by expanding the number of interfaces and data dependencies that shape warehouse work and performance visibility (Nicoletti & Appolloni, 2025).

Applied studies underscore the breadth of AI-enabled decision-making in warehousing. AI-based quality and warehousing management for inbound logistics demonstrates how classification and allocation decisions can be delegated to AI routines, positioning humans as validators and handlers of ambiguous cases (Wu & Tai, 2024). Sustainability-oriented research adds that digital innovations can support sustainable logistics operations, implying that data-mediated competence also involves traceability, documentation, and compliance-related routines that reshape day-to-day work (Saqib & Qin, 2024). Readiness frameworks for digitising logistics operations indicate that these competences require deliberate HR and organisational investment rather than being assumed as automatic by-products of technology acquisition (Gupta et al., 2022), while competency research in adjacent logistics sectors shows that digitalisation reshapes what is expected from operational personnel, particularly around data literacy, systems interaction, and coordination (Lopes et al., 2025). Because automation exposure varies by task, the significance of data-mediated competence also depends on how work is re-bundled and which workers gain access to system-facing activities (Montobbio et al., 2024a; Montobbio et al., 2024b). These competence shifts are further conditioned by organisational learning dynamics and relational capability building during digital integration (Mahroof, 2019; Ekren et al., 2026; Tanveer et al., 2026; Ishaq et al., 2025; Tanveer et al., 2024; Ngo et al., 2024).

2.4. Exception handling and human judgement

A central paradox of AI-intensive warehousing is that as routine components are automated or stabilised, exceptions become more consequential and human judgement becomes more valuable. Task-based automation research implies that technologies most readily displace predictable, codifiable task elements, leaving behind—or amplifying—work characterised by variability, ambiguity, and context dependence (Montobbio et al., 2024a). Warehouses are variability-rich: inbound quality fluctuates, packaging conditions vary, inventory records drift, equipment fails, and demand patterns shift. Under AI-intensive configurations, the operational costs of disruptions can rise because throughput is increasingly produced by tightly coupled, high-velocity processes; small anomalies can propagate rapidly through interconnected subsystems.

The wider evidence base suggests that organisational outcomes depend on how firms manage residual non-routine tasks once technologies reorganise work (Montobbio et al., 2024b). In AI-intensive warehouses, exception handling is therefore not peripheral "troubleshooting" but an organising competence that sustains system performance. Decision-support infrastructures can improve detection and triage, yet they can also generate new classes of exceptions tied to data quality, model limitations, or integration faults (Nemati et al., 2002). When systems route tasks based on imperfect data or misclassify inputs, operational actors must recognise the mismatch, diagnose its origin, and restore flow through interventions and escalation routines.

Research on integrating external AI into smart dynamic warehousing further implies that exception handling expands beyond physical anomalies to include digital anomalies—conflicting system recommendations, non-intuitive optimisation outcomes, or edge cases where standard logic produces undesirable consequences (Hamilton et al., 2024). AI-based warehousing management in inbound contexts similarly indicates that classification and allocation routines remain vulnerable to ambiguous inputs, requiring humans to validate outputs and manage uncertainty (Wu & Tai, 2024). Sustainability-oriented digital innovation research heightens the significance of exceptions because deviations can threaten compliance, traceability, and waste-reduction objectives, making judgement a form of operational risk management (Saqib & Qin, 2024). The ability to sustain such judgement-intensive work is shaped by readiness and human-centric organisational conditions, including how workers perceive technology, the legitimacy of escalation practices, and the support provided for learning (Mahroof, 2019; Gupta et al., 2022; Ekren et al., 2026). Competency agendas emphasise that exception expertise is a composite capability—technical-system literacy, operational domain knowledge, and coordination—already recognised as increasingly critical across logistics contexts (Lopes et al., 2025), and it is further conditioned by relational and organisational capabilities that either enable or block sustained learning under transition pressures (Tanveer et al., 2026; Ishaq et al., 2025; Tanveer et al., 2024; Ngo et al., 2024; Nicoletti & Appolloni, 2025).

2.5. Authority and accountability redistribution

AI-intensive warehousing redistributes authority and accountability by relocating decision-making into algorithmic systems while keeping humans responsible for outcomes. In integrated decision-support environments, the locus of "knowing" and "deciding" shifts toward codified rules, optimisation logics, and system-generated recommendations (Nemati et al., 2002). Discretion increasingly concerns whether to follow system guidance, when to override it, and how to justify deviations in environments where deviations may be auditable and performance is continuously measured.

Technology–occupation research emphasises that organisational mediation shapes how automation affects authority structures, because task redesign alters who controls sequencing, evaluation, and error attribution (Montobbio et al., 2024b). In warehouses, robotics and AI scheduling can centralise control through dashboards and algorithmic allocation, narrowing frontline discretion while intensifying monitoring. At the same time, automation can create new authoritative roles—system coordinators or exception managers—whose legitimacy derives from system literacy and the ability to translate digital signals into operational interventions. Warehousing 5.0 perspectives sharpen the normative stakes by arguing that human-centric design must include fair responsibility allocation and safe, transparent socio-technical governance (Ekren et al., 2026).

The governance challenge is compounded when external AI is integrated into internal warehousing systems, because decision logic may be partially opaque and shaped by multiple actors (vendors, IT teams, operations leaders) (Hamilton et al., 2024). This creates a risk of "responsibility without authority," where frontline workers are held accountable for outcomes they cannot meaningfully influence, such as model-driven allocations or system configurations. Ecosystem-level transformation models similarly suggest that authority can be distributed across interfaces and platforms, embedding external constraints into internal warehouse operations and diffusing accountability (Nicoletti & Appolloni, 2025). Sustainability-focused digital innovation adds accountability pressures because performance may be evaluated not only through cost and speed but also through compliance and traceability regimes that require disciplined data practices (Saqib & Qin, 2024). These accountability dynamics feed back into task recomposition and competence development: they influence who is trained, who is authorised to override, and how exception work is recognised and rewarded (Montobbio et al., 2024a; Lam et al., 2024; Mahroof, 2019; Gupta et al., 2022; Lopes et al., 2025; Wu & Tai, 2024).

Capability-oriented supply chain research further suggests that authority and accountability arrangements are stabilised (or destabilised) through learning routines and relational governance mechanisms. Evidence on digital technology integration points to the role of relational capability building in sustaining coordinated action under digital transformation (Tanveer et al., 2026), while work on defensive reasoning in circular transitions highlights how blame dynamics and risk-avoidant routines can obstruct learning and reinforce inequitable responsibility allocation (Ishaq et al., 2025). Procurement-centred and risk-focused studies similarly indicate that adaptive routines condition how organisations distribute and manage responsibilities under sustainability and performance pressures (Tanveer et al., 2024; Ngo et al., 2024). Finally, decision-rights redistribution is inseparable from the knowledge infrastructures that structure what is seen and acted upon, returning attention to the socio-technical nature of decision support in AI-intensive operations (Nemati et al., 2002).

3. CASE STUDY

This chapter draws on an anonymised focal case from a large, globally operating third-party logistics (3PL) provider that manages multi-client warehousing and fulfilment operations across a distributed network of facilities.

3.1. Case setting

The case concerns a high-throughput fulfilment centre that underwent a multi-year automation trajectory centred on the deployment and scaling of autonomous mobile robots (AMRs) integrated with warehouse management and labour orchestration systems. The organisation implemented AMRs through a strategic partnership with a specialist robotics provider, using the technology primarily to augment order picking and internal transport activities while progressively embedding system-based coordination and performance governance into daily operations. To protect confidentiality, organisational names, facility identifiers, customer sectors, and precise deployment figures are withheld; the case is presented as a theoretically representative instance of AI-intensive warehousing rather than as an evaluative account of a specific firm.

The case is theoretically useful because it sits at the intersection of three conditions that make skill recomposition observable with clarity. First, as a 3PL operating in a contract logistics context, the fulfilment centre is structurally exposed to fluctuating demand profiles, diverse product and packaging characteristics, and heterogeneous service-level requirements. This operational variability foregrounds the limits of routinised automation and elevates the importance of exception handling and situated judgement, making it possible to trace how "non-routine" work becomes central as automation scales. Second, the facility's automation pathway is not defined by a single "big bang" replacement of labour but by staged integration and scaling of AMRs within a broader socio-technical system. This makes it analytically appropriate for examining task re-bundling and the emergence of hybrid roles in which residual manual work, system supervision, and coordination labour are recombined rather than cleanly separated.

Third, the case provides a strong setting for analysing data-mediated operational competence and shifting authority because AMR deployments require tight coupling between physical movement, digital work allocation, and performance measurement. As AMR-enabled workflows expand, operational decisions are increasingly enacted through dashboards, alerts, and system recommendations, which reshapes what counts as competence and redistributes decision rights—particularly around when workers can deviate from system instructions, when overrides are legitimate, and how responsibility is attributed when disruptions occur. The facility therefore offers a concentrated context for observing how algorithmically mediated work reorganises accountability and how workers navigate the resulting identity transitions as competence becomes defined through system-facing performance and exception stewardship.

3.2. Task reconfiguration under AI-intensive warehousing

The introduction and scaling of AMRs in the focal fulfilment centre generated a marked reconfiguration of warehouse work that was best captured as a re-bundling of tasks into hybrid role profiles, rather than a linear reduction of labour. Prior to automation intensification, operational roles were organised around physically continuous task sequences—walking-intensive picking, manual internal transport, and locally coordinated replenishment. As AMRs were integrated, these sequences were decomposed and recomposed. Walking and transport components were progressively externalised to robots, while human work was repositioned toward pick execution at interfaces, micro-coordination of robot–human handoffs, and the maintenance of "flow continuity" across zones. In practice, this meant that the facility did not converge on a simple binary of "automated vs. manual" work; instead, it produced hybrid roles that combined residual manual handling with system-facing coordination and safety oversight, consistent with the view that automation exposure and occupational change are uneven and task-specific (Montobbio et al., 2024a; Montobbio et al., 2024b).

A central empirical pattern was the emergence of residual tasks that were not eliminated but reclassified as critical "support" work: managing packaging variability, handling atypical items that failed to fit automated routines, performing ad hoc quality checks, and executing local rework when digital instructions conflicted with physical conditions. These residual activities were not marginal; they became strategically consequential because the performance gains promised by automation were contingent on sustained throughput stability. This aligns with the Warehousing 5.0 framing that future warehousing performance depends on socio-technical redesign in which human work remains integral to resilience and safety (Ekren et al., 2026). Yet the case also highlighted a more critical implication: residual tasks were often less visible within formal performance metrics and therefore at risk of being undervalued, echoing human-centric readiness concerns about whether organisational arrangements recognise and support new forms of work as legitimate expertise (Mahroof, 2019).

In parallel, coordination work expanded and became more granular. The introduction of AMRs altered handoff points, timing, and dependencies between zones, requiring new coordination routines around queue management, congestion avoidance, and prioritisation during demand spikes. Rather than being a purely technical change, this reconfiguration embedded the warehouse more deeply into integrated operating models and performance regimes, where orchestration logic increasingly reflected cross-client service commitments and platform-mediated standards typical of advanced logistics ecosystems (Nicoletti & Appolloni, 2025; Lam et al., 2024). The resulting coordination labour required workers to interact with system-generated task allocations and to negotiate local adaptations within those constraints, highlighting that task redesign and competence requirements co-evolve.

The re-bundling of tasks also interacted with capability development and organisational learning dynamics. The facility's ability to stabilise hybrid roles depended on cross-functional coordination between operations, maintenance/engineering, and IT-facing support, a pattern consistent with arguments that digital integration outcomes are shaped by relational and organisational capabilities rather than technology alone (Tanveer et al., 2026). Where coordination routines were well established, role recomposition created viable pathways for workers to shift into system-facing functions; where routines were weak or contested, task reconfiguration risked producing work intensification and defensive responses that constrained adaptation (Ishaq et al., 2025). In addition, the redefinition of work bundles intersected with broader sustainability and risk considerations. Digital innovation in logistics is increasingly evaluated through sustainability-related operational objectives, which in this case translated into heightened attention to traceability, waste prevention, and data discipline around returns and damaged goods—areas where residual manual work remained essential (Saqib & Qin, 2024; Ngo et al., 2024). Competency discussions in logistics domains similarly anticipate that task reconfiguration will elevate coordination and digital competences as baseline expectations for operational roles (Gupta et al., 2022; Lopes et al., 2025). Finally, the facility's re-bundling dynamics were enabled by the coupling of AMRs with decision-support and data infrastructures that structure work allocation and monitoring, reflecting foundational insights about the integration of AI and data systems in operational environments (Nemati et al., 2002) and contemporary observations on embedding external AI components into warehouse solutions (Hamilton et al., 2024). In this sense, the case illustrates how AMR adoption recomposes work through hybridisation: humans remain central, but the content of that centrality shifts toward coordination-intensive, system-adjacent labour.

3.3. Data-mediated operational competence

A second, closely linked pattern in the focal case was the redefinition of operational competence through data-mediated work. As AMRs scaled, the warehouse increasingly operated as a coupled physical–digital system in which performance was enacted through dashboards, alerts, and algorithmically informed work allocation. Operational actors—both frontline and supervisory—were required to read and respond to system signals, not only to execute tasks. Competence thus became visible in the ability to interpret performance indicators, diagnose anomalies in system outputs, and sustain data integrity through disciplined scanning and exception documentation. This empirical shift is consistent with the long-standing proposition that decision-support environments reorganise work by integrating data warehousing, AI, and knowledge infrastructures that shape what can be known and acted upon (Nemati et al., 2002).

In practice, the facility's daily rhythms were increasingly anchored in system cues: task queues, robot utilisation metrics, pick rate indicators, backlog heatmaps, and exception alerts. Workers who could translate these cues into action—adjusting sequencing, coordinating short-term reallocations, or initiating escalation—were positioned as high-value contributors. This competence was not reducible to general "digital literacy." It combined (i) operational domain knowledge of how flow should behave, (ii) interpretive ability to infer what a signal meant in context, and (iii) communicative competence to coordinate with adjacent functions under time pressure. The facility thereby exemplified how logistics digital transformation tends to produce performance regimes in which operational effectiveness depends on data-driven coordination and analytics-enabled control (Lam et al., 2024).

The case also demonstrated that data-mediated competence is shaped by integration complexity. Because AMRs were embedded through a partnership with a specialised robotics provider, operational actors routinely encountered situations where system behaviour depended on interfaces across platforms (e.g., WMS, labour management, robotics control). This amplified the need for workers to understand "where the signal comes from" and what could be changed locally versus what required technical intervention, paralleling concerns raised in research on incorporating external AI into internal, firm-wide warehousing solutions (Hamilton et al., 2024). Moreover, the warehouse's operating model was influenced by multi-client service commitments and cross-organisational performance reporting, reinforcing the ecosystem argument that digital transformation increasingly entails integrated operations models that distribute visibility, standards, and constraints across networks (Nicoletti & Appolloni, 2025).

A further empirical implication concerned the relationship between data-mediated competence and sustainability-linked operational governance. The facility's performance monitoring increasingly encompassed not only speed and accuracy but also traceability and error documentation. This resonates with findings that digital innovations can support sustainable logistics operations, but also intensify demands for disciplined information practices that make processes auditable and compliant (Saqib & Qin, 2024). Relatedly, the case suggests that data-mediated competence should be treated as a risk-management capability: maintaining data quality reduced downstream disruptions and supported more stable service performance under sustainability-related constraints, consistent with research emphasising the role of dynamic practices in moderating sustainability-related risks and performance outcomes (Ngo et al., 2024).

From a workforce development perspective, the observed competence shift substantiates arguments that digitisation readiness depends on intentional human resource development rather than technology acquisition alone (Gupta et al., 2022). The facility's internal differentiation between workers who could operate effectively through dashboards and those who remained confined to residual manual tasks mirrored sectoral competency discussions highlighting the growing centrality of digital, analytic, and coordination competencies across logistics domains (Lopes et al., 2025). Yet the case also foregrounded a critical tension: data-mediated performance regimes can inadvertently devalue tacit competence that is not easily represented in standard metrics, reinforcing concerns raised in human-centric readiness research about legitimacy, acceptance, and perceived fairness under smart warehousing transitions (Mahroof, 2019). Capability-oriented work further illuminates why this tension matters: sustaining data-mediated performance required cross-functional routines and relational coordination, and was vulnerable to defensive reasoning that could inhibit knowledge sharing or escalate blame (Tanveer et al., 2026; Ishaq et al., 2025; Tanveer et al., 2024). Finally, the case aligns with applied warehousing research showing that AI-enabled management systems reposition humans as monitors and validators who handle ambiguity at the edges of algorithmic routines (Wu & Tai, 2024), while also reflecting the broader labour-market logic that the shifting task composition of occupations produces uneven opportunities for skill upgrading (Montobbio et al., 2024a; Montobbio et al., 2024b). Overall, the focal case demonstrates that AI-intensive warehousing redefines competence through data-mediated orchestration, making interpretive, coordination, and system-facing skills core to operational performance.

3.4. Exception handling and human judgement

The third pattern concerns the centrality of exception handling as the operational locus where human judgement remained indispensable. As AMR-enabled routines stabilised portions of picking and transport, the facility's performance increasingly hinged on the identification, diagnosis, and resolution of disruptions that fell outside standardised flows. Exceptions were not rare anomalies; they were recurrent features of high-velocity operations, arising from item variability, packaging damage, data misalignment, robot congestion, or interface mismatches between systems. This observation supports a critical implication of task-based automation accounts: as technologies automate predictable components, the remaining work tends to concentrate in variability, ambiguity, and context-dependent judgement (Montobbio et al., 2024a).

Empirically, the facility institutionalised escalation routines that translated exception events into coordinated interventions. Frontline workers were expected to classify issues (e.g., item not found, mis-scan, robot unable to complete a route, unsafe congestion) and to trigger appropriate pathways—local correction, supervisor escalation, technical support, or quarantine/rework. Over time, competence was increasingly evaluated by how effectively individuals could keep flow moving under uncertainty. This aligns with broader evidence that employment and skill outcomes of new technologies depend on organisational redesign and the management of residual non-routine work, rather than on automation capacity alone (Montobbio et al., 2024b).

The case also illustrates how exceptions are shaped by data and platform integration. Many disruptions were "hybrid" in the sense that they originated at the interface between physical reality and digital representation: inventory accuracy problems, latency in task updates, or conflicting recommendations across systems. Such phenomena are consistent with foundational insights that decision-support and knowledge infrastructures create new dependencies on data quality and integration fidelity, thereby generating new categories of operational problems alongside their solutions (Nemati et al., 2002). Contemporary work on adding external AI into firm-wide warehousing solutions similarly anticipates that integration complexity can introduce novel failure modes that require organisational routines for diagnosis and recovery (Hamilton et al., 2024). Applied studies of AI-enabled warehousing management also reinforce that algorithmic routines can be effective while remaining vulnerable to ambiguous inputs, positioning humans as the handlers of uncertainty (Wu & Tai, 2024).

Exception handling in the focal facility was further intensified by sustainability-related and risk-governance pressures. Deviations were not only operational inconveniences; they had implications for traceability, waste reduction, and customer accountability, which meant that exception documentation and corrective action were increasingly formalised. This resonates with the argument that digital innovations can enhance sustainable logistics operations while simultaneously expanding information and compliance demands on operational workers (Saqib & Qin, 2024). Sustainability-related risk research further suggests that such pressures can amplify the consequences of disruptions and elevate the value of dynamic management practices that stabilise performance under uncertainty (Ngo et al., 2024). In this setting, exception competence functioned as a practical risk-mitigation capability.

The case also underscores the human-centric and learning dimensions of exception work. Workers' willingness to escalate issues, admit uncertainty, and share corrective knowledge depended on trust and perceived fairness in how exceptions were treated—whether they were framed as learning opportunities or as individual failures. This tension connects directly to human-centric readiness findings that emphasise perception, acceptance, and organisational preparedness in smart warehousing transitions (Mahroof, 2019), as well as to Warehousing 5.0 arguments that resilient, human-centred warehousing requires institutionalising safety, learning, and meaningful roles rather than intensifying surveillance and blame (Ekren et al., 2026). Readiness and competency frameworks further imply that exception handling is not an ad hoc talent but a developable competence that should be embedded in workforce development architectures (Gupta et al., 2022; Lopes et al., 2025).

Finally, the facility's exception practices were shaped by broader governance and capability-building dynamics. Integrated operating models and platform dependencies can relocate where disruptions originate and how quickly they can be resolved, making exception work partly contingent on cross-organisational interfaces and standards (Nicoletti & Appolloni, 2025; Lam et al., 2024). Capability research suggests that organisations that develop relational routines for digital integration are better able to institutionalise effective escalation, whereas defensive reasoning can block the sharing of failure information and inhibit adaptation (Tanveer et al., 2026; Ishaq et al., 2025). Related work on procurement and circular business models further indicates that cross-functional coordination routines can be decisive for translating disruptions into organisational learning rather than into fragmented blame (Tanveer et al., 2024). In sum, the focal case demonstrates that AI-intensive warehousing elevates exception handling into a core operational skill, revealing how human judgement becomes the practical anchor of performance when automation intensifies.

3.5. Authority and accountability redistribution

The final pattern concerns how AMR-enabled orchestration redistributed authority and accountability within the warehouse. As work allocation and performance monitoring became increasingly system-mediated, decision rights shifted from local discretion toward algorithmically structured guidance, while responsibility for outcomes remained anchored in human roles. Operational actors were required to follow system-generated task sequences, yet also to intervene when system instructions produced friction or risk. This produced a distinctive governance tension: the system became the default authority for "what should happen," but humans remained accountable for "what actually happened," particularly when deviations were recorded and auditable.

The case revealed that override rights were stratified. Frontline workers could execute limited local corrections (e.g., re-scans, short reroutes, minor substitutions) but were expected to escalate broader deviations. Supervisors and designated system-facing coordinators held greater authority to reallocate labour, pause zones, or trigger technical interventions, while IT/engineering functions controlled deeper configuration changes. This stratification mirrors foundational arguments that integrated decision-support environments reorganise authority by embedding knowledge, rules, and prioritisation within information infrastructures, thereby shaping how discretion is distributed and legitimised (Nemati et al., 2002). It also resonates with research on external AI integration in warehousing, which suggests that multi-layered systems can increase opacity and shift practical control toward those who can interpret and negotiate platform interfaces (Hamilton et al., 2024).

Accountability in the focal facility was increasingly exercised through audit trails and metric visibility. Exceptions, overrides, and deviations were logged, allowing performance and compliance to be evaluated retrospectively. Such auditability strengthened consistency and traceability, but it also intensified attribution dynamics—how errors were assigned to individuals versus systems, and how responsibility was negotiated when failures emerged from integration issues rather than from individual negligence. This connects with the broader observation that digital transformation in logistics often expands measurement and governance regimes, thereby reshaping not only processes but also labour relations and perceptions of fairness (Lam et al., 2024). The case further suggests that the governance implications of auditability are amplified in integrated operating models where performance reporting and standards are shaped by ecosystem-level interfaces (Nicoletti & Appolloni, 2025).

A critical insight from the case is that authority redistribution was not purely top-down; it was also socially negotiated through readiness conditions and learning routines. Where workers perceived the system as reliable and supportive, compliance and escalation behaviours were relatively stable. Where they perceived system guidance as misaligned with operational realities, they developed informal workaround practices—sometimes productive, sometimes risky—highlighting the human-centric concern that smart warehousing transitions depend on acceptance, trust, and credible governance arrangements (Mahroof, 2019). Warehousing 5.0 discussions reinforce that human-centric design must include transparent responsibility allocation and safe escalation structures, otherwise automation can intensify surveillance and blame without strengthening resilience (Ekren et al., 2026).

The case also highlights how authority and accountability are intertwined with skill development and capability building. As competence became system-facing, workers who developed data-mediated interpretive skills gained informal authority even when formal decision rights remained constrained, reflecting competency agendas that emphasise digital and analytic capabilities as increasingly essential for logistics roles (Lopes et al., 2025) and readiness frameworks that emphasise HR development for digitisation (Gupta et al., 2022). Conversely, workers concentrated in residual manual tasks experienced reduced influence over system-governed performance outcomes, raising the risk of polarised trajectories consistent with task-based accounts of uneven occupational exposure (Montobbio et al., 2024a; Montobbio et al., 2024b).

Finally, capability-oriented supply chain research helps explain why accountability arrangements stabilised in some areas but remained contested in others. Digital integration benefits are more likely to be realised when relational capabilities and cross-functional routines support coordinated action and shared problem solving (Tanveer et al., 2026). Where defensive reasoning dominated, errors became politicised and learning was inhibited, echoing findings on how defensive reasoning can constrain capability development in major transitions (Ishaq et al., 2025). Related evidence on procurement's role in organisational change and on dynamic practices in managing sustainability-related risks suggests that governance routines can moderate whether accountability becomes a learning device or a blame mechanism (Tanveer et al., 2024; Ngo et al., 2024). In addition, sustainability-oriented digital innovation underscores that auditability and traceability increasingly serve broader societal and compliance objectives, thereby raising the stakes of responsible override and error attribution (Saqib & Qin, 2024). In sum, the focal case shows that AI-intensive warehousing redistributes authority through system-mediated orchestration while intensifying accountability through auditability, making governance a central dimension of skill recomposition.

4. CONCLUSION

This chapter examined how AI-intensive warehousing recomposes operational skills through a sustained automation trajectory in an anonymised high-throughput fulfilment centre. The analysis showed that AMR-centred automation does not primarily reduce work in a linear manner; instead, it re-bundles tasks into hybrid roles, elevates data-mediated competence, makes exception handling the practical locus of expertise, and redistributes authority and accountability through increasingly auditable, system-mediated governance. Taken together, these dynamics demonstrate that workforce change in smart warehousing is best understood as a socio-technical reconfiguration of work content, performance criteria, and learning pathways.

4.1. Theoretical implications

This chapter contributes theoretically by repositioning AI-intensive warehousing as a site of skill recomposition in which the core analytical object is the reconstitution of task boundaries, competence criteria, and governance relations rather than a simple substitution of labour. In doing so, it extends task-based accounts of labour-saving automation by showing how automation exposure materialises inside a warehouse labour process through staged re-bundling and hybrid role formation, with residual work becoming strategically consequential for sustaining throughput stability (Montobbio et al., 2024a; Montobbio et al., 2024b). The contribution is not merely to restate uneven exposure, but to specify the organisational mechanism through which unevenness is produced: the coupling of AMR-enabled routines with data infrastructures and orchestration systems that shift the operational centre of gravity from manual execution to system-mediated coordination and judgement. This mechanism clarifies why technology effects on skills cannot be inferred from the presence of robots alone; they depend on how socio-technical architectures reorganise work and allocate discretion.

Second, the chapter advances conceptual understanding of data-mediated operational competence by linking foundational ideas about decision support and knowledge infrastructures to contemporary smart warehousing practice. The case shows how competence is increasingly enacted through dashboards, alert regimes, and system-generated work allocation, thereby extending the relevance of integrated decision-support architectures to frontline operational work (Nemati et al., 2002). This provides a theoretically grounded account of how digital transformation in logistics reshapes performance regimes: operational expertise becomes inseparable from the ability to interpret system signals, maintain data integrity, and coordinate action across interdependent subsystems (Lam et al., 2024). By locating these dynamics within a 3PL fulfilment context, the chapter also contributes to ecosystem-oriented digital transformation scholarship by illustrating how integrated operating models and platform interfaces condition the content of work and the distribution of competence across roles (Nicoletti & Appolloni, 2025).

Third, the chapter strengthens debates on human–machine complementarity by specifying exception handling as the practical locus of human judgement under AI intensification. Rather than treating exceptions as residual anomalies, the case demonstrates that exceptions become structurally central as automation stabilises routine components, because the propagation costs of disruptions increase in tightly coupled, high-velocity systems. This insight reinforces and extends human-centric smart warehousing perspectives that foreground the importance of organisational readiness, trust, and human-centred design for resilient performance (Mahroof, 2019; Ekren et al., 2026). It also aligns with applied warehousing studies that show how AI-enabled systems reposition humans as validators and handlers of ambiguity at the edges of algorithmic routines, while broadening the theoretical interpretation by linking this repositioning to the recomposition of operational expertise and role legitimacy (Wu & Tai, 2024; Hamilton et al., 2024).

Fourth, the chapter contributes to theorising authority and accountability redistribution in algorithmically mediated work by tracing how auditability and override stratification reshape discretion, responsibility attribution, and learning incentives. This extends digital transformation accounts beyond performance improvement to reveal governance as a constitutive dimension of skill change: as work becomes system-mediated, competence includes navigating decision rights, executing legitimate overrides, and managing traceable deviations. The chapter thus complements competency and readiness frameworks that emphasise the need for deliberate workforce development in digitised logistics operations, while sharpening the theoretical point that the content of "essential competence" is partially produced by governance architectures and not only by technical requirements (Gupta et al., 2022; Lopes et al., 2025).

Finally, the chapter integrates a capability lens to explain why skill recomposition outcomes are contingent and potentially uneven. The case indicates that successful transitions depend on relational and organisational capabilities that stabilise cross-functional coordination, support knowledge sharing, and mitigate defensive reasoning that can block adaptation. This extends capability-focused insights on digital technology integration and transition dynamics into the warehousing domain by showing how capability development shapes whether hybrid roles become legitimate upgrading pathways or devolve into intensified control and polarised trajectories (Tanveer et al., 2026; Ishaq et al., 2025). Related evidence on procurement-enabled organisational change and on dynamic practices moderating sustainability-related risks further supports the argument that the organisational infrastructure for learning and coordination conditions both performance and the distribution of transition burdens across roles (Tanveer et al., 2024; Ngo et al., 2024). In this way, the chapter contributes a theoretically integrated account of AI-intensive warehousing that connects task-based automation, digital transformation governance, human-centric readiness, and capability-building as mutually reinforcing explanations of skill recomposition.

4.2. Practical implications

Practically, the chapter indicates that warehouse automation programmes should be managed as workforce redesign projects rather than as equipment upgrades. Managers should anticipate that AMR and AI adoption will not simply "remove walking" or "speed up picking," but will create hybrid roles that combine residual manual handling, safety oversight, system interaction, and coordination work. This implies that job descriptions, staffing models, and performance management systems need to be redesigned in parallel with automation deployment so that newly created coordination and recovery work is formally recognised, adequately resourced, and not treated as invisible "support." If organisations fail to legitimise this work, they risk throughput fragility because the residual and coordination tasks are precisely what stabilise automated flow.

A second implication is that capability development should be targeted toward data-mediated competence. Warehouses should treat dashboard interpretation, data integrity discipline, and signal-based coordination as core operational skills, and build structured pathways for workers to develop them. This includes practical training on how to diagnose data-quality problems, when and how to escalate, and how to translate performance indicators into operational actions without gaming metrics. Importantly, organisations should monitor whether access to system-facing tasks is equitably distributed; otherwise, automation can create a two-tier workforce in which some workers are upgraded into system-facing roles while others are confined to residual manual work with limited progression.

Third, organisations should deliberately design exception-handling architectures. Because exceptions become central under AI intensification, warehouses need clear escalation routines, psychologically safe reporting norms, and rapid cross-functional response mechanisms that prevent blame and support learning. Exception management should be treated as a professional competence with defined roles, rather than as informal heroics. This is especially important during ramp-up phases when integration issues and edge cases are most frequent.

Fourth, governance arrangements must be made explicit. As algorithmic orchestration increases auditability, warehouses should clarify who has authority to override systems, under what conditions, and how deviations should be documented. Transparent override rules reduce risky workarounds and help align operational reality with system logic. At the same time, accountability frameworks should distinguish between human error and system/integration failure so that auditability becomes a learning device rather than a blame mechanism.

Finally, the chapter suggests that responsible automation requires attention to worker identity transitions. Leaders should communicate credibly about how “skill” is being redefined and provide recognised pathways for advancement into coordination, supervision, and system-facing roles. Where possible, organisations should co-design training and role transitions with workers and supervisors to build trust in the new socio-technical regime. Doing so strengthens both performance outcomes and employment equity by ensuring that AI-intensive warehousing becomes a site of inclusive upgrading rather than polarised recomposition.

REFERENCES

Ekren, B. Y., Venkatadri, U., Sgarbossa, F., & Grosse, E. H. (2026). Warehousing 5.0 for the future of the logistics industry. *International Journal of Production Research, 64*(5), 1–11. DOI: 10.1080/00207543.2026.2617791

Gupta, A., Singh, R. K., & Gupta, S. (2022). Developing human resource for the digitization of logistics operations: Readiness index framework. *International Journal of Manpower, 43*(2), 355–379. DOI: 10.1108/IJM-03-2021-0175

Hamilton, J. R., Maxwell, S. J., Ali, S. A., & Tee, S. (2024). Adding external artificial intelligence (ai) into internal firm-wide smart dynamic warehousing solutions. *Sustainability (Basel), 16*(10), 3908. DOI: 10.3390/su16103908

Ishaq, S., Tanveer, U., Hoang, T. G., & Wamba Samuel, F. (2025). From Linear to Circular: Capabilities, Defensive Reasoning and Supply Chain Collaborations in Manufacturers' Circular Economy Transition. *British Journal of Management*, 1467-8551.12932. DOI: 10.1111/1467-8551.12932

Lam, H. Y., Tang, V., & Wong, L. (2024). Raising logistics performance to new levels through digital transformation. *International Journal of Engineering Business Management, 16*, 18479790241231730. DOI: 10.1177/18479790241231730

Lopes, L. S., Nabais, J. L., Pinto, C., Caldeirinha, V., & Pinho, T. (2025). Essential Competencies in Maritime and Port Logistics: A Study on the Current Needs of the Sector. *Sustainability (Basel), 17*(6), 2378. DOI: 10.3390/su17062378

Mahroof, K. (2019). A human-centric perspective exploring the readiness towards smart warehousing: The case of a large retail distribution warehouse. *International Journal of Information Management, 45*, 176–190. DOI: 10.1016/j.ijinfomgt.2018.11.008

Montobbio, F., Staccioli, J., Virgillito, M. E., & Vivarelli, M. (2024a). Labour-saving automation: A direct measure of occupational exposure. *World Economy, 47*(1), 332–361. DOI: 10.1111/twec.13522

Montobbio, F., Staccioli, J., Virgillito, M. E., & Vivarelli, M. (2024b). The empirics of technology, employment and occupations: Lessons learned and challenges ahead. *Journal of Economic Surveys, 38*(5), 1622–1655. DOI: 10.1111/joes.12601

Nemati, H. R., Steiger, D. M., Iyer, L. S., & Herschel, R. T. (2002). Knowledge warehouse: An architectural integration of knowledge management, decision support, artificial intelligence and data warehousing. *Decision Support Systems, 33*(2), 143–161. DOI: 10.1016/S0167-9236(01)00141-5

Ngo, V. M., Quang, H. T., Hoang, T. G., & Binh, A. D. T. (2024). Sustainability-related supply chain risks and supply chain performances: The moderating effects of dynamic supply chain management practices. *Business Strategy and the Environment*, *33*(2), 839–857. DOI: 10.1002/bse.3512

Nicoletti, B., & Appolloni, A. (2025). Digital transformation in ecosystems: Integrated operations model and its application to fifth-party logistics operators. *Journal of Global Operations and Strategic Sourcing*, *18*(1), 91–122. DOI: 10.1108/JGOSS-04-2023-0024

Saqib, Z. A., & Qin, L. (2024). Investigating effects of digital innovations on sustainable operations of logistics: An empirical study. *Sustainability (Basel)*, *16*(13), 5518. DOI: 10.3390/su16135518

Tanveer, U., Hoang, T. G., Ishaq, S., Kamal, M. M., & Attri, R. (2026). Enhancing supplier innovation capabilities through digital technology integration: A relational perspective. *Technological Forecasting and Social Change*, *223*, 124426. DOI: 10.1016/j.techfore.2025.124426

Tanveer, U., Hoang, T. G., Truong, H. Q., Ishaq, S., & Gong, Y. (2024). The critical role of procurement in the emergence of circular business models: Insights from multiple cases of Vietnamese manufacturers. *Business Strategy and the Environment*, *33*(8), 7689–7707. DOI: 10.1002/bse.3888

Wu, P. J., & Tai, Y. C. (2024). Artificial intelligence-based food-quality and warehousing management for food banks' inbound logistics. *Journal of Enterprise Information Management*, *37*(1), 307–325. DOI: 10.1108/JEIM-10-2022-0398

Chapter 9
Algorithmic Control and the Reconfiguration of Worker Autonomy in Logistics

Thi-Phuong Nguyen
http://orcid.org/0009-0009-5017-5013
Department of Science, Technology, and International Projects, Ho Chi Minh University of Economics and Finance, Ho Chi Minh City, Vietnam

Jun Koi Chee
National University of Singapore, Singapore

ABSTRACT

Algorithmic systems are becoming central to logistics operations by shaping routes, distributing tasks, and assessing performance through continuous scoring. Although widely associated with efficiency gains, these tools also reshape autonomy by embedding discretion within system rules and strengthening metric-based supervision. This chapter frames algorithmic management as a distinctive autonomy regime: a governance arrangement in which task allocation, evaluation practices, transparency, expertise, and negotiation interact to influence how autonomy is enacted and challenged. Drawing on an anonymised case of a large parcel-delivery provider introducing dynamic routing and algorithmic performance scoring, the analysis shows that autonomy is not simply diminished but reorganised, with less discretion in planning while execution relies on constrained judgement under high auditability. The chapter indicates that legitimacy hinges on the visibility and contestability of algorithmic decisions, and that worker expertise and identity increasingly shift toward system-facing competence.

DOI: 10.4018/979-8-3373-7826-8.ch009

1. INTRODUCTION

Algorithmic management has become deeply integrated into logistics operations as firms increasingly rely on data-driven systems to distribute work, optimise routing, and assess performance at scale. Within transport and last-mile delivery, predictive routing tools and productivity scoring mechanisms are promoted as means of improving operational precision by minimising variation in sequencing, pacing, and service delivery. However, as logistics activities are more tightly synchronised through algorithmic infrastructures, this technological shift is accompanied by an equally significant transformation in the human organisation of work: discretion is redefined, autonomy is recalibrated, and the standards by which competence and "good performance" are judged are increasingly shaped by system-based logics rather than occupational judgement alone. Accordingly, recent literature has moved beyond treating algorithmic management as a neutral efficiency instrument and instead conceptualises it as a labour process technology that restructures control, accountability, and the quality of work in contemporary logistics labour markets (Altenried, 2019; Barnes et al., 2025; Noponen et al., 2024).

The chapter is motivated by the continuing gap between managerial narratives of algorithmic optimisation and workers' everyday experience of technologically mediated control. Although prior research highlights the dual character of algorithmic management—its capacity to create coordination value while simultaneously intensifying surveillance and constraining discretion—both empirical and conceptual studies suggest that its effects on autonomy are uneven and cannot be reduced to straightforward narratives of "control loss" (Meijerink & Bondarouk, 2023; Ruiner & Klumpp, 2022). This tension is particularly pronounced in logistics because operational work remains exposed to uncertainty at the point of execution, even as algorithms make worker behaviour increasingly measurable and comparable. At the same time, organisational legitimacy is becoming more dependent on whether algorithmic decisions are understandable, open to challenge, and perceived as fair, especially where opaque scoring systems place responsibility for errors on workers themselves (Mendonça & Kougiannou, 2023; Nilsson et al., 2025). These developments extend beyond questions of efficiency, carrying important implications for occupational health, job satisfaction, and broader concerns about decent work under Logistics 4.0 (Aissoug, 2026; Nilsson et al., 2025). The chapter therefore seeks to theorise how autonomy is reorganised in practice under algorithmic governance, and how control operates not only through technological systems but also through managerial mediation, informal adjustments, and collective sensemaking processes (Vieira & Junte, 2025; Cini, 2023; Schaupp, 2022).

Accordingly, the chapter aims to explain how algorithmic management restructures worker autonomy in logistics operations by conceptualising an "autonomy regime" in which task allocation, evaluation, transparency, expertise, and negotiation mechanisms co-produce new conditions of discretion and control. To ground this argument, the chapter draws on an anonymised illustrative case of a large parcel-delivery provider that introduced predictive routing and algorithmic productivity scoring, using the case to show how optimisation is coupled with auditability and how legitimacy is shaped through contestability and managerial mediation.

The chapter is structured as follows. Section 2 develops the conceptual framework, positioning algorithmic management within logistics labour process debates and articulating five analytical dimensions: algorithmic allocation and discretion, metric-based behavioural control, transparency and contestability, expertise and identity-based autonomy, and negotiated autonomy under algorithmic governance (Noponen et al., 2024; Meijerink & Bondarouk, 2023). Section 3 introduces the anonymised case context and justifies its theoretical relevance. Section 4 presents the case findings organised to mirror the framework, demonstrating how autonomy is recomposed across planning and execution, how scoring intensifies oversight, and how fairness, expertise, and negotiation shape the stability of the autonomy regime. Section 5 concludes by summarising contributions and outlining practical implications for firms and policymakers concerned with balancing efficiency, accountability, and sustainable work in digitally governed logistics.

2. LITERATURE REVIEW

2.1. Chapter overview and conceptual positioning

Algorithmic management has become a defining feature of contemporary logistics operations, reshaping how work is allocated, sequenced, evaluated, and disciplined through data-driven systems. Across transport and delivery networks, routing engines, automated task allocation, and continuous performance scoring increasingly mediate the labour process, promising operational precision while altering how autonomy, discretion, and control are experienced in everyday work. Logistics is a particularly revealing domain for examining these dynamics because it combines time-critical service commitments, fragmented and mobile workplaces, and high levels of standardisation with persistent operational uncertainty and customer-facing variability. These characteristics make algorithmic governance highly consequential: it is deployed to tame uncertainty and increase predictability, yet it must operate through workers' situated judgement at the point of execution where disruptions, traffic conditions, customer interactions, and service contingencies remain unavoidable (Altenried, 2019; Barnes et al., 2025).

Within the expanding literature, a first set of debates concerns whether algorithmic management should be understood primarily as an intensification of managerial control or as a new socio-technical arrangement that can also enable certain forms of autonomy. A systematic review frames this tension sharply by asking whether algorithmic management represents "Taylorism on steroids" or a set of tools that can support autonomy depending on design and context (Noponen et al., 2024). HRM scholarship similarly conceptualises a duality in which algorithms can create value—through coordination and optimisation—while simultaneously reorganising autonomy and control, thereby requiring research to analyse the conditions under which algorithmic governance becomes enabling versus disciplinary (Meijerink & Bondarouk, 2023). Empirical work in logistics-driving contexts reinforces that autonomy is rarely erased; rather, it is re-specified. Digital control can tighten target pressures and monitoring while leaving workers responsible for making micro-decisions that keep operations feasible, thereby producing autonomy that is bounded, conditional, and often experienced as intensified responsibility under constrained discretion (Ruiner & Klumpp, 2022). This chapter is positioned within this debate by treating autonomy not as a binary outcome but as a configuration whose form and legitimacy change as algorithmic systems are embedded in operational routines.

A second debate concerns the labour process foundations of algorithmic management in logistics. Research on logistical labour highlights that contemporary logistics is characterised by speed, fragmentation, and multi-tiered subcontracting, with algorithmic systems functioning as infrastructures that coordinate dispersed work while enabling standardised performance comparison (Barnes et al., 2025). The last-mile literature emphasises how logistical urbanism and platformisation reorganise labour through real-time coordination and spatial optimisation, with autonomy reworked through time discipline, route control, and customer-facing pressures (Altenried, 2019). In this setting, algorithmic management should be analysed as a labour process technology that reconfigures the extraction of value and the organisation of control, rather than as an add-on tool layer. Political-economy analyses further strengthen this point by arguing that automation and digital governance in logistics can intensify workplace asymmetries under conditions of market concentration and competitive pressure, shaping how autonomy is distributed and how contestation is managed within and across organisational tiers (Cirillo et al., 2025).

A third debate foregrounds the institutional and social embeddedness of algorithmic control. Schaupp (2022) demonstrates how algorithmic integration can be co-constituted with broader regimes—such as migration and workplace regimes—producing precarious forms of (dis)obedience where compliance and non-compliance are structured by vulnerability, segmentation, and institutional constraints. This perspective suggests that autonomy transformation cannot be understood solely at the level of workplace technology; it must also be examined as a stratified condition shaped by employment relations and wider governance arrangements. Relatedly, research on intraplatform algorithmic changes shows how shifting algorithmic rules can disconnect labour by destabilising predictability and undermining workers' capacity to organise collectively, thereby altering the collective foundations through which autonomy can be defended or expanded (Mendonça & Kougiannou, 2023). Scholarship on platform worker mobilisation further documents the rise and variety of resistance repertoires—ranging from everyday tactical non-compliance to organised collective action—indicating that algorithmic governance is enacted through ongoing contestation and collective agency rather than imposed unilaterally (Cini, 2023).

These debates are also connected to health, well-being, and normative questions about decent work in Logistics 4.0. Comparative evidence in logistics indicates that algorithmic management practices shape occupational health through work intensity, pacing, and recovery time, with organisational choices mediating whether harms are mitigated or intensified (Nilsson et al., 2025). In parallel, work revisiting the concept of decent work argues that Logistics 4.0 and automation reconfigure work values, recognition, and job satisfaction, making autonomy a normative concern tied to dignity and quality of working life rather than only an operational variable (Aissoug, 2026). These contributions suggest that analysing autonomy transformation requires attending to how control and optimisation intersect with well-being and meaning, including how workers interpret fairness, recognition, and the legitimacy of constraints.

At the level of organisational structure, algorithmic management also redefines managerial work and the sites where discretion is exercised. Evidence from the Spanish dark stores sector shows that middle managers do not simply disappear under algorithmic systems; their role evolves toward interpreting system outputs, handling escalations, and mediating tensions between metric compliance and operational realities (Vieira & Junte, 2025). This finding supports a broader proposition that algorithmic control often centralises certain decision logics while simultaneously creating new coordination problems that require human interpretation and conflict resolution. Moreover, consent and compliance under algorithmic management can be produced through disciplinary and subjectivating mechanisms. A Foucauldian analysis of food-delivery work illustrates how workers may come to consent to algorithmic management through internalised norms and self-governance aligned with platform metrics, suggesting that autonomy is shaped by how workers make sense of algorithmic rules, not only by formal discretion (Galière, 2020).

Finally, the chapter positions algorithmic management within wider transformation agendas in logistics and service operations, where digital governance increasingly intersects with sustainability objectives and strategic reconfiguration. Digital technologies are mobilised not only for efficiency but also to support circular practices and social sustainability, often expanding monitoring, auditability, and compliance demands within operational work (Tanveer et al., 2025; Thi Binh et al., 2025). Strategy-oriented perspectives on safe-shoring and resource orchestration indicate that organisational responses to uncertainty and geopolitical risk can intensify standardisation and performance governance, with downstream implications for how autonomy is structured and experienced by operational workers (Do et al., 2025). Collaboration-focused accounts of sustainability transitions likewise imply that digitally enabled governance can redistribute responsibilities across actors and tiers, making autonomy transformation inseparable from inter-organisational arrangements and accountability regimes (Tanveer et al., 2024).

2.2. Algorithmic allocation and the restructuring of discretion

Algorithmic allocation reconfigures autonomy at the point where logistical work is initiated the assignment of routes, tasks, and temporal sequences. In transport and delivery operations, predictive routing systems use historical and real-time data to optimise route choice, stop ordering, and time windows, while algorithmic dispatch allocates tasks based on capacity utilisation, service-level targets, and productivity objectives. The central theoretical implication is that discretion is displaced from workers' situated judgement toward system logics that define "optimal" action in advance, thereby narrowing decision latitude and transforming the value of local knowing. In labour process terms, algorithmic allocation operates as a coordination technology that externalises planning and sequencing from the worker to the system, enabling tighter control over pace and spatial movement while reducing the scope for worker-defined prioritisation (Altenried, 2019; Barnes et al., 2025).

However, the restructuring of discretion should not be interpreted as a simple removal of agency. The literature suggests a recomposition in which autonomy is relocated to micro-moments of execution and contingency management. In digitalised driving and food logistics contexts, autonomy persists in the form of tactical adjustments—navigating traffic, handling customer interactions, and responding to breakdowns—yet it is increasingly subordinated to target pressures and monitoring that constrain how such adjustments can be made without penalty (Ruiner & Klumpp, 2022). Systematic review evidence similarly indicates that algorithmic management can intensify standardisation while also generating new dependencies on workers' practical judgement at the edge of algorithmic routines, particularly where uncertainty cannot be fully modelled (Noponen et al., 2024). This duality underscores why predictive routing should be analysed as a managerial project that redefines discretion: workers may retain responsibility for outcomes while losing influence over the planning premises that structure those outcomes.

Organisationally, the restructuring of discretion is mediated by how decision rights and override pathways are designed. Where dispatch algorithms are implemented as non-negotiable prescriptions, discretion collapses into compliance and workers' local knowing is primarily valued only when it can be translated into system-recognisable categories (e.g., incident codes, delay reasons). Where systems allow structured feedback loops, local knowing can become a resource for continuous improvement rather than a basis for informal resistance. HRM-focused theorising highlights this design contingency by framing algorithmic management as a dual system of control and value creation; allocation algorithms can generate operational value, but the autonomy effects depend on governance choices about discretion, accountability, and human judgement (Meijerink & Bondarouk, 2023).

The restructuring of discretion also has distributive and institutional dimensions. In settings characterised by precarious employment relations and workforce segmentation, algorithmic allocation may compound vulnerability by reducing workers' ability to negotiate assignments, manage fatigue, or balance work with social reproduction demands (Schaupp, 2022). Market-structure arguments further imply that, under concentrated competitive conditions, optimisation logics may be prioritised over worker-centred discretion, reinforcing asymmetries in bargaining power and amplifying the disciplining capacity of allocation systems (Cirillo et al., 2025). These dynamics connect to the broader transformation of logistical labour in which spatial and temporal control becomes a central mechanism of value extraction (Altenried, 2019; Barnes et al., 2025).

Finally, allocation systems are rarely stable. In platform-mediated and digitally governed environments, changes to dispatch rules can rapidly reshape workers' capacity to plan, coordinate, or organise collectively, disconnecting labour by destabilising shared expectations and undermining collective tactics (Mendonça & Kougiannou, 2023). This points to a critical implication for the chapter's later case analysis: predictive routing and algorithmic dispatch should be examined not only as technical optimisation tools but as organisational governance arrangements that re-specify discretion, relocate the practical significance of local knowledge, and set the conditions under which autonomy can be exercised, contested, or transformed.

2.3. Metric-based performance evaluation and behavioural control

If algorithmic allocation reshapes autonomy at task initiation, metric-based evaluation transforms autonomy through the continuous production of behavioural visibility and comparative performance. In logistics operations, productivity scoring systems translate heterogeneous activities—driving, delivery completion, dwell time, customer contact, and compliance behaviours—into quantified indicators that can be monitored in real time and aggregated for ranking, sanctioning, and incentives. The theoretical significance lies in how metrics not only measure performance but constitute what performance is: they standardise expected behaviours and make compliance with operational norms legible, thereby enabling a form of behavioural control that operates through numbers rather than direct supervision.

The algorithmic management literature consistently highlights this evaluative infrastructure as a key mechanism through which control is intensified. Review evidence frames algorithmic management as potentially hyper-Taylorised precisely because it enables granular measurement and continuous optimisation at scale, allowing firms to drive standardisation and pacing through targets that are continuously recalibrated (Noponen et al., 2024). HRM theorising similarly emphasises the duality of evaluation algorithms: they may support value creation by improving coordination and reducing process variance, but they can simultaneously reduce autonomy by narrowing acceptable behaviours to those that are measurable and rewarded, transforming discretion into a risk of metric deviation (Meijerink & Bondarouk, 2023). In logistics-driving contexts, empirical work demonstrates that new modes of digital control can increase pressure and reduce perceived autonomy even where workers retain executional responsibility, because evaluation systems translate local decisions into accountable deviations from algorithmic expectations (Ruiner & Klumpp, 2022).

Metric-based control also reshapes labour process dynamics by reconfiguring pacing and effort extraction. As logistical labour is organised around speed, service reliability, and tight temporal windows, metrics become tools for intensifying time discipline and standardising the labour process across dispersed work settings (Altenried, 2019; Barnes et al., 2025). Political-economy accounts suggest that, under competitive pressure and market concentration, such evaluative infrastructures can deepen workplace asymmetries by strengthening managerial leverage over performance norms and by shifting risk onto workers through individualised accountability (Cirillo et al., 2025). From this perspective, productivity scoring is not a neutral measurement practice but a governance instrument that can redistribute risk, tighten control, and reshape the employment bargain.

The consequences extend beyond performance to health and well-being. Comparative evidence in logistics indicates that algorithmic management practices influence occupational health through work intensity, stress, and reduced recovery time, with organisational practices mediating the extent of harm (Nilsson et al., 2025). A decent-work framing similarly argues that Logistics 4.0 reshapes work values and job satisfaction, implying that metric regimes affect not only efficiency but also dignity, recognition, and the perceived meaningfulness of work (Aissoug, 2026). These arguments reinforce the need to treat metric-based evaluation as a central mechanism through which autonomy is transformed, because it structures how workers understand what is valued and how they experience fairness and legitimacy.

Finally, metric infrastructures interact with organisational hierarchy and managerial roles. As algorithmic evaluation increases visibility, middle management may shift from direct supervision toward interpreting metrics, enforcing compliance, and managing exceptions to the metric regime, rather than exercising discretion grounded in contextual knowledge (Vieira & Junte, 2025). At the same time, workers may respond through compliance, strategic adaptation, or resistance. Consent can be produced when workers internalise metric norms and align self-management with algorithmic expectations, yet this consent remains fragile and contingent on perceived legitimacy (Galière, 2020). In sum, productivity scoring and continuous measurement reorganise autonomy by standardising behavioural expectations, intensifying monitoring, and redefining performance in ways that shape both managerial practice and workers' lived experience.

2.4. Transparency, contestability, and perceived fairness

Transparency and contestability are central to understanding why algorithmic management generates divergent worker responses even under similar technical configurations. Algorithmic systems not only allocate tasks and evaluate performance; they also structure the informational conditions under which workers can interpret decisions, attribute causes of outcomes, and judge legitimacy. Theoretical work on algorithmic management therefore emphasises that autonomy transformation is mediated by how visible algorithmic logics are, whether decision pathways are explainable, and whether workers have meaningful mechanisms to contest errors, appeal outcomes, or influence system parameters (Meijerink & Bondarouk, 2023; Noponen et al., 2024).

In logistics contexts, the opacity of routing and scoring algorithms can shift workers' experience of autonomy from discretion to uncertainty. When workers cannot understand why routes change, why scores fluctuate, or how certain behaviours are weighted, they may interpret governance as arbitrary, producing compliance that is instrumental rather than legitimate. Empirical evidence in driving professions suggests that perceived autonomy and control are shaped not only by monitoring intensity but also by workers' capacity to make sense of digital control systems and to reconcile system demands with practical realities (Ruiner & Klumpp, 2022). In platform-mediated contexts, rule changes that are poorly communicated can destabilise predictability and undermine trust, weakening workers' capacity to coordinate and organise collectively (Mendonça & Kougiannou, 2023). These dynamics indicate that transparency is not simply informational; it is constitutive of fairness perceptions and the possibility of procedural legitimacy.

Contestability—the ability to challenge decisions and correct errors—further shapes compliance and resistance. Where appeal mechanisms exist, workers may treat algorithmic outputs as negotiable inputs to judgement, supporting a more stable governance relationship. Where contestability is absent, workers may rely on informal workarounds, strategic non-compliance, or collective mobilisation to restore a sense of agency. Research on platform worker mobilisations documents the variety of resistance repertoires that emerge under algorithmic control, including collective action that targets the governance rules rather than only immediate working conditions (Cini, 2023). At the same time, studies of algorithmic integration and precarious (dis)obedience suggest that contestation is stratified: vulnerability and institutional constraints can limit the feasibility of overt resistance, producing compliance that is shaped by precariousness rather than consent (Schaupp, 2022).

The fairness implications of transparency and contestability also connect to organisational health and decent work agendas. Comparative research in logistics shows that algorithmic management practices influence occupational health, and that organisational practices—such as communication, dispute resolution, and workload governance—mediate negative outcomes (Nilsson et al., 2025). A decent-work perspective similarly suggests that job satisfaction and work values are shaped by recognition and dignity, which are undermined when workers perceive algorithmic systems as unfair, unaccountable, or punitive (Aissoug, 2026). In this sense, transparency and contestability are not ancillary governance features but core determinants of whether algorithmic management is experienced as legitimate coordination or coercive oversight.

Organisational hierarchy further complicates these dynamics. Middle managers may become key actors in translating algorithmic outputs into socially acceptable decisions, mediating disputes, and restoring a sense of procedural fairness when system outputs misalign with operational reality (Vieira & Junte, 2025). Yet such mediation can also be constrained by auditability and performance pressure, reducing managers' discretion to correct or contextualise algorithmic outcomes. Political-economy accounts imply that, under competitive conditions and market concentration, firms may prioritise efficiency and standardisation over contestability, thereby deepening asymmetries and eroding legitimacy (Cirillo et al., 2025; Barnes et al., 2025). The chapter's later case analysis therefore treats transparency and contestability as central explanatory mechanisms for worker perceptions of fairness, legitimacy, and compliance under algorithmic governance.

2.5. Expertise redefinition and identity-based autonomy

Algorithmic management transforms autonomy not only through allocation and evaluation, but also through the redefinition of expertise and occupational identity. In logistics work, autonomy has historically been anchored in tacit route knowledge, situational time management, customer-handling competence, and the ability to coordinate service delivery under uncertainty. As predictive routing and algorithmic scoring systems become central to operational governance, these forms of expertise may be devalued, re-codified, or repositioned as secondary to system-facing competencies. The theoretical implication is that autonomy becomes increasingly identity-based: workers' perceived agency and status depend on whether their knowledge is recognised within the algorithmic regime and whether they can claim legitimacy as competent actors under system-mediated evaluation.

The autonomy–control literature in logistics-driving contexts illustrates this identity dynamic. Digital systems can tighten control while simultaneously demanding that workers manage contingencies and maintain service quality, producing an experience of responsibility without corresponding recognition of expertise (Ruiner & Klumpp, 2022). In last-mile settings, logistical urbanism and platform coordination reshape the meaning of "good work" by aligning competence with speed and metric performance, potentially reducing the status of relational and situational expertise that is less easily quantified (Altenried, 2019). Review and HRM theorising underscore that algorithmic management reconfigures value creation by specifying which capabilities are rewarded and which are invisible, thereby reshaping professional identities and the distribution of symbolic and material rewards (Noponen et al., 2024; Meijerink & Bondarouk, 2023).

Identity-based autonomy becomes especially salient when systems mediate the translation of expertise into performance categories. If route knowledge and customer competence are not reflected in scoring logic, workers may experience a loss of professional recognition even when their situated judgement sustains service outcomes. Conversely, workers who learn to manage the system—optimising within constraints, anticipating metric consequences, and producing compliant documentation—may acquire new forms of status as "system-competent" operators. This redefinition is not merely individual adaptation; it is organisationally produced by how competence is encoded and how recognition is distributed through evaluation infrastructures.

The literature also suggests that identity transformation is stratified and shaped by institutional conditions. Under precarious employment relations and segmented labour regimes, the capacity to claim professional identity and autonomy may be constrained, producing compliance and self-discipline as survival strategies rather than as forms of empowerment (Schaupp, 2022). Political-economy analyses further indicate that automation and digital control can deepen asymmetries, with expertise redefinition functioning as a mechanism through which managerial power is consolidated by privileging measurable behaviours over tacit skill (Cirillo et al., 2025). At the same time, the quality-of-work literature argues that Logistics 4.0 reshapes work values and job satisfaction; recognition, dignity, and meaningful autonomy become critical dimensions of decent work as digital systems redefine what counts as valuable contribution (Aissoug, 2026).

Organisational roles and managerial mediation also matter. Evidence from dark stores suggests that middle managers' evolving role includes translating system expectations into workable practices and recognising contextual expertise that metrics may miss, thereby shaping whether identity-based autonomy is preserved or eroded (Vieira & Junte, 2025). Where such mediation is weak or constrained, workers may respond through withdrawal, workaround practices, or collective resistance. Mobilisation research indicates that resistance can be motivated not only by earnings or conditions but also by dignity and recognition, as workers contest the terms through which their expertise is valued (Cini, 2023). This perspective aligns with analyses of consent under algorithmic management, which show how workers can internalise system norms, reshaping identity toward metric-aligned self-governance, yet often under conditions of limited alternatives (Galière, 2020). Overall, expertise redefinition is central to autonomy transformation because it determines whether workers experience algorithmic governance as the erosion of professional agency or as a rearticulation of competence with new status pathways.

2.6. Social negotiation of autonomy under algorithmic governance

Although algorithmic management is frequently presented as automated control, autonomy outcomes are produced through social negotiation. Algorithmic systems must be enacted in practice: workers interpret, comply with, or tactically deviate from system directives; supervisors mediate between system outputs and operational realities; and collective norms shape what forms of adaptation are considered legitimate. The theoretical implication is that autonomy under algorithmic governance is neither fully determined by technology nor fully preserved by individual agency. Instead, it is negotiated through everyday practices, institutional constraints, and organisational responses that co-produce the autonomy–control relationship.

The literature provides multiple entry points to conceptualise this negotiation. Studies of driving professions in food logistics show that autonomy is shaped by how workers navigate digital controls and target pressures, often developing practical coping strategies that reconcile system demands with operational feasibility (Ruiner & Klumpp, 2022). In platform and last-mile settings, the labour process is characterised by speed and fragmentation, yet workers still enact situated judgement, and the boundaries of acceptable deviation are often policed through both metrics and peer norms (Altenried, 2019; Barnes et al., 2025). A Foucauldian perspective further suggests that negotiation can occur through subjectivation: workers may come to consent to algorithmic management by internalising metric norms and practising self-governance aligned with system expectations (Galière, 2020). Such consent, however, is contingent and may coexist with quiet forms of non-compliance.

Collective dynamics are particularly important. Intraplatform algorithmic changes can disconnect labour by destabilising predictability and undermining collective organising capacity, indicating that the negotiability of autonomy depends partly on whether workers can coordinate shared interpretations and responses to system governance (Mendonça & Kougiannou, 2023). At the same time, platform worker mobilisation research documents a growing variety of resistance forms, from micro-resistance and strategic compliance to broader collective campaigns aimed at transparency, fair pay, and governance reform (Cini, 2023). These repertoires demonstrate that autonomy negotiation often targets not only immediate work constraints but also the rules and metrics through which algorithmic control is exercised.

Institutional and organisational stratification shapes who can negotiate and how. Schaupp's analysis of precarious (dis)obedience highlights how vulnerability and institutional regimes can delimit overt resistance, producing compliance shaped by precariousness, migration governance, and workplace power relations (Schaupp, 2022). Political-economy perspectives imply that market concentration and competitive pressure can reinforce managerial incentives to standardise and intensify control, thereby narrowing the scope for negotiated discretion and amplifying asymmetries (Cirillo et al., 2025). Yet organisational practices can also widen negotiation space. Comparative research on occupational health in logistics indicates that organisational choices mediate the effects of algorithmic management; communication practices, workload governance, and support mechanisms can shape whether algorithmic systems intensify harm or become more sustainable (Nilsson et al., 2025). This connects with decent-work perspectives that treat dignity, recognition, and perceived fairness as central outcomes in Logistics 4.0 (Aissoug, 2026).

Managerial roles are an additional locus of negotiation. Evidence from dark stores indicates that middle managers are increasingly positioned as mediators who interpret system outputs, manage escalations, and reconcile metric governance with operational realities (Vieira & Junte, 2025). This mediation can either soften algorithmic rigidity—by contextualising decisions and enabling procedural fairness—or intensify control if managers act primarily as enforcers of metric compliance. Finally, broader transformation agendas in logistics and service operations suggest that negotiation is influenced by strategic objectives such as sustainability, circular practices, and safe-shoring, which can expand monitoring and auditability demands and thereby reshape what autonomy can mean in practice (Thi Binh et al., 2025; Do et al., 2025). In sum, autonomy under algorithmic governance is enacted through practice: it is continuously produced at the intersection of system design, organisational mediation, collective norms, and the political economy of logistics.

3. ILLUSTRATIVE CASE STUDY

This chapter draws on an anonymised case of a large international parcel delivery organisation that introduced predictive routing and algorithmically supported performance management across its transport operations. The organisation operates a high-volume last-mile distribution network serving both business-to-business and business-to-consumer markets across multiple metropolitan regions. Its operations involve thousands of daily delivery routes, tight service-level commitments, and strong pressure to optimise fuel consumption, route efficiency, and delivery reliability. These characteristics make transport operations highly data-intensive and operationally interdependent, providing a suitable empirical setting for examining how algorithmic management reshapes worker autonomy in logistics.

The focal organisation began implementing predictive routing systems as part of a broader digital transformation initiative aimed at improving operational efficiency and environmental performance. Prior to this transition, drivers relied heavily on accumulated route knowledge, informal coordination with dispatchers, and individual judgement in sequencing deliveries. Route planning was supported by digital tools but remained substantially shaped by human decision-making. As predictive routing was progressively introduced, algorithmic systems began generating route sequences, estimating arrival times, and dynamically adjusting delivery plans in response to traffic conditions, customer availability, and operational disruptions. Over time, routing became increasingly system-directed, with drivers expected to follow algorithmically generated instructions while maintaining delivery quality and safety standards.

Alongside predictive routing, the organisation introduced algorithmic productivity indicators designed to track route efficiency, schedule adherence, and delivery completion performance. These indicators were derived from telematics data, delivery confirmation systems, and route-tracking applications, allowing performance to be monitored continuously rather than evaluated retrospectively. Supervisors gained access to dashboards that compared performance across routes and drivers, while drivers themselves could view selected indicators related to their own delivery outcomes. The integration of predictive routing with productivity scoring created a tightly coupled system in which allocation, execution, and evaluation became connected through a shared data infrastructure.

This case is theoretically useful because it allows observation of algorithmic management within a conventional employment-based logistics organisation rather than a purely platform-mediated setting. The organisation retains formal managerial hierarchies, collective norms of professional driving, and established operational routines, enabling analysis of how algorithmic governance interacts with existing labour process arrangements instead of replacing them. The transition to predictive routing therefore reveals how discretion is reorganised when system-generated optimisation becomes the default reference for operational decisions, while drivers remain responsible for managing uncertainty on the road. This duality makes the case particularly relevant for examining how algorithmic allocation reshapes decision latitude without eliminating executional responsibility.

The operational scale of the organisation further strengthens the analytical value of the case. Because routing algorithms are deployed across large numbers of routes, performance indicators can be standardised and compared systematically, making behavioural expectations more explicit and measurable. At the same time, the variability inherent in last-mile delivery ensures that algorithmic instructions cannot fully anticipate local contingencies, creating recurring situations in which drivers must reconcile system recommendations with practical realities. These tensions make visible the processes through which autonomy is negotiated, contested, and redefined in everyday work.

Finally, the case provides a coherent organisational context for analysing how predictive routing and productivity scoring jointly reshape autonomy. Algorithmic allocation influences how work is initiated, metric-based evaluation shapes how work is judged, and managerial oversight mediates how deviations are interpreted. Together, these elements create an autonomy regime in which control is technologically mediated but enacted through organisational relationships and operational practice. As such, the case offers a theoretically generative setting for examining the transformation of discretion, fairness perceptions, expertise, and negotiated autonomy in logistics operations under algorithmic management.

4. CASE FINDINGS: ALGORITHMIC MANAGEMENT AND AUTONOMY TRANSFORMATION

4.1. Algorithmic allocation and discretion loss/recomposition

In the focal case, predictive routing operated as the primary mechanism through which algorithmic management reshaped day-to-day autonomy. Historically, drivers' route-based autonomy was anchored in situated knowledge: how to sequence stops to avoid congestion, when to shift priorities to accommodate customer availability, and how to blend tacit route familiarity with service obligations. With the introduction of algorithmic routing, this autonomy was partially displaced. Route sequencing and path recommendations became system-defined, and drivers were increasingly expected to treat the algorithmic plan as the default authority. The most immediate effect was a contraction of discretion at the planning stage: decisions about "what comes next" were less a matter of driver judgement and more a matter of compliance with system logic.

However, the case did not support a simplistic claim of autonomy loss. Instead, discretion was recomposed and relocated to new sites of judgement. Drivers reported that predictive routing reduced their latitude to apply local knowing proactively, but it simultaneously increased the need for tactical discretion at the execution frontier. Congestion, parking constraints, customer interactions, and unplanned pickups generated frequent micro-deviations that the system could not fully anticipate. In these moments, autonomy reappeared as problem-solving under constraints: deciding when to deviate, how to recover schedule, and how to document reasons in system-recognisable categories. This pattern aligns with evidence that digital control can tighten prescriptions while still relying on workers' situated judgement to keep operations feasible, producing bounded autonomy that is experienced as responsibility under intensified expectations (Ruiner & Klumpp, 2022). It also resonates with last-mile labour accounts in which logistical urbanism and platform-style coordination reorganise autonomy through time discipline and spatial control, without eliminating the practical necessity of judgement (Altenried, 2019).

A crucial empirical mechanism in the case was the progressive normalisation of algorithmic authority. As routing recommendations were increasingly dynamic, re-optimisation created a moving target for what counts as "following the plan." Drivers described a shift from exercising discretion to "managing the system," where the practical question was not whether the algorithm was correct, but how to remain compliant while maintaining service quality. This shift reconfigured local knowing from a guiding logic into a latent resource that could be mobilised mainly when the system failed or when disruptions forced deviations. The result is consistent with the broader depiction of logistical labour as increasingly coordinated through infrastructures that standardise and compare dispersed work at scale (Barnes et al., 2025). It also speaks to the duality emphasised in algorithmic management research: allocation algorithms can create value through coordination, but they also transform autonomy by relocating planning and discretion into system logics (Meijerink & Bondarouk, 2023; Noponen et al., 2024).

The case further revealed that discretion recomposition was stratified. Drivers with longer tenure and stronger route familiarity were more capable of identifying when algorithmic guidance was infeasible and of executing rapid recovery, but their ability to translate this expertise into recognised discretion depended on whether deviations could be justified through acceptable codes and whether supervisors would validate them. In other words, discretion was not only a technical matter but an institutional one, shaped by how vulnerability, employment relations, and organisational governance conditioned the legitimacy of deviation. This finding aligns with analyses of precarious (dis)obedience, where the capacity to refuse or contest algorithmic direction is uneven and shaped by institutional constraints and workforce segmentation (Schaupp, 2022). The case also suggests that allocation systems can amplify asymmetries under competitive pressures, as optimisation becomes the overriding rationale for constraining discretion (Cirillo et al., 2025).

Finally, the allocation regime was experienced as unstable because small algorithmic changes had immediate consequences for predictability and planning. Drivers emphasised that recalibrations to routing logic could alter workload distribution, stop density, or timing assumptions, shifting everyday feasibility. This echoes evidence that intraplatform algorithmic changes can disconnect labour by undermining predictability and destabilising collective expectations, thereby weakening workers' ability to coordinate responses (Mendonça & Kougiannou, 2023). Overall, the case demonstrates that predictive routing transforms autonomy through a dual movement: discretion is removed from planning and sequencing, yet reappears as constrained, execution-frontier judgement oriented to compliance, documentation, and recovery.

4.2. Productivity scoring and intensified behavioural oversight

The implementation of algorithmic productivity scoring intensified behavioural oversight by converting diverse aspects of delivery work into continuous, comparable metrics. In the focal case, drivers' performance was increasingly represented through dashboards that combined route adherence indicators, time-at-stop measures, completion rates, and exception frequencies into evaluative scores. These scores were used for coaching, benchmarking, and performance discussions, and they shaped day-to-day behaviour by redefining what counts as acceptable work practice. The empirical effect was an expanded regime of auditability: drivers understood that their pace, sequencing, and deviations were traceable, and that explanations for local contingencies needed to be legible in the organisation's metric language.

This metricisation of work intensified time discipline. Drivers described heightened pressure to maintain pace and to minimise non-delivery time, including micro-decisions about parking, customer interaction length, and administrative documentation. Break-taking and recovery time were experienced as more constrained, not necessarily through explicit prohibition, but through the anticipatory awareness that time not captured as "productive" could register as inefficiency. This finding aligns with broader logistical labour analyses that depict delivery work as governed through speed, fragmentation, and performance comparison, where measurement infrastructures function as mechanisms of effort extraction (Altenried, 2019; Barnes et al., 2025). It is also consistent with systematic review evidence that algorithmic management can intensify Taylorist control by enabling continuous optimisation and granular monitoring (Noponen et al., 2024).

Importantly, the case suggests that optimisation and surveillance became coupled: routing recommendations created the expected tempo, while scoring systems enforced adherence and penalised divergence. This coupling reduced the boundary between operational coordination and behavioural control, illustrating the HRM duality that algorithms may create value by stabilising coordination while simultaneously reshaping autonomy by narrowing acceptable behaviours to those that the system can measure and reward (Meijerink & Bondarouk, 2023). Drivers expressed that the system did not simply "measure" their work; it structured it by making metric-aligned behaviour the safest path. This dynamic also helps explain why workers may consent to algorithmic control: aligning self-management with metric expectations can become a rational adaptation under auditability, even when autonomy is experienced as eroded (Galière, 2020).

The intensified evaluative regime had implications for health and well-being. Drivers linked the continuous pressure of scoring to stress, reduced recovery time, and the experience of constant surveillance, especially during high-volume periods. This pattern corresponds to comparative research in logistics showing that algorithmic management can shape occupational health through pacing and intensity, with organisational practices mediating negative effects (Nilsson et al., 2025). In the focal case, the presence of formal safety and compliance discourses did not fully offset the practical incentives created by productivity indicators; instead, workers perceived tensions between doing "safe work" and doing "scored work." This tension is consistent with decent-work arguments that Logistics 4.0 reconfigures work values and job satisfaction, as recognition becomes tied to metric outputs rather than to broader notions of quality or dignity (Aissoug, 2026).

Managerial roles shifted accordingly. Supervisors increasingly acted as interpreters and enforcers of metric regimes, using dashboards to justify coaching and to resolve performance disputes. This aligns with evidence from dark-store logistics that middle managers' roles evolve under algorithmic management toward managing escalations, interpreting system outputs, and mediating tensions between metric compliance and operational reality (Vieira & Junte, 2025). Finally, political-economy accounts help situate the behavioural effects: under competitive pressure and market concentration, productivity scoring can deepen workplace asymmetries by individualising accountability and intensifying managerial leverage (Cirillo et al., 2025). Overall, the case demonstrates that productivity scoring transforms autonomy by coupling optimisation to surveillance and by reconstituting performance as metric-aligned behaviour, with consequential effects on pacing, recovery, and compliance.

4.3. Fairness, legitimacy, and contestability dynamics

The legitimacy of the autonomy regime in the focal case depended critically on how workers interpreted algorithmic decisions and whether they had meaningful avenues to contest them. Drivers' fairness judgements were shaped less by the abstract presence of algorithms and more by the perceived reasonableness of routing recommendations and the perceived integrity of scoring outputs under real-world constraints. When algorithmic outputs aligned with operational realities, drivers tended to treat them as useful coordination tools. When outputs misaligned—through infeasible sequencing, unrealistic timing assumptions, or apparent misattribution of delays—drivers experienced the system as arbitrary and potentially punitive.

A central empirical dynamic was partial opacity. Drivers could see route sequences, alerts, and summary performance indicators, but they could not fully observe the weighting logic or the reasons why recalibration occurred. This limited explanatory access shaped perceptions of procedural fairness. Workers described that they could often identify why a route was practically difficult, yet struggled to translate this into evidence that was legible to the system. The result was a sense that fairness depended on managerial interpretation rather than on transparent rules. This pattern aligns with broader findings that autonomy and perceived control are shaped by workers' capacity to make sense of digital control systems, not only by monitoring intensity (Ruiner & Klumpp, 2022), and with review arguments that the experience of algorithmic management hinges on design features such as transparency and accountability (Noponen et al., 2024; Meijerink & Bondarouk, 2023).

Contestability mechanisms existed but were uneven. In principle, drivers could flag route issues and challenge certain score anomalies through supervisors, using exception codes and incident documentation. In practice, the effectiveness of contestation depended on managerial discretion, time availability for dispute handling, and the credibility of documentation within the metric regime. This reinforced the perception that contestability was socially mediated rather than structurally guaranteed. It also revealed a key role for middle managers, who served as translators between system outputs and lived operational realities. This is consistent with evidence that middle managers under algorithmic management increasingly act as mediators who interpret outputs, handle escalations, and manage tensions between performance dashboards and practical feasibility (Vieira & Junte, 2025).

The absence of robust contestability in some situations contributed to coping strategies that blurred compliance and resistance. Drivers described selective compliance—following the system when feasible and deviating when necessary—while anticipating how deviations might be interpreted. This anticipatory governance resembles the subjectivation dynamics identified in platform labour, where workers can come to consent to algorithmic management through self-discipline aligned with metric expectations, yet remain aware of the system's punitive potential (Galière, 2020). At the collective level, fairness concerns were also discussed among drivers, shaping shared interpretations of what the system "really values" and when management would support contestation. Such collective sensemaking is consistent with mobilisation research showing that workers develop varied repertoires to contest algorithmic control, including informal knowledge sharing and collective action (Cini, 2023).

The case further suggests that fairness is stratified by institutional vulnerability. Drivers with less tenure, lower perceived status, or greater dependence on stable income reported weaker confidence in contestation and greater incentives to comply even when outputs seemed unreasonable. This resonates with analyses of precarious (dis)obedience in digitalised logistics and manufacturing, where vulnerability conditions the feasibility of resistance and shapes compliance patterns (Schaupp, 2022). It also aligns with arguments that power asymmetries can be amplified under market concentration and competitive pressure, making procedural justice harder to secure (Cirillo et al., 2025).

Finally, fairness and contestability had implications for well-being. When workers experienced algorithmic outcomes as unchallengeable, they reported stress and cynicism, which are consistent with comparative evidence linking algorithmic management practices in logistics to occupational health risks mediated by organisational practices (Nilsson et al., 2025). Decent-work perspectives likewise imply that legitimacy and recognition are central to job satisfaction under Logistics 4.0, and that perceived unfairness undermines dignity and sustainable employment relations (Aissoug, 2026). Overall, the case demonstrates that legitimacy under algorithmic management is not automatic; it is produced through transparency, contestability, and managerial mediation, and it remains fragile when system outputs are opaque or dispute pathways are weak.

4.4. Redefining expertise and autonomy through system-facing competence

The focal case indicates that algorithmic management reshaped autonomy by redefining what constitutes expertise and, consequently, who is recognised as a competent logistics worker. In the pre-algorithmic regime, a "good driver" was widely associated with tacit route knowledge, nuanced time management, local customer familiarity, and the ability to improvise under uncertainty while maintaining service quality. Under predictive routing and productivity scoring, these forms of expertise remained practically important but became less visible as sources of recognised performance. Instead, competence was increasingly defined through system-facing practices: interpreting route signals, anticipating scoring implications, documenting exceptions in acceptable categories, and aligning execution with dashboard expectations.

This shift produced a rearticulation of identity-based autonomy. Drivers' sense of professional agency became linked to their capacity to manage the system rather than to their independent judgement. Those who could translate operational realities into system-recognisable actions—by using appropriate codes, maintaining metric-aligned pacing, and avoiding "unexplained" deviations—were more likely to be recognised as high performers. Conversely, drivers who relied primarily on tacit route judgement but struggled with metric regimes experienced a loss of recognition even when their service outcomes were strong. This pattern reflects the duality identified in algorithmic management scholarship: evaluative infrastructures not only monitor work but redefine value creation and the criteria of competence, thereby reshaping autonomy and professional status (Meijerink & Bondarouk, 2023; Noponen et al., 2024).

The case also illustrates how expertise is reframed as compliance-capable competence. Under auditability, the capacity to justify decisions became as important as the decisions themselves. Drivers described that "knowing the route" was less valuable if it could not be reconciled with the system's sequencing logic and scoring expectations. This echoes broader analyses of last-mile labour where platform-style coordination aligns competence with metric performance, potentially devaluing relational and situational expertise that is harder to quantify (Altenried, 2019). It also aligns with evidence in food logistics driving contexts that digital control can reduce perceived autonomy by rendering local judgement accountable as deviation, producing responsibility without corresponding recognition (Ruiner & Klumpp, 2022).

Identity transformation was uneven and interacted with organisational mediation. Supervisors could sometimes recognise contextual expertise—acknowledging, for example, that customer constraints or area-specific issues justified deviations. Yet such recognition was constrained by the metric regime and by managerial accountability to dashboards. This dynamic parallels findings that middle managers under algorithmic management increasingly operate as mediators and translators who manage tensions between system outputs and operational feasibility, thereby shaping whether contextual expertise retains legitimacy (Vieira & Junte, 2025). Where mediation was effective, drivers could maintain a sense of professional autonomy by having their judgement validated; where mediation was weak, drivers experienced the system as delegitimising their expertise.

The redefinition of expertise also connected to worker well-being and decent work. Drivers' narratives indicated that recognition became more conditional and more tightly tied to quantified outputs, affecting morale and perceived dignity. This aligns with Logistics 4.0 discussions of decent work, which emphasise that work values and job satisfaction are reshaped as digital systems redefine recognition and meaningful contribution (Aissoug, 2026). In addition, the capacity to develop system-facing competence was stratified by institutional and labour process conditions. Workers with greater vulnerability or weaker bargaining power were less able to contest the redefinition of expertise, consistent with precarious (dis)obedience analyses that show how segmentation conditions autonomy and the feasibility of resistance (Schaupp, 2022). Political-economy accounts further suggest that, under concentrated market power, expertise redefinition can function as a mechanism of managerial control by privileging measurable behaviours over tacit skill, deepening asymmetries (Cirillo et al., 2025).

Finally, the chapter's broader sustainability framing provides an additional interpretive layer. As logistics firms pursue digital governance for efficiency and accountability, system-facing competence becomes intertwined with auditability and compliance objectives that extend beyond immediate productivity. Digital transformation agendas linked to circular practices and social sustainability can further expand measurement and reporting demands, intensifying the importance—and the politics—of recognised competence within algorithmic regimes (Tanveer et al., 2025; Thi Binh et al., 2025). In sum, the case shows that autonomy is transformed through the redefinition of expertise: professional agency becomes increasingly tied to the ability to operate within, interpret, and remain legible to algorithmic systems.

4.5. Negotiated autonomy: coping practices, workarounds, and local norms

The autonomy regime observed in the focal case was stabilised and contested through everyday negotiation. Predictive routing and productivity scoring did not produce mechanically uniform behaviour; instead, drivers and supervisors developed local norms and coping practices that made algorithmic governance workable under operational uncertainty. These negotiations centred on when compliance was expected, when deviation was tolerated, and how deviations should be documented to preserve legitimacy within the metric regime. The resulting autonomy was neither purely constrained nor purely preserved; it was enacted through selective compliance, informal problem-solving, and shared sensemaking about the system's expectations.

Drivers described a repertoire of coping practices. One common practice was anticipatory compliance: aligning driving and delivery behaviour with the system's presumed priorities to avoid unexplained deviations, even when alternative actions might have been operationally sensible. Another practice was strategic documentation: using exception codes and incident notes to translate local contingencies into system-legible accounts. A third practice was tactical deviation followed by recovery—deviating from the sequence to address a known local constraint, then returning to the algorithmic plan to minimise the visibility of divergence. These practices resemble forms of subjectivation under algorithmic management, where workers internalise metric norms and govern themselves accordingly, while still exercising bounded agency to keep work feasible (Galière, 2020).

Negotiation was also collective. Drivers shared informal knowledge about which deviations were likely to be penalised, how to "read" the scoring system, and how to handle recurring system misalignments in specific territories. Such collective sensemaking shaped local norms of acceptable practice and created a practical buffer against perceived arbitrariness. This aligns with research on worker mobilisation and resistance, which emphasises that workers develop varied repertoires—ranging from everyday micro-resistance to collective campaigns—to contest algorithmic control and to restore agency (Cini, 2023). It also resonates with arguments that algorithmic changes can disconnect labour by undermining predictability and shared expectations; in the focal case, collective sensemaking functioned as a partial countermeasure to such destabilisation (Mendonça & Kougiannou, 2023).

Supervisors played a pivotal role in negotiation by interpreting system outputs and mediating disputes. In many instances, practical autonomy depended on managerial willingness to contextualise deviations and to advocate for drivers when algorithmic outputs were misaligned with operational reality. This mirrors evidence from dark stores that middle managers increasingly become mediators and translators under algorithmic management, handling escalations and reconciling metric governance with feasibility (Vieira & Junte, 2025). Yet mediation had limits: supervisors were themselves accountable to dashboards and organisational targets, constraining their ability to legitimise deviation systematically. As a result, negotiated autonomy remained fragile and contingent.

Institutional conditions shaped the scope of negotiation. Drivers with greater vulnerability were less likely to deviate openly or to contest decisions, reproducing stratified autonomy consistent with precarious (dis)obedience analyses in digitalised logistics (Schaupp, 2022). Political-economy perspectives suggest that competitive pressures and market concentration can further narrow negotiation space by prioritising standardisation and intensifying managerial leverage (Cirillo et al., 2025). At the same time, organisational practices oriented toward health and decent work can widen negotiation space. Comparative evidence indicates that occupational health outcomes under algorithmic management are mediated by organisational supports and governance practices (Nilsson et al., 2025), and decent-work perspectives highlight the importance of recognition and dignity in sustaining job satisfaction under Logistics 4.0 (Aissoug, 2026). In the focal case, where negotiation practices supported procedural fairness and recognition, compliance was more stable; where negotiation collapsed into enforcement, cynicism and stress increased.

Finally, the negotiation of autonomy should be situated within broader organisational transformation agendas. As logistics firms pursue digital technologies for sustainability goals—such as accountability, traceability, and socially sustainable operations—algorithmic governance can expand auditability and reshape local norms of documentation and compliance (Tanveer et al., 2025; Thi Binh et al., 2025). Strategic reconfiguration agendas, including safe-shoring responses to uncertainty, can further intensify standardisation and performance governance, indirectly constraining the space for negotiated discretion (Do et al., 2025). Collaboration-oriented transition accounts likewise imply that governance arrangements can redistribute responsibilities across actors and tiers, shaping how autonomy is negotiated within interdependent systems (Tanveer et al., 2024). Overall, the case demonstrates that autonomy under algorithmic management is not a fixed property of system design; it is produced through everyday practices and mediated by managerial roles, collective norms, and the political economy of contemporary logistics.

5. CONCLUDING REMARKS

This chapter examined how algorithmic management reshapes worker autonomy in logistics through an anonymised parcel-delivery case involving predictive routing and algorithmic productivity scoring. The findings indicate that autonomy is not simply reduced; it is recomposed. Planning-stage discretion over sequencing and pacing is increasingly relocated into system logics, while executional autonomy persists as bounded judgement oriented to feasibility, recovery, and documentation. Productivity scoring couples optimisation with auditability, tightening behavioural oversight through metricised definitions of performance. Legitimacy depends on workers' capacity to interpret system outcomes and to contest errors through credible dispute pathways, which remain uneven and socially mediated. In parallel, professional identity shifts as "good" work becomes increasingly defined by system-facing competence—managing signals, codes, and metric implications—rather than by tacit route knowledge alone. Across these dynamics, autonomy is continuously negotiated through informal coping practices, collective sensemaking, and managerial mediation.

5.1. Theoretical contributions

The chapter's theoretical contribution is to conceptualise algorithmic management in logistics as an autonomy regime—a patterned governance configuration through which predictive routing and productivity scoring relocate discretion into optimisation logics while recomposing autonomy as bounded executional judgement, metric-accountable pacing, and socially mediated legitimacy. This extends the duality perspective that algorithmic systems may simultaneously enable coordination/value creation and intensify control by showing that, in last-mile operations, autonomy is neither simply removed nor preserved but redistributed across planning, execution, and accountability arrangements (Meijerink & Bondarouk, 2023; Noponen et al., 2024; Ruiner & Klumpp, 2022). It further elaborates labour process and political-economy accounts of logistical work by specifying how allocation and evaluative infrastructures standardise performance expectations and individualise responsibility under competitive pressures (Barnes et al., 2025; Cirillo et al., 2025; Altenried, 2019). Finally, the chapter theorises legitimacy as constitutive of algorithmic governance—shaped by opacity, contestability, managerial mediation, and collective sensemaking—thereby linking autonomy transformation to negotiated compliance, stratified (dis)obedience, and well-being outcomes in digitally governed logistics workplaces (Mendonça & Kougiannou, 2023; Vieira & Junte, 2025; Schaupp, 2022; Galière, 2020; Cini, 2023; Nilsson et al., 2025; Aissoug, 2026).

5.2. Practical implications

Regarding the practical implications, this chapter findings imply that algorithmic management should be designed and governed as a socio-technical workforce system rather than as a purely optimisation tool. Predictive routing should incorporate structured feedback loops that allow frontline local knowledge to be captured, validated, and translated into system improvements, while preserving bounded discretion for executional contingencies. Productivity scoring should be governed with explicit metric principles that distinguish controllable from uncontrollable variability, avoid perverse incentives that compress recovery time, and ensure that safety, service quality, and well-being are not subordinated to narrow efficiency indicators. Transparency mechanisms should be strengthened through explainable outputs, stable communication of rule changes, and credible appeal pathways where workers can contest misattributions and have outcomes corrected without stigma. Managerially, organisations should recognise that supervisors become key mediators; they require discretion, training, and workload capacity to interpret dashboards responsibly and to maintain procedural legitimacy. Workforce development should focus on system-facing competence—signal interpretation, exception documentation, and metric literacy—while also safeguarding the value of tacit expertise and relational work that sustain service outcomes.

REFERENCES

Aissoug, E. L. (2026). Revisiting the concept of decent work: Exploring work values and job satisfaction in the era of Logistics 4.0. *International Journal of Physical Distribution & Logistics Management*, *56*(2), 1–29. DOI: 10.1108/IJPDLM-01-2025-0014

Altenried, M. (2019). On the last mile: Logistical urbanism and the transformation of labour. *Work Organisation, Labour & Globalisation*, *13*(1), 114–129. DOI: 10.13169/workorgalaboglob.13.1.0114

Barnes, T., O'Neill, C., & Kelly, L. (2025). New worlds of logistical labour. *Work Organisation, Labour & Globalisation*, *19*(2), 127–139. DOI: 10.13169/workorgalaboglob.19.2.0001

Cini, L. (2023). Resisting algorithmic control: Understanding the rise and variety of platform worker mobilisations. *New Technology, Work and Employment*, *38*(1), 125–144. DOI: 10.1111/ntwe.12257

Cirillo, V., Massimo, F. S., Rinaldini, M., Staccioli, J., & Virgillito, M. E. (2025). Monopoly power upon the world of work: A workplace analysis in the logistics segment under automation. *Review of Political Economy*, *37*(4), 1599–1631. DOI: 10.1080/09538259.2024.2419611

Do, T. H. M., Tanveer, U., Ishaq, S., & Hoang, T. G. (2025). Safe-shoring and resource orchestration for B2B firms in emerging economies. *Journal of International Management*, *31*(5), 101263. DOI: 10.1016/j.intman.2025.101263

Galière, S. (2020). When food-delivery platform workers consent to algorithmic management: A Foucauldian perspective. *New Technology, Work and Employment*, *35*(3), 357–370. DOI: 10.1111/ntwe.12177

Meijerink, J., & Bondarouk, T. (2023). The duality of algorithmic management: Toward a research agenda on HRM algorithms, autonomy and value creation. *Human Resource Management Review*, *33*(1), 100876. DOI: 10.1016/j.hrmr.2021.100876

Mendonça, P., & Kougiannou, N. K. (2023). Disconnecting labour: The impact of intraplatform algorithmic changes on the labour process and workers' capacity to organise collectively. *New Technology, Work and Employment*, *38*(1), 1–20. DOI: 10.1111/ntwe.12251

Nilsson, K. H., Matilla-Santander, N., Lee, M. K., Brulin, E., Bodin, T., & Håkansta, C. (2025). Algorithmic management and occupational health: A comparative case study of organizational practices in logistics. *Safety Science*, *187*, 106863. DOI: 10.1016/j.ssci.2025.106863

Noponen, N., Feshchenko, P., Auvinen, T., Luoma-aho, V., & Abrahamsson, P. (2024). Taylorism on steroids or enabling autonomy? A systematic review of algorithmic management. *Management Review Quarterly*, *74*(3), 1695–1721. DOI: 10.1007/s11301-023-00345-5

Ruiner, C., & Klumpp, M. (2022). Autonomy and new modes of control in digital work contexts–a mixed-methods study of driving professions in food logistics. *Employee Relations*, *44*(4), 890–912. DOI: 10.1108/ER-04-2021-0139

Schaupp, S. (2022). Algorithmic integration and precarious (dis) obedience: On the co-constitution of migration regime and workplace regime in digitalised manufacturing and logistics. *Work, Employment and Society*, *36*(2), 310–327. DOI: 10.1177/09500170211031458

Tanveer, U., Hoang, T. G., & Ishaq, S. (2025). Exploring the strategic role of digital technologies in supporting circular practices within service-based firms. *Production Planning and Control*, •••, 1–17. DOI: 10.1080/09537287.2025.2577189

Tanveer, U., Ishaq, S., & Hoang, T. G. (2024). Enhancing carbon trading mechanisms through innovative collaboration: Case studies from developing nations. *Journal of Cleaner Production*, *482*, 144122. DOI: 10.1016/j.jclepro.2024.144122

Thi Binh, A. D., Nguyen, T. T. B., Huynh, T. L. D., Cong-Pham, H., Hoang, T. G., & Truong, H. Q. (2025). Multilevel drivers of social sustainability in developing food supply chains: The role of food safety management systems. *Journal of Enterprise Information Management*, 1–36.

Vieira, T., & Junte, S. (2025). Lost in Automation? Algorithmic Management and the Evolving Role of Middle Managers-Insights From the Spanish Dark Stores Sector. *Work and Occupations*, 07308884251398078. DOI: 10.1177/07308884251398078

Chapter 10
Building a Digital Capability Pipeline for AI-Driven Workforce Transformation in Supply Chains

Adilah Hisa
http://orcid.org/0000-0002-5411-2927
Universiti Teknologi Brunei, Brunei

ABSTRACT

Logistics and supply chain operations are increasingly reshaped by AI, automation, robotics, and advanced analytics. These technologies boost efficiency and decision-making but also transform roles, redistribute tasks, and create skill demands that often outpace workforce readiness. This chapter presents a digital capability pipeline grounded in Human Capital Theory, focusing on AI-driven workforce transformation. It integrates digital literacy, AI oversight, structured reskilling, human–AI collaboration, and adaptive learning, addressing role redesign, task augmentation, and career evolution. Coordinated investment across individual, organizational, and ecosystem levels, supported by leadership, process design, and partnerships, enables continuous renewal of AI competencies and operational resilience. Feedback mechanisms support iterative skill development and strategic adaptation. The chapter provides practical, policy, and research insights for building AI-ready, adaptable logistics workforces capable of sustaining long-term competitive advantage.

DOI: 10.4018/979-8-3373-7826-8.ch010

1. INTRODUCTION

Logistics and supply chain (LSC) operations are undergoing rapid technological transformation, increasingly driven by the integration of artificial intelligence (AI) into core workflows (Seyedghorban et al., 2020). The global market for digital solutions in LSC is projected to expand at a computed annual growth rate (CAGR) of 40.9% from 2022 through 2029, rising from US$24.19 billion in 2024 to US$134.26 billion in 2029 (Research and Markets, 2025). This transformation creates a pressing need for upskilling, reskilling, and competence development to ensure that workers remain employable and capable of adding value in AI-enabled environments. With this expansion, AI-enabled technologies—including machine learning analytics, intelligent automation, robotics, and predictive optimization systems—are reshaping operational models, enabling greater efficiency, transparency, and value creation across LSC networks (Liu & Chiu, 2021). Major industry examples illustrate AI's centrality: Amazon deploys AI-driven warehouse robotics and intelligent fulfillment systems; Walmart utilizes AI-based inventory and demand forecasting; UPS employs AI-powered route optimization (ORION); and Maersk integrates AI analytics in maritime logistics (DocShipper, 2025). These applications highlight how AI is transforming not only operational efficiency but also the nature of work with supply chains.

While AI adoption enables improved scalability, accuracy, and responsiveness (Seyedghorban et al., 2020), it simultaneously introduce a central and persistent challenge: a growing skill–technology misalignment. As AI systems take over predictive, analytical, and decision-support tasks, logistics roles are evolving toward human-AI collaboration, algorithmic reasing, system supervision, and exception management. Traditional competencies—manual handling, routine coordination, and standard planning—are no longer sufficient. Employees are now required to interpret AI outputs, monitor system performance, make context-sensitive decisions, and act in partnership with intelligent technologies (Culot et al., 2024; Gupta et al., 2021). Concurrently, global shortages of digitally skilled workers capable of handling and operating such technologies further complicates adaptation, potentially limiting full realization of productivity gains and strategic potential of digital transformation initiatives (Gupta et al., 2021). Recent reports from the World Economic Forum (2025) and the International Labour Organization (2025) indicate that a significant portion of current logistics-related skills risk becoming obsolete within the next five years, with capability gaps emerging as one of the primary barriers to progress in digitalization. Thus, this transformation creates a critical need for upskilling, reskilling, and competence development to ensure that workers remain employable and capable of adding value in AI-enabled environments.

Despite investments in AI infrastructure, workforce preparedness often lags behind technological implementation, limiting the full potential of AI-driven transformation. Shortages of digitally and analytically skilled employees exacerbate these challenges, slowing adoption, increasing operational risk, and potentially undermining service quality (International Labour Organization, 2025; World Economic Forum, 2025). Managing the supply chain system effectively necessitates access to appropriately skilled and capable talent base (Meier et al., 2024). As AI reshapes tasks, roles, and workflows, organizations must deliberately develop strategies to mobilize their workforce toward new competencies, ensuring employees are prepared for emerging tasks, can work effectively with intelligent systems, and maintaining meaningful employment in AI-intensive supply chains.

The Operations and Supply Chain Management (OSCM) literature has largely focused on identifying the competencies and skills necessary for effective supply chain management, paying far less attention to how AI-related capabilities are systematically developed, renewed, and aligned with evolving digital technologies (Banerjee & Sharma, 2025; Patrucco et al., 2021; Subrahmanyam, 2025). In particular, the role of human capital strategies and structured capability development processes in enabling continuous reskilling, AI literacy development, and human-AI collaboration remains marginal in existing research. This constrains current explanations of how LSC organizations maintain workforce readiness, support employability, and ensure operational resilience in AI-driven supply chains.

Addressing this gap requires the development of a structured digital capability pipeline. Such a pipeline mobilizes workforce transformation across three levels:

- Individual level: development of AI literacy, algorithmic reasoning, data interpretation skills, and huma-AI collaboration competencies.
- Organizational level: leadership support, AI-integrated training programs, workforce planning aligned with AI adoption strategies, and a culture that encourages continuous learning.
- Ecosystem level: sector-wide reskilling initiatives, partnerships with educational institutions, and public-private collaboration to support employment and skills development in AI-enabled logistics.

By positioning AI-focused workforce development as a strategic capability, organizations can enhance operational performance, strengthen employability, and ensure a sustainable transition to AI-intensive supply chains.

In this chapter, we examine how LSC organizations can design and implement robust AI capability pipelines to address skill gaps, transform workforce competencies, and promote employment resilience. Specifically, the chapter aims to:

- Examine the skill–AI misalignment in LSC settings and implications for employment and workforce competence.
- Demonstrate why a structured AI capability pipeline is essential for workforce readiness, skill development, and operational resillience.
- Identify gaps in OSCM research regarding human capital strategies for AI-driven workforce transformation.
- Propose a practical, research-informed framework for developing and sustaining AI capability pipeline, integrating AI literacy, reskilling pathways, human–AI collaboration skills, and continuous learning mechanisms.

By centering human capital in AI adoption, this chapter reframes workforce development as a core strategic lever for employment continuity, skill transformation, and operational excellence in the AI-enabled future of LSC work.

In the remainder of this chapter, we will explore the evolving AI-enabled landscape, outlining the challenges associated with skill-AI misalignment. The chapter then introduces the theoretical foundation informing workforce capability development and presents a conceptual framework for digital capability pipeline. Finally, the chapter concludes with implications for practice, research, and policy, offering recommendations to support workforce-centered digital transformation in LSC environments.

2. CHANGING NATURE OF OSCM WORK

2.1 AI-driven technologies and process transformation in OSCM

As AI adoption accelerates, smart technologies such as automation, robotics, digital twins, Internet of Things (IoT), and big data are becoming important to the redesign and reconfiguration of LSC operational processes, shaping how operations are planned, coordinated, and executed (Hughes et al., 2022). Within this technological ecosystem, AI functions as the analytical core, integrating sensor data, coordinating robotic systems, and generating predictive and prescriptive insights that guide operational decisions. Robotics and automation enhance efficiency in repetitive and high-volume tasks, while AI supports proactive maintenance, process improvements, and informed decision-making (Foroughi, 2020). Digital twins enable the creation of virtual replicas of physical systems, facilitating product personalization and scenario testing; IoT offer real-time, integrated end-to-end tracking across supply chains; and big data analytics facilitates the systematic extraction actionable insights from complex datasets (Hughes et al., 2022; Narkhede et al., 2024). These systems increasingly rely on AI-based modelling to convert raw data into actionable operational intelligence.

Given their demonstrated potential to improve efficiency, responsiveness, and visibility, the integration of these technologies also introduces additional layers of structural complexity, requiring new coordination routines, governance mechanisms, and interoperable infrastructures (Fernando & Wulansari, 2020). Algorithmic decision systems steadily generate forecasts, optimization outputs, and anomaly alerts, shifting elements of operational judgement from manual execution toward data-driven recommendation systems (Kokogho et al., 2024)

Evidence suggests that organizations with more mature technology integration demonstrate stronger resilience and adaptability (Ambrogio et al., 2022). However, such performance gains depend heavily on employees' ability to interpret, supervise, and intervene in algorithm-generated processes. Undoubtedly, these technological shifts are not only transforming operational architecture but also employment structures, creating as tasks are redistributed between humans and intelligent systems.

2.2 Reconfiguration of OSCM roles and work practices

Technological advancements in LSC settings are reconfiguring job roles and altering how tasks are performed across functions (Modgil et al., 2025). As machine-learning tools assume responsibility for routine forecasting, scheduling, and monitoring activities, demand for low-skilled, repetitive roles declines, while analytical and interpretive functions expand (Gupta et al., 2021). This evolution contributes to growing shortages in advanced technical and analytical skill areas (Omol, 2023), resulting in roles that are more data-oriented, system-integrated, and cross-functional.

Role boundaries and decision authority are also shifting. With intelligent systems producing real-time recommendations and exception signals, employees are expected to apply judgement in validating outputs, resolving anomalies, and coordinating responses across supply networks. These adjustments elevate the cognitive demands and reduce reliance on experience based solely on task repetition. Performance is therefore tied less to manual execution and more to employees' capacity to exercise critical judgement, synthesize information, and operate within digitally interconnected settings (Chuang, 2022).

At the occupational level, planners now rely on predictive modelling tools that support inventory and demand decisions. Warehouse personnel increasingly supervise robotic systems rather than performing manual picking alone. Drivers utilizes route optimization algorithms that dynamically adjust to traffic and delivery constraints. Supervisors transition toward performance monitoring through dashboards and automated alerts to ensure smooth processes. Analysts interpret system-generated insights to support strategic decisions, inventory optimization, and operational improvements (Albrecht et al., 2024).

These changes reflect employment restructuring rather than simple substitution. Certain routine tasks are displaced, while higher-order responsibilities—oversight, analytical evaluation, and coordination—expand. Career trajectories increasingly involve movement from execution-focused roles toward data interpretation, systems governance, and cross-functional orchestration. Supply chain work is therefore reorganized around collaboration between human expertise and algorithmic guidance, rather than around mechanized automation alone.

2.3 Emerging skill requirements and workforce readiness gaps

With task and responsibilities restructure, the workforce requires enhanced competencies to execute, oversee, and govern intelligent operational systems. Contemporary roles call for stronger data literacy, analytical reasoning, and adaptive problem-solving. Workers must engage in exception management, interpret predictive outputs, and exercise oversight over automated decision processes.

Recent global assessments confirm that skills obsolescence is intensifying across LSC occupations, revealing a growing disconnect between workforce capabilities and technological requirements. Reports from the World Economic Forum (2025) and International Labour Organization (2025) indicate that a substantial proportion of job-relevant capabilities is likely to change or lose relevance within the next decade, particularly those associated with routine planning, execution, and monitoring activities. Importantly, these shifts extend beyond technical positions to supervisory and managerial roles that rely on data interpretation, system oversight, and cross-platform coordination, further widening the skill-technology gap. Such patterns signal structural change in employment profiles rather than temporary adjustment.

Parallel research similarly identifies skills shortfalls as a major constraint on digital transformation, especially in technologically dynamic sectors such as LSC. As digital operations become more sophisticated, workforce development must move beyond episodic interventions. Structured capability pipeline is required to support role transitions, sustain employability, and enable personnel to remain effective within increasingly automated and analytics-intensive environments.

2.4 Strategic role of human capability in intelligent operations

Human capabilities play a key role in supporting successful digital transformation in OSCM. Although algorithmic tools enhance forecasting, optimization, and monitoring, outcomes depend on how organizations mobilize judgement, contextual knowledge, and learning processes alongside these technologies (Modgil et al., 2025;

Schiuma et al., 2024; Subrahmanyam, 2025). Automated systems require monitoring, interpretation, and ethical oversight, reinforcing the continuing importance of skilled human intervention.

To respond effectively to digital disruption, organizations require coordinated development and renewal of managerial, operational, and technical capabilities. Managerial capabilities enable organizations to interpret digital information, recombine knowledge, and translate technological investments into dynamic capabilities; operational expertise support reliable execution with technology-mediated workflows; and technical proficiency underpins effective engagement with modelling tools, analytical platforms and automated interfaces (Inan & Yilmaz, 2025; Modgil et al., 2025). Importantly, these capabilities are collectively enacted and embedded within routines, training systems, and knowledge-sharing infrastructures.

Consistent with this view, prior research identifies human capabilities as important drivers of performance, innovation, and competitiveness in the digital era (Marino-Romero et al., 2022; Saini et al., 2025). In logistics contexts characterized by increasing reliance on predictive modelling and automation, the strategic priority shifts from simply addressing digital skill shortages to deliberately enabling employment mobility, progression pathways, and sustained relevance in evolving role structures.

2.5 Literature gaps and implications for workforce centered approaches

While technological insights are abundant (Culot et al., 2024), existing OSCM and digital transformation literature remains disproportionately weighted toward tools, architectures, and implementation frameworks, with far less attention devoted to workforce-related strategies. Much of the literature positions AI, big data, and digital platforms as the primary drivers of transformation, privileging technology-oriented models while treating human capital considerations secondary or enabling conditions (Foroughi, 2020; Ranjith Kumar et al., 2021; Ueasangkomsate, 2025).

This technology-dominant orientation under-examines how AI adoption reshapes employment structures, role boundaries, task composition, and required competencies within supply chains. Although recent studies call for more human-centered perspectives on digital transformation, including closer examination of workforce transformation dynamics (Banerjee & Sharma, 2025; Subrahmanyam, 2025), these contributions remain fragmented. Existing research offers limited insight into how organizations systematically prepare, redeploy, and sustain employees as intelligent systems assume analytical, predictive, and optimization functions.

Prior studies rarely articulate how workforce development efforts should be structured, sequenced, or institutionalized alongside AI implementation. Training is often treated as an ad hoc or supportive activity rather than as a strategically embedded process that evolves in parallel with algorithmic integration. As a result, organizations receive little guidance on how to design coherent pathways that support reskilling, skill renewal, and career mobility in digitally intensive supply chain environments.

Addressing this imbalance frames the central purpose of this chapter: advancing a workforce-centered perspective by proposing a research-informed framework for building a sustainable digital capability pipeline. By positioning human capital as a strategic asset rather than a reactive consideration, the chapter reinforces the role of employment sustainability, competence transformation, and inclusive skill development in the future of AI-enabled supply chain work.

3. KEY CHALLENGES IN BUILDING A FUTURE-READY SUPPLY CHAIN WORKFORCE

The rapid diffusion of advanced technologies, ranging from AI, automation, robotics to digital twins, highlights an urgent imperative: preparing a workforce capable of thriving in digitally augmented supply chains. Employees are gradually expected to manage complex, AI-driven processes, often without adequate guidance or support. However, workforce preparation has not always progressed at the same pace as technological deployment.

This has contributed to escalating skill deficiencies across supply chain functions (Foroughi, 2020; Mhaske et al., 2025), threatening firms' ability to extract value from AI investments. As a result, firms must go beyond technology acquisition and implement structured, forward-looking strategies to reskill and deploy talent, or risk compromising the performance, underutilizing AI tools, reducing employee confidence, and uneven workforce readiness.

Research further highlights that the digital skills deficit in supply chain training is exacerbated by the fragmented provision of workforce development opportunities and the absence of cohesive training approaches across organizations (Foroughi, 2020). Capability building initiatives are often short-term, unevenly distributed, and weakly aligned with evolving technological requirements. Without continuity and alignment, workforce readiness remains reactive rather than anticipatory.

Ongoing skills shortfalls undermine both employee outcomes and organizational resilience. Employees may experience reduced engagement, limited career mobility, and uncertainty regarding role security, while organizations face operational inefficiencies and constrained adaptability in AI-intensive environments (Ambrogio et al., 2022; Mhaske et al., 2025). Organizational barriers such as budgetary and time constraints, siloed structures, and short-term priorities frequently crowd out long-term investments in skill renewal. These conditions erode the development of coordinated and scalable capability pipelines necessary for sustained workforce transformation (Birou & Hoek, 2021).

Moreover, inequities in access to training and career progression can emerge, privileging certain roles or units while marginalizing others. Such disparities risk producing uneven preparedness across employee groups and may exacerbate employment vulnerability in lower-skilled or routine-oriented positions.

Policy- and ecosystem challenges further compound these issues. Despite the growing demand for AI-relayed competencies, standardized skill frameworks, interoperable certification pathways, and coordinated industry-academic training mechanisms remain underdeveloped (Angel-Urdinola et al., 2025; Foroughi, 2020). These disconnects constrain the creation of inclusive and transferable capability models required to sustain long-term employability in AI-enabled supply chains.

4. THEORETICAL FOUNDATIONS INFORMING WORKFORCE CAPABILITY DEVELOPMENT

Human Capital Theory (Becker, 1964, HCT) frames employees' knowledge, skills, and competencies as productive assets that contribute to organizational value and performance. From this perspective, human capital is not a static or one-time endowment but is accumulated through ongoing, coordinated investment, enhanced through learning and experience, and subject to depreciation as skills become outdated. This fluid nature of human capital is particularly important in AI-enabled and technology-intensive LSC environments, where digital tools, data-driven systems, and automation evolve rapidly. Thus, workforce capability should not be treated as merely an operational necessity but as a strategic lever that shapes organizations' capacity to adapt, innovate, and remain competitive. Through this lens, HCT helps explain how targeted investments in reskilling, upskilling, and continuous learning enhance employees' productive capacity, role adaptability, and employability, thereby enabling LSC organizations to more effectively deploy AI, automation, and other intelligent systems. Such initiatives often bring back organizational returns in the form of higher operational efficiency, reduced disruption, enhanced resilience, and stronger competitive positioning (Mhaske et al., 2025; Wesche & Handke, 2023).

However, the mere adoption of advanced technologies does not guarantee performance, as technology and human capabilities are inherently interdependent (Pedota et al., 2023). Digital systems generate value only when they are complemented by employees who possess the skills to interpret, supervise, and collaborate with these tools. In this sense, sophisticated technologies introduce a shared digital language within the workplace, requiring personnel across functions to acquire at least foundational digital literacy to interact with and utilize these systems effectively (Pedota et al., 2023). As technologies continue to advance, this shared digital language also changes, accelerating skill obsolescence and necessitating the ongoing renewal of human capital to sustain workforce relevance and job security.

Drawing on HCT, workforce capability development in digital supply chain contexts is therefore best understood as cumulative, strategically coordinated investment process rather than a series of isolated training events. A digital capability pipeline represents a structured, long-term mechanisms through which organizations deliberately build, refresh, and strengthen workforce competencies in a progressive and coordinated manner. In contrast to ad hoc or tool-specific training—often reactive, fragmented, and disconnected from career progression, the capability pipeline emphasizes staged learning pathways that integrate foundational digital literacy, role-specific technical expertise, and advanced analytical and adaptive skills over time. This approach reflects the HCT's principle that human capital accumulates through sustained investment and erodes if not continuously replenished, especially in environments characterized by rapid technological innovation. By sequencing development across roles, functions, and career stages, the pipeline allows organizations to align workforce skills with emerging technologies, minimize skill-technology misalignment, and ensure that human capital remains productive, adaptable, and aligned with evolving AI-driven task requirements as operational demands change.

Within this pipeline-oriented approach, the scope of skills being cultivated becomes crucial. An excessive focus on narrow or proprietary digital capabilities can be problematic, as contemporary digital skills frameworks instead emphasize the importance of broader, transferable competencies like digital literacy, data interpretation, and information processing skills that are applicable across diverse work contexts and technological systems (Audrin et al., 2024; Orero-Blat et al., 2022). At the same time, workforce development depends on organizational capacity and ecosystem coordination. Variations in investment, access to resources, infrastructure, and public-private collaboration affect how consistently skills are cultivated and replenished across firms (Mhaske et al., 2025; Minor et al., 2025). Moreover, the responsibility for workforce development cannot rest solely with individual organizations, especially in AI-intensive supply chain contexts where market mechanisms alone underprovide training opportunities. Barriers such as limited access to educational resources, outdated curricula, insufficient infrastructure, lagging regulations, and weak public-private collaboration further constrain skill development (Mhaske et al., 2025). These challenges highlight the need for coordinated investment by organizations, educational institutions, industry consortia, and government actors to support accessible, industry-aligned capability development that enhances long-term employability and equitable workforce participation.

Ultimately, workforce proficiency and adaptability serve as important enablers of AI-enabled transformation in LSC firms, supporting operational efficiency, service performance, and innovation by underpinning a learning-oriented culture, agile practices, and effective utilization of digital technologies (Cichosz et al., 2020). Sustaining OSCM performance therefore requires the continuous development of workforce capabilities—at individual, organizational, and ecosystem levels—alongside the adoption of new technologies, highlighting the strategic role of human capital in driving successful implementation and mitigating technology-induced employment displacement risks (Gupta et al., 2021). Empirical evidence further suggests that human capital investment facilitates technology assimilation, strengthen adaptive and entrepreneurial competencies, and fosters firm-level innovativeness, enabling supply chain operations to leverage digital transformation for competitive advantage, workforce resilience, and improved business performance (Lang et al., 2022).

5. PROPOSED DIGITAL CAPABILITY PIPELINE FRAMEWORK

5.1 Overview of the Framework

The digital capability pipeline conceptualizes capability development as a structured, long-term system through which organizations continuously build, renew, and reconfigure workforce capabilities in response to AI-driven changes in task composition, decision authority, and role structures within supply chains. From a HCT perspective (Becker, 1964), this pipeline reflects strategic investments in employees' knowledge, skills, and competencies that increase productivity, operational performance, and innovation potential in Ai-enabled enabled LSC environments.

The framework addresses workforce challenges arising from the rapid diffusion of AI, automation, and advanced analytics, which are reallocating routine tasks to intelligent systems while expanding the need for analytical oversight, exception management, and human-machine coordination. These shifts have created significant skill gaps and transitional pressures in supply chain employment structures. Organizations therefore have both a strategic and ethical responsibility to ensure systematic reskilling and upskilling so employees can adapt to evolving technological demands and maintain employability amid algorithmic integration (Chuang et al., 2024; Omol, 2023). By formalizing capability development int a pipeline, firms transition from ad hoc training to a coordinated investment logic in which workforce skills co-evolve with AI deployment, support role redesign, and mitigate displacement risks, while delivering measurable organizational value.

Figure 1 illustrates the digital capability pipeline operating across three interrelated levels — individual, organizational, and ecosystem — linked by continuous feedback loops and anchored in HCT principles. Differ from conventional training models that focus narrowly on tool adoption (Bhatt & Muduli, 2022), this framework explicitly connects capability development to employment sustainability, role mobility, and long-term competence transformation in AI-intensive supply chains.

- At the individual level, employees develop and renew AI-relevant competencies—including digital literacy, data interpretation, technical proficiency and collaborative problem-solving—enabling them to transition from execution-oriented roles toward analytical, supervisory, and coordination-based responsibilities. Human capital at this level directly contribute to employability, adaptability, and career progression in evolving job structures.
- At the organizational level, firms institutionalize structured learning architectures through workforce planning, leadership commitment, facilitating culture and technology infrastructure that supports human-AI collaboration. These mechanisms ensure that reskilling efforts are aligned with strategic AI adoption pathways and emerging task reallocation patterns, thereby amplifying returns on human capital investment.
- At the ecosystem level, external actors such as education providers, industry bodies, and policymakers contribute to standardized skill frameworks, certification pathways, and sector-wide talent pipelines that facilitate transferable competencies and inclusive access to AI-related employment opportunities. This level addresses systemic skill shortages and supports labor market mobility across firms and regions.
- Across all levels, feedback mechanisms operate to identify emerging skill gaps, recalibrate development initiatives, and align workforce capabilities with strategic priorities and technological trajectories. This dynamic feedback process ensures that capability investments remain synchronized with AI-induced shifts in job design, preventing skill obsolescence and sustaining workforce resilience over time.

Figure 1. The digital capability pipeline

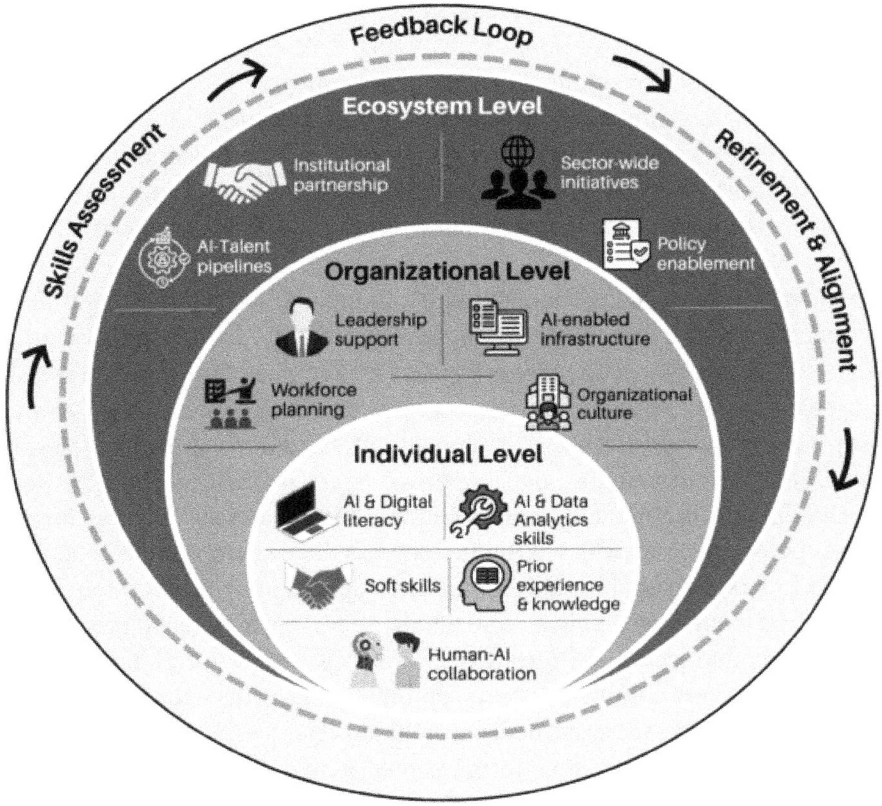

5.2 Building blocks of the Framework

5.2.1 Levels

5.2.1.1 Individual levels

Employees' AI and digital literacy, analytical skills, and problem-solving abilities constitute critical human capital and represent the primary site of skill accumulation within the digital capability pipeline. Investing in these capabilities not only enhances individual performance but also creates value for the organization by enabling effective operation, supervision, and interpretation of AI-driven systems, robotics, and advanced analytics (Becker, 1964). To operate effectively in AI-intensive LSC settings, employees play a central role in acquiring, updating, and applying digital skills that translate technologies into operational performance. Both technical expertise and soft skills are significant, as employees must manage not only AI-supported forecasting, data analytics, and robotic systems, but also to collaborate across functions, adapt to evolving task configurations, and resolve complex operational exceptions. For example, employees managing AI-based inventory systems must simultaneously understand algorithm outputs, validate system recommendations, communicate insights to warehouse supervisors, and coordinate with IT and logistics teams. Essentially, technological and soft significantly impact agility and performance in logistics (Cantoni et al., 2024; Essex et al., 2016; Sangari & Razmi, 2015).

Employees enter this environment with a foundation of AI and digital literacy, analytical reasoning,, prior experience, learning agility, and motivation to keep improving. These initial endowments form the entry point of the pipeline and shape employees' capacity to transition from execution-focused roles toward analytical and supervisory responsibilities. Combined with access to AI-enabled platforms, robotics, cloud-based systems, and supportive organizational mechanisms such as mentoring and cross-functional collaboration, these resources serve as inputs for ongoing competence renewal. Digital literacy has therefore become a foundational capability in modern supply chain and logistics operations. Employees are increasingly required to understand algorithmic logic, supervise automated processes, and intervene exception scenarios (Foroughi, 2020). Proficiency in data analytics allows personnel to interpret complex datasets, optimize routing decisions, anticipate disruptions, and support predictive decision-making (Hughes et al., 2022).

Beyond initial acquisition, renewal is essential, as learning agility enables employees to quickly adapt to new tools and revised workflows, ensuring that performance keeps pace with AI system evolution. Familiarity with digital twins, cloud-based platforms, and IoT monitoring supports planning and simulation functions (Hughes et al., 2022). Given the increased connectivity of digital systems, cybersecurity awareness is also necessary to mitigate privacy risks, protect sensitive information, and ensure the safe operation of algorithmic infrastructures, particularly when connecting less-secure systems (Radanliev et al., 2020).

Equally important are soft skills, as AI-supported supply chains rely on cross-functional coordination and collaborative interpretation of system outputs. Employees must demonstrate teamwork, critical thinking, adaptability, and communication capabilities to coordinate flexibly across units and respond to AI-generated forecasts during disruptions (Cantoni et al., 2024; Hamann-Lohmer et al., 2023; Koh & Yuen, 2022; Wahab et al., 2024). For instance, during demand volatility, personnel must jointly evaluate predictive signals, adjust workflows, and align stakeholders to minimize performance impact.

These capabilities are accumulated and refreshed over time through structured reskilling programs, mentoring, on-the-job learning, AI-assisted learning systems, rotational assignments, and role redesign that embed learning into daily work (Goraya et al., 2024; Gupta et al., 2021; Mhaske et al., 2025). This process strengthens human-AI collaboration, enabling employees to oversee automated processes and exercise judgement in data-driven environments (Hughes et al., 2022).

As a result, employees progressively develop advanced analytics proficiency, stronger cybersecurity awareness, and enhanced collaborative oversight capabilities. Through continuous accumulation and updating of skills, individuals are better able to maintain employability, navigate role restructuring, and assume higher-value analytical and supervisory functions within AI-enabled supply chains.

5.2.1.2 Organizational levels

While individual capabilities are critical, organizational structures, cultures, and processes determine how those skills are coordinated, scaled, and aligned with AI adoption strategies. At this level of the digital capability pipeline, organizations transform individual learning into repeatable, organization-wide capability systems that facilitate task redistribution and role redesign. Effective leadership guides workforce adaptation by articulating a clear AI integration vision, aligning technological investments with employment planning (Subrahmanyam, 2025). Consistent top management commitment ensures resource allocation for systematic reskilling aligned with evolving task architectures (Gupta et al., 2021).

AI-intensive operations require scalable and interoperable infrastructure capable of supporting predictive modelling, automation, and cross-platform analytics. Fragmented or siloed systems can limit visibility, analytics and automation effectiveness (Kalaitzi & Tsolakis, 2022). Scalable infrastructure enables algorithmic processing across suppliers, warehouses, logistics service providers, and customers, while interoperability supports coordinated and timely decision-making (Kalaitzi & Tsolakis, 2022). In parallel, the connected nature of digital supply chain intensifies exposure to cyber risks, making cybersecurity and recovery planning integral to infrastructure (Radanliev et al., 2020). Core technologies such as ERP systems, cloud platforms, IoT networks, and digital twins form the backbone through which AI-supported decision-making becomes embedded in routine operations.

Organizations must also invest deliberately in workforce development, embedding skills within formal structures rather than relying on isolated learning. Targeted learning pathways, digital academies, and protected development time enable personnel to transition into newly emerging AI-related responsibilities. Prior research confirms that human capital development, particularly through systematic training and upskilling, is a key organizational resource for the effective technology assimilation and competitive advantage (Gupta et al., 2021; Mhaske et al., 2025).

Without such investments, organizations risk persistent skill gaps that hinder AI adoption and performance improvements.

However, leadership support, infrastructure, and training investments alone are insufficient to generate sustained value. Their effectiveness depends on how learning is sequenced, embedded, and institutionalized through organizational processes. A structured capability pipeline enables staged progression from foundational literacy to advanced analytics and oversight roles, supporting workforce mobility and minimizing skill obsolescence (Bouwmans et al., 2024; Gupta et al., 2021). Rather than reactive training, the pipeline formalizes role-based development aligned with AI adoption trajectories, transforming dispersed expertise into scalable organizational competence.

Aligned workforce planning further strengthens this process by anticipating emerging AI-related skill requirements and coordinating recruitment, redeployment, and reskilling accordingly (Gupta et al., 2021). Supportive organizational cultures that promote experimentation, continuous learning, innovativeness, and cross-functional collaboration help stimulate knowledge exchange and reduce resistance to technological change and support smooth employment transitions (Lang et al., 2022; Subrahmanyam, 2025).

Collectively, these institutional investments enhance efficiency, agility, and resilience while also mitigating displacement risks and supporting structured career progression in AI-driven operational settings (Becker, 1964; Bouwmans et al., 2024). When combined with advanced technologies, organizational-level coordination enables faster, data-driven decision-making, improved cross-functional and inter-organizational integration, and responsive operations under uncertainty (Kalaitzi & Tsolakis, 2022; Sangari & Razmi, 2015). Beyond operational gains, this institutionalized capability development supports continuous process optimization, service enhancement, and sustained competitive advantage in increasingly digitalized environments.

5.2.1.3 Ecosystem level

Beyond firm boundaries, capability renewal depends on the broader ecosystem in which organizations operate. Within the digital capability pipeline, the ecosystem level functions as the external mechanisms that align education, policy, and industry collaboration with AI-related labor market shifts. The role of external stakeholders such as educational institutions, industry associations, government agencies, and training providers is critical in shaping the availability, relevance, and continuity of AI-relevant competencies across logistics roles. As digital technologies diffuse rapidly across LSC systems, individual organizations often lack the capacity to independently generate all required capabilities, making ecosystem-level coordination essential.

At this level, inputs are primarily shaped by institutional support structures and cross-sector collaboration. Partnerships with universities, vocational institutions, and training providers extend human capital development beyond individual firms, ensuring alignment between curricula and evolving requirements in predictive analytics, automation oversight, and algorithmic decision support (Cantoni et al., 2024; Meier et al., 2024; Mhaske et al., 2025). In parallel, public–private collaboration supports inclusive access to reskilling and upskilling initiatives, particularly through funding schemes, training subsidies, and incentives that lower participation barriers for firms and individuals. Policy frameworks reinforce these efforts by providing regulatory clarity, strategic direction, and long-term institutional commitment to AI-related workforce development (Mhaske et al., 2025).

These ecosystem-level inputs are transformed into capability renewal through a set of coordinated processes. A key process involves the design and delivery of national or sector-wide upskilling programs that address common skill gaps across industries. Such initiatives generate scale efficiencies by standardizing competency benchmarks and addressing shared AI-related skill gaps. Credentialing mechanisms—including micro-credentials and industry-recognized certifications—further support the pipeline by validating competencies and signaling readiness for AI-intensive roles (Lang, 2023). These mechanisms facilitate workforce mobility, promote lifelong learning, and reduce friction during employment transitions.

Knowledge diffusion constitutes another essential ecosystem-level process. Industry forums, collaborative digital platforms, and cross-sector partnerships enable the exchange of best practices, technological insights, and experiential learning related to digital supply chain transformation (Foroughi, 2020). Such interactions reduce duplication of effort, accelerate collective learning, and support the dissemination of emerging capabilities across organizations and sectors. Importantly, they allow for smaller firms and less digitally mature organizations to access expertise and resources that would otherwise remain concentrated among leading firms (Martin-Rios et al., 2022).

The coordinated functioning of these inputs and processes leads to several key outcomes. First, the ecosystem pipeline supports the continuous skill replenishment, ensuring an inclusive and resilient workforce supply that can accommodate diverse segments of the labor market and reduce the risk of structural skill shortages in AI-related logistics occupations (Mhaske et al., 2025). Second, ecosystem-level collaboration facilitates industry-wide capability diffusion (Martin-Rios et al., 2022), allowing digital competencies to spread beyond individual organizations and become embedded across sectors. This collective accumulation of human capital strengthens overall supply chain performance, and resilience (Mhaske et al., 2025).

At its core, the ecosystem-level pipeline anchors long-term employment sustainability by aligning institutional training systems with AI-induced changes in job design. By reinforcing skills beyond the firm, this level ensures that the organizational capability systems are continuously supplied with relevant talent, supporting labor market adaptability and inclusive participation in AI-driven supply chains.

5.2.2 Cross-level linkages

The effectiveness of the digital capability pipeline rests on coherent alignment across individual, organizational, and ecosystem levels, particularly in responding to AI-driven changes to logistics roles and task structures. AI systems do not merely introduce new tools; they decide authority, shift routine work toward automation, and expand oversight and analytical responsibilities. The pipeline explains how these employment shifts are coordinated and sustained across levels.

At the individual level, employees develop competencies that enable them to supervise AI systems, interpret outputs, and manage exceptions. However, these capabilities only reshape employment structures when organizations institutionalize them. At the organizational level, firms embed AI-related responsibilities into formal job designs, clarify accountability between human and algorithmic decisions, and create progression pathways linking operational roles to more advanced analytical or supervisory positions. This prevents upskilling from remaining isolated and ensures that role redesign aligns with strategic objectives.

Ecosystem actors reinforce this alignment by updating training standards, certifications, and educational programs to reflect emerging AI-related role requirements. Through coordinated curriculum development and credentialing, external institutions reduce skill mismatches and support workforce mobility across firms adapting to similar AI-enabled operating models.

Through these cross-level linkages, the pipeline ensures that AI adoption translates into structured employment transformation—through redesigned roles, clearer career pathways, and coordinated capability renewal—rather than ad hoc adjustments at the employee level.

5.2.3 Feedback loop

The digital capability pipeline is not linear but iterative. AI systems generate new data, performance insights, and operational patterns that, in turn, redefine required skills and job structures. The feedback loop ensures that workforce development co-evolves with these AI-driven changes, generating sustained operational and competitive value (Becker, 1964). Given the rapid pace of technological change and increasing complexity of supply chain systems, digital capabilities must be continuously monitored, assessed, and updated rather than developed through one-off interventions (Mhaske et al., 2025). Feedback processes identify deficiencies early, refine training programs iteratively, and maintain alignment with strategic objectives and technological demands (Baker, 2010).

At the individual level, feedback mechanisms assess not only technical proficiency but also employees' effectiveness in human–AI collaboration. Performance metrics increasingly capture the quality of AI-assisted decisions, the handling of system exceptions, and the ability to interpret predictive outputs. Where gaps emerge, for example, difficulty interpreting model uncertainty or responding to automated disruptions—targeted reskilling interventions can be introduced. This prevents capability erosion and supports continuous role adaptation.

At the organizational level, feedback from AI system performance, operational disruptions, and employee engagement informs job redesign and workforce planning (Atanassova et al., 2025; Subrahmanyam, 2025). For example, if AI deployment shifts workload toward exception management, firms may formalize specialized escalation roles or redistribute responsibilities across teams. If automation reduces routine task intensity but increases analytical demands, training priorities and recruitment profiles are adjusted accordingly. Feedback also captures broader employment effects, such as uneven workload distribution or emerging skill polarization. Addressing these issues may require redefining role boundaries or strengthening progression pathways to maintain workforce sustainability.

At the ecosystem level, industry signals regarding emerging AI applications, labor shortages, and shifting competence requirements inform updates to sector-wide training programs, certification standards, and policy frameworks (Mhaske et al., 2025). As AI capabilities expand, from predictive analytics to autonomous systems, education providers, and industry associations revise curricula and credentials structures accordingly. This maintains alignment between labor market supply and AI-transformed logistics roles.

By connecting individual learning, organizational processes, and ecosystem interventions, the feedback loop transforms the pipeline into an adaptive employment governance mechanism. Rather than treating workforce development as a one-time response to AI implementation, it establishes continuous recalibration of skills, roles, and career pathways. This dynamic alignment supports resilient employment systems, responsible AI integration, and sustained competitive performance in logistics operation.

5.3 Implementation strategies

Implementing the digital capability pipeline requires translating its conceptual design into actionable initiatives that directly addresses AI-driven changes to logistics employment structures. Rather than treating capability development as a general digital initiative, implementation should begin with a clear diagnosis of how AI reshapes tasks, roles, and decision authority across LSC.

A critical first step is to identify where AI adoption is altering work most significantly—such as AI-assisted demand forecasting, warehouse automation, predictive maintenance, or autonomous transport routing. Organizations should map how these systems redistribute tasks between humans and algorithms, distinguishing between:

- Tasks likely to be automated
- Tasks augmented by AI-assisted decision support
- Tasks that remain human-centric (e.g., exception handling, coordination, ethical judgement)

This mapping clarifies priority skill transitions, such as movement from manual execution to AI supervision, from routine scheduling to analytics interpretation, or from transactional processing to cross-functional coordination. Executive sponsorship is critical to align workforce redesign with AI deployment strategies and to prevent capability development from lagging behind technological implementation (Gupta et al., 2021).

A phased deployment approach is recommended to manage complexity of AI integration and reduce risk. Pilot programs can be launched in selected units or functions not only to test AI systems, but also to test redesigned job roles, revised performance metrics, and new competency requirements. For example, when implementing AI-based warehouse optimization, firms can pilot AI oversight roles responsible for monitoring system outputs, structured exception-handling protocols, and training modules focused on data interpretation and systems intervention. Insights from pilots should inform broader scaling decisions, including recruitment profiles, revised job descriptions, and new progression pathways toward analytics-intensive roles (Bellantuono et al., 2021).

Successful implementation also requires embedding AI-related competencies into formal HR and operational systems. Capability development should be integrated into performance management (i.e., quality of AI-assisted decisions), career pathways (e.g., operator→ AI supervisor → analytics specialist), and succession planning for digitally intensive roles. Synchronizing AI rollout with targeted training maximizes skill transfer. Technologies such as simulation-based learning, digital twins, and AI-enabled adaptive training systems can accelerate workforce readiness (Ambrogio et al., 2022). Aligning these tools with AI-enabled work redesign rather than deployed as generic digital training solutions ensures that investments in skills and technology generate measurable impact (Mhaske et al., 2025).

At the ecosystem level, firms should formalize partnerships with universities, vocational institutions, and industry bodies to co-develop AI-relevant curricula. Sector-wide collaboration can standardize competencies in areas such as applied logistics analytics, algorithmic oversight, automation coordination, and digital risk management (Martin-Rios et al., 2022; Meier et al., 2024; Mhaske et al., 2025). Such coordination reduces skill mismatches and supports mobility across firms facing similar AI-driven restructuring, strengthening the external labor market for AI-enabled logistics roles.

AI adoption often introduces uncertainty regarding job security, role displacement, and career viability. Effective change management should therefore explicitly address employment implications. Transparent communication about role evolution, reskilling pathways, and new progression opportunities can mitigate resistance and reinforce trust. Managers should be trained to lead hybrid human-AI teams, model responsible AI use, and facilitate continuous learning (Subrahmanyam, 2025).

Through these implementation strategies, the digital capability pipeline becomes a structured mechanism for governing AI-induced employment transformation rather than a generic digital training initiative.

6. IMPLICATIONS

6.1 Implications for Practice

The implementation of digital capability pipeline offers managers a structured approach to managing AI-driven workforce transformation in logistics. Managers should begin with systematic AI impact assessments that identify roles most exposed to automation, roles undergoing augmentation, and emerging hybrid roles (e.g., AI operations coordinator, analytics translator). This assessment clarifies where immediate reskilling is necessary and where longer-term career pathway redesign is required.

Following needs assessment, workforce segmentation should reflect AI interaction intensity rather than generic digital proficiency. For example, operational supervisors require AI monitoring and exception-handling skills, planners and analysts require advanced data interpretation and model validation capabilities, and frontline operators require system interaction literacy and collaborative coordination skills. Competency frameworks should also provide a clear roadmap for progression pathways from routine operational roles toward AI-intensive positions.

Moreover, AI transitions career structures from hierarchical progression based on tenure toward skill-based mobility anchored in analytics and system expertise. Managers should formalize transitions such as warehouse operator to automation supervisor, transport scheduler to predictive analytics coordinator, and inventory controller to AI-assisted demand planner (Bessen, 2018; Brynjolfsson & Mitchell, 2017). Making these pathways visible reduces displacement anxiety and increases workforce engagement (Parker et al., 2017).

AI implementation decisions should consider not only cost and productivity, but also workforce sustainability. Human oversight capacity, workload distribution, and skill polarization risks should be actively managed to avoid long-term employment fragmentation. When effectively implemented, the capability pipeline enhances agility, improves human-AI collaboration quality, and supports resilient employment systems aligned with AI-enabled operations.

The capability pipeline represents an investment in human capital that generates sustained value for both employees and organizations. Managers who operationalize these frameworks create environments where workforce development, strategic priorities, and technological adoption reinforce one another, supporting continuous improvement, innovation, and competitive advantage in increasingly digitalized supply chains (Becker, 1964; Gupta et al., 2021).

6.2 Implications for Policy

AI-driven restructuring in logistics requires coordinated policy responses that address both skill supply and employment stability. Policymakers should develop AI-specific logistics competency frameworks, support micro-credentials in applied AI oversight and analytics, incentivize firm-level reskilling over displacement, and promote public-private training partnerships aligned with AI adoption trajectories.

Policy interventions can also mitigate regional or sectoral skill polarization by subsidizing reskilling in automation-exposed roles (Martin-Rios et al., 2022; Mhaske et al., 2025). By aligning education systems, labor market policy, and industry collaboration with AI-induced role transformation, policymakers strengthen ecosystem-level resilience and reduce structural skill shortages.

As highlighted by Meier et al. (2024), policies can be designed to shape the labor market, ensuring that career pathways, educational opportunities, and professional growth for supply chain workers are aligned with industry demand. By coordinating the supply of skilled workers with evolving operational needs, these policies contribute to a larger, more competent talent pool, improving the resilience and competitiveness of the sector. Moreover, well-designed policy frameworks can embed continuous capability development mechanisms, supporting iterative updates to curricula, certifications, and training programs in response to technological change. By strengthening the ecosystem-level dimension of the digital capability pipeline, such policies ensure that workforce readiness is sustained, inclusive, and adaptive to future disruptions.

6.3 Implications for Research

The proposed digital capability pipeline framework highlights several avenues for future empirical investigation. While the conceptual model integrates individual, organizational, and ecosystem-level dimensions of workforce development, there is limited empirical evidence on how these levels interact in practice, particularly in digitally enabled LSC. Future research should examine how AI adoption reshapes employment structures, including task redistribution between humans and AI systems, shifts from hierarchical to skill-based mobility, and the balance between augmentation and displacement outcomes, as well as emerging patterns of skill polarization across AI-enabled supply chains.

One key research gap lies in the measurement and operationalization of the digital capability pipeline. Scholars could develop and validate metrics for AI oversight capability, exception-handling proficiency, human-AI collaboration quality, and progression pathways from routine roles toward AI-intensive positions. Longitudinal studies are especially needed to track role evolution, carer pathways shifts, and workforce segmentation based on AI interaction intensity across firms with different levels of digital pipeline maturity.

Additionally, interdisciplinary research bridging the domains of OSCM, human resource management (HRM), and digital transformation should examine how HR practices, such as structured training, workforce planning, and cultural initiatives, interact with intelligence systems, and how public–private partnerships, educational institutions, and policy frameworks shape sector-wide digital capability development. Such studies could provide deeper insights into how organizations adapt to AI transformation, sustain human capital development, and translate workforce investments into measurable improvements in productivity, resilience, and innovation.

7. CONCLUSION

AI is redefining logistics work by redistributing tasks, reshaping decision authority, and altering skill composition across supply chain roles. While AI offers substantial improvements in efficiency, visibility, and value creation, its successful integration depends on deliberate workforce adaptation. Without systematic and coordinated workforce development, investments in AI risk failing to deliver sustained operational and strategic outcomes.

This chapter's core contribution is the digital capability pipeline: a multi-level framework that explains how individual skills, organizational systems, and ecosystem institutions can be aligned to govern AI-driven employment transformation in logistics.

Rather than viewing workforce development as a peripheral support activity, the pipeline positions capability formation as a central mechanism for managing task augmentation, role redesign, and career pathway evolution under AI adoption. Through structured reskilling, institutionalized learning pathways, and ecosystem coordination, organizations can convert AI deployment from a source of disruption into a driver of sustainable performance and resilient employment systems.

By anchoring workforce strategy explicitly in AI-induced changes to work, the digital capability pipeline provides managers, policymakers, and researchers with a coherent framework for understanding and shaping the future employment in AI-enabled logistics.

REFERENCES

Albrecht, T., Baier, M.-S., Gimpel, H., Meierhöfer, S., Röglinger, M., Schlüchtermann, J., & Will, L. (2024). Leveraging Digital Technologies in Logistics 4.0: Insights on Affordances from Intralogistics Processes. *Information Systems Frontiers*, *26*(2), 755–774. DOI: 10.1007/s10796-023-10394-6

Ambrogio, G., Filice, L., Longo, F., & Padovano, A. (2022). Workforce and supply chain disruption as a digital and technological innovation opportunity for resilient manufacturing systems in the COVID-19 pandemic. *Computers & Industrial Engineering*, *169*, 108158. DOI: 10.1016/j.cie.2022.108158 PMID: 35431410

Angel-Urdinola, D. F., Chinen, M., & Rodon, G. (2025). *Digital Skills Development: Competence Frameworks, Assessment Tools, and Pedagogical Approaches* (Education Working Paper, Issue. https://thedocs.worldbank.org/en/doc/a607bb6e3b76d2be0f3db8db34dcf73e-0140022025/related/3EDU-WP-14-Digital-skills-development.pdf

Atanassova, I., Bednar, P., Khan, H., & Khan, Z. (2025). Managing the VUCA environment: The dynamic role of organizational learning and strategic agility in B2B versus B2C firms. *Industrial Marketing Management*, *125*, 12–28. 10.1016/j.indmarman.2024.12.008. DOI: 10.1016/j.indmarman.2024.12.008

Audrin, B., Audrin, C., & Salamin, X. (2024). Digital skills at work – Conceptual development and empirical validation of a measurement scale. *Technological Forecasting and Social Change*, *202*, 123279. 10.1016/j.techfore.2024.123279. DOI: 10.1016/j.techfore.2024.123279

Baker, N. (2010). Employee feedback technologies in the human performance system. *Human Resource Development International*, *13*(4), 477–485. DOI: 10.1080/13678868.2010.501994

Banerjee, P., & Sharma, N. (2025). Digital transformation and talent management in industry 4.0: A systematic literature review and the future directions [Review]. *The Learning Organization*, *32*(4), 620–640. DOI: 10.1108/TLO-10-2023-0183

Becker, G. S. (1964). *Human Capital: A Theoretical Analysis with Special Reference to Education*. Columbia University Press.

Bellantuono, N., Nuzzi, A., Pontrandolfo, P., & Scozzi, B. (2021). Digital Transformation Models for the I4.0 Transition: Lessons from the Change Management Literature. *Sustainability (Basel)*, *13*(23), 12941. https://www.mdpi.com/2071-1050/13/23/12941. DOI: 10.3390/su132312941

Bessen, J. (2018). Artificial intelligence and jobs: The role of demand. In *The economics of artificial intelligence: an agenda* (pp. 291–307). University of Chicago Press.

Bhatt, P., & Muduli, A. (2022). Artificial intelligence in learning and development: A systematic literature review. *European Journal of Training and Development, 47*(7-8), 677–694. DOI: 10.1108/EJTD-09-2021-0143

Birou, L., & Hoek, R. V. (2021). Supply chain management talent: The role of executives in engagement, recruitment, development and retention. *Supply Chain Management, 27*(6), 712–727. DOI: 10.1108/SCM-08-2020-0418

Bouwmans, M., Lub, X., Orlowski, M., & Nguyen, T.-V. (2024). Developing the digital transformation skills framework: A systematic literature review approach. *PLoS One, 19*(7), e0304127. DOI: 10.1371/journal.pone.0304127 PMID: 38968253

Brynjolfsson, E., & Mitchell, T. (2017). What can machine learning do? Workforce implications. *Science, 358*(6370), 1530–1534. /doi:10.1126/science.aap8062. DOI: 10.1126/science.aap8062 PMID: 29269459

Cantoni, F., Ricciardi, A., Bisogni, P. G., & Zsifkovits, H. (2024). The unravelled role of soft skills in the logistics and supply chain management field. *Journal of Innovation & Knowledge, 9*(4), 100615. 10.1016/j.jik.2024.100615. DOI: 10.1016/j.jik.2024.100615

Chuang, S. (2022). Indispensable skills for human employees in the age of robots and AI. *European Journal of Training and Development, 48*(1-2), 179–195. DOI: 10.1108/EJTD-06-2022-0062

Chuang, S., Shahhosseini, M., Javaid, M., & Wang, G. G. (2024). Machine learning and AI technology-induced skill gaps and opportunities for continuous development of middle-skilled employees. *Journal of Work-Applied Management*. Advance online publication. DOI: 10.1108/JWAM-08-2024-0111

Cichosz, M., Wallenburg, C. M., & Knemeyer, A. M. (2020). Digital transformation at logistics service providers: Barriers, success factors and leading practices. *International Journal of Logistics Management, 31*(2), 209–238. DOI: 10.1108/IJLM-08-2019-0229

Culot, G., Podrecca, M., & Nassimbeni, G. (2024). Artificial intelligence in supply chain management: A systematic literature review of empirical studies and research directions. *Computers in Industry, 162*, 104132. 10.1016/j.compind.2024.104132. DOI: 10.1016/j.compind.2024.104132

DocShipper. (2025). *AI Changing Logistics & Supply Chain – 2025*. https://docshipper.com/logistics/ai-changing-logistics-supply-chain-2025/

Essex, A., Subramanian, N., & Gunasekaran, A. (2016). The relationship between supply chain manager capabilities and performance: Empirical evidence. *Production Planning and Control*, *27*(3), 198–211. DOI: 10.1080/09537287.2015.1091519

Fernando, Y., & Wulansari, P. (2020). Perceived understanding of supply chain integration, communication and teamwork competency in the global manufacturing companies. *European Journal of Management and Business Economics*, *30*(2), 191–210. DOI: 10.1108/EJMBE-06-2020-0157

Foroughi, A. (2020). Supply chain workforce training: Addressing the digital skills gap. *Higher Education, Skills and Work-based Learning*, *11*(3), 683–696. DOI: 10.1108/HESWBL-07-2020-0159

Goraya, M. A. S., Yaqub, M. Z., Khan, M. A., Akram, M. S., & Alofaysan, H. (2024). Transforming performance: How agility, response, resilience and support shape success in digital strategies. *Information Technology & People*. Advance online publication. DOI: 10.1108/ITP-05-2024-0592

Gupta, A., Singh, R. K., & Gupta, S. (2021). Developing human resource for the digitization of logistics operations: Readiness index framework. *International Journal of Manpower*, *43*(2), 355–379. DOI: 10.1108/IJM-03-2021-0175

Hamann-Lohmer, J., Bendig, M., & Lasch, R. (2023). Investigating the impact of digital transformation on relationship and collaboration dynamics in supply chains and manufacturing networks – A multi-case study. *International Journal of Production Economics*, *262*, 108932. 10.1016/j.ijpe.2023.108932. DOI: 10.1016/j.ijpe.2023.108932

Hughes, L., Dwivedi, Y. K., Rana, N. P., Williams, M. D., & Raghavan, V. (2022). Perspectives on the future of manufacturing within the Industry 4.0 era. *Production Planning and Control*, *33*(2-3), 138–158. DOI: 10.1080/09537287.2020.1810762

Inan, G. G., & Yilmaz, G. (2025). Developing Organisational Capabilities for Digital Transformation. In *Digital Transformation: A Business Imperative* (pp. 12-28). *L* DOI: 10.4324/9781003626640-3

International Labour Organization. I. (2025). *World Employment and Social Outlook: Trends 2025*. I. L. Organization. https://www.ilo.org/publications/flagship-reports/world-employment-and-social-outlook-trends-2025

Kalaitzi, D., & Tsolakis, N. (2022). Supply chain analytics adoption: Determinants and impacts on organisational performance and competitive advantage. *International Journal of Production Economics*, *248*, 108466. 10.1016/j.ijpe.2022.108466. DOI: 10.1016/j.ijpe.2022.108466

Koh, L. Y., & Yuen, K. F. (2022). Emerging competencies for logistics professionals in the digital era: A literature review [Systematic Review]. *Frontiers in Psychology, Volume 13 - 2022.* /DOI: 10.3389/fpsyg.2022.965748

Kokogho, E., Odio, P. E., Ogunsola, O. Y., & Nwaozomudoh, M. O. (2024). AI-powered economic forecasting: Challenges and opportunities in a data-driven world. *International Journal of Management and Organizational Research*, *3*(6), 74–83. 10.54660/IJMOR.2024.3.6.74-83. DOI: 10.54660/IJMOR.2024.3.6.74-83

Lang, J. (2023). Workforce upskilling: Can universities meet the challenges of lifelong learning? *International Journal of Information and Learning Technology*, *40*(5), 388–400. DOI: 10.1108/IJILT-01-2023-0001

Lang, L. D., Behl, A., Phuong, N. N. D., Gaur, J., & Dzung, N. T. (2022). Toward SME digital transformation in the supply chain context: The role of structural social and human capital. *International Journal of Physical Distribution & Logistics Management*, *53*(4), 448–466. DOI: 10.1108/IJPDLM-12-2021-0525

Liu, K. P., & Chiu, W. (2021). Supply Chain 4.0: The impact of supply chain digitalization and integration on firm performance. *Asian Journal of Business Ethics*, *10*(2), 371–389. DOI: 10.1007/s13520-021-00137-8

Marino-Romero, J. A., Palos-Sanchez, P. R., & Velicia-Martin, F. (2022). Improving KIBS performance using digital transformation: Study based on the theory of resources and capabilities. *Journal of Service Theory and Practice*, *33*(2), 169–197. DOI: 10.1108/JSTP-04-2022-0095

Martin-Rios, C., Erhardt, N. L., & Manev, I. M. (2022). Interfirm collaboration for knowledge resources interaction among small innovative firms. *Journal of Business Research*, *153*, 206–215. 10.1016/j.jbusres.2022.08.024. DOI: 10.1016/j.jbusres.2022.08.024

Meier, E., Brown, A. N., Chovitz, B., Zwinkels, D., Egharevba, M., McHenry, B., Kabatende, J., & Gege Buki, I. K. (2024). Systems thinking approach to human resources development in public health supply chains. *Journal of Humanitarian Logistics and Supply Chain Management*, *15*(3), 276–293. DOI: 10.1108/JHLSCM-10-2023-0097

Mhaske, P., Bhattacharjee, B., Haldar, N., Upadhyay, P., & Mandal, A. (2025). Bridging digital skill gaps in the global workforce: A synthesis and conceptual framework building. *Research in Globalization, 11*, 100311. 10.1016/j.resglo.2025.100311

Minor, K., McLoughlin, E., & Carlisle, S. (2025). The Digital Skills Gap – Is it Time to Rethink the Needs of Tourism and Hospitality Organizations in the UK? *Journal of Hospitality & Tourism Education*, *37*(3), 301–312. DOI: 10.1080/10963758.2024.2316338

Modgil, S., Singh, R. K., & Agrawal, S. (2025). Developing human capabilities for supply chains: An industry 5.0 perspective. *Annals of Operations Research*, *348*(3), 2075–2105. DOI: 10.1007/s10479-023-05245-1

Narkhede, G., Chinchanikar, S., Narkhede, R., & Chaudhari, T. (2024). Role of Industry 5.0 for driving sustainability in the manufacturing sector: An emerging research agenda. *Journal of Strategy and Management*. Advance online publication. DOI: 10.1108/JSMA-06-2023-0144

Omol, E. J. (2023). Organizational digital transformation: From evolution to future trends. *Digital Transformation and Society*, *3*(3), 240–256. DOI: 10.1108/DTS-08-2023-0061

Orero-Blat, M., Jordán, H. D. J., & Palacios-Marqués, D. (2022). The measurement of digital skills and competences: A bibliometric analysis. *International Journal of Intellectual Property Management*, *12*(2), 185–199. DOI: 10.1504/IJIPM.2022.122297

Parker, S. K., Van den Broeck, A., & Holman, D. (2017). Work Design Influences: A Synthesis of Multilevel Factors that Affect the Design of Jobs. *The Academy of Management Annals*, *11*(1), 267–308. DOI: 10.5465/annals.2014.0054

Patrucco, A. S., Rivera, L., Mejía-Argueta, C., & Sheffi, Y. (2021). Can you grow your supply chain without skills? The role of human resource management for better supply chain management in Latin America. *International Journal of Logistics Management*, *33*(1), 53–78. DOI: 10.1108/IJLM-11-2020-0426

Pedota, M., Grilli, L., & Piscitello, L. (2023). Technology adoption and upskilling in the wake of Industry 4.0. *Technological Forecasting and Social Change*, *187*, 122085. 10.1016/j.techfore.2022.122085. DOI: 10.1016/j.techfore.2022.122085

Radanliev, P., De Roure, D., Page, K., Nurse, J. R. C., Mantilla Montalvo, R., Santos, O., Maddox, L. T., & Burnap, P. (2020). Cyber risk at the edge: Current and future trends on cyber risk analytics and artificial intelligence in the industrial internet of things and industry 4.0 supply chains. *Cybersecurity*, *3*(1), 13. DOI: 10.1186/s42400-020-00052-8

Ranjith Kumar, R., Ganesh, L. S., & Rajendran, C. (2021). Quality 4.0 – a review of and framework for quality management in the digital era. *International Journal of Quality & Reliability Management*, *39*(6), 1385–1411. DOI: 10.1108/IJQRM-05-2021-0150

Research and Markets. (2025). *AI in Logistics and Supply Chain Management Market Report 2025: AI-Powered Platforms Revolutionizing Logistics and Supply Chain Efficiency Through Optimization and Risk Mitigation – Forecast to 2034*. https://www.globenewswire.com/news-release/2025/05/12/3078941/0/en/AI-in-Logistics-and-Supply-Chain-Management-Market-Report-2025-AI-Powered-Platforms-Revolutionizing-Logistics-and-Supply-Chain-Efficiency-Through-Optimization-and-Risk-Mitigation-F.html

Saini, M., Singh, D., Kataria, A., & Singh, R. (2025). Digital transformation and environmental sustainability: Reviewing the role of human capital. *Journal of Organizational Change Management*, •••, 1–24. DOI: 10.1108/JOCM-03-2025-0289

Sangari, M. S., & Razmi, J. (2015). Business intelligence competence, agile capabilities, and agile performance in supply chain: An empirical study. *International Journal of Logistics Management*, *26*(2), 356–380. DOI: 10.1108/IJLM-01-2013-0012

Schiuma, G., Santarsiero, F., Carlucci, D., & Jarrar, Y. (2024). Transformative leadership competencies for organizational digital transformation. *Business Horizons*, *67*(4), 425–437. 10.1016/j.bushor.2024.04.004. DOI: 10.1016/j.bushor.2024.04.004

Seyedghorban, Z., Tahernejad, H., Meriton, R., & Graham, G. (2020). Supply chain digitalization: Past, present and future. *Production Planning and Control*, *31*(2-3), 96–114. DOI: 10.1080/09537287.2019.1631461

Subrahmanyam, S. (2025). Human Factors and Workforce Adaptation in Digital Transition. In Martínez-Falcó, J., Sánchez-García, E., & Marco-Lajara, B. (Eds.), *Navigating Digital Transformation Through Business Process Management* (pp. 95–126). IGI Global Scientific Publishing., DOI: 10.4018/979-8-3373-3336-6.ch005

Ueasangkomsate, P. (2025). Building a future-ready workforce: A sociotechnical approach to digital transformation in Thai food SMEs. *Journal of the International Council for Small Business*, 1-22. /DOI: 10.1080/26437015.2025.2457631

Wahab, S. N., Tan, A., & Roche, O. (2024). Identifying supply chain manager leadership skills and competencies gaps in Malaysia. *Higher Education, Skills and Work-based Learning*, *14*(5), 921–937. DOI: 10.1108/HESWBL-07-2023-0179

Wesche, J. S., & Handke, L. (2023). Digitisation and automation in training and development: A meta-review of new opportunities and challenges. *Personnel Review*, *53*(3), 771–790. DOI: 10.1108/PR-09-2022-0660

World Economic Forum. W. (2025). *The Future of Jobs Report 2025*. W. E. Forum. https://www.weforum.org/publications/the-future-of-jobs-report-2025/

Chapter 11
Designing Just Reskilling Pathways for AI-Driven Logistics Transformation

Nguyen Vu Thao Huynh
http://orcid.org/0009-0002-2238-2313
RMIT University, Vietnam

ABSTRACT

Reskilling is often presented as a positive response to AI-driven change in logistics, assuming workers can easily move from routine tasks to digital and AI-related roles once training is offered. This chapter argues that such assumptions are incomplete. Reskilling is not only a technical issue of training design but also a socio-political process shaped by organisational priorities, unequal learning support, and workers' access to opportunity. Drawing on a case study of a logistics organisation, the chapter shows that workers began reskilling from unequal starting points. Outcomes were shaped by workload, digital confidence, education, supervisory support, scheduling flexibility, language ability, and assumptions about who was considered "trainable." As a result, reskilling benefits were unevenly distributed: some workers moved into more secure analytical roles, while others remained excluded from these gains. The chapter proposes an equity-oriented reskilling model to explain these unequal outcomes.

1. INTRODUCTION

Artificial intelligence is reshaping logistics at once operationally, organisationally, and socially. The sector has become a central arena for AI deployment because it combines data-intensive flows, time-critical decision-making, and enduring pres-

DOI: 10.4018/979-8-3373-7826-8.ch011

sure to improve cost efficiency, visibility, resilience, and service performance. AI is now increasingly integrated into demand forecasting, route optimisation, warehouse orchestration, inventory planning, supplier coordination, customer service, document processing, and predictive maintenance. This expansion has led both practitioners and scholars to argue that the future of logistics will not be defined simply by labour replacement, but by the reorganisation of work into new forms of human–AI complementarity (Richey Jr et al., 2023; Samuels, 2025; Riad et al., 2024). Within this framing, reskilling has become a dominant policy and managerial response: workers whose roles are altered by automation are expected to acquire new competencies, adjust to AI-enabled workplaces, and transition into jobs centred on interpretation, judgement, exception management, cross-functional coordination, and digital oversight.

At first sight, this emphasis on reskilling appears both reasonable and progressive. If AI transforms work, then workers should be supported in learning; if logistics requires more digitally capable employees, then training systems should evolve accordingly. A growing body of research on workforce readiness, future competencies, and human–AI collaboration reinforces this position by advocating continuous capability renewal, more agile learning systems, and proactive organisational investment in upskilling and reskilling (Li, 2024; Tenakwah and Watson, 2025; Asiedu and Tenakwah, 2025; da SILVA, 2025). Recent review studies likewise show that reskilling has become central to governmental, higher education, and corporate responses to digital transformation and AI disruption (Ersanlı et al., 2025; Shimray and Subaveerapandiyan, 2025; Vuc et al., 2025).

Yet the dominant discourse on reskilling carries an important limitation. It often treats reskilling as a neutral and universally available good, presuming that workers will benefit from training so long as organisations provide the appropriate programmes. Such an assumption masks the unequal realities of technological transition. Workers do not encounter AI transformation from equivalent starting points: they differ in educational background, contract security, language ability, technological familiarity, time availability, caregiving responsibilities, health conditions, and managerial recognition. Organisations, moreover, do not distribute training opportunities in an even or impartial manner. Decisions regarding who is selected, which roles are prioritised, what forms of learning are valued, and how much support is provided are shaped by power relations, cost considerations, performance pressures, and strategic priorities. Under these conditions, reskilling can function not only as a mechanism of adaptation, but also as a process of sorting, stratification, and exclusion.

This issue is particularly acute in logistics. Logistics firms often operate with layered occupational hierarchies, strict time discipline, performance metrics, variable scheduling, and segmented workforces spanning warehouse operators, drivers, clerical staff, planners, analysts, supervisors, and outsourced service personnel. AI does not affect these groups in identical ways. Some roles become more augmented, others more monitored, and others more vulnerable to redesign or reduction. The promise of reskilling therefore cannot be evaluated only by whether programmes exist. It must be examined in terms of who actually gets access to meaningful transition pathways and who remains trapped in increasingly peripheral roles.

This chapter addresses that problem by critically examining reskilling through the lens of equity. Rather than asking only whether AI-related training was provided, it asks how reskilling was structured, how workers were positioned within it, and why outcomes diverged across groups. The chapter draws on an anonymous logistics organisation that launched an internal reskilling initiative during an AI-led operational transformation. The initiative was presented as a future-oriented workforce development strategy intended to prepare employees for a more digital logistics environment. Yet the case shows that reskilling was not experienced as a flat opportunity landscape. Access, participation, confidence, and outcomes varied systematically. Formal training design mattered, but so did hidden selection practices, informal managerial sponsorship, role-based scheduling flexibility, and the uneven availability of learning support.

The central argument advanced here is that reskilling in AI-driven logistics must be understood as a socio-political process embedded in organisational power relations and institutional constraints. The chapter therefore makes two related contributions. Empirically, it demonstrates how workers' capacity to benefit from AI reskilling depends on more than curriculum content or skill demand. It is mediated by structural inequality inside the organisation. Theoretically, it develops an equity-oriented reskilling model that explains how structural barriers, institutional interests, and informal filtering mechanisms shape differentiated access to AI-relevant opportunity. This model challenges the assumption that reskilling is inherently inclusive and instead positions it as an arena where just and unjust transitions are actively produced.

The chapter proceeds as follows. Section 2 reviews the literature on human capital, learning inequality, and the politics of reskilling in digital transformation. Section 3 presents the case study of reskilling practices in an anonymous logistics organisation. Section 4 develops the equity-oriented reskilling model and discusses its broader implications. Section 5 concludes by outlining principles for designing more inclusive and socially responsive reskilling pathways in AI-driven logistics transformation.

2. LITERATURE BACKGROUND: HUMAN CAPITAL, LEARNING INEQUALITY, AND RESKILLING POLITICS

2.1 Reskilling as the dominant response to AI-driven workforce change

Across management, policy, and practitioner discourse, reskilling has become the preferred answer to the labour market disruptions associated with AI. Rather than framing AI solely as a threat of displacement, contemporary studies increasingly position it as a catalyst for occupational redesign, capability renewal, and new forms of human-machine collaboration (Tenakwah and Watson, 2025; Asiedu and Tenakwah, 2025). This shift is partly strategic. Purely substitution-focused narratives risk social resistance and reputational backlash, whereas reskilling enables organisations and policymakers to present technological change as manageable, developmental, and future-oriented. It also resonates with the broader language of employability, adaptability, and lifelong learning that has shaped human resource development and labour market policy over the past two decades.

Recent reviews confirm the scale of this turn. Ersanlı et al. (2025) show that global reskilling and upskilling initiatives have proliferated across public and private sectors as AI adoption accelerates. Shimray and Subaveerapandiyan (2025), through bibliometric analysis, similarly identify reskilling as a central theme in debates on job creation and job displacement under AI. Li (2024) argues that future-ready workforces require integrated models of technical, cognitive, and adaptive skill development, especially in Industry 4.0 and post-Industry 4.0 environments. da SILVA (2025) extends this view by proposing a future competencies cycle in which workforce development must be continuous, iterative, and responsive to technological change rather than episodic or reactive.

These contributions are important because they move beyond simplistic binaries of jobs lost versus jobs gained. They emphasise transition, capability formation, and the need to prepare workers for roles that combine technical proficiency with judgement, problem solving, and collaboration. Yet much of this literature remains optimistic in a way that can understate organisational inequality. The analytical focus often falls on what skills are needed, how institutions can supply them, and how organisations can cultivate readiness. Less attention is given to the political economy of access. In other words, the literature is stronger in specifying the content of reskilling than in explaining the uneven conditions under which workers can actually participate in and benefit from it.

2.2 Human capital theory and its limits in digital transitions

Human capital theory remains one of the most influential frameworks for understanding workforce development. In its classical form, it treats skills, knowledge, and education as productive assets that enhance individual employability and organisational performance. From this perspective, reskilling is a rational investment. Workers improve their productivity and market value, while firms strengthen their adaptive capacity and innovation potential. This logic is clearly visible in current debates on AI-readiness, where calls for upskilling and reskilling are often justified in terms of competitiveness, employability, and return on investment (Asiedu and Tenakwah, 2025; Vuc et al., 2025).

In logistics, the appeal of human capital reasoning is particularly strong. AI implementation requires new combinations of digital literacy, systems awareness, data interpretation, and process coordination. Employees who were previously evaluated largely in terms of speed, compliance, or repetitive execution may now be expected to interface with dashboards, exception alerts, automated recommendations, and digitally integrated workflows. Reskilling thus appears as a means of aligning labour capabilities with new technological demands. Studies on AI competencies in logistics underscore this point. Shatat and Shatat (2024) identify a set of AI-related competencies, including data interpretation, digital tool use, and technology-enabled decision support, as increasingly relevant for logistics management. Richey Jr et al. (2023) similarly note that AI in logistics changes the skill profile of many roles, making human capability development a necessary complement to technological investment.

Yet human capital theory has significant limitations when applied uncritically to AI-driven transitions. First, it tends to individualise responsibility. If workers are told that they must remain employable by continuously reskilling, then structural inequalities can be reframed as personal deficits rather than institutional failures. Second, it often assumes that access to capability development is open and meritocratic. In practice, however, training opportunities are distributed through organisational structures that are neither neutral nor fully transparent. Third, human capital approaches can reduce learning to measurable competencies while neglecting the power relations that determine which competencies are recognised, funded, and rewarded.

These limitations matter because digital transformation does not occur on a level playing field. Workers with higher prior education, more stable contracts, greater confidence with digital systems, and closer proximity to managerial networks are usually better positioned to capture the gains of technological transition. Those in routine, precarious, or physically demanding roles may face the opposite condition: they are told that reskilling is available, but the organisational conditions necessary for successful learning are weak or absent. Human capital theory can therefore help explain why reskilling is valorised, but it is insufficient for explaining why its benefits are distributed unevenly.

2.3 Learning inequality and differentiated capacity to adapt

A more critical perspective emerges when reskilling is examined through the lens of learning inequality. Learning opportunities are not merely offered; they are mediated by material and institutional conditions. Workers differ in their available time, their exposure to learning-supportive environments, their familiarity with formal education formats, and their confidence in navigating digital knowledge systems. Even when the same programme is formally available to all, the real capacity to benefit may vary sharply.

This issue has become increasingly visible in debates on digital transition. Vuc et al. (2025), in the higher education context, show that resilience-oriented human capital development under AI requires more than curriculum reform; it depends on institutional support systems that enable diverse learners to engage meaningfully. Li (2024) likewise highlights that future-ready workforce preparation demands flexible learning architectures rather than one-size-fits-all training delivery. These insights are highly relevant to workplace settings. In organisations, learning inequality may stem from shift design, role fragmentation, hierarchical communication, resource scarcity, uneven digital exposure, or the tacit assumption that some workers are inherently more "developable" than others.

Learning inequality is especially consequential in logistics because the sector includes a wide range of occupations with very different relations to formal learning. Managers and analysts may already work with digital systems and abstract decision tools, making AI training an extension of existing routines. Warehouse workers, transport coordinators, customer service staff, or clerical employees may instead experience AI-related learning as discontinuous with their prior work histories. The same programme can therefore function as advancement for some and as alienation for others. Research on business intelligence and analytics in SMEs provides an important analogy. Hoang and Bui (2023) show that technology adoption is not simply a matter of tool availability, but of practice maturity, organisational readiness, and the ability to translate technological systems into meaningful use. The same principle applies to workforce transformation. Reskilling cannot be reduced to access to content. It requires interpretive support, time for practice, contextual translation, and organisational reinforcement. Without these conditions, formal participation may conceal substantive exclusion.

2.4 Reskilling politics and the hidden governance of opportunity

To understand why reskilling often produces unequal outcomes, it is necessary to move beyond capability discourse and examine the politics of reskilling. Organisational training systems are not neutral delivery mechanisms. They are shaped by managerial priorities, efficiency calculations, labour control concerns, and assumptions about future organisational value. Consequently, decisions about reskilling are also decisions about workforce stratification. Three dimensions are especially important. The first is prioritisation. Organisations rarely reskill everyone equally. Under budget constraints and performance pressure, firms often invest first in employees deemed strategically important, easier to retrain, or more likely to remain with the organisation. The second is categorisation. Workers are not only trained; they are classified. Some are labelled as high-potential, digitally ready, flexible, or promotable, while others are treated as operationally necessary but developmentally peripheral. The third is support allocation. Even when workers are formally enrolled in the same programme, the quality of mentoring, time release, supervisory encouragement, and follow-up opportunities may vary substantially.

These dynamics are visible across emerging discussions of workforce preparation for AI. Tenakwah and Watson (2025) argue that organisations need deliberate strategies for preparing humans and machines to work together, but they also imply that success depends on leadership choices and organisational design. Asiedu and Tenakwah (2025) similarly highlight HR's role in future-proofing the workforce, which points to the gatekeeping power of internal talent systems. da SILVA (2025) proposes cyclical competency development, yet such cycles are always governed by institutional decisions about who enters, who progresses, and what counts as evidence of readiness. A political reading of reskilling therefore highlights a crucial tension. Organisations frequently present AI reskilling as inclusive and empowering, but they also use it to support operational efficiency, redeploy labour selectively, and reduce workforce redundancy. This creates a structural contradiction between the rhetoric of inclusive development and the practice of strategic filtering. Workers may be told that learning is for everyone, while internal systems quietly channel meaningful opportunities toward those already closest to managerial trust and organisational advantage.

2.5 AI transformation in logistics and the changing content of work

The logistics context intensifies the stakes of reskilling because AI is not entering a static work system. It is interacting with a sector already shaped by volatility, time compression, data integration, and resilience pressure. Research increasingly shows that AI in logistics is being adopted not only to automate tasks, but also to improve prediction, responsiveness, coordination, and exception handling across the supply chain (Richey Jr et al., 2023; Modgil et al., 2022; Riad et al., 2024; Samuels, 2025). These developments are often linked to broader shifts from Industry 4.0 toward more networked, intelligent, and anticipatory systems. This matters for labour because the content of work changes in layered ways. Some tasks are automated. Some are augmented through decision support. Some become more visible and measurable. Some are elevated in strategic importance because human oversight is still needed when algorithms fail, conflict, or encounter uncertainty. In supply chain resilience research, AI is often framed as enhancing forecasting, adaptation, and recovery capacity (Modgil et al., 2022; Riad et al., 2024). Yet this resilience depends on workers who can interpret signals, coordinate across functions, and act when automated systems cannot fully resolve disruption. AI therefore does not eliminate the need for human capability; it redistributes where and how that capability matters.

In logistics firms, this redistribution produces new skill hierarchies. Data literacy, systems integration awareness, exception management, digital communication, and cross-functional problem solving become more valuable. Workers lacking these capabilities may find their roles narrowed, more closely monitored, or rendered more vulnerable to replacement. Those able to acquire and demonstrate them may gain access to more stable or upwardly mobile roles. Reskilling thus becomes the hinge between technological change and social mobility inside the organisation. However, recent logistics and supply chain studies mostly emphasise implementation, performance, resilience, and innovation rather than distributive fairness. For example, Tanveer et al. (2026) show how digital technology integration can enhance supplier innovation capabilities through relational mechanisms. Although their focus is inter-organisational rather than workforce-centred, the study underscores a broader point: digital transformation produces advantage when actors have the relational and organisational capacity to translate technology into new forms of value creation. The same is true at the employee level. Reskilling is not simply about learning tools; it is about gaining access to the organisational conditions under which those tools can be meaningfully converted into opportunity.

2.6 The missing focus on equity, power, and access

Taken together, the literature establishes that reskilling is important, AI is changing workforce demands, and logistics is a critical site of transformation. Yet an important gap remains. Much of the existing discussion treats reskilling as a practical necessity without interrogating how access to that necessity is organised. Human capital perspectives explain why skills matter. Transition literature explains why adaptability matters. Logistics and AI studies explain why new competencies matter. But the literature remains comparatively weak in theorising how power, inequality, and institutional design shape who actually benefits from reskilling. This gap is not minor. Without attention to equity, reskilling can become a legitimising discourse that masks exclusion. Organisations can claim social responsibility by offering training while leaving intact the structural barriers that prevent many workers from succeeding. Workers can be invited into transformation rhetorically while being filtered out materially. Such dynamics are especially likely in sectors like logistics, where labour is segmented and operational pressure often constrains genuine developmental support. This chapter addresses that omission by treating reskilling not as a neutral intervention but as a socially differentiated organisational process. It examines how workers are selected, supported, judged, and repositioned during AI-related transition. In doing so, it opens a more critical conversation about just reskilling pathways in logistics and beyond.

3. CASE STUDY: RESKILLING PRACTICES IN AN ANONYMOUS LOGISTICS ORGANISATION

3.1 Organisational background and AI transformation context

The case organisation, here referred to as LogistiCo, is a large integrated logistics firm operating across warehousing, domestic transport coordination, customer order management, and supply chain visibility services. Over several years, the firm expanded its digital infrastructure and began embedding AI-enabled systems into selected operational processes. These included predictive demand support, route planning assistance, exception alerting, automated document classification, dashboard-based workforce monitoring, and decision-support tools for inventory and service coordination. The organisation's transformation programme was framed by senior management as necessary for competitiveness, resilience, and service quality in a more volatile logistics environment.

Officially, the workforce strategy accompanying this transformation emphasised "future readiness." Leaders argued that AI would not simply replace jobs but would redesign them. Existing employees were told that the organisation intended to help them transition into more value-adding positions through internal reskilling. Training materials highlighted digital fluency, analytical capability, cross-functional collaboration, and AI-assisted decision making as the competencies of the future. The programme's formal narrative was therefore developmental rather than reductive: the organisation was not only implementing technology but also investing in people. Yet this strategic framing coexisted with clear efficiency pressures. The

AI initiative was linked to productivity targets, lower error rates, faster response times, and leaner staffing structures in selected functions. Managers were expected to maintain operational continuity while supporting capability development. The reskilling initiative was therefore launched inside a context of tension. It had to satisfy both a moral and reputational expectation of inclusive development and a managerial demand for measurable returns.

3.2 The formal design of the reskilling programme

The reskilling programme consisted of three broad streams. The first was foundational digital training, aimed at improving comfort with digital systems, dashboards, workflow platforms, and data interpretation. The second involved role-specific AI exposure, such as understanding how automated recommendations were generated, how to manage exceptions, and how to validate system outputs. The third focused on transition-oriented pathways for employees considered suitable for movement into higher-order roles such as operations analysts, AI-support coordinators, digital process specialists, and cross-functional planning staff. From a policy perspective, the programme appeared comprehensive. Training modules were modular, internal communication emphasised openness to participation, and managers were instructed to identify employees with development potential. Some learning resources were delivered asynchronously through internal platforms, while other components took the form of workshops, supervised practice, and pilot-based experiential learning. Certificates of completion were used to signal progress. In internal presentations, the programme was described as a mechanism for democratising access to the future of work.

However, the formal structure obscured several practical filters. Participation in advanced modules required managerial nomination. Time release was uneven across departments. Some roles had more flexibility to attend workshops or complete online content during working hours, while others had to learn outside shift time or during fragmented breaks. The organisation also assumed a baseline of digital and language competence that was not distributed evenly across the workforce. As a result, the programme's design contained an important contradiction: it was framed as broadly inclusive but operationalised in ways that advantaged those already closer to organisational privilege.

3.3 Selection, nomination, and the hidden sorting of workers

One of the most consequential features of LogistiCo's reskilling initiative was the hidden governance of selection. Officially, employees interested in developing could express willingness to join. In practice, meaningful access to transition-oriented pathways depended heavily on managerial nomination and informal sponsorship. Supervisors were asked to identify "suitable" employees who could be released from routine duties and who, in their view, possessed the right attitude, learning agility, and long-term fit for future roles. This process appeared reasonable on efficiency grounds. Managers under operational pressure did not want to nominate staff whom they believed would struggle, disengage, or leave the organisation shortly after training. Yet the criteria used were often tacit and socially loaded. Employees who already communicated confidently with managers, demonstrated comfort with software interfaces, had prior exposure to reporting tasks, or were perceived as proactive were more likely to be selected. By contrast, workers in tightly scheduled operational roles, those with weaker English skills, older staff, and employees whose strengths were associated with reliability rather than digital adaptability were less likely to be prioritised.

The result was a quiet sorting process. Formal inclusion remained intact because the programme existed for the workforce as a whole, but the pathways most likely to lead to internal mobility were channelled toward a narrower group. Several workers described the reskilling initiative as open "in theory" yet difficult to access without managerial backing. Others noted that nomination decisions often appeared to confirm prior assumptions about who was already seen as office-track or future-track rather than genuinely discovering hidden potential. This mattered because selection shaped not only entry into training but also the confidence with which workers interpreted the programme. Being nominated signalled organisational recognition. Being overlooked signalled the opposite. Thus, reskilling functioned not merely as skill development but as symbolic classification. It told workers who the organisation imagined as part of its future.

3.4 Unequal learning conditions and the burden of self-adaptation

Even among those who entered the programme, the capacity to benefit varied substantially. A central reason was unequal learning conditions. Workers in administrative, planning, or hybrid coordination roles often had more predictable schedules, easier access to computers, and greater opportunity to discuss course content with peers or supervisors. By contrast, warehouse and frontline operational staff frequently encountered reskilling as an additional burden layered on top of performance-intensive work. For them, online modules were harder to complete, workshops could conflict with shifts, and practice opportunities were limited. This created an important pattern: workers were expected to demonstrate adaptability, but the organisational support necessary for adaptation was unevenly distributed. Some participants could experiment with dashboards, ask follow-up questions, and apply learning to everyday work. Others completed training in a more symbolic fashion, with limited reinforcement and little opportunity to translate formal content into occupational repositioning. The programme therefore rewarded not only motivation but also the pre-existing capacity to create learning continuity.

Language and educational background also shaped experience. Although most materials were presented in accessible internal language, the programme still relied on concepts associated with analytics, automation logic, process mapping, and system reasoning. Employees with prior tertiary education or office-based reporting experience absorbed these ideas more quickly. Others found them abstract and struggled to connect them with their own tasks. In such cases, the organisation's rhetoric of self-directed learning placed the burden back onto the individual. When workers failed to progress, this could be interpreted as a lack of readiness rather than a mismatch between programme design and learner conditions. The case therefore reveals that reskilling success was not simply about who was willing to learn. It depended on whether the organisation had created equitable conditions for learning. Where those conditions were weak, reskilling became a test of self-compensation: workers had to overcome structural disadvantage through individual effort.

3.5 Divergent outcomes: transition, stagnation, and marginalisation

The outcomes of the reskilling initiative were highly differentiated. For a relatively advantaged subgroup, the programme generated real opportunity. These employees moved into new or expanded roles involving analytics support, digital workflow coordination, exception management, and AI-assisted planning. Their previous participation in training became visible evidence of potential, and they often received additional mentoring or stretch assignments. For them, reskilling worked as both capability development and career mobility. A second group experienced partial benefit. They gained greater familiarity with AI-enabled systems and became somewhat more effective in their existing roles, but they did not obtain significant advancement. Their work changed in content but not in status. They were expected to interface with new systems, monitor algorithmic outputs, or follow AI-informed procedures, yet their remuneration, influence, and job security remained largely unchanged. In this sense, reskilling enabled functional adaptation without substantially altering their organisational position.

A third group became increasingly marginalised. These workers were included in the transformation narrative but not meaningfully incorporated into its gains. Some completed only the most basic modules. Others were repeatedly unable to participate due to workload, scheduling, or limited support. A number of operational employees felt that AI transformation was moving "around" them rather than "with" them. Their roles became more monitored, more standardised, or less central to future planning, while reskilling did little to alter that trajectory. This divergence is theoretically significant. It shows that reskilling can operate simultaneously as a mechanism of inclusion, adaptation, and exclusion. The same initiative that helps one group transition upward may leave another group in place and push a third toward peripheralisation. Organisational narratives of universal future-readiness can therefore conceal a stratified reality.

3.6 The tension between corporate efficiency and inclusive development

At the centre of the case lies a persistent tension between efficiency and inclusion. LogistiCo's leaders genuinely recognised that AI transformation would require workforce development. Many managers also expressed sincere concern about supporting employees through change. Yet the organisation's operational imperatives limited how inclusive the programme could become. Releasing too many frontline workers for learning created staffing strain. Investing deeply in employees perceived as less likely to progress appeared inefficient. Building tailored support structures for different groups required time and money that were difficult to justify under performance pressure. As a result, the reskilling initiative drifted toward a pragmatic compromise. It remained broad enough to support the organisation's developmental narrative, but selective enough to protect short-term efficiency. This compromise was not accidental. It reflected the institutional logic of the organisation. In a tightly managed logistics environment, inclusive development was desirable only insofar as it did not disrupt operational discipline or dilute investment returns.

This does not mean that the programme was cynical. Rather, it means that reskilling was governed by competing logics. One logic framed employees as stakeholders in a shared technological future. The other framed them as differentiated assets whose development should be calibrated according to likely organisational payoff. The inequities observed in the case emerged from the interaction of these logics rather than from a simple absence of good intentions.

3.7 Interpreting the case

The case illustrates four broader points. First, reskilling cannot be understood solely through formal programme design because hidden selection mechanisms powerfully shape access. Second, workers' outcomes depend on unequal learning conditions, not just on motivation or curriculum quality. Third, organisational support for reskilling is filtered through efficiency logics that make inclusive development conditional rather than unconditional. Fourth, AI-related reskilling can become a social sorting device that redistributes opportunity unevenly while maintaining the appearance of organisational modernity and care. These insights provide the foundation for the theoretical discussion that follows. The challenge is not merely to improve training delivery. It is to conceptualise reskilling as an equity problem embedded in organisational transformation.

4. DISCUSSION: THE EQUITY-ORIENTED RESKILLING MODEL

4.1 Why existing reskilling models are insufficient

Most conventional models of reskilling are built around a pipeline logic. Technological change creates new skill demand; organisations or institutions provide training; workers acquire competencies; improved fit then generates employability, mobility, or productivity. This model is useful for identifying broad transition dynamics, but it is too linear to explain the empirical realities revealed in the case. It assumes that the main challenge is matching skills to future roles. It pays less attention to the conditions under which workers are recognised as eligible for transition, supported through learning, and positioned to convert training into actual opportunity.

The case shows that between skill provision and skill outcome lie multiple filtering processes. Workers do not move directly from programme availability to successful transition. They pass through institutional gates shaped by organisational politics, managerial interpretation, workload distribution, and hidden assumptions about trainability. Moreover, outcomes are not binary. Reskilling may produce upward mobility, functional adaptation without advancement, or deeper marginalisation. A more adequate model therefore needs to explain not only learning, but also selection, support, conversion, and inequality.

4.2 Core premises of the equity-oriented reskilling model

The equity-oriented reskilling model proposed in this chapter rests on five core premises:

- The first premise is that reskilling is socially situated rather than neutral. Workers encounter learning opportunities from unequal structural positions. These positions are shaped by education, role type, schedule control, language ability, digital familiarity, contractual stability, and proximity to managerial networks. Thus, the same programme does not represent the same opportunity for everyone.

- The second premise is that reskilling is institutionally filtered. Organisational actors decide who is nominated, who is released, who is mentored, and who is judged likely to succeed. These decisions are rarely random. They reflect strategic priorities and tacit classifications of value. As a result, reskilling opportunities are governed, not merely offered.
- The third premise is that learning requires support infrastructures. Access to content is insufficient when workers lack time, coaching, peer reinforcement, opportunities for practice, or role transitions that allow new capabilities to be recognised. Where support infrastructures are unequal, learning outcomes will also be unequal.
- The fourth premise is that reskilling outcomes depend on conversion, not acquisition alone. A worker may complete training but still fail to convert new knowledge into advancement if organisational pathways are blocked or if newly acquired capabilities are not legible to decision-makers. Training certificates do not automatically translate into job redesign, promotion, or security.
- The fifth premise is that reskilling is normatively consequential because it shapes the justice of technological transition. AI transformation does not only alter tasks; it redistributes futures. Reskilling therefore must be evaluated in terms of whether it expands substantive opportunity across the workforce or selectively protects those already advantaged.

4.3 Structural barriers in the model

At the first layer of the model are structural barriers. These are the pre-existing conditions that shape workers' starting positions before they encounter formal reskilling opportunities. In the case, these barriers included uneven educational background, differences in digital confidence, limited schedule flexibility, physically and cognitively intensive frontline work, and variable access to computers and quiet learning space. Such barriers are often treated as external to programme design, but they are central to explaining outcome inequality. Structural barriers matter because they influence both entry and endurance. Workers facing intense shift pressure or low digital confidence are less likely to volunteer, less likely to be perceived as strong candidates, and more likely to struggle during the programme. If organisations ignore these barriers, they effectively convert inequality of condition into inequality of outcome while preserving the fiction of meritocracy. In theoretical terms, this expands the human capital discussion. Skills are not accumulated in a vacuum. The capacity to invest in one's own learning is itself unequally distributed. Therefore, any serious model of reskilling must include the social conditions of learnability.

4.4 Institutional interests and strategic calibration

The second layer of the model concerns institutional interests. Organisations do not pursue reskilling solely for worker benefit. They reskill to support strategic adaptation, maintain competitiveness, protect continuity, and enhance the value captured from technological investments. This is not inherently illegitimate. However, it means that reskilling design is always calibrated against organisational return. In the case, institutional interest manifested through selective investment. Employees most likely to serve the organisation's future operating model received stronger support. Training was prioritised where managers believed it could generate measurable benefit. Inclusive development was therefore constrained by a logic of strategic payoff. Workers whose development required greater resource commitment or whose future role within the organisation was less clear were less likely to receive intensive support. This layer helps explain why reskilling often becomes narrower in practice than in rhetoric. Public narratives emphasise inclusivity, but internal decisions often seek efficiency. The equity-oriented reskilling model does not treat this as hypocrisy alone. It treats it as a structural feature of organisational transformation. Firms are not welfare institutions; they are strategic actors. The problem arises when this strategic logic is concealed behind universalist claims that obscure unequal access.

4.5 Hidden selection mechanisms and organisational categorisation

The third layer of the model focuses on hidden selection mechanisms. These are the informal or semi-formal processes through which workers are categorised as suitable or unsuitable for future-oriented roles. In the case, nomination, supervisory sponsorship, and prior reputational cues shaped access to advanced training and mobility-linked pathways. Workers were judged not only by current performance, but also by perceived digital agility, attitude, communication style, and presumed developmental potential. This is a crucial theoretical insight because it reveals that reskilling functions as a classificatory system. Organisations do not simply teach; they sort. They identify who belongs to the future and who remains tied to the present. The criteria for this sorting are often not codified, which makes them difficult to contest. Yet they can systematically reproduce inequality because workers who already fit managerial expectations are more likely to receive developmental opportunities. This mechanism connects reskilling to broader debates on power and recognition. Access to transition depends partly on whether workers are seen as investable. Such visibility is unequally distributed. Employees in operationally dense or lower-status roles may be overlooked not because they lack potential, but because the organisation has weaker mechanisms for recognising it.

4.6 Unequal support infrastructures and learning conversion

The fourth layer of the model concerns support infrastructures and capability conversion. Even when workers are admitted into reskilling programmes, outcomes depend on the extent to which learning is scaffolded and socially translated into opportunity. Support infrastructures include time release, mentoring, practical application, peer learning, supervisor encouragement, accessible content, and organisational pathways for redeployment. In the case, uneven support infrastructures produced diverging trajectories. Some employees received not only training but also project exposure, follow-up feedback, and expanded responsibilities. Others completed modules with little integration into subsequent work. This distinction is central. Learning becomes valuable when organisations create conditions for conversion. Without conversion, training may improve familiarity without changing occupational destiny.

The concept of conversion also helps distinguish symbolic inclusion from substantive inclusion. A programme can be formally open and still fail to produce equitable outcomes if workers cannot translate participation into recognised capability or job movement. The justice of reskilling therefore lies not in enrolment statistics alone, but in whether learning is converted into meaningful opportunity across diverse groups.

4.7 Outcome pathways: advancement, adaptive retention, and marginalisation

The final layer of the model specifies three broad outcome pathways.

- The first is *advancement*. Workers gain both capability and improved organisational positioning. They enter more secure, influential, or better-remunerated roles that are aligned with AI-enabled transformation.
- The second is *adaptive retention*. Workers become able to function within new systems and retain relevance in their current roles, but without major improvements in status, security, or mobility. They adapt, yet do not advance.
- The third is *marginalisation*. Workers remain outside meaningful transition pathways. They may receive minimal training or symbolic inclusion, but their roles become narrower, more monitored, or less central to the future organisation.

These pathways show why reskilling must be analysed distributionally. A single initiative can produce all three simultaneously. Success for one group can coexist with stagnation or exclusion for others. From an equity perspective, the question is not whether reskilling works in aggregate, but how its benefits and burdens are distributed.

4.8 The model's contribution to theory

The equity-oriented reskilling model contributes to several bodies of literature. First, it extends human capital reasoning by showing that skill development is conditioned by unequal access, organisational recognition, and support infrastructures. Human capital matters, but its development is socially mediated. Second, it contributes to AI and workforce transition debates by challenging the assumption that reskilling is inherently inclusive. AI transitions generate not only new competency demands but also new mechanisms of labour sorting.

Third, it adds a labour-sensitive perspective to logistics transformation research. Much logistics scholarship has focused on performance, resilience, and technology implementation (Richey Jr et al., 2023; Modgil et al., 2022; Riad et al., 2024; Samuels, 2025). This chapter complements that literature by showing that workforce development under AI is also a question of distributive justice. Fourth, it contributes to organisational learning discussions by emphasising that the capacity to learn is institutionally organised. Learning is not merely an individual attribute. It is supported, constrained, and recognised through social structures. This insight resonates with wider evidence that digital capability development depends on organisational maturity and practice conditions rather than technology access alone (Hoang and Bui, 2023; Tanveer et al., 2026).

4.9 Practical implications: toward just reskilling pathways

The model also has practical implications. If organisations want reskilling to support a just transition rather than selective adaptation, five design principles follow. The first is *equity diagnosis before programme launch*. Firms should identify which groups face the greatest barriers to participation, including shift constraints, language issues, digital confidence gaps, and limited supervisory support. Without this diagnosis, programmes will reflect the biases of existing structures. The second is *transparent and contestable selection criteria*. Access to advanced pathways should not depend primarily on opaque managerial nomination. Workers should be able to understand how selection occurs and how to appeal or prepare for future entry.

The third is *differentiated support rather than uniform provision*. Workers with fewer prior advantages require more scaffolding, not less. Tailored learning time, coaching, peer support, and contextualised delivery are essential if formal equality is to become substantive equality. The fourth is *conversion pathways embedded into workforce planning*. Training must be linked to real role redesign, internal mobility options, and recognition systems. Otherwise, reskilling risks becoming performative. The fifth is *justice-oriented metrics*. Organisations should evaluate reskilling not only by completion rates or productivity gains, but by who advances, who stagnates, and who exits or becomes peripheral. Equity should be a measurable outcome, not a rhetorical aspiration.

These implications are forward-looking because AI transformation in logistics is likely to deepen rather than recede. As more functions become datafied and algorithmically assisted, the question of who can transition into AI-complementary work will become increasingly central. Firms that ignore the equity dimension may achieve short-term efficiency while generating long-term exclusion, morale erosion, and legitimacy risks.

5. CONCLUSION AND IMPLICATIONS

This chapter has argued that reskilling in AI-driven logistics transformation must be understood as more than a technical response to changing skill demand. It is a socio-political process in which workers' futures are distributed unevenly through organisational structures, institutional interests, and hidden selection mechanisms. The case of LogistiCo demonstrates that reskilling outcomes depend not only on what is taught, but on who is chosen, who is supported, and who is able to convert learning into opportunity. The analysis reveals three major insights. First, workers do not enter AI transition from equal positions. Structural inequalities in education, time availability, digital familiarity, language confidence, and role design shape the capacity to participate. Second, organisations govern reskilling strategically. Even when programmes are framed as inclusive, meaningful opportunities are often channelled toward those already seen as more investable or future-fit. Third, the outcomes of reskilling are stratified. Some workers advance into AI-complementary roles, some merely adapt within existing positions, and others become increasingly marginalised.

The chapter's main theoretical contribution is the equity-oriented reskilling model. This model explains how structural barriers, institutional interests, hidden selection, and uneven support infrastructures interact to shape differentiated transition outcomes. In doing so, it advances current debates on workforce development by moving beyond neutral or technocratic accounts of reskilling. It shows that reskilling is not only about capability formation, but also about the justice of access to transformation. The practical implication is straightforward but demanding. Organisations cannot claim that reskilling supports a just AI transition merely because training modules exist. They must design pathways that recognise unequal starting points, reduce hidden gatekeeping, provide differentiated support, and link learning to real occupational mobility. In logistics, where AI is increasingly central to operational strategy, this challenge is urgent. The future of work in the sector will not be judged only by how intelligent its systems become, but by how fairly workers are enabled to move with them. From a policy perspective, the chapter also suggests that governments, industry associations, and education providers should be cautious about endorsing reskilling as a universal remedy without addressing access conditions. Public-private programmes that celebrate digital transition while overlooking learning inequality risk reproducing exclusion under the language of opportunity. More socially responsive interventions will require attention to worker diversity, organisational incentives, and the distributional effects of internal talent systems.

For future research, several directions emerge. Comparative studies across logistics segments could examine how reskilling differs between warehousing, transport, platform logistics, and integrated supply chain services. Longitudinal studies could explore whether workers who are initially marginalised later find alternative pathways or are permanently excluded from AI-driven advancement. Research could also investigate how unions, worker voice mechanisms, or public regulation affect the fairness of internal reskilling systems. Finally, greater dialogue is needed between logistics scholarship and critical labour studies so that technological transformation is analysed not only in terms of efficiency and resilience, but also in terms of justice, recognition, and social inclusion. A just reskilling pathway is therefore not one that merely prepares labour for technology. It is one that reorganises opportunity so that technological transformation does not deepen existing inequalities. That is the central challenge for AI-driven logistics, and it is likely to become one of the defining workforce questions of the coming decade.

REFERENCES

Asiedu, E., & Tenakwah, E. S. (2025). Future-proofing your workforce: Upskilling and reskilling as HR's top priorities. *Strategic HR Review*, *24*(4), 169–173. DOI: 10.1108/SHR-01-2025-0008

da SILVA, C. A. G. (2025). The Future Competencies & Skills Development Cycle: A New Workforce Model in the Context of Digital Transformation and Artificial Intelligence. *Journal of Human Resource Management*, *28*(2), 139–155.

Ersanlı, C. Y., Çelik, F., Barjesteh, H., Duran, V., & Manoochehrzadeh, M. (2025). A review of global reskilling and upskilling initiatives in the age of AI. *AI and Ethics*, *5*(6), 1–10. DOI: 10.1007/s43681-025-00767-9

Hoang, T. G., & Bui, M. L. (2023). Business intelligence and analytic (BIA) stage-of-practice in micro-, small-and medium-sized enterprises (MSMEs). *Journal of Enterprise Information Management*, *36*(4), 1080–1104. DOI: 10.1108/JEIM-01-2022-0037

Li, L. (2024). Reskilling and upskilling the future-ready workforce for industry 4.0 and beyond. *Information Systems Frontiers*, *26*(5), 1697–1712. DOI: 10.1007/s10796-022-10308-y PMID: 35855776

Modgil, S., Singh, R. K., & Hannibal, C. (2022). Artificial intelligence for supply chain resilience: Learning from Covid-19. *International Journal of Logistics Management*, *33*(4), 1246–1268. DOI: 10.1108/IJLM-02-2021-0094

Riad, M., Naimi, M., & Okar, C. (2024). Enhancing supply chain resilience through artificial intelligence: Developing a comprehensive conceptual framework for AI implementation and supply chain optimization. *Logistics (Basel)*, *8*(4), 111. DOI: 10.3390/logistics8040111

Richey, R. G.Jr, Chowdhury, S., Davis-Sramek, B., Giannakis, M., & Dwivedi, Y. K. (2023). Artificial intelligence in logistics and supply chain management: A primer and roadmap for research. *Journal of Business Logistics*, *44*(4), 532–549. DOI: 10.1111/jbl.12364

Samuels, A. (2025). Examining the integration of artificial intelligence in supply chain management from Industry 4.0 to 6.0: A systematic literature review. *Frontiers in Artificial Intelligence*, *7*, 1477044. DOI: 10.3389/frai.2024.1477044 PMID: 39902380

Shatat, A. S., & Shatat, A. S. (2024). Artificial intelligence competencies in logistics management: An empirical insight from Bahrain. *Journal of Information & Knowledge Management*, *23*(01), 2350059. DOI: 10.1142/S0219649223500594

Shimray, S. R., & Subaveerapandiyan, A. (2025). AI and workforce dynamics: A bibliometric analysis of job creation, displacement and reskilling. *Global Knowledge, Memory and Communication*. Advance online publication. DOI: 10.1108/GKMC-12-2024-0824

Tanveer, U., Hoang, T. G., Ishaq, S., Kamal, M. M., & Attri, R. (2026). Enhancing supplier innovation capabilities through digital technology integration: A relational perspective. *Technological Forecasting and Social Change*, *223*, 124426. DOI: 10.1016/j.techfore.2025.124426

Tenakwah, E. S., & Watson, C. (2025). Embracing the AI/automation age: Preparing your workforce for humans and machines working together. *Strategy and Leadership*, *53*(1), 32–48. DOI: 10.1108/SL-05-2024-0040

Vuc, D. E., Stroe, V. D., Fanea-Ivanovici, M., Pană, M. C., & Maftei, R. (2025). Higher Education in Romania in the Age of AI: Reskilling for Resilience and Sustainable Human Capital Development. *Sustainability (Basel)*, *18*(1), 137. DOI: 10.3390/su18010137

Chapter 12
Reimagining Procurement and Logistics Transformation Through Artificial and Generative Intelligence: A Critical Review

James Kanyepe
http://orcid.org/0000-0002-6871-8831
University of Botswana, Botswana

Chisungo Chisungo
http://orcid.org/0000-0001-7759-2276
Chinhoyi University of Technology, Zimbabwe

ABSTRACT

Procurement and logistics have evolved from transactional tasks to strategic capabilities driving performance, competitiveness, and innovation. The complexity of global supply chains, data proliferation, and demand for agility have created opportunities for Artificial Intelligence (AI) and Generative AI (GenAI) to transform procurement and logistics. Despite growing adoption, literature remains fragmented, with limited integration of adoption trends, role shifts, workforce implications, skill barriers, and performance outcomes. This chapter uses a qualitative, literature-based approach underpinned by a systematic review. It examines the extent of AI and GenAI adoption in procurement and logistics, analyses how AI reshapes procurement roles, explores

DOI: 10.4018/979-8-3373-7826-8.ch012

barriers to AI-driven skills, and evaluates workforce implications in logistics systems, while identifying research gaps and offering actionable insights for scholars, practitioners, and policymakers.

INTRODUCTION

Procurement and logistics have undergone a profound transformation over the past few decades, evolving from predominantly transactional functions to strategically critical capabilities that directly shape organizational performance, competitiveness, and innovation (Nsabigaba, 2024). Traditionally, these functions focused primarily on sourcing and purchasing goods and services at the lowest possible cost. In contemporary business environments, however, procurement and logistics are increasingly recognized as drivers of value creation, influencing not only operational efficiency but also strategic objectives, organizational agility, and resilience (Vaka, 2024). This evolution is driven by multiple factors, including globalization, the rapid pace of technological innovation, the riseof data-intensive business processes, and heightened competition across industries (Adebayo et al., 2024).

Modern procurement and logistics encompass a wide array of activities beyond simple purchasing or transportation management, including supplier relationship management, contract lifecycle management, risk assessment, compliance monitoring, demand forecasting, and strategic decision-making (Adebayo et al., 2024). Organizations that successfully integrate these functions can leverage them as strategic levers, enhancing efficiency, reducing costs, and simultaneously enabling innovation and competitive advantage (Joice, 2024). The growing recognition of these functions as strategic capabilities reflects an awareness that supply chain performance is intrinsically linked to organizational success, particularly in industries where timely access to quality resources, risk mitigation, and process efficiency are critical (Handfield et al., 2015).

Global supply chains are exposed to diverse risks, ranging from geopolitical disruptions to market volatility and natural disasters (Krykavskyy et al., 2023). In addition, procurement and logistics systems generate massive volumes of data, including transaction histories, supplier performance metrics, demand forecasts, and market intelligence (Olaleye et al., 2024). Traditional manual processes struggle to process this information efficiently, leaving organizations vulnerable to delays, suboptimal decision-making, and inefficiencies (Adebayo et al., 2024). Consequently, organizations are under mounting pressure to adopt technological solutions capable of automating routine tasks, analysing complex datasets, and generating actionable insights that support both operational and strategic decisions (Rane et al., 2024). Artificial intelligence (AI) has emerged as a transformative enabler in this context, providing computational capabilities to process large volumes of data and perform tasks that traditionally require human intelligence (Russell & Norvig, 2021). Core AI techniques, including machine learning, expert systems, natural language processing, and predictive analytics, enable systems to identify patterns, detect anomalies, and generate insights that support timely and effective decision-making (Agrawal, Gans, & Goldfarb, 2019). In procurement and logistics, AI applications include supplier selection, contract analysis, spend management, demand forecasting, and risk assessment, delivering measurable benefits in operational efficiency, cost optimization, and strategic alignment (Guida, Caniato, Moretto, & Ronchi, 2023).

Building on traditional AI, generative artificial intelligence (GenAI) represents a significant advancement, with the ability to produce novel outputs such as synthetic text, scenario simulations, automated reports, and predictive models (Goodfellow et al., 2014; Singh et al., 2025). Foundational frameworks such as generative adversarial networks (GANs) enable realistic scenario generation, whereas transformer-based architectures underpin modern large language models (LLMs), allowing efficient processing of complex sequences and human-like output generation (Vaswani et al., 2017). These capabilities position GenAI as a powerful tool for procurement and logistics functions that require scenario planning, predictive modelling, and knowledge automation.

While AI and GenAI offer substantial operational benefits, they also have profound implications for employment and skills (Yavetz & Nakash, 2026). Tasks may be automated, augmented, or transformed, altering decision-making authority and creating new roles such as procurement and logistics analysts, AI coordinators, and data-driven planners (Adepoju, 2025). This transformation raises new skill requirements, including digital literacy, data analytics, and AI-assisted decision-making capabilities, while revealing organizational capability gaps that can limit effective adoption. Despite the growing attention given to AI adoption, the empirical understanding of its impact on workforce roles, skill needs, and organizational readiness in logistics and procurement remains limited, particularly in complex, engineering-intensive contexts and emerging economies. Addressing these gaps requires a systematic synthesis of the literature aiming to do the following:

RO1: Examine the extent of AI and generative AI adoption in procurement and logistics functions.
RO2: Analyse how AI integration reshapes the role of procurement.
RO3: Examine the barriers to affecting AI-driven skills in procurement and logistics.
RO4: Evaluating the workforce implications of AI and generative AI adoption in logistics systems.

This chapter is positioned as a theory-informed systematic review that goes beyond descriptive synthesis to develop an integrative conceptual framework explaining how AI and generative AI reshape employment structures and skill configurations in logistics and procurement. By integrating insights from sociotechnical systems (STS) theory, the technology acceptance model (TAM), and skill-biased technological change perspectives, this chapter advances a structured model that links technological adoption patterns to task transformation, role reconfiguration, and competency evolution. In doing so, it contributes not only to the synthesis of existing evidence but also to a conceptual foundation for future empirical research on AI-driven workforce transformation in logistics.

THEORETICAL GROUNDING

This study draws from the Technology Acceptance Model (TAM) and Socio-Technical Systems (STS) Theory. The Technology Acceptance Model (TAM), developed by Davis (1989), posits that the primary determinants of technology adoption are perceived usefulness and perceived ease of use. These perceptions influence users' attitudes toward a system, shaping their behavioral intentions and, ultimately, actual technology use. Within procurement and logistics, the TAM is particularly relevant because successful adoption of AI and GenAI depends on how professionals perceive the value, usability, and workforce impact of these technologies. For example, AI-driven spend analytics, predictive forecasting, automated supplier evaluation, and contract lifecycle management are more likely to be adopted if users believe that they enhance decision quality, improve efficiency, reduce cognitive workload, and support workforce capabilities by enabling higher-value tasks. TAM also emphasizes the role of organizational support, workflow integration, and training programs in shaping adoption outcomes. Applying the TAM allows this study to examine how individual perceptions of AI influence engagement, skill development, and workforce adaptation, highlighting variations in adoption and capability utilization across diverse logistics and procurement environments.

On the other hand, the sociotechnical systems (STS) theory emphasizes the interdependence of social and technical subsystems within organizations (Trist & Emery, 2015; Cherns, 1976). STS theory asserts that organizational effectiveness cannot be achieved through technological optimization alone; technology must be aligned with the social subsystem, which includes people, roles, skills, work practices, and organizational culture. Misalignment between social and technical elements can lead to inefficiencies, workforce resistance, and underperformance. STS principles such as equifinality and minimal critical specification highlight the importance of context-sensitive system design. In procurement and logistics,

STS theory underscores that AI and GenAI adoption directly affects employment structures, task allocation, and required competencies. Aligning technology with human workflows ensures not only efficiency and performance but also workforce engagement, role evolution, and the development of new skills necessary for AI-augmented operations.

METHODOLOGY

This study adopts a qualitative, literature-based research design to examine the adoption and integration of artificial intelligence (AI) and generative artificial intelligence (GenAI) in procurement and logistics, with a particular focus on workforce implications, employment, and skill requirements. Literature-based research is widely recognized as a rigorous approach for exploring emerging and complex phenomena, especially in contexts where empirical evidence is dispersed or rapidly evolving (Webster & Watson, 2002). A systematic literature review (SLR) was conducted to ensure comprehensiveness, transparency, and methodological rigor. The review drew upon major academic and professional databases, including Scopus, ScienceDirect, IEEE Xplore, Emerald Insight, and Google Scholar, covering publications from 2010--2025. This period captures foundational research on AI adoption in procurement and logistics as well as recent studies addressing applications of generative AI and their impacts on workforce roles, task allocation, and skill evolution. The search terms included "artificial intelligence in procurement," "generative AI," "digital procurement," "AI adoption," "procurement performance," and "AI workforce impact." Inclusion criteria focused on peer-reviewed journal articles, technical reports, and industry white papers offering empirical or conceptual insights into AI-driven practices and their effects on employment, skills, and workforce transformation. Each study was evaluated for relevance, methodological rigor, and theoretical or practical contributions, ensuring that only high-quality evidence was synthesized. Figure 1 illustrates the research design and process flow.

Figure 1. Research design and process flow (Author, 2025)

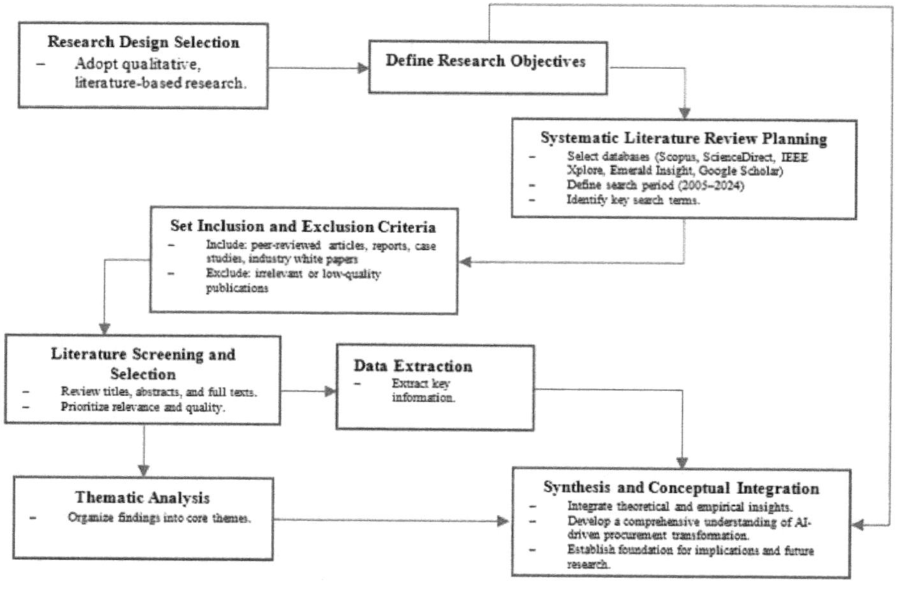

The literature was analysed thematically following Braun and Clarke's (2006) six-step approach. The analysis was structured around four dimensions aligned with the chapter's objectives. This approach enables the synthesis of both conceptual and empirical evidence, providing a critical understanding of AI's role in procurement transformation. The methodology explicitly links literature findings to the research objectives (RO1–RO4), offering insights into AI and GenAI adoption patterns, operational and strategic benefits, implementation challenges, workforce implications, and impacts on employment and skill requirements in procurement and logistics. Anchoring the methodology in established research practices enhances academic rigor, credibility, and replicability (Saunders et al., 2000). While literature-based research provides a comprehensive overview of AI and GenAI adoption, it is limited by reliance on published studies and potential publication bias. Nevertheless, this approach establishes a robust foundation for future research and offers practical implications for scholars, practitioners, and policymakers seeking to leverage AI technologies in procurement.

LITERATURE REVIEW

Artificial Intelligence (AI)

Artificial intelligence (AI) refers to computational systems capable of performing tasks that traditionally require human intelligence, including reasoning, learning, problem-solving, perception, and decision-making. By leveraging algorithms and data-driven models, AI can process large and complex datasets, uncover patterns, and generate insights that inform timely and accurate decisions. Core AI techniques include machine learning, which enables systems to learn from historical data and improve predictions over time; expert systems, which codify domain knowledge for rule-based decision-making; natural language processing, which allows computers to interpret and generate human language; and robotics, which automates physical or repetitive processes (Rane et al., 2024).

Generative artificial intelligence (GenAI)

Generative artificial intelligence (GenAI) is a specialized subset of AI designed to produce novel outputs, such as content, solutions, or data, on the basis of learned patterns from existing information. Unlike conventional AI, which focuses primarily on prediction, classification, or optimization, GenAI emphasizes creation and simulation, enabling systems to mimic human-like creativity. Key GenAI models, including generative adversarial networks (GANs), can produce text, images, simulations, and structured outputs, significantly expanding the scope of AI applications across domains. GenAI extends the capabilities of traditional AI by supporting higher-order, strategic tasks. Applications include automated contract drafting, scenario-based decision-making, predictive modelling, and knowledge synthesis (Zhang et al., 2025). For example, GenAI can simulate multiple supply chain scenarios to assess risk exposure, generate automated reports summarizing procurement performance, or assist in creating innovative sourcing strategies (Khlie et al., 2024).

RESULTS

Extent and Patterns of AI and Generative AI Adoption in Procurement and Logistics Functions

The adoption of artificial intelligence (AI) and generative AI (GenAI) in procurement and logistics functions has accelerated in recent years, reflecting a broader shift from rule-based automation toward data-driven, intelligence-enabled decision-making (Hashmi et al., 2025). Specifically, AI enables organizations to process large volumes of structured and unstructured data, enhances predictive accuracy, and improves strategic sourcing, risk assessment, and operational decision-making across supply chains (Handfield, Jeong, & Choi, 2019). Generative AI complements these functionalities by supporting automated document generation, knowledge synthesis, and scenario modelling, thereby enhancing the cognitive and strategic dimensions of AI-enabled procurement and logistics systems (Dwivedi et al., 2023). Within procurement, AI adoption encompasses supplier evaluation and selection, spend analysis, contract management, demand forecasting, and risk monitoring (Muntala 2021). For example, machine learning algorithms facilitate the continuous assessment of supplier performance, identification of emerging risks, and adaptive sourcing strategies, enabling procurement teams to anticipate disruptions and optimize contract terms in real time (Sakala & Bwalya, 2023). Furthermore, routine administrative tasks, such as purchase order processing, invoice reconciliation, and compliance verification, have been increasingly automated, allowing procurement personnel to focus on higher-value activities, including strategic supplier engagement, negotiation, and value creation (Strohmer et al., 2020).

Nevertheless, the adoption of AI remains uneven. Large multinational enterprises tend to implement integrated AI platforms across all procurement stages, whereas SMEs often adopt task-specific applications, such as spend categorization or supplier scoring, reflecting differences in resources, digital maturity, and workforce capabilities (Rashid & Kausik, 2024). In logistics, AI applications span transportation, warehousing, inventory management and distribution. Specifically, predictive analytics, route optimization, autonomous vehicles, and automated warehouse systems improve operational efficiency, reduce costs, and enhance delivery reliability (Mohsen, 2024; Sodiya et al., 2024). Notably, large-scale e-commerce and manufacturing firms were early adopters of comprehensive AI-driven logistics systems, leveraging predictive and cognitive capabilities to support real-time decision-making, multitier supply chain coordination and risk mitigation (Rainy & Chowdhury, 2022). In contrast, the adoption of generative AI in logistics is still emerging, as it primarily supports knowledge-intensive tasks such as scenario modelling, operational risk assessment, and the synthesis of large datasets.

However, adoption among SMEs and organizations in regions with limited digital infrastructure remains selective and is often restricted to basic forecasting, inventory alerts, or routing recommendations rather than fully integrated, intelligence-driven systems (Schwaeke et al., 2025). The extent and sophistication of AI and GenAI adoption in procurement and logistics are shaped by organizational, technological, and contextual factors. For example, large organizations, particularly multinational corporations, exhibit higher adoption levels because of their capacity to invest in integrated IT infrastructure, advanced analytics platforms, and dedicated AI implementation teams (Akinlade et al., 2024). Consequently, these firms can deploy end-to-end AI solutions that span supplier evaluation, predictive forecasting, and logistics optimization, thereby achieving strategic intelligence across the supply chain (Nweje & Taiwo, 2025). In contrast, SMEs often demonstrate incremental or task-specific adoption, reflecting their resource constraints and limited digital capabilities. Furthermore, digital maturity is a critical determinant; organizations with interoperable, high-quality data architectures are better positioned to exploit predictive and cognitive AI functionalities, whereas those reliant on legacy or fragmented systems face considerable barriers (Sánchez et al., 2025; Toumi et al., 2025). Furthermore, leadership and strategic alignment play pivotal roles. Organizations that integrate AI adoption within broader digital transformation initiatives, secure senior management commitment, and align technology deployment with workforce development and governance frameworks are more likely to achieve extensive and sustainable adoption (Fenwick et al., 2024).

AI Integration Reshapes the Logistics and Procurement Roles

The integration of artificial intelligence (AI) and generative AI (GenAI) drives structural transformation within procurement and logistics functions. Beyond generating operational efficiency gains, AI reshapes work processes, redistributes cognitive responsibilities, and redefines professional authority across supply networks. By embedding predictive analytics, machine learning, and cognitive automation into sourcing and logistics workflows, procurement is evolving from a transactional support function into an intelligence-driven, strategic capability. Consequently, this transformation affects task allocation, professional identity, governance responsibilities, and competency requirements (Sharma 2022; Rashid 2023). Importantly, AI integration does not merely automate discrete activities; rather, it fundamentally alters the architecture of decision making within procurement systems. As a result, algorithmic tools increasingly inform sourcing, risk assessment, and supplier management, creating hybrid human–AI environments in which professionals must exercise interpretive judgment and contextual oversight (Seyedan and Mafakheri, 2020).

Transformation of Tasks

AI reconfigures procurement and logistics tasks through automation, augmentation, and cognitive improvements. Specifically, routine and rule-based activities, including purchase order processing, invoice reconciliation, spending classification, compliance checks, and supplier performance monitoring, are increasingly executed through robotic process automation and machine learning systems (Sharma, 2022). Empirical evidence suggests that such automation reduces manual workload, enhances accuracy, and accelerates procurement cycles (Rashid, 2023). Nevertheless, the transformation extends beyond the efficiency gains. Predictive analytics tools support demand forecasting, price trend analysis, and supplier risk assessment, thereby enabling real-time visibility and scenario-based planning (Seyedan and Mafakheri, 2020). In this context, AI augments rather than replaces professional expertise, as procurement professionals increasingly rely on dynamic dashboards and simulation models to evaluate alternative sourcing strategies and anticipate supply chain disruptions.

Moreover, generative AI further enhances cognitive capabilities by synthesizing large datasets, drafting contracts, summarizing supplier communications, and modelling sourcing scenarios (Singh et al., 2026). Consequently, cognitive effort shifts from data compilation and procedural execution to analytical interpretation, strategic alignment, and exception management. This reallocation signifies a transition from manual processing to intelligence-enabled orchestration of the entire process. However, a greater reliance on algorithmic outputs introduces governance complexities. Professionals must evaluate data integrity, assess model robustness, and mitigate risks associated with bias, opacity, and compliance (Bibi, 2024). Thus, automation is accompanied by expanded oversight responsibilities rather than diminished accountability.

Reconfiguration of Professional Roles

As task structures evolve, professional roles in procurement and logistics undergo substantive redefinition. Specifically, operational and compliance-focused responsibilities are increasingly complemented by strategic advisory and analytical functions (Onotole et al., 2022). For example, procurement professionals now leverage AI-generated insights to optimize supplier portfolios, manage cost volatility, and assess multidimensional risks across financial, geopolitical, and operational domains. In addition, responsibilities related to algorithm validation, data governance, and ethical oversight are becoming integral to professional practice, requiring the critical evaluation of AI outputs and adherence to regulatory standards (Bibi, 2024). In this respect, AI elevates the function's strategic influence while simultaneously intensifying accountability. Furthermore, leadership roles are increasingly aligned with digital transformation strategies, influencing cross-functional coordination in logistics, finance, sustainability, and enterprise risk management (Rice, 2024). Conversely, intermediate roles centered on documentation and routine reporting are declining, reflecting structural shifts toward intelligence-intensive and digitally mediated work environments (Appiah, 2025).

Evolution of the Required Skill Sets

The restructuring of tasks and roles necessitates a comprehensive evolution of professional competency (Arranz Lahuerta et al., 2026). First, technical literacy, which encompasses familiarity with AI platforms, data analytics tools, and machine learning outputs, has become foundational. Second, analytical competencies, including systems thinking, scenario evaluation, and risk modelling, enable professionals to contextualize AI-generated recommendations within broader organizational objectives (Annapureddy et al., 2025). Such skills ensure that algorithmic outputs are critically assessed rather than uncritically adopted. Simultaneously, sociocognitive and relational competencies remain indispensable in the field. Adaptability, critical thinking, collaborative problem solving, and ethical reasoning facilitate responsible human–AI interactions and effective stakeholder engagement (Asrifan et al., 2025).

Organizational and structural implications

Thus, AI integration positions procurement and logistics as intelligence-enabled orchestrators within digitally interconnected supply systems. Specifically, automation reallocates human effort toward higher-value activities, role reconfiguration enhances strategic influence, and evolving competencies strengthen cross-functional integration (Tatini 2025). Nevertheless, the extent and inclusiveness of this transformation depend on organizational readiness. Investments in digital infrastructure, leadership alignment, and reskilling programs significantly influence whether AI adoption yields capability enhancement or structural dislocation (Appiah 2025).

Barriers to effective AI-driven skill development in procurement and logistics

A complex interplay of structural, organizational, technological, and human barriers constrains the implementation of AI-driven skill transformation in procurement and logistics. While artificial intelligence (AI) and generative AI (GenAI) create demand for advanced digital, analytical, and governance competencies, the transition toward an AI-enabled workforce is neither automatic nor uniform. In practice, multiple factors impede the effective development of AI-related skills in procurement and logistics functions.

Digital Infrastructure and Data Limitations

A primary barrier is inadequate digital infrastructure and fragmented data ecosystems. AI systems depend on high-quality, interoperable, and real-time data;

however, many procurement and logistics functions continue to operate within legacy systems characterized by siloed databases and inconsistent data standards (Oyeyemi et al., 2025). Consequently, poor data governance, limited system integration, and insufficient cybersecurity frameworks undermine both AI deployment and the development of associated skills (Mahmood et al., 2024). Without practical exposure to functional AI systems, workforce upskilling efforts often remain theoretical rather than applied, limiting the acquisition of actionable competencies (Da Silva, 2025).

Skill Gaps and Educational Constraints

AI-driven transformation requires competencies in data analytics, machine learning interpretation, algorithmic oversight, and digital system integration (Banerjee, 2025). However, procurement and logistics professionals traditionally possess expertise in negotiation, supplier management, and operational coordination rather than advanced technical analytics (Handfield, Jeong, & Choi, 2019). This misalignment creates significant skill gaps that impede workforce preparedness. Furthermore, higher education and professional training programs in many regions have been slow to incorporate AI-specific curricula tailored to logistics contexts, reducing the availability of qualified personnel for organizational adoption (Abbasi et al., 2025).

Financial and Resource Constraints

Effective reskilling initiatives require substantial investments in training programs, digital tools, and expert facilitation (Sundaram, 2025). SMEs, which constitute a large proportion of logistics networks, often lack the financial capacity to implement comprehensive upskilling strategies. Even in larger organizations, prioritizing short-term operational returns over long-term human capital development can result in underinvestment in workforce transformation, thereby limiting the strategic impact of AI adoption (Chauhan & Puhan, 2025).

Organizational Resistance and Cultural Barriers

Workforce resistance is another significant impediment to AI-driven skill development. Employees may perceive AI technologies as threats to job security, leading to reluctance to participate in training initiatives (Zhang et al., 2025). Additionally, organizational cultures that emphasize hierarchical decision-making or risk aversion can inhibit experimentation with AI-enabled workflows (Murire 2024). Managerial skepticism regarding the reliability of AI-generated insights may further delay adoption, reduce motivation for skill acquisition, and diminish the effectiveness of training programs (Chaturvedi & Dasgupta, 2024).

Leadership and Strategic Misalignment

The success of AI-driven skill transformation depends on a clear strategic direction and leadership commitment. However, in many procurement and logistics environments, AI adoption is often pursued primarily as a technological upgrade rather than as a comprehensive organizational change initiative (Kulkov et al., 2024). When AI implementation is not integrated with human capital strategies, reskilling efforts tend to be fragmented, reactive, and unsustainable (Tiaraningrum and Sekti, 2026). Consequently, the absence of a coherent roadmap linking AI capabilities to workforce development undermined long-term transformation.

Ethical, regulatory, and governance challenges

AI systems introduce new governance requirements, including algorithmic transparency, bias mitigation, and regulatory compliance (Bahangulu and Owusu-Berko, 2025). Nevertheless, many organizations lack established frameworks to guide the ethical deployment of AI. Uncertainty regarding legal liability, data privacy regulations, and accountability structures can discourage investment in AI-specific competencies (Spulbar 2025). Moreover, employees may lack clarity regarding their responsibilities in overseeing algorithmic decisions, creating ambiguity in role definitions and further limiting effective skill development (Parker and Grote, 2022).

Workforce Implications of AI and Generative AI Adoption in Logistics Systems

The adoption of artificial intelligence (AI) and generative AI (GenAI) within logistics systems has profound implications for workforce transformation, extending beyond operational efficiency to the restructuring of roles, skills, and organizational design. While these technologies improve forecasting accuracy, supplier evaluation, and real-time decision-making, their most significant impact lies in reshaping human work across procurement and logistics functions (Rainy and Chowdhury, 2022). Specifically, AI applications in logistics, such as predictive analytics, machine learning–based demand forecasting, automated inventory optimization, and supplier performance monitoring, reduce reliance on manual, transaction-oriented processes (Richey et al., 2023). Similarly, in procurement, AI-enabled systems facilitate continuous supplier risk assessment, automated spending analysis, and enhanced regulatory compliance (Sakala & Bwalya, 2023). Consequently, routine administrative tasks, including purchase order processing, invoice reconciliation, and documentation management, are increasingly automated, diminishing the demand for low-skill, repetitive activities and prompting task reallocation and role restructuring within operational units.

Workforce transformation is characterized less by wholesale job elimination and more by task reallocation and role augmentation. As AI systems assume data processing and optimization functions, human workers increasingly perform supervisory, interpretive, and strategic activities (Adepoju, 2025). Procurement and logistics professionals are repositioned toward higher-value responsibilities, including supplier relationship management, negotiation strategies, risk mitigation, and cross-functional coordination (Helmold & Terry, 2016). In this context, decision-making becomes data driven, whereas human judgment remains central to contextualizing algorithmic outputs, resolving exceptions, and managing complex stakeholder relationships (Ashal & Morshed, 2024). Therefore, AI adoption shifts the workforce profile from execution-oriented roles to analytical and governance-focused responsibilities. GenAI tools enable automated report generation, contract drafting, scenario simulations, and large-scale data synthesis (Yandrapalli, 2023). However, these technologies also reshape knowledge-intensive roles. Middle-management functions centered on documentation and routine analysis may diminish, whereas new roles may emerge in AI oversight, prompt design, compliance monitoring, and digital knowledge governance (Oyetade & Zuva, 2025).

A critical implication of AI and GenAI adoption is the evolution of the skill requirements within logistics systems. Organizations face a growing demand for digital literacy, data analytics expertise, systems integration capabilities, and AI governance competencies (Ren, 2025). Employees must be able to interpret predictive models, assess algorithmic recommendations and translate AI-generated insights into operational decisions. Concurrently, soft skills, including adaptability, critical thinking, and collaborative problem solving, gain prominence in managing technologically mediated work environments (Gayathri et al., 2025). These developments align with skill-biased technological change theory, which posits that advanced technologies increase the demand for higher-skilled labor while reducing routine task intensity. However, the effectiveness of workforce transformation depends on organizational readiness. Furthermore, strategic alignment between AI implementation and broader organizational objectives is essential to prevent skill mismatches and the underutilization of technological investments (Appiah, 2025).

DISCUSSION

The findings of this review indicate that the adoption of AI and GenAI in procurement and logistics extends beyond incremental process improvement, reflecting a broader sociotechnical transformation. Rather than continuing traditional rule-based automation, AI adoption represents a structural shift toward intelligence-enabled decision architectures that reconfigure how organizations generate, interpret, and act on information. Specifically, AI enhances forecasting accuracy, supplier evaluation, demand management, and real-time operational decision-making (Hashmi, Ali, & Al-Masri, 2025), whereas generative AI extends these capabilities by automating knowledge-intensive tasks, such as document generation, scenario modelling, and strategic synthesis (Dwivedi et al., 2023).

Across studies, AI and GenAI have reshaped decision-making authority, reoriented professional cognition, and redefined organizational processes. For example, procurement and logistics functions increasingly operate within algorithmically mediated environments, where human expertise is augmented but also constrained by AI-driven insights (Seyedan & Mafakheri, 2020). This pattern indicates that AI adoption fundamentally transforms the balance between human judgment and machine-assisted decision-making, transitioning organizations from execution-oriented operations to analytics-driven coordination and oversight.

Analysis across studies reveals that adoption patterns are highly contingent on an organization's size, resources, and digital maturity. Large multinational enterprises tend to implement integrated AI platforms across all procurement and logistics stages, whereas SMEs often adopt task-specific tools because of limited resources and infrastructure (Rashid & Kausik, 2024; Schwaeke et al., 2025). Similarly, firms in developed economies leverage advanced digital infrastructure and supportive regulatory environments, whereas organizations in emerging economies rely on incremental and selective adoption (Fenwick et al., 2024; Zuiderwijk et al., 2021). These patterns suggest that ecosystem readiness, governance stability, and absorptive capacity are critical enablers of AI adoption. Consequently, without coordinated investment in digital infrastructure and workforce capabilities, AI may exacerbate the existing capability gaps between firms and regions.

The literature consistently shows that workforce transformation is characterized less by job elimination and more by task reallocation and role augmentation (Adepoju, 2025). AI automates routine, low-skill activities, such as purchase order processing, invoice reconciliation, and inventory tracking, thereby increasing the demand for analytical, supervisory, and strategic roles (Sharma, 2022; Singh et al., 2026). Similarly, generative AI extends automation into cognitive domains, supporting report generation, contract drafting, scenario simulation, and large-scale data synthesis (Yandrapalli, 2023; Oyetade & Zuva, 2025). These developments indicate a shift toward human–AI collaboration, in which knowledge-intensive roles increasingly require interpretive judgment, scenario evaluation, and exception management. However, this transformation is not without challenges. Professionals may experience cognitive overload when they are required to validate AI outputs without the full transparency of model architectures. Additionally, GenAI introduces risks such as hallucinations, accountability ambiguity, and legal liability (Oyetade & Zuva, 2025; Yandrapalli, 2023). These findings underscore the need for governance literacy and critical digital judgment as central competencies in AI-mediated procurement and logistics roles.

Across studies, skill requirements evolve along three interdependent dimensions. First, technical literacy and data analytics expertise have become foundational, enabling professionals to navigate AI platforms and interpret algorithmic outputs (Arranz Lahuerta et al., 2026; Annapureddy et al., 2025). Second, analytical competencies, such as systems thinking, scenario evaluation, and risk modelling, are essential for translating AI-generated insights into actionable decisions. Third, sociocognitive and relational skills, including adaptability, ethical reasoning, cross-functional collaboration, and negotiation, remain critical for effective human–AI interaction and stakeholder engagement (Asrifan et al., 2025; Veershetty, 2026). These findings align with skill-biased technological change theory, which posits that advanced technologies increase the demand for higher-order cognitive skills while reducing reliance on routine labor.

Despite these opportunities, several structural and organizational barriers constrain effective workforce transformations. Fragmented digital infrastructure, siloed data systems, and limited interoperability reduce the practical integration of AI competencies (Oyeyemi et al., 2025; Mahmood et al., 2024). Skill gaps persist because of historical professional training models that emphasize operational execution over advanced analytics (Handfield et al., 2019). Moreover, financial limitations, cultural resistance, and leadership misalignment hinder systematic reskilling efforts (Sundaram, 2025; Chauhan & Puhan, 2025). Ethical and regulatory uncertainties, including algorithmic transparency, bias mitigation, and accountability, further complicate skill development initiatives (Bahangulu & Owusu-Berko, 2025). These patterns reveal that studies have comprehensively examined AI adoption in SMEs or emerging economies, leaving an incomplete understanding of context-specific barriers and adoption strategies. Likewise, empirical evidence of the long-term effectiveness of reskilling programs and governance mechanisms remains limited, highlighting the need for longitudinal and comparative research. Figure 2 shows an integrative conceptual model of AI-driven employment and skill transformation in logistics.

Figure 2. Integrative framework of AI-driven workforce transformation in logistics and procurement

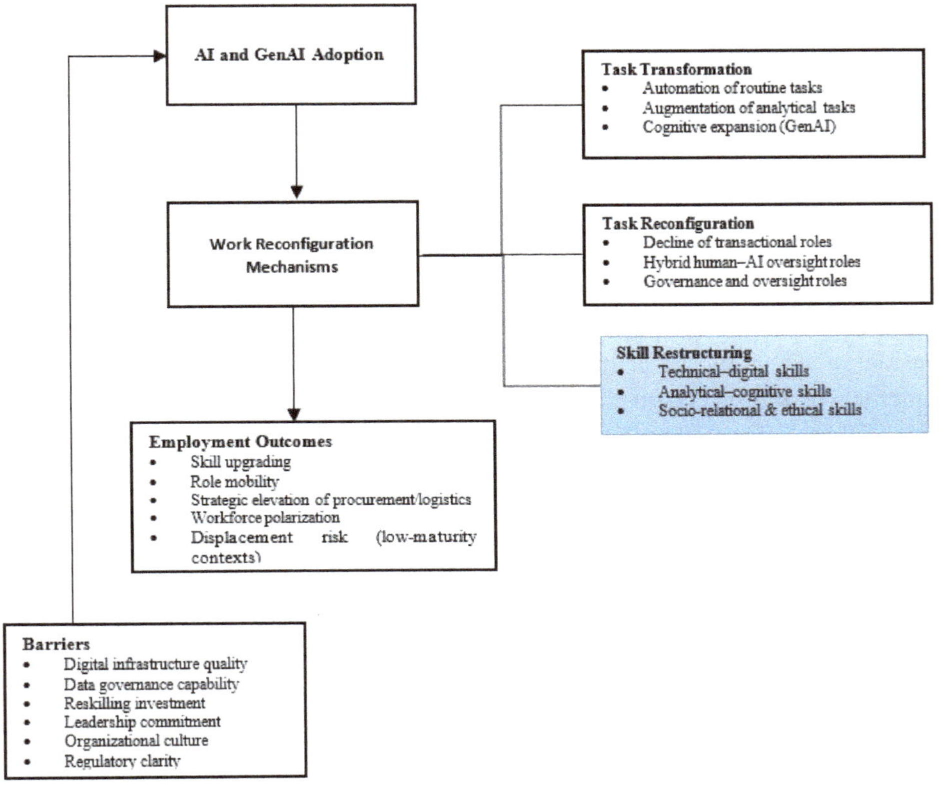

Figure 2 depicts a multilevel sociotechnical framework in which AI and generative AI adoption initiates task, role, and competency reconfiguration processes that mediate employment and skill outcomes in logistics. These relationships are moderated by structural and organizational conditions such as digital infrastructure quality, governance mechanisms, and human capital development investments, which determine whether AI adoption results in capability enhancement or workforce polarization.

CONCLUSION AND IMPLICATIONS

This review demonstrates that the adoption of artificial intelligence (AI) and generative AI (GenAI) in procurement and logistics involves not only technological transformation but also workforce transformation. While AI delivers operational efficiencies such as automation, predictive forecasting, and supplier performance monitoring and strategic benefits such as enhanced risk management, these outcomes are contingent on how organizations manage employment transitions, reskill staff, and develop human capital. AI adoption can redefine job roles, shift task allocations, and create new competencies, highlighting the need for proactive workforce planning. Persistent knowledge gaps remain regarding how AI reshapes labor demand, job quality, and long-term career pathways, underscoring the need for longitudinal and comparative research on workforce impacts alongside technological performance.

Practical Implications

For organizations seeking to leverage AI in logistics and procurement, workforce considerations should be central to adoption strategies. First, organizations must implement reskilling and upskilling programs to equip employees with data literacy, analytical capabilities, and AI-augmented decision-making skills. In addition, job redesign initiatives should clarify evolving roles, integrate human oversight in AI-driven processes, and ensure that employees remain meaningfully engaged. Third, organizational leaders should proactively manage employment transitions, including role shifts, redeployment, and change management, to mitigate resistance and maintain workforce morale. Moreover, cross-functional collaboration and executive sponsorship remain critical to align AI adoption with both organizational goals and workforce development priorities. Additionally, a phased adoption approach starting with lower-risk, high-value use cases allows employees to gradually adapt to AI-enabled workflows, supporting a smoother transition and building confidence in new technologies.

Theoretical Implications

This review advances the theoretical understanding of AI adoption by emphasizing its workforce and organizational dimensions. Integrating sociotechnical systems (STS) theory and the technology acceptance model (TAM), the findings suggest that the value of AI depends not only on technical sophistication but also on human capital readiness, learning orientation, and workforce engagement. Successful adoption requires alignment between social and technical subsystems, including workforce skills, task reallocation, and employee acceptance. The uneven returns on AI investment observed across sectors can be partly explained by differences in workforce preparedness, highlighting the importance of complementary processes such as training, continuous learning, and human-centered governance. This study provides a foundation for future research on AI-driven workforce transformation, including employment transitions, skill development, and career pathway redesign, alongside organizational and technological performance.

Limitations

This study is subject to several limitations. First, its reliance on a systematic review of literature means that the findings are inherently dependent on the quality, scope, and reporting of prior studies. As a result, emerging, experimental, or context-specific AI practices in procurement may not be fully captured, potentially limiting the generalizability of the insights. Second, the rapid pace of technological advancement in AI and generative AI implies that certain applications, tools, or regulatory frameworks may evolve quickly, rendering some findings less current over time. Finally, the study does not provide primary empirical evidence regarding the long-term effects of AI adoption on procurement performance, organizational learning, or fairness in decision-making processes. These limitations underscore the need for longitudinal, comparative, and context-specific research to validate, refine, and extend the conceptual and practical insights generated by this review.

REFERENCES

Abbasi, B. N., Wu, Y., & Luo, Z. (2025). Exploring the impact of artificial intelligence on curriculum development in global higher education institutions. *Education and Information Technologies*, *30*(1), 547–581. DOI: 10.1007/s10639-024-13113-z

Adebayo, V. I., Paul, P. O., & Eyo-Udo, N. L. (2024). The role of data analysis and reporting in modern procurement: Enhancing decision-making and supplier management. *GSC Advanced Research and Reviews, 20*(1), 088-097.

Adepoju, A. S. (2025). Transforming administrative functions through AI: Strategic planning, task automation, and resource optimization. *International Journal of Research Publication and Reviews*, *6*(1), 4300–4316. DOI: 10.55248/gengpi.6.0125.0622

Adepoju, A. S. (2025). Transforming administrative functions through AI: Strategic planning, task automation, and resource optimization. *International Journal of Research Publication and Reviews*, *6*(1), 4300–4316. DOI: 10.55248/gengpi.6.0125.0622

Agrawal, A., Gans, J., & Goldfarb, A. (2019). *The economics of artificial intelligence: An agenda*. University of Chicago Press., DOI: 10.7208/chicago/9780226613475.001.0001

Akinlade, I. A., Adebayo, M. A., Tijani, A. O., Ezenwaka, C. P., & Fadeyi, G. (2024). A Framework for AI Adoption and Strategic Decision Efficiency in Global Strategy Teams. *Applied Sciences, Computing, and Energy*, *1*(1), 231–245.

Annapureddy, R., Fornaroli, A., & Gatica-Perez, D. (2025). Generative AI literacy: Twelve defining competencies. *Digital Government: Research and Practice*, *6*(1), 1–21. DOI: 10.1145/3685680

Appiah, R. I. (2025). Corporate Strategies for Successful Workforce Upskilling and Reskilling in Response to AI Adoption-What Works, What Does not, and Why. *International Journal of Emerging Research in Engineering and Technology*, *6*(1), 91–99.

Arranz Lahuerta, L., López Ramajo, M. R., & Gandía, A. (2026). Artificial intelligence and organisational transformation: Technical skills, job insecurity and adoption. *Management Decision*, •••, 1–16. DOI: 10.1108/MD-05-2025-1462

Ashal, N., & Morshed, A. (2024). Balancing data-driven insights and human judgment in supply chain management: The role of business intelligence, big data analytics, and artificial intelligence. *Journal of Infrastructure. Policy and Development*, *8*(6), 3941. DOI: 10.24294/jipd.v8i6.3941

Asrifan, A., Widyaningrum, A., Ramli, R. B., Riyanti, R., & Sultan, S. (2025). Navigating the AI Era: Enhancing Critical Thinking Skills for Global Challenges. In *Enhancing Classroom Instruction and Student Skills With AI* (pp. 449-480). IGI Global Scientific Publishing.

Bahangulu, J. K., & Owusu-Berko, L. (2025). Algorithmic bias, data ethics, and governance: Ensuring fairness, transparency and compliance in AI-powered business analytics applications. *World Journal of Advanced Research and Reviews*, *25*(2), 1746–1763. DOI: 10.30574/wjarr.2025.25.2.0571

Banerjee, D. (2025). Digital Transformation Strategies for AI-Driven Organizations. [IJEETR]. *International Journal of Engineering & Extended Technologies Research*, *7*(6), 11046–11051.

Bibi, P. (2024). Establishing transparency and accountability in AI: Ethical standards for data governance and automated systems. *Birkstedt, T., Minkkinen, M., Tandon, A., & Mäntymäki, M.(2023). AI governance: themes, knowledge gaps and future agendas. Internet Research*, *33*(7), 133–167.

Braun, V., & Clarke, V. (2006). Using thematic analysis in psychology. *Qualitative Research in Psychology*, *3*(2), 77–101. DOI: 10.1191/1478088706qp063oa

Chaturvedi, A., & Dasgupta, M. (2024). Managerial perception of AI in strategic decision-making. *Journal of Computer Information Systems*, •••, 1–13. DOI: 10.1080/08874417.2024.2418403

Chauhan, S., & Puhan, A. (2025). Human capital valuation and economic resilience: A theoretical framework for workforce investments in the disruptive era. *People, Profits, and Policy: Redefining Workforce Economics and Financial Strategy in a*, 22.

Cherns, A. (1976). The principles of sociotechnical design. *Human Relations*, *29*(8), 783–792. DOI: 10.1177/001872677602900806

Da Silva, C. A. G. (2025). The Future Competencies & Skills Development Cycle: A New Workforce Model in the Context of Digital Transformation and Artificial Intelligence. *Journal of Human Resource Management*, *28*(2), 139–155.

Davis, F. D. (1989). Technology acceptance model: TAM. *Al-Suqri, MN, Al-Aufi, AS: Information seeking behavior and technology adoption, 205*(219), 5.

Dwivedi, Y. K., Kshetri, N., Hughes, L., Slade, E. L., Jeyaraj, A., Kar, A. K., Baabdullah, A. M., Koohang, A., Raghavan, V., & Ahuja, M. (2023). So what if ChatGPT wrote it? Multidisciplinary perspectives on opportunities, challenges and implications of generative artificial intelligence. *International Journal of Information Management*, *71*, 102642. DOI: 10.1016/j.ijinfomgt.2023.102642

Fenwick, A., Molnar, G., & Frangos, P. (2024). The critical role of HRM in AI-driven digital transformation: A paradigm shift to enable firms to move from AI implementation to human-centric adoption. *Discover Artificial Intelligence*, *4*(1), 34. DOI: 10.1007/s44163-024-00125-4

Francis Onotole, E., Ogunyankinnu, T., Adeoye, Y., Osunkanmibi, A. A., Aipoh, G., & Egbemhenghe, J. (2022). The role of generative AI in developing new supply chain strategies-future trends and innovations. *International Journal of Supply Chain Management*, *11*(4), 325–338.

Gayathri, K. C., Jayaprakash, M., Bhaskar, K. V., & Agoramoorthy, M. (2025, March). Optimizing Workforce Development through Machine Learning: A Comprehensive Analysis of Skill Gaps and Predictive Insights. In *2025 International Conference on Intelligent Computing and Control Systems (ICICCS)* (pp. 1179-1184). IEEE. DOI: 10.1109/ICICCS65191.2025.10984732

Goodfellow, I. J., Pouget-Abadie, J., Mirza, M., Xu, B., Warde-Farley, D., Ozair, S., Courville, A., & Bengio, Y. (2014). Generative adversarial networks. *arXiv*. https://arxiv.org/abs/1406.2661

Guida, M., Caniato, F., Moretto, A., & Ronchi, S. (2023). The role of artificial intelligence in the procurement process: State of the art and research agenda. *Journal of Purchasing and Supply Management*, *29*(2), 100823. Advance online publication. DOI: 10.1016/j.pursup.2023.100823

Handfield, R., Jeong, S., & Choi, T. (2019). Emerging procurement technology: Data analytics and cognitive analytics. *International Journal of Physical Distribution & Logistics Management*, *49*(10), 972–1002. DOI: 10.1108/IJPDLM-11-2017-0348

Handfield, R. B., Cousins, P. D., Lawson, B., & Petersen, K. J. (2015). How can supply management really improve performance? A knowledge-based model of alignment capabilities. *The Journal of Supply Chain Management*, *51*(3), 3–17. DOI: 10.1111/jscm.12066

Hashmi, M. S., Ali, A., & Al-Masri, R. (2025). Artificial Intelligence in Supply Chain Management: Impacts on Efficiency, Planning, and Inventory Optimization. *Journal for Current Sign*, *3*(3), 617–637.

Helmold, M., & Terry, B. (2016). Global sourcing and supply management excellence in China. *Singapur: Springer Verlag.*

Joice, J. (2024). The Role of Strategic Sourcing in Competitive Advantage: A Procurement Perspective. *International Journal of Emerging Research in Engineering and Technology*, *5*(4), 1–10. DOI: 10.63282/3050-922X.IJERET-V5I4P101

Khlie, K., Benmamoun, Z., Jebbor, I., & Serrou, D. (2024). Generative AI for enhanced operations and supply chain management. *Journal of Infrastructure. Policy and Development*, *8*(10), 6637.

Krykavskyy, Y., Shandrivska, O., & Pawłyszyn, I. (2023). A study of macroeconomic and geopolitical influences and security risks in supply chains in times of disruptions. *LogForum, 19*(3).

Kulkov, I., Kulkova, J., Rohrbeck, R., Menvielle, L., Kaartemo, V., & Makkonen, H. (2024). Artificial intelligence-driven sustainable development: Examining organizational, technical, and processing approaches to achieving global goals. *Sustainable Development (Bradford)*, *32*(3), 2253–2267. DOI: 10.1002/sd.2773

Mahmood, H. S., Abdulqader, D. M., Abdullah, R. M., Rasheed, H., Ismael, Z. N. R., & Sami, T. M. G. (2024). Conducting in-depth analysis of AI, IoT, web technology, cloud computing, and enterprise systems integration for enhancing data security and governance to promote sustainable business practices. *Journal of Information Technology and Informatics*, *3*(2), 297–332.

Mohsen, B. M. (2024). AI-driven optimization of urban logistics in smart cities: Integrating autonomous vehicles and IoT for efficient delivery systems. *Sustainability (Basel)*, *16*(24), 11265. DOI: 10.3390/su162411265

Muntala, P. S. R. P. (2021). Prescriptive AI in Procurement: Using Oracle AI to Recommend Optimal Supplier Decisions. *International Journal of AI, BigData. Computational and Management Studies*, *2*(1), 76–87.

Murire, O. T. (2024). Artificial intelligence and its role in shaping organizational work practices and culture. *Administrative Sciences*, *14*(12), 316. DOI: 10.3390/admsci14120316

Nsabigaba, F. (2024). The role of procurement practice in shaping competitive advantage. *Journal of procurement & supply chain.*

Nweje, U., & Taiwo, M. (2025). Leveraging Artificial Intelligence for predictive supply chain management, focus on how AI-driven tools are revolutionizing demand forecasting and inventory optimization. *International Journal of Science and Research Archive*, *14*(1), 230–250. DOI: 10.30574/ijsra.2025.14.1.0027

Olaleye, I. A., Mokogwu, C., Olufemi-Phillips, A. Q., & Adewale, T. T. (2024). Optimizing procurement efficiency: Frameworks for data-driven cost reduction and strategic vendor management. *International Journal of Management Studies*, *6*(4), 121–130.

Oyetade, K., & Zuva, T. (2025). A Review of Generative AI's Impact on Workforce Transformation and Future Skill Requirements. *OIDA International Journal of Sustainable Development*, *18*(12), 187–196.

Oyeyemi, B. B., John, A. O., & Awodola, M. (2025). Infrastructure and regulatory barriers to AI supply chain systems in Nigeria vs. the US. *Engineering Science and Technology*, *6*(4), 155–172. DOI: 10.51594/estj.v6i4.1912

Parker, S. K., & Grote, G. (2022). Automation, algorithms, and beyond: Why work design matters more than ever in a digital world. *Applied Psychology*, *71*(4), 1171–1204. DOI: 10.1111/apps.12241

Rainy, T. A., & Chowdhury, A. R. (2022). The Role Of Artificial Intelligence In Vendor Performance Evaluation Within Digital Retail Supply Chains: A Review Of Strategic Decision-Making Models. *American Journal of Scholarly Research and Innovation*, *1*(01), 220–248. DOI: 10.63125/96jj3j86

Rane, N. L., Paramesha, M., Choudhary, S. P., & Rane, J. (2024). Artificial intelligence, machine learning, and deep learning for advanced business strategies: A review. *SSRN*, *2*(3), 147–171. DOI: 10.2139/ssrn.4835661

Rashid, A. B., & Kausik, M. A. K. (2024). AI revolutionizing industries worldwide: A comprehensive overview of its diverse applications. *Hybrid Advances*, *7*, 100277. DOI: 10.1016/j.hybadv.2024.100277

Rashid, H. (2023). Quantitative Analysis of the Cost-Saving Potential of Procurement Automation Tools in Large-Scale Manufacturing. *IJLRP-International Journal of Leading Research Publication, 4*(12).

Ren, X. (2025). The Impact of Generative AI-Driven Job Reshaping on Creativity Sustainability. *The Frontiers of Society, Science and Technology, 7*(7).

Rice, A. J. (2024). The rise of intelligent procurement: Embracing AI and data analytics for crossfunctional synergy. *Journal of Supply Chain Management. Logistics and Procurement*, *6*(4), 319–329. DOI: 10.69554/ZGFA3030

Richey, R. G.Jr, Chowdhury, S., Davis-Sramek, B., Giannakis, M., & Dwivedi, Y. K. (2023). Artificial intelligence in logistics and supply chain management: A primer and roadmap for research. *Journal of Business Logistics*, *44*(4), 532–549. DOI: 10.1111/jbl.12364

Russell, S., & Norvig, P. (2021). *Artificial intelligence: A modern approach* (4th ed.). Pearson Education.

Sakala, C. M., & Bwalya, S. M. (2023). The role of artificial intelligence in optimizing supply chain performance. *Journal of Procurement and Supply Chain Management*, *2*(1), 1–14.

Sánchez, E., Calderón, R., & Herrera, F. (2025). Artificial Intelligence Adoption in SMEs: Survey Based on TOE–DOI Framework, Primary Methodology and Challenges. *Applied Sciences (Basel, Switzerland)*, *15*(12), 6465. DOI: 10.3390/app15126465

Saunders, M. N., Lewis, P., & Thornhill, A. (2000). Research Methods for Business Students: Lecturers' Guide.

Schwaeke, J., Peters, A., Kanbach, D. K., Kraus, S., & Jones, P. (2025). The new normal: The status quo of AI adoption in SMEs. *Journal of Small Business Management*, *63*(3), 1297–1331. DOI: 10.1080/00472778.2024.2379999

Seyedan, M., & Mafakheri, F. (2020). Predictive big data analytics for supply chain demand forecasting: Methods, applications, and research opportunities. *Journal of Big Data*, *7*(1), 53. DOI: 10.1186/s40537-020-00329-2

Sharma, A. (2022). The future of procurement: Integrating AI, automation, and blockchain for next-generation supply chains. *International Journal of Artificial Intelligence, Data Science, and Machine Learning*, *3*(4), 1–10. DOI: 10.63282/3050-9262.IJAIDSML-V3I4P101

Singh, V., Hughes, L., Albashrawi, M. A., Jeon, I., & Dwivedi, Y. K. (2026). Generative artificial intelligence (GenAI) in procurement and supply chain management: Applications, opportunities and challenges. *Journal of Systems and Information Technology*, *28*(1), 123–144. DOI: 10.1108/JSIT-03-2025-0139

Sodiya, E. O., Umoga, U. J., Amoo, O. O., & Atadoga, A. (2024). AI-driven warehouse automation: A comprehensive review of systems. *GSC Advanced Research and Reviews*, *18*(2), 272–282. DOI: 10.30574/gscarr.2024.18.2.0063

Spulbar, L. F. (2025). Legal frameworks for AI-driven markets and their challenges and opportunities in the digital economy. *Revista de Stiinte Politice*, (86), 288–304.

Strohmer, M. F., Easton, S., Eisenhut, M., Epstein, E., Kromoser, R., Peterson, E. R., & Rizzon, E. (2020). *Disruptive procurement: Winning in a digital world*. Springer Nature. DOI: 10.1007/978-3-030-38950-5

Sundaram, S. (2025). Innovating for the Future: Sustainable Corporate Strategies for Workforce Upskilling and Reskilling. *International Journal of Research in Entrepreneurship & Business Studies*, *6*(3), 33–46. DOI: 10.47259/ijrebs.2025.633

Tatini, P. R. (2025). Transforming sourcing and supply chain management: The evolution of AI agents in modern procurement. *International Journal of Scientific Research in Computer Science. Engineering and Information Technology*, *11*, 1219–1226.

Tiaraningrum, L., & Sekti, B. A. (2026). Empowering the Future Workforce: Reskilling Strategies in the Age of Human-AI Augmentation. In *Redefining Global Creative Sectors Through AI and Human Augmentation* (pp. 85-118). IGI Global Scientific Publishing.

Toumi, A., Fosso Wamba, S., & Hafsi, M. (2025). Enterprise architecture as a knowledge management discipline: Evolution, challenges and AI-enabled future. *Journal of Enterprise Information Management*, •••, 1–26. DOI: 10.1108/JEIM-04-2025-0319

Trist, E. R. I. C., & Emery, F. R. E. D. (2015). Sociotechnical systems theory. In *Organizational behavior 2* (pp. 169–194). Routledge.

Vaka, D. K. (2024). Procurement 4.0: Leveraging Technology for Transformative Processes. *Journal of Scientific and Engineering Research*, *11*(3), 278–282.

Veershetty, G. (2026). AI-Driven Supplier Relationship Management in the Digital Enterprise: Quantifying Value and Resilience with SAP Ariba. *International Journal of Artificial Intelligence, Data Science, and Machine Learning*, *7*(1), 82–86. DOI: 10.63282/3050-9262.IJAIDSML-V7I1P116

Webster, J., & Watson, R. T. (2002). Analyzing the past to prepare for the future: Writing a literature review. *Management Information Systems Quarterly*, *26*(2), xiii–xxiii. DOI: 10.2307/4132319

Yandrapalli, V. (2023). Revolutionizing supply chains using power of generative ai. *International Journal of Research Publication and Reviews*, *4*(12), 1556–1562. DOI: 10.55248/gengpi.4.1223.123417

Yavetz, G., & Nakash, M. (2026). Adopting GenAI applications in the workplace: Managerial implications and insights from ICT professionals. *EuroMed Journal of Business*, •••, 1–19. DOI: 10.1108/EMJB-08-2024-0217

Zhang, Y., Liu, X., Yan, Q., & Na, M. (2025). Empowering workforces in AI-driven environments: Co-skilling, organizational support, and mitigating job insecurity. *Frontiers in Psychology*, *16*, 1700129. DOI: 10.3389/fpsyg.2025.1700129 PMID: 41488962

Zuiderwijk, A., Chen, Y.-C., & Salem, F. (2021). Implications of the use of artificial intelligence in public governance: A systematic literature review. *Government Information Quarterly*, *38*(3), 101577. DOI: 10.1016/j.giq.2021.101577

Chapter 13

Skill Transitions in AI Augmented Road Freight Operations

Duy Le Anh Tran
http://orcid.org/0000-0001-9979-045X
Ho Chi Minh City University of Economics and Finance, Vietnam

Frederic Gautier
IAE Paris Sorbonne, France

Long Ngoc Dinh
International University, Vietnam National University Ho Chi Minh City, Vietnam

ABSTRACT

Artificial intelligence applications such as intelligent route optimisation, condition based maintenance analytics, and semi autonomous vehicle control are transforming work in road freight transport. This chapter examines how the driver's role shifts from direct mechanical control toward technologically mediated system oversight requiring monitoring capacity, analytical judgement, and structured risk governance. Drawing on four anonymised empirical cases representing advanced AI integration in freight operations, the analysis shows that automation reshapes expertise by redistributing cognitive authority between human operators and algorithmic systems. Tacit experiential knowledge is reconfigured, and occupational identity is renegotiated. The chapter develops a hybrid stewardship model explaining how AI does not merely substitute or augment labour but restructures accountability, decision prerogatives, and skill boundaries in digitally augmented transport systems.

DOI: 10.4018/979-8-3373-7826-8.ch013

1. INTRODUCTION

Road freight is entering a phase in which algorithmic systems participate directly in the organisation of mobility, safety, and asset reliability. AI-enabled routing platforms increasingly determine the "optimal" movement of vehicles across space and time; predictive maintenance systems transform how vehicle health is sensed, interpreted, and acted upon; and semi-autonomous driving and advanced driver-assistance systems (ADAS) redistribute micro-decisions about lane keeping, stability, and hazard response. While these developments are often represented as incremental "assistance" to drivers, their cumulative effect is more profound. They reorder how work is coordinated, how decision quality is evaluated, and how responsibility is allocated across human and machine actors.

Research on the digitalisation of transport has long emphasised that transport systems are shaped by ongoing interactions between infrastructures, institutions, and behavioural adaptations (Lyons, 2015). Contemporary AI systems intensify this interaction by inserting algorithmic inference into decision points previously governed by local experience and professional judgement. In logistics, digital transformation is widely documented as uneven and contested, shaped by ecosystem dynamics, organisational capability, and external pressures (Cichosz et al., 2020; Mikl et al., 2021). It is increasingly linked to business model change through data, platforms, and digital servitization, where predictive and optimisation services become strategic differentiators rather than back-office tools (Zare & Persaud, 2025; Kmiecik & Skórnóg, 2025). These shifts matter because road freight is simultaneously an economic backbone and a safety-critical domain. When AI becomes embedded in planning, diagnosis, and driving support, its consequences are not limited to operational metrics; they reshape what counts as expertise, how accountability is evidenced, and how occupational legitimacy is sustained.

The central claim of this chapter is that AI in road freight changes professional driving primarily by reorganising the epistemic foundations of expertise and the relational architecture of accountability. When algorithmic outputs become authoritative inputs to routing, maintenance scheduling, and driving interventions, competence becomes less about continuous manual control and more about supervisory attention, interpretive judgement, and risk-bearing decision-making under uncertainty. Simultaneously, the institutional definition of "good driving" becomes increasingly mediated by data traces, system compliance metrics, and platform-generated narratives of events, altering both worker identity and legitimacy. This dual shift—toward interpretive oversight and toward data-mediated evaluation—creates a distinctive pattern of skill transition: drivers increasingly operate as operational governors of socio-technical systems rather than as isolated executors of physical tasks.

To theorise these changes, the chapter proposes a hybrid stewardship framework. "Stewardship" is used here as a socio-technical governance function at the operational edge, where human workers translate algorithmic guidance into safe, reliable action; absorb residual risk; and sustain legitimacy among managers, regulators, customers, and technology providers. The framing is deliberately hybrid: it treats the driver's role as neither a residual after automation nor a simple "human-in-the-loop" placeholder, but as a reconstituted professional position whose value is expressed through monitoring, interpretation, escalation, and justified intervention. The chapter develops this framework using four anonymised cases (Case A–D) that represent leading-edge adoption of AI-enabled routing, predictive maintenance, semi-autonomous driving/ADAS, and AI safety telematics. These cases are used not to claim universal representativeness, but to surface mechanisms that recur across different adoption loci and that together illuminate how stewardship becomes a stabilising solution to the tensions of semi-automation.

The remainder of the chapter proceeds as follows. Section 2 introduces the conceptual background and develops the theoretical framework in four linked dimensions: cognitive redistribution, cognitive accountability, skill boundary reconfiguration, and occupational identity/legitimacy. Section 3 outlines the multiple-case research design and justifies the selection of four cases that collectively capture distinct but interdependent points of algorithmic influence in road freight. Section 4 presents the findings by pairing within-case analysis with cross-case synthesis, thereby showing how stewardship is enacted through common patterns that nonetheless vary by technology locus. Section 5 concludes with a brief summary and articulates theoretical contributions and practical implications for carriers, technology providers, and policymakers.

2. LITERATURE REVIEW AND THEORETICAL FRAMING

2.1. Background concepts and problem setting

AI adoption in transport is frequently discussed through the performance language of optimisation, efficiency, and safety. In road freight, this language is reinforced by the long-standing role of computational techniques in route planning and traffic modelling, now extended by AI-augmented optimisation and predictive analytics (Rauf & Umer, 2023). Yet a critical limitation of purely performance-centred accounts is that they treat AI as a set of tools added to a stable division of labour. Such accounts may successfully describe *what* improves (for example, lower fuel use or fewer incidents), while under-specifying *how* work itself is reorganised, *who* gains or loses authority, and *why* accountability disputes intensify even as automation increases.

At the level of everyday operations, drivers increasingly encounter AI not as a single artefact but as an ecology of interdependent systems that collectively govern freight work across the operational cycle. Routing systems embed models of congestion, service-time uncertainty, compliance constraints, and cost trade-offs; predictive maintenance systems embed probabilistic failure models, sensor thresholds, and scheduling heuristics; and ADAS systems embed assumptions about safe trajectories, acceptable interventions, and boundary conditions under which assistance should engage or disengage. Importantly, these systems are rarely deterministic in a way that eliminates judgement. They are probabilistic and context-sensitive, meaning their outputs are best understood as recommendations or risk signals that demand interpretation, calibration, and occasional contestation.

AI in road freight also sits within wider, overlapping transitions that shape both adoption trajectories and workforce consequences. First, transport's "digital age transition" is characterised by the expansion of data infrastructures, platform-based coordination, and new governance arrangements that alter how mobility is planned and regulated (Lyons, 2015). Second, sustainability transitions are increasingly intertwined with digital transformation. Reviews of sustainability and the digital transition highlight both enabling pathways (for example, improved resource efficiency through data-driven coordination) and new risks (for example, intensified dependencies and unequal distribution of benefits) (Rosário & Dias, 2022; Nieddu et al., 2022). Recent discussions of AI-augmented sustainability management further suggest that algorithms do not merely improve decision-making; they reconfigure how decision authority is established and justified, raising questions of accountability and legitimacy in complex supply chains (Gupta, 2026).

Third, policy debates increasingly recognise the need for "just technology transition" agendas to minimise adverse social impacts on transport workers and to govern reskilling and employment reconfiguration (Pronello & Fedeli, 2025). This orientation is particularly salient in road freight, where safety accountability remains socially and legally consequential, and where changes in work identity can be as destabilising as changes in task composition. Finally, empirical research on logistics service providers indicates that digital transformation is shaped by barriers and success factors such as data quality, integration architectures, organisational culture, and leadership capability (Cichosz et al., 2020). Ecosystem perspectives similarly emphasise that disruptive technology transitions in global logistics unfold through interdependencies among carriers, technology vendors, regulators, and customers, rather than within isolated firms (Mikl et al., 2021).

These overlapping transitions converge in a core occupational puzzle. Road freight work has traditionally combined embodied skills, local route knowledge, and tacit judgement about vehicle behaviour and road conditions. AI changes the conditions under which these competences matter by transferring parts of planning, diagnosis, and micro-control to algorithmic systems. Yet, in many semi-automated settings, formal accountability for safe and reliable operation remains with human workers and the carrier. This produces a hybrid configuration in which drivers must oversee algorithmic systems, interpret recommendations, and manage exceptions while remaining answerable for outcomes. The chapter conceptualises the emerging role as *system stewardship*: a hybrid position in which professional authority, responsibility, and identity are renegotiated at the boundary between human judgement and algorithmic inference.

To develop this argument, the next subsections specify four theoretical dimensions that together explain stewardship formation. First, human–AI complementarity is reframed as cognitive redistribution (Section 2.2). Second, cognitive accountability is introduced to capture how justificatory burdens intensify under algorithmic decision support (Section 2.3). Third, skill transitions are theorised as boundary reconfiguration rather than linear deskilling or upskilling (Section 2.4). Fourth, occupational identity and legitimacy are positioned as mechanisms shaping whether stewardship becomes a valued professional pathway or a contested site of surveillance and blame (Section 2.5).

2.2. Human–AI complementarity as cognitive redistribution

A growing body of research frames AI as enabling new value creation and business model change through data-driven capabilities and digital servitization. In logistics and related service sectors, these shifts often manifest as platform-based coordination, predictive services, and embedded intelligence that transforms how firms compete and deliver value (Zare & Persaud, 2025; Kmiecik & Skórnóg, 2025). Such accounts are important for understanding why firms adopt AI and how adoption relates to strategic differentiation. However, they can inadvertently naturalise a managerial viewpoint in which "augmentation" is primarily an efficiency lever. From a work and skills perspective, the more consequential question concerns how AI alters the distribution of judgement, authority, and interpretive labour within the operational system.

This chapter therefore reframes complementarity as *cognitive redistribution*. Cognitive redistribution emphasises that AI adoption changes which actor is presumed competent to decide, what becomes cognitively salient, and what counts as evidence in operational decision-making. In road freight, routing platforms can standardise or dynamically recompute route choices that were previously shaped by individual route mastery; predictive maintenance can relocate diagnostic judgement toward sensor analytics and fleet-level models; and semi-autonomous features can shift micro-control functions toward embedded control systems. The consequence is not a simple shift from "manual" to "automated," but a reorganisation of attention and judgement. Drivers spend less time constructing plans or continuously micro-controlling the vehicle and more time monitoring system states, interpreting outputs, and managing anomalies.

The notion of cognitive redistribution is also consistent with the broader movement toward "physical AI," where intelligent systems increasingly operate in complex physical environments that require adaptive perception and real-time responses (Thakur et al., 2025). Even when these systems do not fully automate driving, they alter how control is exercised and how competence is demonstrated. This is particularly relevant in semi-autonomous road freight contexts, where the system may manage micro-control while the human remains responsible for situational comprehension and safe intervention. Under such conditions, complementarity is unstable: it varies with weather, traffic, road infrastructure, and the unpredictable behaviour of other road users. The practical implication is that professional competence is increasingly expressed through *trust calibration* and *boundary recognition*—knowing when system outputs are reliable and when they are mis-specified for local contexts.

By conceptualising complementarity as redistribution, the framework also links work change to broader digital transformation dynamics. Digital transformation research in logistics shows that the benefits of new technologies are mediated by integration quality, organisational routines, and the alignment of digital tools with operational realities (Cichosz et al., 2020). Ecosystem perspectives further suggest that technology transitions are shaped by interdependent actors and standards (Mikl et al., 2021). From a stewardship standpoint, these insights imply that redistribution is rarely "clean." Authority may shift to algorithms, but the supporting routines for escalation, learning, and contestation may lag behind, producing ambiguity about what drivers should do when the system is wrong or incomplete.

The framework therefore expects that the most consequential skill transitions occur at the routine–exception boundary. In routine conditions, algorithmic recommendations may be treated as authoritative and efficiency-enhancing. In non-routine conditions, drivers must diagnose when model assumptions misfit local contexts and decide whether to comply, override, or escalate. Stewardship emerges as the occupational solution to this boundary problem: drivers become responsible not only for executing tasks but for governing the interface between algorithmic inference and situated action.

2.3. Cognitive accountability and risk-work under algorithmic decision support

In safety- and reliability-critical operations, AI does not remove accountability; it reallocates and reframes it. A distinctive feature of semi-automated work is that the relationship between control and responsibility becomes asymmetric. As AI systems become more influential in shaping operational decisions, humans may remain the primary accountability holders for outcomes. This accountability condition is not merely legalistic; it reorganises everyday work by generating a requirement for *cognitive accountability*: the obligation to justify how decisions were made, including how algorithmic guidance was interpreted, trusted, contested, or overridden.

Cognitive accountability becomes particularly salient when algorithmic systems generate post hoc evidence. Logs, alerts, and dashboards do not merely record events; they structure how events are interpreted and how causality is attributed. In road freight, this means that a driver's decision can be judged not only by its outcome but by its alignment with system recommendations and by how well it can be reconstructed from data traces. This changes the work of risk management. Instead of risk being managed primarily through anticipatory judgement and embodied caution, it is managed through a combination of operational action and justificatory preparedness. Drivers must be able to explain why they deviated from a recommended route, delayed a maintenance action, or intervened when assistance systems engaged.

The framework conceptualises this as *risk-work*: a set of practices through which workers manage uncertainty, safety, and service reliability under constraints while also maintaining defensible accounts of decision-making. Risk-work is already central to supply chain operations in disruption contexts, where organisations must respond to volatility, interdependencies, and service requirements while managing reputational and contractual consequences (Duong et al., 2025). AI can strengthen risk management through earlier detection, improved forecasting, and faster coordination. However, it also introduces new epistemic vulnerabilities: model errors, data biases, and opacity can amplify uncertainty and complicate responsibility allocation. When systems are treated as authoritative without adequate mechanisms for contestation and learning, the risk shifts from "operational uncertainty" to "accountability uncertainty"—uncertainty about how decisions will be evaluated after the fact.

Socio-technical research on AI-driven digital servitization in other service industries underscores that AI adoption generates tensions around control, accountability, and alignment between technical systems and organisational routines (Sathiskumar & Andersen, 2025). Road freight shares these dynamics, but with higher stakes due to safety and regulatory accountability. The stewardship role emerges precisely where drivers must hold together operational safety, organisational compliance, and legitimate justification under algorithmically mediated decision processes.

Cognitive accountability also links to just transition concerns. If accountability remains concentrated at the frontline while systems increasingly shape the conditions of decision-making, workers may experience heightened stress, reduced autonomy, and greater exposure to blame. Policy-oriented discussions of just technology transition in transport therefore become relevant not only for employment outcomes but also for the governance of accountability and fairness in semi-automated work (Pronello & Fedeli, 2025). From this perspective, stewardship is not only a new skills profile; it is an institutional arrangement that must be supported through clear override rights, escalation protocols, and fair incident review practices.

2.4. Tacit knowledge, skill boundaries, and the reconstitution of expertise

Skill transitions in AI-augmented work are often narrated in terms of deskilling and reskilling, with a focus on whether automation removes tasks or creates new ones. While useful, these narratives can obscure the relational nature of expertise in road freight, where competence has historically been embedded in embodied skills, local knowledge, and tacit judgement. The analytic priority, therefore, is not merely to list new skills but to explain how AI redraws *skill boundaries*: the demarcations of what drivers, dispatchers, maintenance personnel, and technology vendors are authorised to decide, and how that authority is validated.

Career transition research on middle-skilled workers facing disruptive technologies shows that transitions are shaped by workers' capacity to develop new competences, reframe identities, and mobilise organisational opportunities (Chen et al., 2019). In road freight, this implies that driver transitions depend not only on individual learning but also on whether organisations reconfigure roles, training, evaluation, and cross-functional coordination in ways that support new forms of expertise. Logistics capability research similarly suggests that survival in turbulent contexts depends on adaptability, data literacy, and integrative coordination across functions and partners (Merkert et al., 2023). These insights help explain why the stewardship role is not simply "more digital skills." It requires the capacity to translate between algorithmic representations and situated operational realities.

AI reconfigures how tacit knowledge is valued and expressed. Routing optimisation can weaken the organisational premium on individual route mastery, particularly when algorithms can recompute routes dynamically. Yet it can elevate other forms of knowledge that were previously secondary, such as anomaly detection, customer-facing problem solving, and rapid re-planning under constraint. Predictive maintenance can formalise diagnostic knowledge through sensor signals and probabilistic thresholds, reconfiguring how "vehicle feel" and embodied judgement are incorporated into maintenance workflows. ADAS can reduce the frequency of certain manual micro-skills, potentially attenuating embodied competence, while increasing the value of attention management, boundary recognition, and hazard interpretation.

Digital transformation scholarship indicates that these changes are not frictionless. Barriers related to data integration, process redesign, and organisational culture shape whether new technologies enable learning and empowerment or produce rigid compliance regimes (Cichosz et al., 2020). Ecosystem perspectives further emphasise that technology transitions unfold through interdependencies among actors, standards, and infrastructures (Mikl et al., 2021). In road freight, this means that skill boundaries are negotiated not only within firms but also across supply chain partners and technology providers. When platforms define performance via compliance metrics, safety scores, or exception rates, they create new pathways through which competence is recognised and rewarded, but also new vulnerabilities where legitimate expertise is marginalised because it is difficult to render machine-readable. From a stewardship standpoint, the central skill transition is therefore boundary navigation. Drivers must learn to interpret system outputs, recognise when outputs misfit local contexts, translate tacit observations into system-compatible categories, and coordinate with dispatch and maintenance teams when escalation is required. The result is a reconstitution of expertise: the "good driver" is increasingly evaluated not only by smooth vehicle handling but by the ability to govern socio-technical interfaces under uncertainty and constraint.

2.5. Occupational identity and legitimacy in algorithmically mediated driving

AI adoption affects not only tasks and skills but also the symbolic and relational foundations of occupational identity. Professional driving has historically been associated with autonomy, responsibility, and craft-like capacity to manage uncertainty. Algorithmic systems introduce alternative scripts of professionalism that emphasise compliance with recommendations, metric-based safety performance, and continuous monitoring. This can create identity tension, particularly when systems are experienced as surveillance infrastructures or as managerial instruments that narrow discretion without recognising the interpretive labour required to make algorithms operationally viable.

Workforce identity shifts under digital transformation have been documented in transport governance contexts, where professionals must adapt their roles and legitimacy claims amid changing technologies, public expectations, and data-driven decision regimes (Kussl, 2025). In logistics more broadly, business model innovation and digital transformation reshape organisational narratives of value and competence (Zare & Persaud, 2025; Kmiecik & Skórnóg, 2025), which can reclassify frontline work from experiential craft to data-mediated compliance. These narratives are consequential because they shape what kinds of work are recognised as skilled, what kinds of learning are supported, and what kinds of judgement are considered legitimate.

The stewardship concept offers a mechanism-sensitive way to interpret these tensions. Stewardship identity implies that professionalism is increasingly tied to attentive oversight, interpretive judgement, and accountable intervention rather than to continuous manual mastery alone. However, stewardship identity is not automatic. It is co-produced through institutional arrangements such as training content, performance evaluation, incident review procedures, and managerial framing of the driver's contribution. Where organisations treat AI as an unchallengeable authority and drivers as compliance subjects, identity tensions are likely to intensify, and resistance may increase. Where organisations recognise that algorithms are fallible and that frontline interpretive labour is essential for safe and reliable operations, stewardship can become a credible professional pathway.

Just transition scholarship in transport argues that policy and organisational agendas must actively minimise social harms and support workforce adaptation (Pronello & Fedeli, 2025). This implies that identity and legitimacy are not peripheral concerns; they are central mechanisms shaping whether AI-driven change produces sustainable operational improvements or fragile systems dependent on coerced compliance. Sustainability and digital transition scholarship similarly cautions that technological change can generate uneven social outcomes even when efficiency improves (Rosário & Dias, 2022; Nieddu et al., 2022). In road freight, legitimacy hinges on whether the new measurement and accountability regimes are perceived as fair, transparent, and aligned with road realities.

Taken together, sections 2.2–2.5 specify the theoretical framework used in the analysis: AI-driven change in road freight produces (i) cognitive redistribution, (ii) intensified cognitive accountability and risk-work, (iii) skill boundary reconfiguration and reconstituted expertise, and (iv) occupational identity and legitimacy renegotiation. The next section introduces the multiple-case design used to examine how these mechanisms appear across different adoption loci in road freight.

3. RESEARCH DESIGN AND CASE SETTING: FOUR ANONYMISED CASES

This chapter uses a multiple-case design to develop and illustrate the hybrid stewardship framework across distinct but interrelated AI adoption loci in road freight. The analytic objective is theory elaboration: to explain how system stewardship emerges through the redistribution of cognitive authority, the intensification of cognitive accountability, the reconfiguration of skill boundaries, and the renegotiation of occupational identity. A multiple-case design is appropriate because AI in road freight is not a single technology but a layered socio-technical arrangement. Examining varied adoption loci enables the identification of recurring mechanisms and boundary conditions across contexts, strengthening analytical generalisation.

The selection logic is grounded in theoretical sampling rather than representativeness. Each case represents an advanced adoption site where AI meaningfully shapes operational decisions and where frontline actors remain accountable for outcomes. Together, the cases provide variation across the freight work system: pre-trip and in-route planning, asset health governance, in-vehicle control support, and post-event evidence/performance governance. This variation is important because stewardship is expected to form not from one isolated tool but from the way multiple systems redistribute authority and accountability across the operational cycle. The design therefore enables the chapter to treat stewardship as an integrative role that emerges across planning, execution, maintenance, and evaluation.

The cases are anonymised as Case A–D to focus analytic attention on mechanisms rather than brand-specific performance claims. The anonymisation also reflects the chapter's purpose: it uses well-known adoption exemplars as theoretically generative cases rather than as benchmarking exercises. While each case corresponds to a recognisable organisational context, the analysis abstracts to the level of work organisation and socio-technical governance.

Case A represents AI-enabled route optimisation and dynamic routing, conceptualised as a cognitive-authority shift in planning and execution. The case corresponds to a large-scale carrier context in which algorithmic routing becomes the default planning logic and frontline route ownership is reshaped into exception handling and compliance-with-optimisation. This case is theoretically valuable because it makes cognitive redistribution visible in a domain where route planning was historically a major source of tacit expertise and autonomy.

Case B represents connected-fleet predictive maintenance and maintenance-on-demand logics, conceptualised as risk-work and boundary reconfiguration in asset health governance. The case captures how sensor-driven analytics produce probabilistic signals that reallocate diagnostic authority and reshape the relationship between driver judgement and maintenance expertise. It is theoretically valuable because predictive regimes can render failures retrospectively "foreseeable," thereby intensifying accountability negotiations and reshaping how expertise is validated.

Case C represents advanced driver assistance and semi-autonomous driving features, conceptualised as frontline supervisory labour and intensified cognitive accountability. The case captures how embedded intelligence performs parts of control while maintaining the driver as the accountable safety actor. It is theoretically valuable because it concentrates the stewardship paradox: direct control is partially displaced, yet the duty to monitor, intervene, and justify remains.

Case D represents AI-enabled telematics, safety analytics, and in-cab coaching systems, conceptualised as algorithmic oversight, justificatory regimes, and identity politics. The case captures how AI systems construct evidence about "good driving," govern behaviour through metrics and alerts, and reshape how incidents are interpreted. It is theoretically valuable because it makes the legitimacy dimension explicit: identity, dignity, and autonomy are negotiated through data traces and evaluation practices.

Across the four cases, the unit of analysis is the stewardship configuration: the patterned ways in which cognitive authority, accountability, skills, and identity are reorganised around AI systems. The analysis proceeds by presenting findings in four sections aligned with the theoretical framework. Each findings section first provides within-case discussion across Cases A–D and then develops a cross-case synthesis that identifies common mechanisms and salient variations.

4. FINDINGS: STEWARDSHIP FORMATION ACROSS FOUR CASES

4.1. Reconfiguring cognitive authority: from route ownership to supervisory and interpretive labour

In Case A, AI-enabled routing becomes the primary organiser of daily work, shifting the centre of gravity of expertise away from route ownership and toward supervisory enactment. Drivers encounter the route not as a product of their own planning but as an algorithmically generated sequence that optimises a multi-constraint problem. This reconfiguration is consequential because it changes where discretion is located. Rather than deciding the route, drivers increasingly decide when, how, and whether to deviate, and how to manage the operational consequences of deviations. The immediate outcome is that interpretive labour expands. Drivers monitor feasibility, detect local misfits such as access constraints, customer-specific delivery realities, and unexpected congestion, and judge whether the optimisation output remains robust under changing conditions. Over time, this produces a new form of expertise grounded in boundary recognition: knowing when the model's assumptions are likely to be adequate and when they are likely to be mis-specified.

In Case B, cognitive authority shifts from episodic driver judgement about vehicle condition to continuous sensing and analytics. Predictive maintenance systems generate risk signals that reframe what counts as knowledge about vehicle health. Drivers' experiential cues are not eliminated, but they are repositioned as contextual supplements that must be translated into system-relevant categories. Crucially, the system's signals often determine what receives attention and when. This creates an authority asymmetry that is not necessarily illegitimate, but it does require new skills: drivers must learn how to interpret warnings, how to triage competing signals, and how to communicate observations in ways that are legible within predictive regimes. Here, stewardship involves making analytics operationally meaningful, particularly when signals are uncertain or when operational constraints limit immediate compliance.

In Case C, cognitive authority is redistributed at the point of vehicle control. ADAS features execute micro-adjustments and stabilisation responses, while the driver is repositioned as a supervisor who must maintain situational awareness, monitor system state, and be prepared to intervene. Expertise is expressed through vigilance and boundary recognition—knowing when the system is reliable and when contextual volatility requires reassertion of human control. Importantly, this is not a passive role. It involves continuous sensemaking about system engagement, road conditions, and other road users' behaviour, coupled with readiness to intervene in a time-critical manner.

In Case D, cognitive authority is redistributed through evaluative narratives produced by AI safety systems. These systems classify events, generate risk scores, and provide coaching prompts that shape what counts as "safe" or "appropriate" driving. Authority therefore shifts not only in-the-moment but also retrospectively, because incident interpretation and performance evaluation become anchored in algorithmic representations. Drivers confront a dual authority shift: immediate guidance and post hoc judgement, where the organisation may treat the system's classification as the default explanation for why an event occurred.

Cross-case, AI becomes an authoritative participant in planning, diagnosis, control, and evaluation. This authority is enacted through different mechanisms—optimisation sequences, risk signals, control interventions, and evidentiary narratives—but in each case it relocates the driver's expertise from direct action toward supervisory and interpretive labour. The finding strengthens the argument that complementarity should be understood as cognitive redistribution rather than as additive assistance, and it is consistent with broader accounts of digital transformation as reorganisation of decision architectures rather than tool-level upgrades (Cichosz et al., 2020; Zare & Persaud, 2025). When interpreted through the lens of physical AI, the finding also suggests that as intelligent systems increasingly operate within complex physical environments, the human role is likely to be defined by governance of boundaries and exceptions rather than by continuous micro-control (Thakur et al., 2025).

4.2. Cognitive accountability and risk-work: override decisions, escalation, and blame pathways

In Case A, deviations from algorithmic routing are consequential because they can be interpreted as inefficiency, non-compliance, or a failure to follow the "best" plan. Drivers therefore perform risk-work by deciding when to override, how to document reasons, and when to escalate to dispatch or supervisors. The accountability burden is cognitive as well as operational: drivers must justify not only outcomes but also the reasoning process behind deviations. When service failures occur, accountability becomes contested across three potential sources—model adequacy, execution quality, and environmental uncertainty. As a result, drivers' decision-making is increasingly shaped by anticipatory accountability, in which the plausibility of a future explanation influences present action.

In Case B, predictive maintenance intensifies cognitive accountability by rendering failure as potentially foreseeable. When a component fails despite predictive analytics, accountability is negotiated across drivers, maintenance teams, and system providers. Drivers are expected to respond appropriately to risk signals, yet the signals may be probabilistic, ambiguous, or operationally burdensome to address within schedules. Risk-work therefore includes interpreting warnings, negotiating maintenance windows, and managing the reputational consequences of being associated with "ignored" signals. Importantly, the case shows how predictive infrastructures can shift the moral economy of failure: breakdowns become framed less as unfortunate events and more as governance failures, thereby elevating the stakes of compliance and documentation.

In Case C, the accountability paradox is acute. Semi-autonomous features can alter vehicle behaviour in ways that are difficult to anticipate or fully explain at the moment. Yet the driver remains accountable for safety. Risk-work therefore shifts toward monitoring system states, recognising boundary conditions, and intervening promptly. The driver's liability is not only tied to driving outcomes but also to whether the driver is judged to have supervised the system "properly." Where incident review practices privilege system logs without acknowledging model limitations, blame displacement toward the driver as "insufficient supervisor" becomes more likely. This pattern is significant because it illustrates how accountability can become decoupled from actionable control: the driver may be responsible for supervising system behaviour without having full transparency into system reasoning.

In Case D, cognitive accountability becomes institutionalised through scorecards, alerts, and coaching regimes. Drivers are evaluated through algorithmic classifications of events and risk levels, creating a constant requirement to align behaviour with machine-readable definitions of safety. When drivers contest classifications, the dispute concerns evidentiary legitimacy rather than merely behaviour. The case indicates that accountability is not simply a post-event requirement; it becomes an ongoing discipline that shapes how drivers understand their own professionalism and how they prioritise attention during the workday.

Cross-case, AI intensifies the demand that drivers justify decisions where algorithms shape both action and evaluation. Cognitive accountability becomes a defining component of stewardship, complementing socio-technical accounts of AI adoption that foreground tensions around control and responsibility (Sathiskumar & Andersen, 2025). The cases also show that accountability is not redistributed proportionally with control, reinforcing just transition concerns in transport: if workers are required to absorb residual risk and justify decisions under increasingly algorithmic governance, fairness and wellbeing become central to the sustainability of adoption (Pronello & Fedeli, 2025). This conclusion also aligns with risk perspectives in disruption contexts, where uncertainty and interdependence amplify the stakes of who is held responsible and on what evidentiary basis (Duong et al., 2025).

4.3. Skill boundary shifts: revaluing tacit knowledge, formalising judgement, and redistributing expertise

In Case A, algorithmic routing reduces the organisational value of certain forms of tacit route mastery, particularly when dynamic routing updates plans in real time. Yet it elevates anomaly detection, customer-facing problem solving, and rapid re-planning when routes become infeasible. Drivers' competence is expressed through "edge judgement," namely the capacity to interpret when the algorithm's plan remains viable and when local contingencies require intervention. However, the case also reveals a boundary tension: when the system is treated as the default authority, driver discretion risks being rendered as deviation rather than expertise. Consequently, drivers must learn to translate local knowledge into forms that are organisationally legible—through documented reasons, structured escalation, and narratives that align with performance expectations.

In Case B, predictive maintenance reorganises the boundary between driver expertise and maintenance expertise. System signals can trigger maintenance actions even when drivers perceive no immediate problem, while drivers' concerns may be deprioritised if not corroborated by analytics. This reconfiguration transforms the driver's role from an initiator of maintenance attention to a translator and coordinator within a predictive regime. Drivers develop new competences in interpreting diagnostics, recognising false positives, and communicating across professional languages. The skill transition is therefore simultaneously technical and relational: success depends on the ability to mediate between embodied cues, probabilistic signals, and organisational scheduling constraints.

In Case C, ADAS reduces the frequency of some manual micro-skills while increasing the value of attentive monitoring and boundary recognition. Drivers must learn the operational envelope of assistance systems, interpret warning signals, and maintain readiness to intervene. A critical vulnerability is that reduced practice of manual skills can increase dependence on systems and raise the stakes of system failure. The case thus illustrates that reskilling is not merely additive; it can involve substitution of embodied competence with supervisory competence, with potential consequences for resilience when systems behave unexpectedly.

In Case D, telematics and AI coaching formalise judgement through metric regimes. Skill becomes measured through compliance with system-defined behaviours and minimisation of flagged events. Drivers may learn to "drive to the metric," which can support safety objectives, but also risk superficial compliance and reduced recognition of nuanced situational judgement. The case therefore highlights a boundary struggle over what counts as competence: whether it is the production of favourable scores or the capacity to manage complex road realities that may not be fully captured by sensor classifications.

Cross-case, AI redraws skill boundaries and changes how competence is recognised and rewarded. Rather than producing a linear deskilling narrative, the cases reveal layered respecification of skill. Some tacit competences are devalued by standardisation, while new interpretive, diagnostic, and translational competences become critical. This pattern aligns with career transition scholarship on disruptive technologies, which emphasises that transitions involve strategic adaptation, learning, and opportunity structures rather than mere task replacement (Chen et al., 2019). It also resonates with logistics capability debates that stress adaptability and data fluency as essential for survival in volatile environments (Merkert et al., 2023). From a digital transformation perspective, the cases suggest that the stability of new skill boundaries depends on organisational routines and integration quality (Cichosz et al., 2020), and on ecosystem alignment among actors and standards (Mikl et al., 2021). Stewardship, in this sense, is a boundary competence: it holds together multiple expert domains by translating and governing the interface between algorithmic representations and situated operations.

4.4. Occupational identity and legitimacy: autonomy, dignity, and the emergence of stewardship identity

In Case A, route autonomy is reduced, challenging identities grounded in craft-like ownership of route choice and local knowledge. For some drivers, the algorithmic plan is experienced as managerial control encoded in technology, shifting dignity from autonomous judgement to compliance. For others, identity adapts by reframing professionalism as reliable execution and intelligent exception management. Whether stewardship identity emerges depends on whether the organisation recognises interpretive labour as expertise—valuing drivers' capacity to detect model misfits and manage customer realities—or whether it treats deviations as non-compliance.

In Case B, identity is reshaped through the reframing of "knowing the truck." Predictive maintenance can be interpreted as undermining embodied expertise if system signals are consistently privileged over experiential judgement. Yet stewardship identity can also emerge when drivers are recognised as critical translators who contextualise analytics and prevent failures by integrating signals with situated cues. Legitimacy depends on whether organisational routines treat drivers as partners in diagnosis or as passive recipients of alerts. The case indicates that identity and competence become intertwined: when drivers' interpretive work is institutionalised through collaborative maintenance processes, their professional identity is more likely to shift toward stewardship.

In Case C, semi-autonomous driving creates a visible shift from hands-on control to vigilant supervision. Drivers may experience status loss if manual mastery is central to identity, particularly if supervisory work is framed as "watching the machine" rather than as skilled vigilance. Conversely, professional elevation becomes possible when monitoring competence is legitimised through training, evaluation, and incident review narratives that acknowledge the complexity of supervising assistance systems. The case shows that identity transition depends on organisational storytelling: whether the driver is portrayed as a residual controller of last resort or as a central safety steward sustaining the reliability of semi-autonomous operations.

In Case D, identity politics become explicit. AI safety systems can be framed as empowerment—supporting self-improvement and reducing incident risk—or as surveillance that erodes trust and autonomy. Legitimacy is negotiated through the fairness and transparency of scoring systems, the ability to contest classifications, and the extent to which coaching is developmental rather than punitive. Where evaluation is opaque or misaligned with road realities, drivers are more likely to interpret systems as disciplinary rather than supportive, undermining stewardship identity and encouraging workarounds.

Cross-case, occupational identity becomes a contested terrain where professionalism is renegotiated through algorithmic authority and metric regimes. The evidence suggests that stewardship identity is more likely to stabilise when organisations explicitly recognise the driver's oversight and interpretive work as skilled, legitimate labour rather than as residual tasks. This finding aligns with research on identity adaptation under digital transformation in transport governance (Kussl, 2025) and supports policy agendas that argue for just technology transitions attentive to social impacts, dignity, and fairness (Pronello & Fedeli, 2025). It also resonates with broader sustainability–digital transition debates, which caution that efficiency-enhancing digitalisation can still generate unequal or contested social outcomes if legitimacy and accountability are not governed (Rosário & Dias, 2022; Nieddu et al., 2022). In road freight, the emergence of stewardship identity can therefore be read as a key organisational capability: it indicates whether the workforce has a credible narrative and institutional pathway through which to integrate AI into professional practice.

5. CONCLUSION AND IMPLICATIONS

This chapter has argued that AI in road freight reshapes professional driving by reorganising cognitive authority, accountability, skills, and identity. Using four anonymised cases spanning routing optimisation, predictive maintenance, semi-autonomous driving support, and AI safety telematics, the analysis shows that drivers' roles shift toward system stewardship: a hybrid position combining supervisory attention, interpretive judgement, boundary navigation, and accountable intervention. The core insight is that AI does not simply augment labour by adding tools; it restructures the epistemic and relational foundations of work by changing how decisions are made, justified, and evaluated.

The cases collectively illustrate that stewardship is not an optional "soft skill" add-on; it is a functional requirement created by semi-automation. As algorithmic systems become authoritative planners, diagnosticians, micro-controllers, and evaluators, the operational system requires actors who can calibrate trust, manage exceptions, and maintain defensible accounts of decision-making. In practice, this means that the transformation of road freight work is less about the disappearance of the driver and more about the emergence of a new occupational configuration in which human judgement is concentrated at boundaries—between routine and non-routine conditions, between probabilistic signals and operational constraints, and between system classifications and lived road realities.

5.1. Theoretical contributions

The chapter contributes a hybrid stewardship framework that advances theorising of AI-enabled work in logistics in three interrelated ways. First, it reframes human–AI complementarity as cognitive redistribution. This conceptual move matters because it shifts analysis from the presence of AI tools to the reallocation of decision rights and interpretive labour. Across the cases, the key transformations were not reducible to "more automation" but to where authority was relocated: routes became system-owned plans, maintenance became analytics-led governance, driving control became shared with embedded intelligence, and safety performance became interpreted through algorithmic narratives. By emphasising redistribution, the framework clarifies why skill transitions concentrate at the routine–exception boundary, where drivers must interpret algorithmic outputs, detect misfits, and stabilise coordination between system inference and situated reality. This reframing complements optimisation-oriented accounts of AI in transport (Rauf & Umer, 2023) and aligns with strategic discussions of digital transformation and business model change by showing how value creation depends on reorganised judgement rather than on tools alone (Zare & Persaud, 2025; Kmiecik & Skórnóg, 2025).

Second, the chapter theorises cognitive accountability as a defining mechanism of semi-automated logistics. Across cases, drivers remained accountable for outcomes while algorithms shaped both action and retrospective evaluation. The framework specifies how risk-work becomes justificatory as well as operational, and why blame pathways can become asymmetrical when control is partially displaced but responsibility remains concentrated. This contribution complements socio-technical accounts of AI-driven servitization tensions that foreground misalignments between technical systems and organisational routines (Sathiskumar & Andersen, 2025). It also extends disruption-era risk perspectives by demonstrating that algorithmic infrastructures produce new epistemic vulnerabilities and responsibility negotiations, not only new forecasting capacity (Duong et al., 2025). The implication is that accountability is a central design variable in AI-enabled freight systems, not a residual legal issue addressed after deployment.

Third, the framework reconceptualises skill transitions as boundary reconfiguration and legitimacy renegotiation rather than linear deskilling or upskilling. The cases show that expertise is reconstituted through changing decision rights, metric regimes, and translation demands across professional groups. Some forms of tacit knowledge are devalued by standardisation; other forms become newly important because they enable detection of model misfits, context interpretation, and cross-functional coordination. This aligns with career transition scholarship on disruptive technologies that emphasises adaptation strategies and opportunity structures (Chen et al., 2019) and with logistics skills debates that highlight adaptability, data literacy, and coordination capacities as central to resilience in volatile environments (Merkert et al., 2023). By explicitly incorporating identity and legitimacy, the framework also explains why stewardship is an occupational transformation whose stability depends on institutional recognition and just transition governance (Pronello & Fedeli, 2025; Kussl, 2025). In this sense, stewardship functions as a conceptual bridge between micro-level work change and macro-level debates about digital and sustainability transitions (Rosário & Dias, 2022; Nieddu et al., 2022; Gupta, 2026).

5.2. Practical implications

For freight carriers, the primary implication is that AI adoption should be treated as workforce redesign rather than technology deployment. Training must move beyond system operation toward interpretive competence, anomaly diagnosis, and boundary recognition. Because cognitive accountability intensifies, organisations should establish explicit override rights, escalation protocols, and documentation practices that support defensible decision-making without unfairly transferring blame to drivers. Incident review routines should be redesigned to treat algorithmic outputs as fallible inputs rather than as definitive truth claims, thereby preventing simplistic attribution of failure to "non-compliance" when models misfit local contexts.

Carriers should also reconsider performance evaluation regimes. Where scorecards or compliance metrics dominate, drivers may be incentivised toward superficial "driving to the metric," potentially undermining nuanced situational judgement. Evaluation should therefore recognise stewardship labour—monitoring, interpretation, coordination, and risk-bearing intervention—as a measurable and rewardable component of professionalism. This also suggests the need for organisational roles and routines that support stewardship, such as dedicated escalation channels, joint driver–maintenance diagnostics forums, and feedback loops in which frontline observations inform system refinement.

For technology providers, the findings underscore the need to design for accountable use at the point of operation. Interfaces should provide forms of explainability that are meaningful to frontline users, including clarity about confidence, boundary conditions, and the practical implications of warnings or recommendations. Systems should also enable structured contestation and learning: drivers need mechanisms to flag misclassifications, report contextual constraints, and contribute to iterative model improvement. Designs that position drivers primarily as compliance subjects risk undermining legitimacy and fostering resistance, whereas designs that position drivers as partners in socio-technical learning can strengthen safety, reliability, and adoption sustainability.

For policymakers and industry bodies, the chapter supports a just technology transition agenda in transport. Governance should recognise that AI reshapes occupations through new accountability burdens and skill boundary shifts, not only through job displacement. Certification and labour standards may need to evolve to reflect stewardship competences, including interpretive judgement, system oversight, and risk management. Policy frameworks concerned with the sustainability–digital nexus should also attend to the distributive and legitimacy dimensions of AI adoption, ensuring that efficiency gains do not come at the expense of fairness, dignity, and accountable governance. This aligns with policy calls to minimise social impacts of automation on transport workforces (Pronello & Fedeli, 2025) and with scholarship emphasising careful governance of algorithmic decision-making in sustainability transitions (Rosário & Dias, 2022; Gupta, 2026).

In forward-looking terms, the strategic question for road freight is not only the quantity of driving jobs but the quality and governance of the emerging stewardship occupation. AI-augmented freight will increasingly depend on frontline workers who can hold together operational safety, algorithmic guidance, and legitimate accountability. Whether this transition becomes a pathway to professional elevation or a site of intensified surveillance and blame will be shaped by organisational design choices, technology design practices, and public policy commitments to equitable workforce transformation.

REFERENCES

Chen, Q., Wang, J. A., Ou, R., Sun, J., & Chang, L. C. (2019). Disruptive technologies and career transition strategies of middle-skilled workers. *Career Development International*, *24*(5), 475–490. DOI: 10.1108/CDI-06-2018-0172

Cichosz, M., Wallenburg, C. M., & Knemeyer, A. M. (2020). Digital transformation at logistics service providers: Barriers, success factors and leading practices. *International Journal of Logistics Management*, *31*(2), 209–238. DOI: 10.1108/IJLM-08-2019-0229

Duong, A. T. B., Ta, T. D., Truong, D. Q., Hoang, T. G., Pham, H., Hoang, T. H., & Truong Quang, H. (2025). Direct and indirect effect of risk on construction supply chain in disruption era: A service-oriented view. *Engineering, Construction, and Architectural Management*. Advance online publication. DOI: 10.1108/ECAM-04-2024-0456

Gupta, S. K. (2026). AI-augmented sustainability management in agri-food supply chain: Rethinking decision-making in the era of algorithms. *Journal of Agribusiness in Developing and Emerging Economies*, •••, 1–16. DOI: 10.1108/JADEE-09-2025-0412

Kmiecik, M., & Skórnóg, D. (2025). Impact of generative AI on logistics companies' business models. *International Journal of Logistics Research and Applications*, 1-25.

Kussl, S. (2025). Identity and Adaptation: The Evolving Role of Public Sector Professionals in the Digital Transformation of Road Transportation. *International Journal of Public Administration*, •••, 1–20. DOI: 10.1080/01900692.2025.2542310

Lyons, G. (2015). Transport's digital age transition. *Journal of Transport and Land Use*, *8*(2), 1–19.

Merkert, R., Hoberg, K., & Mahadevan, K. (2023). Logistics and Supply Chain Superpowers and Skills for Survival in the "New Normal" Globalized World. *Transportation Journal*, *62*(4), 369–396. DOI: 10.5325/transportationj.62.4.0369

Mikl, J., Herold, D. M., Pilch, K., Ćwiklicki, M., & Kummer, S. (2021). Understanding disruptive technology transitions in the global logistics industry: The role of ecosystems. *Review of International Business and Strategy*, *31*(1), 62–79. DOI: 10.1108/RIBS-07-2020-0078

Nieddu, M., Bertani, F., & Ponta, L. (2022). The sustainability transition and the digital transformation: Two challenges for agent-based macroeconomic models. *Review of Evolutionary Political Economy*, *3*(1), 193–226. DOI: 10.1007/s43253-021-00060-5

Pronello, C., & Fedeli, E. (2025). Just technology transition. A policy agenda to minimise the social impacts of digitalisation and automation on the transport workforce. *Transportation Research Interdisciplinary Perspectives*, *34*, 101670. DOI: 10.1016/j.trip.2025.101670

Rauf, H., & Umer, M. (2023). Development of AI-Augmented optimization technique for analysis & prediction of modal mix in road transportation. *PLoS One*, *18*(11), e0288493. DOI: 10.1371/journal.pone.0288493 PMID: 37917657

Rosário, A. T., & Dias, J. C. (2022). Sustainability and the digital transition: A literature review. *Sustainability (Basel)*, *14*(7), 4072. DOI: 10.3390/su14074072

Sathiskumar, N. N., & Andersen, P. H. (2025). Tensions in AI-driven digital servitization in the banking industry: A socio-technical view. *International Journal of Bank Marketing*, •••, 1–35. DOI: 10.1108/IJBM-05-2025-0353

Thakur, A., Kaipa, K., Banerjee, A. G., Cappelleri, D. J., Krovi, V. N., & Gupta, S. (2025). Physical artificial intelligence for powering the next revolution in robotics. *Journal of Computing and Information Science in Engineering*, *25*(12), 120809. DOI: 10.1115/1.4070122

Zare, J., & Persaud, A. (2025). Digital transformation and business model innovation: A bibliometric analysis of existing research and future perspectives. *Management Review Quarterly*, *75*(3), 1999–2032. DOI: 10.1007/s11301-024-00426-z

Compilation of References

Abbasi, B. N., Wu, Y., & Luo, Z. (2025). Exploring the impact of artificial intelligence on curriculum development in global higher education institutions. *Education and Information Technologies*, *30*(1), 547–581. DOI: 10.1007/s10639-024-13113-z

Abyaneh, A. G., Ghanbari, H., Mohammadi, E., Amirsahami, A., & Khakbazan, M. (2025). An analytical review of artificial intelligence applications in sustainable supply chains. *Supply Chain Analytics*, 100173.

Adebayo, V. I., Paul, P. O., & Eyo-Udo, N. L. (2024). The role of data analysis and reporting in modern procurement: Enhancing decision-making and supplier management. *GSC Advanced Research and Reviews, 20*(1), 088-097.

Adepoju, A. S. (2025). Transforming administrative functions through AI: Strategic planning, task automation, and resource optimization. *International Journal of Research Publication and Reviews*, *6*(1), 4300–4316. DOI: 10.55248/gengpi.6.0125.0622

Adjekum, D. K., & Tosun, O. (2024). Occupational safety and health implications of Industry 4.0: A review of literature. *Safety Science*, *172*, 106420.

Agrawal, A., Gans, J., & Goldfarb, A. (2019). *The economics of artificial intelligence: An agenda*. University of Chicago Press., DOI: 10.7208/chicago/9780226613475.001.0001

Agrawal, A., Gans, J., & Goldfarb, A. (2023). The distributional effects of technology: AI and labor. *Brookings Papers on Economic Activity*, *2023*(1), 1–45.

Aissoug, E. L. (2026). Revisiting the concept of decent work: Exploring work values and job satisfaction in the era of Logistics 4.0. *International Journal of Physical Distribution & Logistics Management*, *56*(2), 1–29. DOI: 10.1108/IJPDLM-01-2025-0014

Akinlade, I. A., Adebayo, M. A., Tijani, A. O., Ezenwaka, C. P., & Fadeyi, G. (2024). A Framework for AI Adoption and Strategic Decision Efficiency in Global Strategy Teams. *Applied Sciences, Computing, and Energy*, *1*(1), 231–245.

Albayrak, Ö., & Zeren, F. (2023). The impact of digitalization on the carbon footprint in logistics: An empirical investigation. *Environmental Science and Pollution Research International*, *30*(15), 44642–44655.

Albrecht, T., Baier, M.-S., Gimpel, H., Meierhöfer, S., Röglinger, M., Schlüchtermann, J., & Will, L. (2024). Leveraging Digital Technologies in Logistics 4.0: Insights on Affordances from Intralogistics Processes. *Information Systems Frontiers*, *26*(2), 755–774. DOI: 10.1007/s10796-023-10394-6

AlSheikh, M., Morshed, A., Alkhodary, D., Khrais, L. T., & Altarawneh, R. (2025). Beyond efficiency: Unpacking AI's dual role in driving sustainable and energy-conscious logistics in North Africa. *Technological Sustainability*, *4*(3), 293–310. DOI: 10.1108/TECHS-05-2025-0101

Altenried, M. (2019). On the last mile: Logistical urbanism and the transformation of labour. *Work Organisation, Labour & Globalisation*, *13*(1), 114–129. DOI: 10.13169/workorgalaboglob.13.1.0114

Althaqafi, T. (2023). Cultivating sustainable supply chain practises in electric vehicle manufacturing: A MCDM approach to assessing GSCM performance. *World Electric Vehicle Journal*, *14*(10), 290. DOI: 10.3390/wevj14100290

Aly, H. (2022). Digital transformation, development and productivity in developing countries: Is artificial intelligence a curse or a blessing? *Review of Economics and Political Science*, *7*(4), 238–256. DOI: 10.1108/REPS-11-2019-0145

Ambrogio, G., Filice, L., Longo, F., & Padovano, A. (2022). Workforce and supply chain disruption as a digital and technological innovation opportunity for resilient manufacturing systems in the COVID-19 pandemic. *Computers & Industrial Engineering*, *169*, 108158. DOI: 10.1016/j.cie.2022.108158 PMID: 35431410

Angel-Urdinola, D. F., Chinen, M., & Rodon, G. (2025). *Digital Skills Development: Competence Frameworks, Assessment Tools, and Pedagogical Approaches* (Education Working Paper, Issue. https://thedocs.worldbank.org/en/doc/a607bb6e3b76d2be0f3db8db34dcf73e-0140022025/related/3EDU-WP-14-Digital-skills-development.pdf

Annapureddy, R., Fornaroli, A., & Gatica-Perez, D. (2025). Generative AI literacy: Twelve defining competencies. *Digital Government: Research and Practice*, *6*(1), 1–21. DOI: 10.1145/3685680

Appiah, R. I. (2025). Corporate Strategies for Successful Workforce Upskilling and Reskilling in Response to AI Adoption-What Works, What Does not, and Why. *International Journal of Emerging Research in Engineering and Technology*, *6*(1), 91–99.

Arranz Lahuerta, L., López Ramajo, M. R., & Gandía, A. (2026). Artificial intelligence and organisational transformation: Technical skills, job insecurity and adoption. *Management Decision*, •••, 1–16. DOI: 10.1108/MD-05-2025-1462

Ashal, N., & Morshed, A. (2024). Balancing data-driven insights and human judgment in supply chain management: The role of business intelligence, big data analytics, and artificial intelligence. *Journal of Infrastructure. Policy and Development*, *8*(6), 3941. DOI: 10.24294/jipd.v8i6.3941

Asiedu, E., & Tenakwah, E. S. (2025). Future-proofing your workforce: Upskilling and reskilling as HR's top priorities. *Strategic HR Review*, *24*(4), 169–173. DOI: 10.1108/SHR-01-2025-0008

Asrifan, A., Widyaningrum, A., Ramli, R. B., Riyanti, R., & Sultan, S. (2025). Navigating the AI Era: Enhancing Critical Thinking Skills for Global Challenges. In *Enhancing Classroom Instruction and Student Skills With AI* (pp. 449-480). IGI Global Scientific Publishing.

Atanassova, I., Bednar, P., Khan, H., & Khan, Z. (2025). Managing the VUCA environment: The dynamic role of organizational learning and strategic agility in B2B versus B2C firms. *Industrial Marketing Management*, *125*, 12–28. 10.1016/j.indmarman.2024.12.008. DOI: 10.1016/j.indmarman.2024.12.008

Audrin, B., Audrin, C., & Salamin, X. (2024). Digital skills at work – Conceptual development and empirical validation of a measurement scale. *Technological Forecasting and Social Change*, *202*, 123279. 10.1016/j.techfore.2024.123279. DOI: 10.1016/j.techfore.2024.123279

Azadeh, K., de Koster, R., & Roy, D. (2019). Robotized and automated warehouse systems: Review and recent developments. *Transportation Science*, *53*(4), 917–945. DOI: 10.1287/trsc.2018.0873

Babai, M. Z., Dallery, Y., Boubaker, S., & Kalai, R. (2019). A new method to forecast intermittent demand in the presence of inventory obsolescence. *International Journal of Production Economics*, *209*, 30–41. DOI: 10.1016/j.ijpe.2018.01.026

Babashahi, L., Barbosa, C. E., Lima, Y., Lyra, A., Salazar, H., Argôlo, M., Almeida, M. A., & Souza, J. M. (2024). AI in the workplace: A systematic review of skill transformation in the industry. *Administrative Sciences*, *14*(6), 127. Advance online publication. DOI: 10.3390/admsci14060127

Bag, S., Gupta, S., Kumar, A., & Sivarajah, U. (2021). An integrated artificial intelligence framework for achieving sustainable development goals. *Journal of Cleaner Production*, *292*, 126010.

Bag, S., Routray, S., Saikouk, T., & Roubaud, D. (2025). Generative AI-Powered Innovation on Data-Driven Financial Decision-Making in Operations and Supply Chain Management: A Moderated Mediation Analysis. *Information Systems Frontiers*, •••, 1–30. DOI: 10.1007/s10796-025-10662-7

Bahangulu, J. K., & Owusu-Berko, L. (2025). Algorithmic bias, data ethics, and governance: Ensuring fairness, transparency and compliance in AI-powered business analytics applications. *World Journal of Advanced Research and Reviews*, *25*(2), 1746–1763. DOI: 10.30574/wjarr.2025.25.2.0571

Baker, N. (2010). Employee feedback technologies in the human performance system. *Human Resource Development International*, *13*(4), 477–485. DOI: 10.1080/13678868.2010.501994

Banerjee, D. (2025). Digital Transformation Strategies for AI-Driven Organizations. [IJEETR]. *International Journal of Engineering & Extended Technologies Research*, *7*(6), 11046–11051.

Banerjee, P., & Sharma, N. (2025). Digital transformation and talent management in industry 4.0: A systematic literature review and the future directions [Review]. *The Learning Organization*, *32*(4), 620–640. DOI: 10.1108/TLO-10-2023-0183

Baptista, J., Stein, M.-K., Klein, S., Watson-Manheim, M. B., & Lee, J. (2020). Digital work and organisational transformation: Emergent Digital/Human work configurations in modern organisations. *The Journal of Strategic Information Systems*, *29*(2), 101618. DOI: 10.1016/j.jsis.2020.101618

Bárcia de Mattos, F., Eisenbraun, J., Kucera, D., & Rossi, A. (2021). Disruption in the apparel industry? Automation, employment and reshoring. *International Labour Review*, *160*(4), 519–536. DOI: 10.1111/ilr.12213

Barnes, T., O'Neill, C., & Kelly, L. (2025). New worlds of logistical labour. *Work Organisation, Labour & Globalisation*, *19*(2), 127–139. DOI: 10.13169/workorgalaboglob.19.2.0001

Baryannis, G., Dani, S., & Antoniou, G. (2019). Predictive analytics and artificial intelligence in supply chain management: Review and implications for the future. *Computers & Industrial Engineering*, *137*, 106024.

Baxter, G., & Sommerville, I. (2011). Socio-technical systems: From design methods to systems engineering. *Interacting with Computers*, *23*(1), 4–17. DOI: 10.1016/j.intcom.2010.07.003

Becker, G. S. (1964). *Human Capital: A Theoretical Analysis with Special Reference to Education*. Columbia University Press.

Bellantuono, N., Nuzzi, A., Pontrandolfo, P., & Scozzi, B. (2021). Digital Transformation Models for the I4.0 Transition: Lessons from the Change Management Literature. *Sustainability (Basel)*, *13*(23), 12941. https://www.mdpi.com/2071-1050/13/23/12941. DOI: 10.3390/su132312941

Bentalha, B. (2023). A Framework for Exploring the Global Performance of Service Supply Chain Management: A Qualitative Study. *Government Impact on Sustainable and Responsible Supply Chain Management*, 106-129.

Bessen, J. (2018). Artificial intelligence and jobs: The role of demand. In *The economics of artificial intelligence: an agenda* (pp. 291–307). University of Chicago Press.

Bhatt, P., & Muduli, A. (2022). Artificial intelligence in learning and development: A systematic literature review. *European Journal of Training and Development*, *47*(7-8), 677–694. DOI: 10.1108/EJTD-09-2021-0143

Bibi, P. (2024). Establishing transparency and accountability in AI: Ethical standards for data governance and automated systems. *Birkstedt, T., Minkkinen, M., Tandon, A., & Mäntymäki, M.(2023). AI governance: themes, knowledge gaps and future agendas. Internet Research*, *33*(7), 133–167.

Birou, L., & Hoek, R. V. (2021). Supply chain management talent: The role of executives in engagement, recruitment, development and retention. *Supply Chain Management*, *27*(6), 712–727. DOI: 10.1108/SCM-08-2020-0418

Bouwmans, M., Lub, X., Orlowski, M., & Nguyen, T.-V. (2024). Developing the digital transformation skills framework: A systematic literature review approach. *PLoS One*, *19*(7), e0304127. DOI: 10.1371/journal.pone.0304127 PMID: 38968253

Boyd, R., & Holton, R. J. (2018). Technology, innovation, employment and power: Does robotics and artificial intelligence really mean social transformation? *Journal of Sociology (Melbourne, Vic.)*, *54*(3), 331–345. DOI: 10.1177/1440783317726591

Boysen, N., de Koster, R., & Weidinger, F. (2019). Warehousing in the e-commerce era: A survey. *European Journal of Operational Research*, *277*(2), 396–411. DOI: 10.1016/j.ejor.2018.08.023

Braun, V., & Clarke, V. (2006). Using thematic analysis in psychology. *Qualitative Research in Psychology*, *3*(2), 77–101. DOI: 10.1191/1478088706qp063oa

Brunetti, M., Mes, M., & Lalla-Ruiz, E. (2024). Smart logistics nodes: Concept and classification. *International Journal of Logistics*, *27*(11), 1984–2020. DOI: 10.1080/13675567.2024.2327394

Brynjolfsson, E., & Mitchell, T. (2017). What can machine learning do? Workforce implications. *Science*, *358*(6370), 1530–1534. /doi:10.1126/science.aap8062. DOI: 10.1126/science.aap8062 PMID: 29269459

Bui, T. D., Chan, F. T., Kumpimpa, T., Tan, K., Sethanan, K., & Tseng, M. L. (2025). A supply chain finance risk management model for the electric vehicle supply chain: A data-driven analysis. *International Journal of Logistics*, *28*(12), 1422–1453. DOI: 10.1080/13675567.2024.2351561

Burton, J. W., Stein, M.-K., & Jensen, T. B. (2020). A systematic review of algorithm aversion in augmented decision making. *Journal of Behavioral Decision Making*, *29*(6), 543–565. DOI: 10.1002/bdm.2155

Busch, P., Pares, F., Chandra, M., Kendall, A., & Tal, G. (2024). Future of global electric vehicle supply chain: Exploring the impact of global trade on electric vehicle production and battery requirements. *Transportation Research Record: Journal of the Transportation Research Board*, *2678*(11), 1468–1482. DOI: 10.1177/03611981241244797

Cantoni, F., Ricciardi, A., Bisogni, P. G., & Zsifkovits, H. (2024). The unravelled role of soft skills in the logistics and supply chain management field. *Journal of Innovation & Knowledge*, *9*(4), 100615. 10.1016/j.jik.2024.100615. DOI: 10.1016/j.jik.2024.100615

Carbonneau, R., Laframboise, K., & Vahidov, R. (2008). Application of machine learning techniques for supply chain demand forecasting. *European Journal of Operational Research*, *184*(3), 1140–1154. DOI: 10.1016/j.ejor.2006.12.004

Chaturvedi, A., & Dasgupta, M. (2024). Managerial perception of AI in strategic decision-making. *Journal of Computer Information Systems*, •••, 1–13. DOI: 10.1080/08874417.2024.2418403

Chauhan, S., & Puhan, A. (2025). Human capital valuation and economic resilience: A theoretical framework for workforce investments in the disruptive era. *People, Profits, and Policy: Redefining Workforce Economics and Financial Strategy in a*, 22.

Chen, Q., Wang, J. A., Ou, R., Sun, J., & Chang, L. C. (2019). Disruptive technologies and career transition strategies of middle-skilled workers. *Career Development International, 24*(5), 475–490. DOI: 10.1108/CDI-06-2018-0172

Chen, W., Men, Y., Fuster, N., Osorio, C., & Juan, A. A. (2024). Artificial intelligence in logistics optimization with sustainable criteria: A review. *Sustainability (Basel), 16*(21), 9145. DOI: 10.3390/su16219145

Cheon, S. H. (2023). Data-driven automated management in logistics warehouse operations: The case of CJ Logistics in South Korea. *Geoforum, 141*, 103737.

Cherns, A. (1976). The principles of socio-technical design. *Human Relations, 29*(8), 783–792. DOI: 10.1177/001872677602900806

Choi, T.-M., Kumar, S., Yue, X., & Chan, H.-L. (2022). Disruptive Technologies and Operations Management in the Industry 4.0 Era and Beyond. *Production and Operations Management, 31*(1), 9–31. DOI: 10.1111/poms.13622

Chuang, S. (2024). Indispensable skills for human employees in the age of robots and AI. *European Journal of Training and Development, 48*(1/2), 179–195. DOI: 10.1108/EJTD-06-2022-0062

Chuang, S., Shahhosseini, M., Javaid, M., & Wang, G. G. (2024). Machine learning and AI technology-induced skill gaps and opportunities for continuous development of middle-skilled employees. *Journal of Work-Applied Management*. Advance online publication. DOI: 10.1108/JWAM-08-2024-0111

Cichosz, M., Wallenburg, C. M., & Knemeyer, A. M. (2020). Digital transformation at logistics service providers: Barriers, success factors and leading practices. *International Journal of Logistics Management, 31*(2), 209–238. DOI: 10.1108/IJLM-08-2019-0229

Cini, L. (2023). Resisting algorithmic control: Understanding the rise and variety of platform worker mobilisations. *New Technology, Work and Employment, 38*(1), 125–144. DOI: 10.1111/ntwe.12257

Cini, L. (2023). Resisting the algorithmic boss: Guessing, gaming, and grieving in the gig economy. [REMOVED HYPERLINK FIELD]. *New Technology, Work and Employment, 38*(2), 278–294.

Cirillo, V., Massimo, F. S., Rinaldini, M., Staccioli, J., & Virgillito, M. E. (2025). Monopoly power upon the world of work: A workplace analysis in the logistics segment under automation. *Review of Political Economy*, *37*(4), 1599–1631. DOI: 10.1080/09538259.2024.2419611

Crainic, T. G., Fu, X., Gendreau, M., Rei, W., & Wallace, S. W. (2011). Progressive hedging-based metaheuristics for stochastic network design. *Networks*, *58*(2), 114–124. DOI: 10.1002/net.20456

Culot, G., Podrecca, M., & Nassimbeni, G. (2024). Artificial intelligence in supply chain management: A systematic literature review of empirical studies and research directions. *Computers in Industry*, *162*, 104132. 10.1016/j.compind.2024.104132. DOI: 10.1016/j.compind.2024.104132

da SILVA, C. A. G. (2025). The Future Competencies & Skills Development Cycle: A New Workforce Model in the Context of Digital Transformation and Artificial Intelligence. *Journal of Human Resource Management*, *28*(2), 139–155.

Davis, F. D. (1989). Technology acceptance model: TAM. *Al-Suqri, MN, Al-Aufi, AS: Information seeking behavior and technology adoption, 205*(219), 5.

Delfanti, A. (2021). Machinic dispossession and augmented despotism: Digital work in an Amazon warehouse. *New Media & Society*, *23*(1), 49–67. DOI: 10.1177/1461444819891613

Dellermann, D., Ebel, P., Söllner, M., & Leimeister, J. M. (2019). Hybrid intelligence. *Business & Information Systems Engineering*, *61*(5), 637–643. DOI: 10.1007/s12599-019-00595-2

Dencik, L., & Stevens, A. (2023). Regimes of justification in the datafied workplace: The case of warehousing. *Work, Employment and Society*.

Dhamija, P., Bedi, M., & Gupta, M. L. (2021). Industry 4.0 and supply chain management: A methodological review. *Research Anthology on Cross-Industry Challenges of Industry*, *4*(0), 192–217. DOI: 10.4018/978-1-7998-8548-1.ch011

Dhanaraj, C., & Parkhe, A. (2006). Orchestrating Innovation Networks. *Academy of Management Review*, *31*(3), 659–669. DOI: 10.5465/amr.2006.21318923

Ding, Y., Zhang, H., & Evans, S. (2023). Smart production lines and energy conservation in manufacturing. *Journal of Cleaner Production*, *386*, 135803.

DocShipper. (2025). *AI Changing Logistics & Supply Chain – 2025*. https://docshipper.com/logistics/ai-changing-logistics-supply-chain-2025/

Do, T. H. M., Tanveer, U., Ishaq, S., & Hoang, T. G. (2025). Safe-shoring and resource orchestration for B2B firms in emerging economies. *Journal of International Management, 31*(5), 101263. DOI: 10.1016/j.intman.2025.101263

du Plessis, M. J., Gerber, R., Goedhals-Gerber, L. L., & van Eeden, J. (2025). Shaping the Future of Freight Logistics: Use Cases of Artificial Intelligence. *Sustainability (Basel), 17*(4), 1355. DOI: 10.3390/su17041355

Dubey, R., & Gunasekaran, A. (2015). The role of the truck driver in sustainable transportation and logistics. *Industrial and Commercial Training, 47*(3), 127–134. DOI: 10.1108/ICT-08-2014-0053

Duggan, J., Sherman, U., Carbery, R., & McDonnell, A. (2020). Algorithmic management and app-work in the gig economy: A research agenda for employment relations and HRM. *International Journal of Human Resource Management, 31*(1), 114–132.

Duong, A. T. B., Ta, T. D., Truong, D. Q., Hoang, T. G., Pham, H., Hoang, T. H., & Truong Quang, H. (2025). Direct and indirect effect of risk on construction supply chain in disruption era: A service-oriented view. *Engineering, Construction, and Architectural Management*. Advance online publication. DOI: 10.1108/ECAM-04-2024-0456

Du, P., Shi, Y., Cao, H., Garg, S., Alrashoud, M., & Shukla, P. K. (2024). AI-enabled trajectory optimization of logistics UAVs with wind impacts in smart cities. *IEEE Transactions on Consumer Electronics, 70*(1), 3885–3897. DOI: 10.1109/TCE.2024.3355061

Dwivedi, Y. K., Ismagilova, E., Hughes, D. L., Carlson, J., Filieri, R., Jacobson, J., Jain, V., Karjaluoto, H., Kefi, H., Krishen, A. S., Kumar, V., Rahman, M. M., Raman, R., Rauschnabel, P. A., Rowley, J., Salo, J., Tran, G. A., & Wang, Y. (2021). Setting the future of digital and social media marketing research: Perspectives and research propositions. *International Journal of Information Management, 59*, 102168. DOI: 10.1016/j.ijinfomgt.2020.102168

Dwivedi, Y. K., Kshetri, N., Hughes, L., Slade, E. L., Jeyaraj, A., Kar, A. K., Baabdullah, A. M., Koohang, A., Raghavan, V., & Ahuja, M. (2023). So what if ChatGPT wrote it? Multidisciplinary perspectives on opportunities, challenges and implications of generative artificial intelligence. *International Journal of Information Management, 71*, 102642. DOI: 10.1016/j.ijinfomgt.2023.102642

Ekren, B. Y., Venkatadri, U., Sgarbossa, F., & Grosse, E. H. (2026). Warehousing 5.0 for the future of the logistics industry. *International Journal of Production Research, 64*(5), 1–11. DOI: 10.1080/00207543.2026.2617791

Ersanlı, C. Y., Çelik, F., Barjesteh, H., Duran, V., & Manoochehrzadeh, M. (2025). A review of global reskilling and upskilling initiatives in the age of AI. *AI and Ethics*, *5*(6), 1–10. DOI: 10.1007/s43681-025-00767-9

Essex, A., Subramanian, N., & Gunasekaran, A. (2016). The relationship between supply chain manager capabilities and performance: Empirical evidence. *Production Planning and Control*, *27*(3), 198–211. DOI: 10.1080/09537287.2015.1091519

European Commission. (2024). *Corporate sustainability due diligence directive*. EU Publications.

Faraj, S., Pachidi, S., & Sayegh, K. (2018). Working and organizing in the age of the learning algorithm. *Information and Organization*, *28*(1), 62–70. DOI: 10.1016/j.infoandorg.2018.02.005

Fenwick, A., Molnar, G., & Frangos, P. (2024). The critical role of HRM in AI-driven digital transformation: A paradigm shift to enable firms to move from AI implementation to human-centric adoption. *Discover Artificial Intelligence*, *4*(1), 34. DOI: 10.1007/s44163-024-00125-4

Fernández-Macías, E., Bisello, M., & Sarkar, S. (2023). The platformisation of work: Evidence from the JRC CODE survey. *European Economic Review*, *158*, 104555.

Fernando, Y., & Wulansari, P. (2020). Perceived understanding of supply chain integration, communication and teamwork competency in the global manufacturing companies. *European Journal of Management and Business Economics*, *30*(2), 191–210. DOI: 10.1108/EJMBE-06-2020-0157

Ferreira, B., & Reis, J. (2023). A Systematic Literature Review on the Application of Automation in Logistics. *Logistics (Basel)*, *7*(4), 80. Advance online publication. DOI: 10.3390/logistics7040080

Flecker, J., & Meil, P. (2010). Organisational restructuring and emerging service value chains: Implications for work and employment. *Work, Employment and Society*, *24*(4), 680–698. DOI: 10.1177/0950017010380635

Foroughi, A. (2020). Supply chain workforce training: Addressing the digital skills gap. *Higher Education, Skills and Work-based Learning*, *11*(3), 683–696. DOI: 10.1108/HESWBL-07-2020-0159

Francis Onotole, E., Ogunyankinnu, T., Adeoye, Y., Osunkanmibi, A. A., Aipoh, G., & Egbemhenghe, J. (2022). The role of generative AI in developing new supply chain strategies-future trends and innovations. *International Journal of Supply Chain Management*, *11*(4), 325–338.

Galière, S. (2020). When food-delivery platform workers consent to algorithmic management: A Foucauldian perspective. *New Technology, Work and Employment, 35*(3), 357–370. DOI: 10.1111/ntwe.12177

Gayathri, K. C., Jayaprakash, M., Bhaskar, K. V., & Agoramoorthy, M. (2025, March). Optimizing Workforce Development through Machine Learning: A Comprehensive Analysis of Skill Gaps and Predictive Insights. In *2025 International Conference on Intelligent Computing and Control Systems (ICICCS)* (pp. 1179-1184). IEEE. DOI: 10.1109/ICICCS65191.2025.10984732

GhanavatiNejad, M., Tavakoli, M., Sheikhalishahi, M., Aydın, N., & Aria, S. S. (2025). An integrated smart framework for fast-moving consumer goods online market logistics: A digital twin framework. *Journal of Industrial and Production Engineering, 42*(5), 533–549. DOI: 10.1080/21681015.2025.2470244

Glikson, E., & Woolley, A. W. (2020). Human trust in artificial intelligence: Review of empirical research. *The Academy of Management Annals, 14*(2), 627–660. DOI: 10.5465/annals.2018.0057

Goodfellow, I. J., Pouget-Abadie, J., Mirza, M., Xu, B., Warde-Farley, D., Ozair, S., Courville, A., & Bengio, Y. (2014). Generative adversarial networks. *arXiv*. https://arxiv.org/abs/1406.2661

Goraya, M. A. S., Yaqub, M. Z., Khan, M. A., Akram, M. S., & Alofaysan, H. (2024). Transforming performance: How agility, response, resilience and support shape success in digital strategies. *Information Technology & People*. Advance online publication. DOI: 10.1108/ITP-05-2024-0592

Gracious, L. A., Jasmine, R. M., Pooja, E., Anish, T. P., Johncy, G., & Subramanian, R. S. (2023, October). Machine Learning and Deep Learning Transforming Healthcare: An Extensive Exploration of Applications, Algorithms, and Prospects. In *2023 4th IEEE Global Conference for Advancement in Technology (GCAT)* (pp. 1-6). IEEE.

Guida, M., Caniato, F., Moretto, A., & Ronchi, S. (2023). The role of artificial intelligence in the procurement process: State of the art and research agenda. *Journal of Purchasing and Supply Management, 29*(2), 100823. Advance online publication. DOI: 10.1016/j.pursup.2023.100823

Gupta, A., Singh, R. K., & Gupta, S. (2022). Developing human resource for the digitization of logistics operations: Readiness index framework. *International Journal of Manpower, 43*(2), 355–379. DOI: 10.1108/IJM-03-2021-0175

Gupta, S. K. (2026). AI-augmented sustainability management in agri-food supply chain: Rethinking decision-making in the era of algorithms. *Journal of Agribusiness in Developing and Emerging Economies*, •••, 1–16. DOI: 10.1108/JADEE-09-2025-0412

Hamann-Lohmer, J., Bendig, M., & Lasch, R. (2023). Investigating the impact of digital transformation on relationship and collaboration dynamics in supply chains and manufacturing networks – A multi-case study. *International Journal of Production Economics*, *262*, 108932. 10.1016/j.ijpe.2023.108932. DOI: 10.1016/j.ijpe.2023.108932

Hamilton, J. R., Maxwell, S. J., Ali, S. A., & Tee, S. (2024). Adding external artificial intelligence (ai) into internal firm-wide smart dynamic warehousing solutions. *Sustainability (Basel)*, *16*(10), 3908. DOI: 10.3390/su16103908

Handfield, R. B., Cousins, P. D., Lawson, B., & Petersen, K. J. (2015). How can supply management really improve performance? A knowledge-based model of alignment capabilities. *The Journal of Supply Chain Management*, *51*(3), 3–17. DOI: 10.1111/jscm.12066

Handfield, R., Jeong, S., & Choi, T. (2019). Emerging procurement technology: Data analytics and cognitive analytics. *International Journal of Physical Distribution & Logistics Management*, *49*(10), 972–1002. DOI: 10.1108/IJPDLM-11-2017-0348

Hansen, N. W. (2016). International company restructuring and the effects on high-skilled employees in lead companies. *Competition & Change*, *20*(4), 237–254. DOI: 10.1177/1024529416646695

Hashemi-Petroodi, S. E., Dolgui, A., Kovalev, S., Kovalyov, M. Y., & Thevenin, S. (2021). Workforce reconfiguration strategies in manufacturing systems: A state of the art. *International Journal of Production Research*, *59*(22), 6721–6744. DOI: 10.1080/00207543.2020.1823028

Hashmi, M. S., Ali, A., & Al-Masri, R. (2025). Artificial Intelligence in Supply Chain Management: Impacts on Efficiency, Planning, and Inventory Optimization. *Journal for Current Sign*, *3*(3), 617–637.

Helmold, M., & Terry, B. (2016). Global sourcing and supply management excellence in China. *Singapur: Springer Verlag*.

Hoang, T. G., & Bui, M. L. (2023). Business intelligence and analytic (BIA) stage-of-practice in micro-, small-and medium-sized enterprises (MSMEs). *Journal of Enterprise Information Management*, *36*(4), 1080–1104. DOI: 10.1108/JEIM-01-2022-0037

Hryhorak, M., Kulak, N., & Galkin, A. (2023). Artificial intelligence in logistics and supply chain management of hazardous materials. *Transportation Research Procedia*, *72*, 147–154.

Hughes, L., Dwivedi, Y. K., Rana, N. P., Williams, M. D., & Raghavan, V. (2022). Perspectives on the future of manufacturing within the Industry 4.0 era. *Production Planning and Control*, *33*(2-3), 138–158. DOI: 10.1080/09537287.2020.1810762

Inan, G. G., & Yilmaz, G. (2025). Developing Organisational Capabilities for Digital Transformation. In *Digital Transformation: A Business Imperative* (pp. 12-28). L DOI: 10.4324/9781003626640-3

International Labour Organization. I. (2025). *World Employment and Social Outlook: Trends 2025*. I. L. Organization. https://www.ilo.org/publications/flagship-reports/world-employment-and-social-outlook-trends-2025

Ishaq, S., Tanveer, U., Hoang, T. G., & Wamba Samuel, F. (2025). From Linear to Circular: Capabilities, Defensive Reasoning and Supply Chain Collaborations in Manufacturers' Circular Economy Transition. *British Journal of Management*, 1467-8551.12932. DOI: 10.1111/1467-8551.12932

Ivanov, D., & Dolgui, A. (2020). A digital supply chain twin for managing the disruption risks and resilience in the era of Industry 4.0. *Production Planning and Control*, *32*(9), 775–788. DOI: 10.1080/09537287.2020.1768450

Ivanov, D., Dolgui, A., & Sokolov, B. (2019). The impact of digital technology and Industry 4.0 on the ripple effect and supply chain risk analytics. *International Journal of Production Research*, *57*(3), 829–846. DOI: 10.1080/00207543.2018.1488086

Jaffrin, L. C., Nithya, T., & Divya, J. (2025, April). IoT for Sustainable Development: Enhancing Environmental Efficiency and Resource Optimization. In *2025 5th International Conference on Trends in Material Science and Inventive Materials (ICTMIM)* (pp. 1224-1230). IEEE.

Jagani, S., Marsillac, E., & Hong, P. (2024). The electric vehicle supply chain ecosystem: Changing roles of automotive suppliers. *Sustainability (Basel)*, *16*(4), 1570. DOI: 10.3390/su16041570

Jahangir, S., Xie, R., Iqbal, A., & Hussain, M. (2025). The influence of sustainable human resource management practices on logistics agility: The mediating role of artificial intelligence. *Sustainability (Basel)*, *17*(7), 3099. DOI: 10.3390/su17073099

Jarrahi, M. H. (2018). Artificial intelligence and the future of work: Human–AI symbiosis in organizational decision making. *Business Horizons*, *61*(4), 577–586. DOI: 10.1016/j.bushor.2018.03.007

Jia, N., Luo, X., Fang, Z., & Liao, C. (2024). WHEN AND HOW ARTIFICIAL INTELLIGENCE AUGMENTS EMPLOYEE CREATIVITY. *Academy of Management Journal*, *67*(1), 5–32. DOI: 10.5465/amj.2022.0426

Joice, J. (2024). The Role of Strategic Sourcing in Competitive Advantage: A Procurement Perspective. *International Journal of Emerging Research in Engineering and Technology*, *5*(4), 1–10. DOI: 10.63282/3050-922X.IJERET-V5I4P101

Joosten, J., Bilgram, V., Hahn, A., & Totzek, D. (2024). Comparing the Ideation Quality of Humans with Generative Artificial Intelligence. *IEEE Engineering Management Review*, *52*(2), 153–164. DOI: 10.1109/EMR.2024.3353338

Kalaitzi, D., Matopoulos, A., & Clegg, B. (2019). Managing resource dependencies in electric vehicle supply chains: A multi-tier case study. *Supply Chain Management*, *24*(2), 256–270. DOI: 10.1108/SCM-03-2018-0116

Kalaitzi, D., & Tsolakis, N. (2022). Supply chain analytics adoption: Determinants and impacts on organisational performance and competitive advantage. *International Journal of Production Economics*, *248*, 108466. 10.1016/j.ijpe.2022.108466. DOI: 10.1016/j.ijpe.2022.108466

Kellogg, K. C., Valentine, M. A., & Christin, A. (2020). Algorithms at work: The new contested terrain of control. *The Academy of Management Annals*, *14*(1), 366–410. DOI: 10.5465/annals.2018.0174

Khan, M. N. M.Md Nazmuddin Moin Khan. (2025). Artificial intelligence driven big data and business analytics: A comprehensive review of multi-sectoral applications in healthcare, finance, supply chain, and organizational innovation. *Pacific Journal of Business Innovation and Strategy*, *2*(4), 122–137. DOI: 10.70818/pjbis.v02i04.0130

Khlie, K., Benmamoun, Z., Jebbor, I., & Serrou, D. (2024). Generative AI for enhanced operations and supply chain management. *Journal of Infrastructure. Policy and Development*, *8*(10), 6637.

Klumpp, M. (2018). Automation and artificial intelligence in business logistics systems: Human reactions and collaboration requirements. *International Journal of Logistics*, *21*(3), 224–242. DOI: 10.1080/13675567.2017.1384451

Klumpp, M., & Zijm, H. (2019). Logistics innovation and social sustainability: How to prevent an artificial divide in human–computer interaction. *Journal of Business Logistics*, *40*(3), 265–278. DOI: 10.1111/jbl.12198

Kmiecik, M., & Skórnóg, D. (2025). Impact of generative AI on logistics companies' business models. *International Journal of Logistics Research and Applications*, 1-25.

Koh, L. Y., & Yuen, K. F. (2022). Emerging competencies for logistics professionals in the digital era: A literature review. *Frontiers in Psychology*, *13*, 965748. Advance online publication. DOI: 10.3389/fpsyg.2022.965748 PMID: 36389597

Kokogho, E., Odio, P. E., Ogunsola, O. Y., & Nwaozomudoh, M. O. (2024). AI-powered economic forecasting: Challenges and opportunities in a data-driven world. *International Journal of Management and Organizational Research*, *3*(6), 74–83. 10.54660/IJMOR.2024.3.6.74-83. DOI: 10.54660/IJMOR.2024.3.6.74-83

Krykavskyy, Y., Shandrivska, O., & Pawłyszyn, I. (2023). A study of macroeconomic and geopolitical influences and security risks in supply chains in times of disruptions. *LogForum, 19*(3).

Kuaites, T., & Thungwha, S. (2025). Enabling Smart Cold Chain Logistics Through Standardization and Digital Transformation: A Structural Model for Reducing Food Loss in Thailand's Agri-Food Sector. *Sustainability (Basel)*, *17*(13), 6085. Advance online publication. DOI: 10.3390/su17136085

Kulkov, I., Kulkova, J., Rohrbeck, R., Menvielle, L., Kaartemo, V., & Makkonen, H. (2024). Artificial intelligence-driven sustainable development: Examining organizational, technical, and processing approaches to achieving global goals. *Sustainable Development (Bradford)*, *32*(3), 2253–2267. DOI: 10.1002/sd.2773

Kumar, V., Ashraf, A. R., & Nadeem, W. (2024). AI-powered marketing: What, where, and how? *International Journal of Information Management*, *77*, 102783. Advance online publication. DOI: 10.1016/j.ijinfomgt.2024.102783

Kussl, S. (2025). Identity and Adaptation: The Evolving Role of Public Sector Professionals in the Digital Transformation of Road Transportation. *International Journal of Public Administration*, •••, 1–20. DOI: 10.1080/01900692.2025.2542310

Lakhani, T., Kuruvilla, S., & Avgar, A. (2013). From the firm to the network: Global value chains and employment relations theory. *British Journal of Industrial Relations*, *51*(3), 440–472. DOI: 10.1111/bjir.12015

Lam, H. Y., Tang, V., & Wong, L. (2024). Raising logistics performance to new levels through digital transformation. *International Journal of Engineering Business Management*, *16*, 18479790241231730. DOI: 10.1177/18479790241231730

Lang, J. (2023). Workforce upskilling: Can universities meet the challenges of lifelong learning? *International Journal of Information and Learning Technology*, *40*(5), 388–400. DOI: 10.1108/IJILT-01-2023-0001

Lang, L. D., Behl, A., Phuong, N. N. D., Gaur, J., & Dzung, N. T. (2022). Toward SME digital transformation in the supply chain context: The role of structural social and human capital. *International Journal of Physical Distribution & Logistics Management*, *53*(4), 448–466. DOI: 10.1108/IJPDLM-12-2021-0525

Lata, A., Chandani, A., & Sharma, S. (2023). Sustainable development goals and gig economy: A bibliometric analysis and future research agenda. *International Journal of Innovation and Sustainable Development*, *17*(1), 1–26.

Leonardi, P. M. (2011). When flexible routines meet flexible technologies: Affordance, constraint, and the imbrication of human and material agencies. *Management Information Systems Quarterly*, *35*(1), 147–167. DOI: 10.2307/23043493

Liang, H., Fan, J., & Wang, Y. (2025). Artificial intelligence, technological innovation, and employment transformation for sustainable development: Evidence from China. *Sustainability (Basel)*, *17*(9), 3842. DOI: 10.3390/su17093842

Li, B., Yang, Y., Zhao, Z., Ni, X., & Zhang, D. (2024). A Novel Ensemble Learning Approach for Intelligent Logistics Demand Management. *Wangji Wanglu Jishu Xuekan*, *25*(4), 507–515. DOI: 10.70003/160792642024072504002

Li, J., Wang, Z., & Li, X. (2024). The impact of artificial intelligence on sustainable development performance of public healthcare supply chain. *Frontiers in Public Health*, *12*, 1368953.

Li, L. (2024). Reskilling and upskilling the future-ready workforce for industry 4.0 and beyond. *Information Systems Frontiers*, *26*(5), 1697–1712. DOI: 10.1007/s10796-022-10308-y PMID: 35855776

Lin, K. Y. (2025). Generative artificial intelligence–driven sustainable supply chain management: a UNISONE framework for smart logistics and predictive analytics under Industry 5.0. *International Journal of Logistics Research and Applications*, 1-32.

Liu, K. P., & Chiu, W. (2021). Supply Chain 4.0: The impact of supply chain digitalization and integration on firm performance. *Asian Journal of Business Ethics*, *10*(2), 371–389. DOI: 10.1007/s13520-021-00137-8

Liu, Q., Ma, Y., Chen, L., Pedrycz, W., Skibniewski, M. J., & Chen, Z.-S. (2024). Artificial intelligence for production, operations and logistics management in modular construction industry: A systematic literature review. *Information Fusion*, *109*, 102423. Advance online publication. DOI: 10.1016/j.inffus.2024.102423

Lopes, L. S., Nabais, J. L., Pinto, C., Caldeirinha, V., & Pinho, T. (2025). Essential Competencies in Maritime and Port Logistics: A Study on the Current Needs of the Sector. *Sustainability (Basel), 17*(6), 2378. DOI: 10.3390/su17062378

Lyons, G. (2015). Transport's digital age transition. *Journal of Transport and Land Use, 8*(2), 1–19.

Ma, H., Gao, Q., Li, X., & Zhang, Y. (2022). AI development and employment skill structure: A case study of China. *Economic Analysis and Policy, 73*, 242–254. DOI: 10.1016/j.eap.2021.11.007

Mahmood, H. S., Abdulqader, D. M., Abdullah, R. M., Rasheed, H., Ismael, Z. N. R., & Sami, T. M. G. (2024). Conducting in-depth analysis of AI, IoT, web technology, cloud computing, and enterprise systems integration for enhancing data security and governance to promote sustainable business practices. *Journal of Information Technology and Informatics, 3*(2), 297–332.

Mahroof, K. (2019). A human-centric perspective exploring the readiness towards smart warehousing: The case of a large retail distribution warehouse. *International Journal of Information Management, 45*, 176–190. DOI: 10.1016/j.ijinfomgt.2018.11.008

Marino-Romero, J. A., Palos-Sanchez, P. R., & Velicia-Martin, F. (2022). Improving KIBS performance using digital transformation: Study based on the theory of resources and capabilities. *Journal of Service Theory and Practice, 33*(2), 169–197. DOI: 10.1108/JSTP-04-2022-0095

Martin-Rios, C., Erhardt, N. L., & Manev, I. M. (2022). Interfirm collaboration for knowledge resources interaction among small innovative firms. *Journal of Business Research, 153*, 206–215. 10.1016/j.jbusres.2022.08.024. DOI: 10.1016/j.jbusres.2022.08.024

Masood, A., Irshad, M., & Ahmad, F. (2023). Artificial Intelligence and Green Human Resource Management: A synergistic approach for environmental sustainability in the manufacturing industry. *Sustainability, 15*(18), 13838.

Meier, E., Brown, A. N., Chovitz, B., Zwinkels, D., Egharevba, M., McHenry, B., Kabatende, J., & Gege Buki, I. K. (2024). Systems thinking approach to human resources development in public health supply chains. *Journal of Humanitarian Logistics and Supply Chain Management, 15*(3), 276–293. DOI: 10.1108/JHLSCM-10-2023-0097

Meijerink, J., & Bondarouk, T. (2023). The duality of algorithmic management: Toward a research agenda on HRM algorithms, autonomy and value creation. *Human Resource Management Review, 33*(1), 100876. DOI: 10.1016/j.hrmr.2021.100876

Mendonça, P., & Kougiannou, N. K. (2023). Disconnecting labour: The impact of intraplatform algorithmic changes on the labour process and workers' capacity to organise collectively. *New Technology, Work and Employment, 38*(1), 1–20. DOI: 10.1111/ntwe.12251

Merkert, R., Hoberg, K., & Mahadevan, K. (2023). Logistics and Supply Chain Superpowers and Skills for Survival in the "New Normal" Globalized World. *Transportation Journal, 62*(4), 369–396. DOI: 10.5325/transportationj.62.4.0369

Mhaske, P., Bhattacharjee, B., Haldar, N., Upadhyay, P., & Mandal, A. (2025). Bridging digital skill gaps in the global workforce: A synthesis and conceptual framework building. *Research in Globalization, 11*, 100311. 10.1016/j.resglo.2025.100311

Mikl, J., Herold, D. M., Pilch, K., Ćwiklicki, M., & Kummer, S. (2021). Understanding disruptive technology transitions in the global logistics industry: The role of ecosystems. *Review of International Business and Strategy, 31*(1), 62–79. DOI: 10.1108/RIBS-07-2020-0078

Minor, K., McLoughlin, E., & Carlisle, S. (2025). The Digital Skills Gap – Is it Time to Rethink the Needs of Tourism and Hospitality Organizations in the UK? *Journal of Hospitality & Tourism Education, 37*(3), 301–312. DOI: 10.1080/10963758.2024.2316338

Mirbabaie, M., Brünker, F., Möllmann Frick, N. R. J., & Stieglitz, S. (2022). The rise of artificial intelligence – understanding the AI identity threat at the workplace. *Electronic Markets, 32*(1), 73–99. DOI: 10.1007/s12525-021-00496-x

Modgil, S., Singh, R. K., & Agrawal, S. (2025). Developing human capabilities for supply chains: An industry 5.0 perspective. *Annals of Operations Research, 348*(3), 2075–2105. DOI: 10.1007/s10479-023-05245-1

Modgil, S., Singh, R. K., & Hannibal, C. (2022). Artificial intelligence for supply chain resilience: Learning from Covid-19. *International Journal of Logistics Management, 33*(4), 1246–1268. DOI: 10.1108/IJLM-02-2021-0094

Mohsen, B. M. (2024). AI-Driven Optimization of Urban Logistics in Smart Cities: Integrating Autonomous Vehicles and IoT for Efficient Delivery Systems. *Sustainability (Basel), 16*(24), 11265. Advance online publication. DOI: 10.3390/su162411265

Mohsen, B. M., & Mohsen, M. (2025). AI-Driven Energy Optimization in Urban Logistics: Implications for Smart SCM in Dubai. *Sustainability (Basel), 17*(18), 8301. DOI: 10.3390/su17188301

Montobbio, F., Staccioli, J., Virgillito, M. E., & Vivarelli, M. (2024a). Labour-saving automation: A direct measure of occupational exposure. *World Economy*, *47*(1), 332–361. DOI: 10.1111/twec.13522

Montobbio, F., Staccioli, J., Virgillito, M. E., & Vivarelli, M. (2024b). The empirics of technology, employment and occupations: Lessons learned and challenges ahead. *Journal of Economic Surveys*, *38*(5), 1622–1655. DOI: 10.1111/joes.12601

Moorthy, K. S., Balakrishnan, G., Kumar, S. S., Raja, L., & Vijayalakshmi, A. (2024). Embracing circular economy principles for sustainable green supply chain management in manufacturing industries. In *Convergence of Human Resources Technologies and Industry 5.0* (pp. 85–110). IGI Global Scientific Publishing. DOI: 10.4018/979-8-3693-1343-5.ch005

Morales, P., & Stecher, A. (2023). Algorithmic management and precarious labour in the platform economy: The case of riders in Chile. *Work Organisation, Labour & Globalisation*, *17*(1), 68–87.

Movahed, A. B., Movahed, A. B., & Nozari, H. (2024). Opportunities and challenges of smart supply chain in Industry 5.0. *Information Logistics for Organizational Empowerment and Effective Supply Chain Management*, 108-138.

Muntala, P. S. R. P. (2021). Prescriptive AI in Procurement: Using Oracle AI to Recommend Optimal Supplier Decisions. *International Journal of AI, BigData. Computational and Management Studies*, *2*(1), 76–87.

Murire, O. T. (2024). Artificial intelligence and its role in shaping organizational work practices and culture. *Administrative Sciences*, *14*(12), 316. DOI: 10.3390/admsci14120316

Narkhede, G., Chinchanikar, S., Narkhede, R., & Chaudhari, T. (2024). Role of Industry 5.0 for driving sustainability in the manufacturing sector: An emerging research agenda. *Journal of Strategy and Management*. Advance online publication. DOI: 10.1108/JSMA-06-2023-0144

Nemati, H. R., Steiger, D. M., Iyer, L. S., & Herschel, R. T. (2002). Knowledge warehouse: An architectural integration of knowledge management, decision support, artificial intelligence and data warehousing. *Decision Support Systems*, *33*(2), 143–161. DOI: 10.1016/S0167-9236(01)00141-5

Ngo, V. M., Quang, H. T., Hoang, T. G., & Binh, A. D. T. (2024). Sustainability-related supply chain risks and supply chain performances: The moderating effects of dynamic supply chain management practices. *Business Strategy and the Environment*, *33*(2), 839–857. DOI: 10.1002/bse.3512

Nguyen, T. H., Le, D. A., & Pham, T. T. (2025). The impact of green logistics management and Industry 4.0 on sustainable performance in Vietnam. *Journal of Science and Technology - IUH, 77*(5), 89–102.

Nguyen, A. H., Hoang, T. G., Ngo, V. M., Nguyen, L. Q. T., & Nguyen, H. H. (2023). Sustainability-oriented supply chain finance in Vietnam: Insights from multiple case studies. *Operations Management Research : Advancing Practice Through Research*, *16*(1), 259–279. DOI: 10.1007/s12063-022-00303-6

Nicoletti, B. (2025a). AI transformation of logistics. In *Artificial Intelligence for Logistics 5.0: From Foundation Models to Agentic AI* (pp. 107–131). Springer Nature Switzerland. DOI: 10.1007/978-3-031-94046-0_4

Nicoletti, B., & Appolloni, A. (2025). Digital transformation in ecosystems: Integrated operations model and its application to fifth-party logistics operators. *Journal of Global Operations and Strategic Sourcing*, *18*(1), 91–122. DOI: 10.1108/JGOSS-04-2023-0024

Nieddu, M., Bertani, F., & Ponta, L. (2022). The sustainability transition and the digital transformation: Two challenges for agent-based macroeconomic models. *Review of Evolutionary Political Economy*, *3*(1), 193–226. DOI: 10.1007/s43253-021-00060-5

Nilsson, K. H., Matilla-Santander, N., Lee, M. K., Brulin, E., Bodin, T., & Håkansta, C. (2025). Algorithmic management and occupational health: A comparative case study of organizational practices in logistics. *Safety Science*, *187*, 106863. DOI: 10.1016/j.ssci.2025.106863

Noponen, N., Feshchenko, P., Auvinen, T., Luoma-aho, V., & Abrahamsson, P. (2024). Taylorism on steroids or enabling autonomy? A systematic review of algorithmic management. *Management Review Quarterly*, *74*(3), 1695–1721. DOI: 10.1007/s11301-023-00345-5

Nsabigaba, F. (2024). The role of procurement practice in shaping competitive advantage. *Journal of procurement & supply chain.*

Nweje, U., & Taiwo, M. (2025). Leveraging Artificial Intelligence for predictive supply chain management, focus on how AI-driven tools are revolutionizing demand forecasting and inventory optimization. *International Journal of Science and Research Archive*, *14*(1), 230–250. DOI: 10.30574/ijsra.2025.14.1.0027

OECD. (2025). *Algorithmic management and the labour process in logistics*. OECD Publishing.

Olaleye, I. A., Mokogwu, C., Olufemi-Phillips, A. Q., & Adewale, T. T. (2024). Optimizing procurement efficiency: Frameworks for data-driven cost reduction and strategic vendor management. *International Journal of Management Studies*, *6*(4), 121–130.

Olan, F., Arakpogun, E. O., Jayawickrama, U., Suklan, J., & Liu, S. (2022a). Sustainable supply chain finance and supply networks: The role of artificial intelligence. *IEEE Transactions on Engineering Management*, *71*, 13296–13311. DOI: 10.1109/TEM.2021.3133104

Olan, F., Liu, S., Suklan, J., Jayawickrama, U., & Arakpogun, E. O. (2022b). The role of Artificial Intelligence networks in sustainable supply chain finance for food and drink industry. *International Journal of Production Research*, *60*(14), 4418–4433. DOI: 10.1080/00207543.2021.1915510

Omidi, F., & Zarei, A. (2023). The impact of algorithmic management on the labour process in the platform economy: A systematic review. *New Technology, Work and Employment*.

Omol, E. J. (2023). Organizational digital transformation: From evolution to future trends. *Digital Transformation and Society*, *3*(3), 240–256. DOI: 10.1108/DTS-08-2023-0061

Oncioiu, I., Mândricel, D. A., & Hojda, M. H. (2025). Artificial intelligence-enabled digital transformation in circular logistics: A structural equation model of organizational, technological, and environmental drivers. *Logistics (Basel)*, *9*(3), 102. DOI: 10.3390/logistics9030102

Orero-Blat, M., Jordán, H. D. J., & Palacios-Marqués, D. (2022). The measurement of digital skills and competences: A bibliometric analysis. *International Journal of Intellectual Property Management*, *12*(2), 185–199. DOI: 10.1504/IJIPM.2022.122297

Oyetade, K., & Zuva, T. (2025). A Review of Generative AI's Impact on Workforce Transformation and Future Skill Requirements. *OIDA International Journal of Sustainable Development*, *18*(12), 187–196.

Oyeyemi, B. B., John, A. O., & Awodola, M. (2025). Infrastructure and regulatory barriers to AI supply chain systems in Nigeria vs. the US. *Engineering Science and Technology*, *6*(4), 155–172. DOI: 10.51594/estj.v6i4.1912

Padmavathi, V., & Saminathan, R. (2023). Fundamentals of IOT, artificial intelligence, and blockchain approaches for applications in Supply Chain Management. In *Blockchain, IoT, and AI Technologies for Supply Chain Management* (pp. 1-18). CRC Press. DOI: 10.1201/9781003264521-1

Palpacuer, F. (2000). Competence-based strategies and global production networks a discussion of current changes and their implications for employment. *Competition & Change*, *4*(4), 353–400. DOI: 10.1177/102452940000400401

Parasuraman, R., Sheridan, T. B., & Wickens, C. D. (2000). A model for types and levels of human interaction with automation. *IEEE Transactions on Systems, Man, and Cybernetics. Part A, Systems and Humans*, *30*(3), 286–297. DOI: 10.1109/3468.844354 PMID: 11760769

Parent-Rocheleau, X., & Parker, S. K. (2022). Algorithms as work designers: How algorithmic management influences the quality of jobs. *Human Resource Management Review*, *32*(3), 100838. DOI: 10.1016/j.hrmr.2021.100838

Parker, S. K., & Grote, G. (2022). Automation, algorithms, and beyond: Why work design matters more than ever in a digital world. *Applied Psychology*, *71*(4), 1171–1204. DOI: 10.1111/apps.12241

Parker, S. K., Van den Broeck, A., & Holman, D. (2017). Work Design Influences: A Synthesis of Multilevel Factors that Affect the Design of Jobs. *The Academy of Management Annals*, *11*(1), 267–308. DOI: 10.5465/annals.2014.0054

Pasupuleti, V., Thuraka, B., Kodete, C. S., & Malisetty, S. (2024). Enhancing Supply Chain Agility and Sustainability through Machine Learning: Optimization Techniques for Logistics and Inventory Management. *Logistics (Basel)*, *8*(3), 73. Advance online publication. DOI: 10.3390/logistics8030073

Patrucco, A. S., Rivera, L., Mejía-Argueta, C., & Sheffi, Y. (2021). Can you grow your supply chain without skills? The role of human resource management for better supply chain management in Latin America. *International Journal of Logistics Management*, *33*(1), 53–78. DOI: 10.1108/IJLM-11-2020-0426

Pedota, M., Grilli, L., & Piscitello, L. (2023). Technology adoption and upskilling in the wake of Industry 4.0. *Technological Forecasting and Social Change*, *187*, 122085. 10.1016/j.techfore.2022.122085. DOI: 10.1016/j.techfore.2022.122085

Pham, N. T., Tučková, Z., & Jabbour, C. J. C. (2020). Greening the hospitality industry: How do green human resource management practices influence organizational citizenship behavior in hotels? A mixed-methods approach. *Tourism Management*, *78*, 104054.

Pradhan, I. P., & Saxena, P. (2023). Reskilling workforce for the artificial intelligence age: Challenges and the way forward. In Tyagi, P., Chilamkurti, N., Grima, S., Sood, K., & Balusamy, B. (Eds.), *The adoption and effect of artificial intelligence on human resources management, Part B* (pp. 181–197). Emerald Publishing Limited., DOI: 10.1108/978-1-80455-662-720230011

Prasath, R., Kumar, V. V., Jaisankari, V., & Sivasubramani, R. (2025). Semantic Search for IoT-Based Object Recognition Using Clustering and Classification. In *Utilizing AI in Network and Mobile Security for Threat Detection and Prevention* (pp. 151–172). IGI Global Scientific Publishing. DOI: 10.4018/979-8-3693-9919-4.ch009

Pronello, C., & Fedeli, E. (2025). Just technology transition. A policy agenda to minimise the social impacts of digitalisation and automation on the transport workforce. *Transportation Research Interdisciplinary Perspectives*, *34*, 101670. DOI: 10.1016/j.trip.2025.101670

Radanliev, P., De Roure, D., Page, K., Nurse, J. R. C., Mantilla Montalvo, R., Santos, O., Maddox, L. T., & Burnap, P. (2020). Cyber risk at the edge: Current and future trends on cyber risk analytics and artificial intelligence in the industrial internet of things and industry 4.0 supply chains. *Cybersecurity*, *3*(1), 13. DOI: 10.1186/s42400-020-00052-8

Rainy, T. A., & Chowdhury, A. R. (2022). The Role Of Artificial Intelligence In Vendor Performance Evaluation Within Digital Retail Supply Chains: A Review Of Strategic Decision-Making Models. *American Journal of Scholarly Research and Innovation*, *1*(01), 220–248. DOI: 10.63125/96jj3j86

Raisch, S., & Krakowski, S. (2021). Artificial intelligence and management: The automation–augmentation paradox. *Academy of Management Review*, *46*(1), 192–210. DOI: 10.5465/amr.2018.0072

Rane, N. L., Paramesha, M., Choudhary, S. P., & Rane, J. (2024). Artificial intelligence, machine learning, and deep learning for advanced business strategies: A review. *SSRN*, *2*(3), 147–171. DOI: 10.2139/ssrn.4835661

Ranjith Kumar, R., Ganesh, L. S., & Rajendran, C. (2021). Quality 4.0 – a review of and framework for quality management in the digital era. *International Journal of Quality & Reliability Management*, *39*(6), 1385–1411. DOI: 10.1108/IJQRM-05-2021-0150

Rashid, H. (2023). Quantitative Analysis of the Cost-Saving Potential of Procurement Automation Tools in Large-Scale Manufacturing. *IJLRP-International Journal of Leading Research Publication, 4*(12).

Rashid, A. B., & Kausik, M. A. K. (2024). AI revolutionizing industries worldwide: A comprehensive overview of its diverse applications. *Hybrid Advances*, *7*, 100277. DOI: 10.1016/j.hybadv.2024.100277

Rauf, H., & Umer, M. (2023). Development of AI-Augmented optimization technique for analysis & prediction of modal mix in road transportation. *PLoS One*, *18*(11), e0288493. DOI: 10.1371/journal.pone.0288493 PMID: 37917657

Rehman, A. U., & Shakeel Sadiq Jajja, M. (2025). Strategic adaptation in the electric vehicle supply chain: Navigating transformative trends in the automobile industry. *Journal of Enterprise Information Management*, *38*(3), 745–767. DOI: 10.1108/JEIM-10-2024-0554

Ren, X. (2025). The Impact of Generative AI-Driven Job Reshaping on Creativity Sustainability. *The Frontiers of Society, Science and Technology, 7*(7).

Research and Markets. (2025). *AI in Logistics and Supply Chain Management Market Report 2025: AI-Powered Platforms Revolutionizing Logistics and Supply Chain Efficiency Through Optimization and Risk Mitigation – Forecast to 2034*. https://www.globenewswire.com/news-release/2025/05/12/3078941/0/en/AI-in-Logistics-and-Supply-Chain-Management-Market-Report-2025-AI-Powered-Platforms-Revolutionizing-Logistics-and-Supply-Chain-Efficiency-Through-Optimization-and-Risk-Mitigation-F.html

Riad, M., Naimi, M., & Okar, C. (2024). Enhancing supply chain resilience through artificial intelligence: Developing a comprehensive conceptual framework for AI implementation and supply chain optimization. *Logistics (Basel)*, *8*(4), 111. DOI: 10.3390/logistics8040111

Rice, A. J. (2024). The rise of intelligent procurement: Embracing AI and data analytics for crossfunctional synergy. *Journal of Supply Chain Management. Logistics and Procurement*, *6*(4), 319–329. DOI: 10.69554/ZGFA3030

Richey, R. G.Jr, Chowdhury, S., Davis-Sramek, B., Giannakis, M., & Dwivedi, Y. K. (2023). Artificial intelligence in logistics and supply chain management: A primer and roadmap for research. *Journal of Business Logistics*, *44*(4), 532–549. DOI: 10.1111/jbl.12364

Ronchini, A., Guida, M., Moretto, A., & Caniato, F. (2024). The role of artificial intelligence in the supply chain finance innovation process. *Operations Management Research*, 1-31.

Rosário, A. T., & Dias, J. C. (2022). Sustainability and the digital transition: A literature review. *Sustainability (Basel)*, *14*(7), 4072. DOI: 10.3390/su14074072

Rose, R. M., Varun, C. M., Sivasakthi, K., Kennady, R., & Lekha, D. (2025, May). Leveraging AI and IoT Data for Predictive Modelling and Preventive Healthcare. In *2025 Third International Conference on Augmented Intelligence and Sustainable Systems (ICAISS)* (pp. 628-633). IEEE. DOI: 10.1109/ICAISS61471.2025.11041733

Ruiner, C., & Klumpp, M. (2022). Autonomy and new modes of control in digital work contexts–a mixed-methods study of driving professions in food logistics. *Employee Relations*, *44*(4), 890–912. DOI: 10.1108/ER-04-2021-0139

Russell, S., & Norvig, P. (2021). *Artificial intelligence: A modern approach* (4th ed.). Pearson Education.

Saini, M., Singh, D., Kataria, A., & Singh, R. (2025). Digital transformation and environmental sustainability: Reviewing the role of human capital. *Journal of Organizational Change Management*, •••, 1–24. DOI: 10.1108/JOCM-03-2025-0289

Sakala, C. M., & Bwalya, S. M. (2023). The role of artificial intelligence in optimizing supply chain performance. *Journal of Procurement and Supply Chain Management*, *2*(1), 1–14.

Samuels, A. (2025). Examining the integration of artificial intelligence in supply chain management from Industry 4.0 to 6.0: A systematic literature review. *Frontiers in Artificial Intelligence*, *7*, 1477044. DOI: 10.3389/frai.2024.1477044 PMID: 39902380

Sánchez, E., Calderón, R., & Herrera, F. (2025). Artificial Intelligence Adoption in SMEs: Survey Based on TOE–DOI Framework, Primary Methodology and Challenges. *Applied Sciences (Basel, Switzerland)*, *15*(12), 6465. DOI: 10.3390/app15126465

Sanders, N. R., Boone, T., Ganeshan, R., & Wood, J. D. (2019). Sustainable supply chains in the age of AI and digitization: Research challenges and opportunities. *Journal of Business Logistics*, *40*(3), 229–240. DOI: 10.1111/jbl.12224

Sangari, M. S., & Razmi, J. (2015). Business intelligence competence, agile capabilities, and agile performance in supply chain: An empirical study. *International Journal of Logistics Management*, *26*(2), 356–380. DOI: 10.1108/IJLM-01-2013-0012

Saqib, Z. A., & Qin, L. (2024). Investigating effects of digital innovations on sustainable operations of logistics: An empirical study. *Sustainability (Basel)*, *16*(13), 5518. DOI: 10.3390/su16135518

Sarker, S., Chatterjee, S., Xiao, X., & Elbanna, A. (2019). The sociotechnical axis of cohesion for the IS discipline: Its historical legacy and its continued relevance. *Management Information Systems Quarterly*, *43*(3), 695–719. DOI: 10.25300/MISQ/2019/13747

Sathiskumar, N. N., & Andersen, P. H. (2025). Tensions in AI-driven digital servitization in the banking industry: A socio-technical view. *International Journal of Bank Marketing*, •••, 1–35. DOI: 10.1108/IJBM-05-2025-0353

Sathya, U., Hashini, S., Lakshmipriya, C., Varun, C. M., & Nalini, M. (2024, December). Emerging Trends and Future Prospects in Internet of Things (IoT) Technology. In *2024 International Conference on Sustainable Communication Networks and Application (ICSCNA)* (pp. 79-85). IEEE.

Saunders, M. N., Lewis, P., & Thornhill, A. (2000). Research Methods for Business Students: Lecturers' Guide.

Schaupp, S. (2022). Algorithmic governance in smart cities: The case of Barcelona. *Theory, Culture & Society*, *39*(4), 169–189.

Schaupp, S. (2022). Algorithmic integration and precarious (dis) obedience: On the co-constitution of migration regime and workplace regime in digitalised manufacturing and logistics. *Work, Employment and Society*, *36*(2), 310–327. DOI: 10.1177/09500170211031458

Schiuma, G., Santarsiero, F., Carlucci, D., & Jarrar, Y. (2024). Transformative leadership competencies for organizational digital transformation. *Business Horizons*, *67*(4), 425–437. 10.1016/j.bushor.2024.04.004. DOI: 10.1016/j.bushor.2024.04.004

Schwaeke, J., Peters, A., Kanbach, D. K., Kraus, S., & Jones, P. (2025). The new normal: The status quo of AI adoption in SMEs. *Journal of Small Business Management*, *63*(3), 1297–1331. DOI: 10.1080/00472778.2024.2379999

Sekti, B. A. (2025a). AI Technology Management Concepts and Strategies. In *AI Technology Management and Value Creation* (pp. 1–32). DOI: 10.4018/979-8-3373-2497-5.ch001

Sekti, B. A. (2025b). Foundations of Artificial Intelligence Ethics. In *Navigating Social Trust in the AI Era* (pp. 23–47). DOI: 10.4018/979-8-3373-7011-8.ch002

Sekti, B. A. (2025c). Machine learning and artificial intelligence (AI) in manufacturing. In *Integrating Digital Innovation and Integrated Frameworks in Manufacturing* (pp. 255–292). DOI: 10.4018/979-8-3373-1082-4.ch011

Sekti, B. A. (2025d). Machine Learning vs. AI: Key Concepts. In *Implementing Enterprise Cybersecurity With AI* (pp. 1–27). DOI: 10.4018/979-8-3373-2252-0.ch001

Seyedan, M., & Mafakheri, F. (2020). Predictive big data analytics for supply chain demand forecasting: Methods, applications, and research opportunities. *Journal of Big Data*, *7*(1), 1–22. DOI: 10.1186/s40537-020-00329-2

Seyedghorban, Z., Tahernejad, H., Meriton, R., & Graham, G. (2020). Supply chain digitalization: Past, present and future. *Production Planning and Control*, *31*(2-3), 96–114. DOI: 10.1080/09537287.2019.1631461

Sharma, A. (2022). The future of procurement: Integrating AI, automation, and blockchain for next-generation supply chains. *International Journal of Artificial Intelligence, Data Science, and Machine Learning*, *3*(4), 1–10. DOI: 10.63282/3050-9262.IJAIDSML-V3I4P101

Shatat, A. S., & Shatat, A. S. (2024). Artificial intelligence competencies in logistics management: An empirical insight from Bahrain. *Journal of Information & Knowledge Management*, *23*(01), 2350059. DOI: 10.1142/S0219649223500594

Shen, Y., & Zhang, X. (2024). The impact of artificial intelligence on employment: The role of virtual agglomeration. *Humanities & Social Sciences Communications*, *11*(1), 122. DOI: 10.1057/s41599-024-02647-9

Shimray, S. R., & Subaveerapandiyan, A. (2025). AI and workforce dynamics: A bibliometric analysis of job creation, displacement and reskilling. *Global Knowledge, Memory and Communication*. Advance online publication. DOI: 10.1108/GKMC-12-2024-0824

Shobhana, N. (2024). AI-powered supply chains towards greater efficiency. In *Complex AI dynamics and interactions in management* (pp. 229–249). IGI Global Scientific Publishing. DOI: 10.4018/979-8-3693-0712-0.ch011

Singh, V., Hughes, L., Albashrawi, M. A., Jeon, I., & Dwivedi, Y. K. (2026). Generative artificial intelligence (GenAI) in procurement and supply chain management: Applications, opportunities and challenges. *Journal of Systems and Information Technology*, *28*(1), 123–144. DOI: 10.1108/JSIT-03-2025-0139

Sodiya, E. O., Umoga, U. J., Amoo, O. O., & Atadoga, A. (2024). AI-driven warehouse automation: A comprehensive review of systems. *GSC Advanced Research and Reviews*, *18*(2), 272–282. DOI: 10.30574/gscarr.2024.18.2.0063

Spulbar, L. F. (2025). Legal frameworks for AI-driven markets and their challenges and opportunities in the digital economy. *Revista de Stiinte Politice*, (86), 288–304.

Strohmer, M. F., Easton, S., Eisenhut, M., Epstein, E., Kromoser, R., Peterson, E. R., & Rizzon, E. (2020). *Disruptive procurement: Winning in a digital world*. Springer Nature. DOI: 10.1007/978-3-030-38950-5

Subrahmanyam, S. (2025). Human Factors and Workforce Adaptation in Digital Transition. In Martínez-Falcó, J., Sánchez-García, E., & Marco-Lajara, B. (Eds.), *Navigating Digital Transformation Through Business Process Management* (pp. 95–126). IGI Global Scientific Publishing., DOI: 10.4018/979-8-3373-3336-6.ch005

Subramanian, G., & Thampy, A. S. (2021). Implementation of hybrid blockchain in a pre-owned electric vehicle supply chain. *IEEE Access : Practical Innovations, Open Solutions*, *9*, 82435–82454. DOI: 10.1109/ACCESS.2021.3084942

Sundaram, S. (2025). Innovating for the Future: Sustainable Corporate Strategies for Workforce Upskilling and Reskilling. *International Journal of Research in Entrepreneurship & Business Studies*, *6*(3), 33–46. DOI: 10.47259/ijrebs.2025.633

Sundari, V. M., Rose, R. M., Sassirekha, S. M., Nalini, M., & Girija, P. (2024, November). Deep Learning: Techniques, Taxonomy, Applications, and Future Directions. In *2024 International Conference on Smart Technologies for Sustainable Development Goals (ICSTSDG)* (pp. 1-5). IEEE.

Sun, Y., Zhu, Q., & Li, X. (2025). Electric vehicle adoption in logistics supply chain. *International Journal of Production Research*, •••, 1–20.

Tan, C. N. L., Liu, D., Dou, J., & Chung, H. F. (2025). AI capabilities and sustainable competitiveness in logistics: A mediated moderation model of resilience, government support, and intervention. *Journal of Enterprise Information Management*, •••, 1–36. DOI: 10.1108/JEIM-06-2025-0494

Tang, Y. M., Chau, K. Y., Lau, Y.-Y., & Zheng, Z. (2023). Data-Intensive Inventory Forecasting with Artificial Intelligence Models for Cross-Border E-Commerce Service Automation. *Applied Sciences (Basel, Switzerland)*, *13*(5), 3051. Advance online publication. DOI: 10.3390/app13053051

Tanveer, U., Hoang, T. G., & Ishaq, S. (2025). Exploring the strategic role of digital technologies in supporting circular practices within service-based firms. *Production Planning and Control*, •••, 1–17. DOI: 10.1080/09537287.2025.2577189

Tanveer, U., Hoang, T. G., & Ishaq, S. (2025). Reshaping global trade finance and supply chains through digital supply chain finance platforms. *Journal of Business Logistics*, *46*(3), e70022. DOI: 10.1111/jbl.70022

Tanveer, U., Hoang, T. G., Ishaq, S., Kamal, M. M., & Attri, R. (2026). Enhancing supplier innovation capabilities through digital technology integration: A relational perspective. *Technological Forecasting and Social Change*, *223*, 124426. DOI: 10.1016/j.techfore.2025.124426

Tanveer, U., Hoang, T. G., Truong, H. Q., Ishaq, S., & Gong, Y. (2024). The critical role of procurement in the emergence of circular business models: Insights from multiple cases of Vietnamese manufacturers. *Business Strategy and the Environment*, *33*(8), 7689–7707. DOI: 10.1002/bse.3888

Tanveer, U., Ishaq, S., & Hoang, T. G. (2024). Enhancing carbon trading mechanisms through innovative collaboration: Case studies from developing nations. *Journal of Cleaner Production*, *482*, 144122. DOI: 10.1016/j.jclepro.2024.144122

Tatini, P. R. (2025). Transforming sourcing and supply chain management: The evolution of AI agents in modern procurement. *International Journal of Scientific Research in Computer Science. Engineering and Information Technology*, *11*, 1219–1226.

Tenakwah, E. S., & Watson, C. (2025). Embracing the AI/automation age: Preparing your workforce for humans and machines working together. *Strategy and Leadership*, *53*(1), 32–48. DOI: 10.1108/SL-05-2024-0040

Thakur, A., Kaipa, K., Banerjee, A. G., Cappelleri, D. J., Krovi, V. N., & Gupta, S. (2025). Physical artificial intelligence for powering the next revolution in robotics. *Journal of Computing and Information Science in Engineering*, *25*(12), 120809. DOI: 10.1115/1.4070122

Thi Binh, A. D., Nguyen, T. T. B., Huynh, T. L. D., Cong-Pham, H., Hoang, T. G., & Truong, H. Q. (2025). Multilevel drivers of social sustainability in developing food supply chains: The role of food safety management systems. *Journal of Enterprise Information Management*, 1–36.

Tiaraningrum, L., & Sekti, B. A. (2026). Empowering the Future Workforce: Re-skilling Strategies in the Age of Human-AI Augmentation. In *Redefining Global Creative Sectors Through AI and Human Augmentation* (pp. 85-118). IGI Global Scientific Publishing.

Toth, Z., Goga, A. S., & Bo coianu, M. (2025). AI Integration in Fundamental Logistics Components: Advanced Theoretical Framework for Knowledge Process Capabilities and Dynamic Capabilities Hybridization. *Logistics (Basel)*, *9*(4), 140. DOI: 10.3390/logistics9040140

Toumi, A., Fosso Wamba, S., & Hafsi, M. (2025). Enterprise architecture as a knowledge management discipline: Evolution, challenges and AI-enabled future. *Journal of Enterprise Information Management*, •••, 1–26. DOI: 10.1108/JEIM-04-2025-0319

Trist, E. L., & Bamforth, K. W. (1951). Some social and psychological consequences of the longwall method of coal-getting. *Human Relations*, *4*(1), 3–38. DOI: 10.1177/001872675100400101

Trist, E. R. I. C., & Emery, F. R. E. D. (2015). Sociotechnical systems theory. In *Organizational behavior 2* (pp. 169–194). Routledge.

Tschang, F. T., & Almirall, E. (2021). Artificial intelligence as augmenting automation: Implications for employment. *The Academy of Management Perspectives*, *35*(4), 642–659. DOI: 10.5465/amp.2019.0062

Ueasangkomsate, P. (2025). Building a future-ready workforce: A sociotechnical approach to digital transformation in Thai food SMEs. *Journal of the International Council for Small Business*, 1-22. /DOI: 10.1080/26437015.2025.2457631

Ulle, R. S., Yogananthan, S., Kumar, V. V., & Reddy, T. (2024). A review on the adoption of AI-powered supply chain and logistics management for effective organizational performance in smes in India. *Cross-Industry AI Applications*, 60-72.

Vaka, D. K. (2024). Procurement 4.0: Leveraging Technology for Transformative Processes. *Journal of Scientific and Engineering Research*, *11*(3), 278–282.

Vaseei, M., & Paris, G. (2024). The twin transition in logistics: Balancing digitalisation and decarbonisation. *International Journal of Logistics Management*, *35*(1), 22–45.

Veershetty, G. (2026). AI-Driven Supplier Relationship Management in the Digital Enterprise: Quantifying Value and Resilience with SAP Ariba. *International Journal of Artificial Intelligence, Data Science, and Machine Learning*, *7*(1), 82–86. DOI: 10.63282/3050-9262.IJAIDSML-V7I1P116

Vidal, T., Laporte, G., & Matl, P. (2020). A concise guide to existing and emerging vehicle routing problem variants. *European Journal of Operational Research*, *286*(2), 401–416. DOI: 10.1016/j.ejor.2019.10.010

Vieira, T., & Junte, S. (2025). Lost in Automation? Algorithmic Management and the Evolving Role of Middle Managers-Insights From the Spanish Dark Stores Sector. *Work and Occupations*, 07308884251398078. DOI: 10.1177/07308884251398078

Vuc, D. E., Stroe, V. D., Fanea-Ivanovici, M., Pană, M. C., & Maftei, R. (2025). Higher Education in Romania in the Age of AI: Reskilling for Resilience and Sustainable Human Capital Development. *Sustainability (Basel)*, *18*(1), 137. DOI: 10.3390/su18010137

Wahab, S. N., Tan, A., & Roche, O. (2024). Identifying supply chain manager leadership skills and competencies gaps in Malaysia. *Higher Education, Skills and Work-based Learning*, *14*(5), 921–937. DOI: 10.1108/HESWBL-07-2023-0179

Webster, J., & Watson, R. T. (2002). Analyzing the past to prepare for the future: Writing a literature review. *Management Information Systems Quarterly*, *26*(2), xiii–xxiii. DOI: 10.2307/4132319

Wesche, J. S., & Handke, L. (2023). Digitisation and automation in training and development: A meta-review of new opportunities and challenges. *Personnel Review*, *53*(3), 771–790. DOI: 10.1108/PR-09-2022-0660

Wood, A. J. (2021). *Algorithmic management: Consequences for work organisation and working conditions*. International Labour Organization.

World Economic Forum. W. (2025). *The Future of Jobs Report 2025*. W. E. Forum. https://www.weforum.org/publications/the-future-of-jobs-report-2025/

Wu, P. J., & Tai, Y. C. (2024). Artificial intelligence-based food-quality and warehousing management for food banks' inbound logistics. *Journal of Enterprise Information Management*, *37*(1), 307–325. DOI: 10.1108/JEIM-10-2022-0398

Wurman, P. R., D'Andrea, R., & Mountz, M. (2008). Coordinating hundreds of cooperative, autonomous vehicles in warehouses. *AI Magazine*, *29*(1), 9–20.

Yandrapalli, V. (2023). Revolutionizing supply chains using power of generative ai. *International Journal of Research Publication and Reviews*, *4*(12), 1556–1562. DOI: 10.55248/gengpi.4.1223.123417

Yavetz, G., & Nakash, M. (2026). Adopting GenAI applications in the workplace: Managerial implications and insights from ICT professionals. *EuroMed Journal of Business*, •••, 1–19. DOI: 10.1108/EMJB-08-2024-0217

Zare, J., & Persaud, A. (2025). Digital transformation and business model innovation: A bibliometric analysis of existing research and future perspectives. *Management Review Quarterly*, *75*(3), 1999–2032. DOI: 10.1007/s11301-024-00426-z

Zhang, Y., Liu, X., Yan, Q., & Na, M. (2025). Empowering workforces in AI-driven environments: Co-skilling, organizational support, and mitigating job insecurity. *Frontiers in Psychology*, *16*, 1700129. DOI: 10.3389/fpsyg.2025.1700129 PMID: 41488962

Zhang, Z. (2023). The impact of the artificial intelligence industry on the number and structure of employments in the digital economy environment. *Technological Forecasting and Social Change*, *197*, 122881. DOI: 10.1016/j.techfore.2023.122881

Zhou, E., & Lee, D. (2024). Generative artificial intelligence, human creativity, and art. *PNAS Nexus*, *3*(3), pgae052. Advance online publication. DOI: 10.1093/pnasnexus/pgae052 PMID: 38444602

Zhu, D., Han, Z., Du, X., Zuo, D., Cai, L., & Xue, C. (2025). Hybrid Model Integrating Fuzzy Systems and Convolutional Factorization Machine for Delivery Time Prediction in Intelligent Logistics. *IEEE Transactions on Fuzzy Systems*, *33*(1), 406–417. DOI: 10.1109/TFUZZ.2024.3472043

Zuiderwijk, A., Chen, Y.-C., & Salem, F. (2021). Implications of the use of artificial intelligence in public governance: A systematic literature review. *Government Information Quarterly*, *38*(3), 101577. DOI: 10.1016/j.giq.2021.101577

About the Contributors

Thinh Gia Hoang holds a Ph.D. in Business and Management from RMIT University. His research expertise encompasses sustainable business models, supply chain sustainability, innovation and technology management, and circular economy practices. He has actively participated in numerous research projects funded by both domestic and international organizations, including the National Foundation for Science and Technology Development (NAFOSTED), the Friedrich Naumann Foundation for Freedom, and the Hinrich Foundation. Dr. Hoang's research contributes to advancing sustainability and innovation in business practices, particularly in the context of emerging economies. His work has been published in leading academic journals such as British Journal of Management, Business Strategy and the Environment, Technological Forecasting and Social Change, International Journal of Production Economics, and Journal of Cleaner Production, among others. In addition to his academic contributions, he is a contributing writer for Bloomberg Businessweek, where he analyzes industrial development strategies, value chain transformations, and trade policies in Vietnam and the ASEAN region. He currently serves as an Associate Editor of the journal Technology Analysis & Strategic Management; and serves in Editorial Board of Discover Sustainability and Humanities and Social Science Communications.

Umair Tanveer joined Exeter Business School in 2022 as Senior Lecturer in Operations Management. Prior to joining Exeter, Umair was a Senior Lecturer in Operations Management and Director of Resources and Work Allocation at University of Bristol. Over the past 14 years, Umair has worked as senior leader, consultant, lecturer and a mentor in top institutions (i.e. University of Bristol, UCL, University of Warwick and Exxon Mobil). Umair's research interests are interdisciplinary, within the area of Operations and Supply Chain Management. His research predominantly adopts the analytical and empirical approaches. His current research interests include Food sustainability, social media research, Circular Economy and sustainable supply chains.

***

Long Dinh is a lecturer and researcher in entrepreneurship and business management, currently affiliated with International University – Vietnam National University Ho Chi Minh City. His research interests focus on entrepreneurship, management, and business innovation, with particular attention to sustainable ventures and innovation-driven business models.

Faiz Izaz Fathoni is a technology researcher with experience in software development and applied computing systems. His work encompasses the development of application-oriented solutions and embedded system integration, with particular interest in mobile technologies and Internet of Things (IoT). He is actively engaged in technical implementation and scientific inquiry related to system design, data processing, and software-based optimization. His research interests focus on scalable computing solutions, interconnected systems, and the application of computational methodologies to real-world technological challenges.

Manisha G is an Assistant Professor in the Department of Computer Science and Engineering at R.M.D Engineering College, Kavaraipettai, Tamil Nadu, India. She is dedicated to teaching and mentoring students while contributing to academic and research activities in computer science. Her areas of interest include emerging technologies and enhancing student learning through innovative approaches.

Frédéric Gautier is a professor of industrial and logistics management. He is academic director of the Sorbonne Business School and co-director of the Risk Chair. He has experience as an auditor in an international firm and as an industrial management controller. His doctoral work, carried out in the aeronautics sector and focusing on the economic management of new product design and development projects, was honored with the thesis prize awarded by the FNEGE. His current work focuses on the management of logistics chains in public hospitals and in a major chemical company.

Adilah Hisa is a lecturer at the School of Business, Universiti Teknologi Brunei and an Assistant Researcher at the School of Business and Economics, Universiti Brunei Darussalam. She holds a Ph.D. in Management from Universiti Teknologi Brunei and a Bachelor's degree in Petroleum Engineering from the University of New South Wales, Australia. She has presented her research in various professional meetings and is currently immersed in an array of forthcoming publications and collaborative projects with esteemed researchers from Universiti Brunei Darussalam. Her research interest include Innovation Management, Leadership, Human Capital Development, Youth Employability, Knowledge Management, Organizational Behavior, and Supply Chain Management.

Le Anh Duy Tran holds a Ph.D. in Management from Sorbonne Panthéon University in France. His educational background includes a Master of Science (MSc) in Logistics and Supply Chain Management from Manchester Metropolitan University, United Kingdom (UK). Over the past seven years, he has gained experience as a lecturer in several universities in Vietnam. In his research endeavors, he regularly contributes to numerous research papers in the supply chain management and logistics field.

Dinesh M G is a faculty member in the Department of Artificial Intelligence and Data Science at Easa College of Engineering and Technology, Coimbatore. He is actively involved in teaching, research, and academic mentoring in emerging computing technologies. His interests include data analytics, intelligent systems, and applied research in AI-driven solutions. Dr. Dinesh contributes to curriculum development and supports student innovation and projects. He is committed to academic excellence and industry-relevant engineering education.

Jihad Mohammad is a distinguished academic and Assistant Professor at the UCSI Graduate Business School, UCSI University, Malaysia. With an extensive background in international higher education, he has previously held faculty positions at Qatar University and the Azman Hashim International Business School (AHIBS) at Universiti Teknologi Malaysia (UTM). Throughout his career, Prof. Jihad has been consistently recognized for his academic excellence, receiving multiple prestigious awards for his research performance and high-impact publications. His research expertise lies at the intersection of Organizational Behavior, Corporate Social Responsibility (CSR), and Sustainability. Prof. Jihad has published over 60 scholarly articles in top-tier journals, such as Internet Research and the Journal of Global Marketing. His work explores the complexities of green management, work ethics, and sustainable consumer behavior. Beyond empirical research, he is a noted authority on academic methodology; his influential book, "Crafting Literature Review: A Guide for Doctoral Students," has become a vital resource for scholars navigating the rigors of thesis development and high-level academic writing. In addition to his prolific research output, Prof. Jihad is deeply committed to mentorship and academic leadership. He has successfully supervised more than 25 doctoral and MBA candidates and serves on the editorial boards of several international journals, including Industrial Management & Data Systems. At UCSI

University, he continues to lead impactful research projects—often supported by national grants like the FRGS—while fostering a culture of ethical inquiry. His dedication to bridging the gap between theoretical frameworks and practical business sustainability makes him a key figure in the regional academic landscape.

Thi-Phuong Nguyen is research fellow of Department of Science, Technology and International Projects, University of Economics and Finance, Ho Chi Minh City, Vietnam. Dr NGUYEN graduated her PhD (Management) in RMIT university. Her research interests span a wide array of fields, including leadership, corporate governance, strategic management, sustainability, supply chain management, and marketing, etc. With over a decade of experience in the higher education sector, Dr. NGUYEN has cultivated a diverse skill set encompassing international program franchise, academic research, fundraising for research projects, and teaching at both undergraduate and postgraduate levels in global institutions such as RMIT University, Birmingham City University, Leipzig University, Liverpool John Moores University, Western Sydney University, and others. She has held various management roles in higher education projects within both for-profit and non-profit sectors.

Jayabharathi P is an Assistant Professor at St. Joseph's College of Engineering, OMR, Chennai – 119. She is actively involved in teaching and mentoring students in her domain, contributing to academic excellence. Her interests include research, student development, and the application of modern engineering concepts in education.

Vinoth R is an academic professional in the Department of Computer Science and Engineering at R.M.K College of Engineering and Technology, Tamil Nadu, India. He is actively involved in teaching, research, and academic development, with interests in core and emerging areas of computer science. His work focuses on enhancing technical knowledge, innovation, and student learning through research-oriented approaches.

S. Anbu is a Professor in the Department of Artificial Intelligence and Data Science at Vel Tech Multi Tech Dr. Rangarajan Dr. Sakunthala Engineering College, Avadi, Chennai. He is actively involved in teaching, research, and academic leadership in the field of AI and data science. His interests focus on advancing intelligent systems, data-driven solutions, and fostering innovation among students and researchers.

Binastya Anggara Sekti has been a lecturer at the Faculty of Computer Science, Esa Unggul University, Jakarta, since 2016. He is actively involved in the Artificial Intelligence and Information Security Study Group. He holds a Bachelor's degree in

Informatics Engineering from the Bandung Institute of Technology and a Master's degree in Information Systems Management from Trisakti University, Jakarta. Prior to entering academia, he accumulated over 25 years of professional experience as an IT practitioner in various companies across Jakarta. His work focused on developing data centers for internet service providers and delivering IT solutions for the manufacturing and oil & gas sectors. His research interests include artificial intelligence, cybersecurity, and the development of IT infrastructure.

Thilagam T is an academician in the Department of Computer Science and Engineering at Vel Tech Rangarajan Dr. Sagunthala R&D Institute of Science and Technology, Chennai, India. She is engaged in teaching and research, with a focus on advancing knowledge in computer science and related technologies. Her interests include fostering innovation, academic excellence, and student-centered learning in emerging computing domains.

Vu Hai Nam is the Vice-Director of the Institute of International Training and Cooperation at BaRia VungTau University. A strategic leader in higher education, he orchestrates global academic partnerships and manages cross-border educational initiatives, ensuring the university's alignment with international standards. Mr. Vu's scholarly trajectory is defined by a long-standing commitment to the complexities of global markets. His research has evolved from foundational International Business strategies to a specialized focus on Environmental, Social, and Governance (ESG) frameworks. Currently a Doctoral Researcher at UCSI University, Malaysia, his work investigates the integration of sustainable governance within international trade. Over the years, his research has consistently sought to bridge the gap between corporate profitability and ethical responsibility, contributing to the discourse on how emerging markets navigate the demands of a green global economy. Beyond his executive role, Mr. Vu is deeply invested in social welfare and grassroots governance. Serving as the Vice-Head of his local neighborhood, he applies his leadership skills to community development, prioritizing social security and maintaining a close connection with the people to ensure effective local administration.

Index

A

O

P

R

S

T

W

www.ingramcontent.com/pod-product-compliance
Lightning Source LLC
LaVergne TN
LVHW060006031026
849161LV00025B/1495